Mourning the Nation

BHASKAR SARKAR

Mourning the Nation

Indian Cinema

in the Wake of

Partition

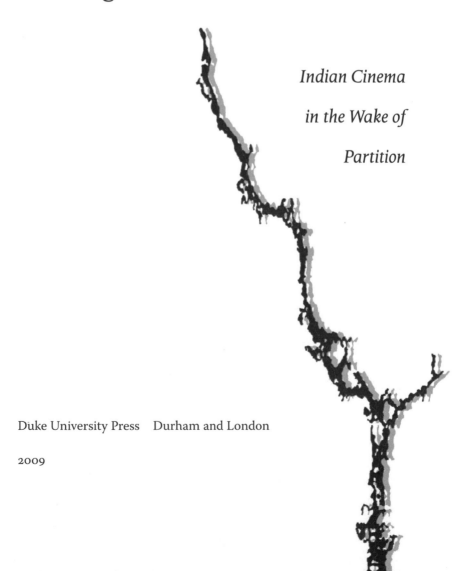

Duke University Press   Durham and London

2009

Designed by C. H. Westmoreland
Typeset in Warnock with Octavian display
by Tseng Information Systems, Inc.
Library of Congress Cataloging-in-Publication data
appear on the last printed page of this book.

for my parents

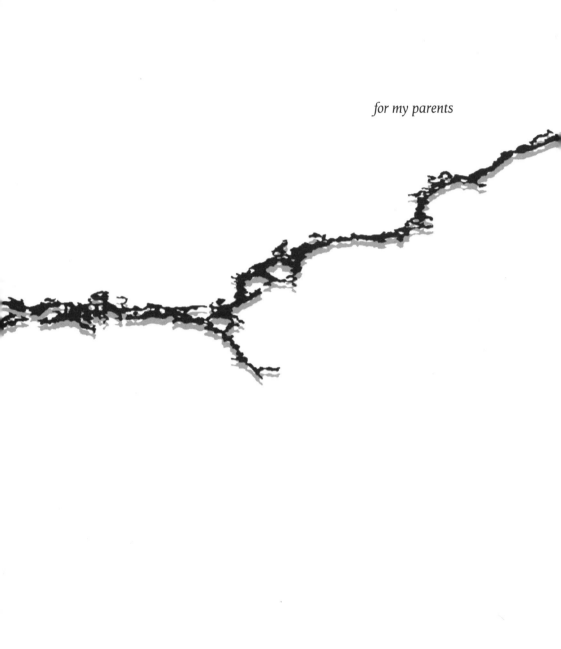

Contents

Acknowledgments

MANY ARE THE DEBTS OF A FIRST BOOK. This one grew out of my doctoral work at the University of Southern California: I must first thank my dissertation committee. My adviser, Marsha Kinder, took a chance and supported my application to film school at a point when I had minimal training in the humanities; she guided me through every step of the research and writing process and remains an inspiring mentor. David James instilled an appreciation of criticality in me, encouraged me to think in a comparative register, and provided me with invaluable feedback. Michael Renov helped me overcome my suspicion of psychoanalytic models and formulate the overarching framework of my project. Hayward Alker broadened my intellectual horizons by introducing me to relevant political theories and nudged my thinking in interesting directions. Besides fueling my general interest in the popular, Lynn Spigel had a significant influence on this work in its formative stages. Beyond my dissertation committee, I also owe a word of gratitude to Timur Kuran, who inspired me to venture into unfamiliar territories and ask unusual questions.

My graduate school peers at USC had an immeasurable impact on my intellectual growth. I fondly remember the many, many hours spent with Rich Cante, Mary Kearney, Jim Moran, Hilary Neroni, Angelo Restivo, Luisa Rivi, Lucia Saks, Valentin Stoilov, Roland Tolentino, Alison

Trope, Dan Walkup, and Chiachi Wu—surely not all in academic pursuit, but nurturing all the same. Across town, at UCLA, David Pendleton and Marc Siegel were important allies.

My wonderful colleagues at the University of California, Santa Barbara have sustained me through the writing and revisions. I thank Michael Berry, Kum-Kum Bhavnani, Peter Bloom, Edward Branigan, Jungbong Choi, Anna Everett, Alison Fraunhar, Roger Friedland, Mary Hancock, Dick Hebdige, Sukyoung Kim, and Constance Penley for all their support and good cheer. I am especially grateful to Swati Chattopadhyay, Lisa Parks, Cristina Venegas, Janet Walker, and Charles Wolfe, who read parts of my manuscript and provided extensive comments. Staff members of the film and media studies department—Kathy Carnahan, Flora Furlong and Joe Palladino—have helped me in more ways than they know.

Colleagues and friends in the fields of cinema studies, South Asia studies, and trauma studies constitute a vibrant conversational community. My audiences and interlocutors at the annual meetings of the Society for Cinema and Media Studies and the Association for Asian Studies, South Asia Studies conferences at UC Berkeley, and the University of Wisconsin, Madison, Oberlin College, Ohio State University, UC Davis, UC Santa Cruz, University of Iowa, University of Pennsylvania, and Utah State University have helped me hone my arguments. In India, Subhabrata Bhattacharya, Brinda Bose, Suresh Chhabria, Nabaneeta Dev Sen, Amrit Gangar, Kaushik Ghosh, Sohini Ghosh, Ranjit Haskote, P. K. Nair, and Manas Ray have been most supportive. Moinak Biswas, Tapati Guha Thakurta, Ashis Nandy, Ashish Rajadhyaksha, and Ravi Vasudevan helped define my project early on. Gayatri Chatterjee continues to share her encyclopedic knowledge of Indian cinema with me and has been a caring friend during my long sojourns in Pune. In the United States, Anjali Arondekar, Anustup Basu, Manishita Das, Sangita Gopal, Akhil Gupta, Lucas Hilderbrand, Priya Jaikumar, Suvir Kaul, Akira Lippit, Philip Lutgendorf, Purnima Mankekar, Gyan Pandey, Geeta Patel, Amit Rai, Rajeshwari Sundar Rajan, Sudipta Sen, Maurice Stevens, Jyotika Virdi, Kamala Viswesaran, and Esther Yau have asked tough questions and offered endless encouragement. I am especially grateful to Corey Creekmur and Parama Roy for all their support and words of wisdom.

In Kolkata, Gita and Satyen Basuroy, Ratnabali Ghosh, Sudharani Roy, Meera and Anil Sarkar, Amitava Sen, and Subha and Kanti Prasanna Sengupta have afforded moral support. My friends Anuradha Bagadthey, Indrani Bagchi, Suman Basuroy, Sukanya Ghosh, Susmita Ghosh, Tufan Ghosh, Praveen Mohanty, Pramit Pal Chaudhury, Jija Roy, Piku

Roy, Antara Sen, and Charanpreet Singh have egged me on and hosted me in Delhi and Mumbai. In Los Angeles, Conerly Casey, Alex Rabrenovich, and Afzal Shah have provided much-needed sustenance over the long period of writing.

Industry insiders Shyam Benegal, Biswaranjan Chatterjee, Bhaskar Ghose, Govind Nihalani, Dilip Sarkar, B. R. Chopra, and Yash Chopra took time off from their busy schedules to speak with me. I thank them for their generosity and illuminating thoughts. Amar Kanwar, M. S. Sathyu, and Supriyo Sen furnished video copies of their works. Parimal Roy provided me with open access to his fantastic collection of film memorabilia. The wonderful staff at the National Film Archives of India in Pune, and Nandan Library in Kolkata deserve a special word of gratitude.

The research for this project was supported by a junior fellowship from the American Institute for Indian Studies; a grant from the Taraknath Das Foundation at Columbia University; funding from the Academic Senate, the Dean's Office, and the Interdisciplinary Humanities Center at UCSB; and a grant from the University of California President's Office.

I am indebted to my editors, Ken Wissoker and Courtney Berger, and the staff at Duke University Press for their guidance and help at various stages of the publication process. Two anonymous referees offered thoughtful, perspicuous suggestions that took my work that extra mile. Sydney Duncan and Dan Reynolds helped with the formatting of the manuscript. Rahul Mukherjee prepared the index.

Long phone conversations with Jozsef Borocz, Cesare Casarino, and Mahua Sarkar helped me retain my sanity over the years. In many ways, my parents inspired the project: the book is dedicated to them with much love. Finally, this book owes its existence to the affectionate support of Bishnupriya Ghosh—co-conspirator, critic, playmate.

National Cinema's Hermeneutic
of Mourning

THAT INDIA'S INDEPENDENCE from colonial occupation in 1947 constitutes a watershed in the annals of global decolonization is well established. What remained far less acknowledged for decades was the salience of that historic conjuncture as a catastrophe with haunting repercussions for community life in South Asia. The end of the British Raj led to the birth of two sovereign nation-states: on August 14, Pakistan came into existence; the next day, India was born. This truncation, referred to as the Partition of August 1947, was a bloody and protracted affair, coming as it did at the end of intense political bickering and parlaying. The event played itself out over a year: roughly a million people were butchered in murderous riots that broke out all over a volatile northern India; as huge masses of terrorized people fled in search of security, 10 to 12 million lost their homes and became hapless refugees. For a few days in mid-August, there was confusion in some areas of Bengal and Punjab (the two provinces that were actually cut up) about their inclusion in the two incipient territories. Partition, as the underside of independence, remains a festering wound in the collective psyche of South Asia; yet public discourse, following a trajectory set by nationalist historiography, has celebrated 1947 mainly as the end of alien occupation, downplaying the violent episode as an aberration within an otherwise harmonious tradition.[1]

With nationhood emerging as *the* modern form of collective political organization, the leaders of a nascent nationalism in the subcontinent had worked to splice together a secular national identity that could withstand the centrifugal challenges of a polity marked by dizzying differences of race, class, creed, caste, language, and regional lifestyles. The slogan "unity in diversity" encapsulated the hope for a national *imaginaire* that would transcend all difference. The realization of the invidious two-nation theory in 1947—one country for Hindus, one for Muslims—rendered a crushing blow to this hope, undermining the belief that a united India could exist in the face of confounding diversity. The rancor and violence raised serious questions regarding the very possibility of continuing community life in South Asia. In spite of the widespread disavowal of 1947 and its reduction to a historical anomaly, Partition emerged as a national trauma—an experience whose memory cast its long, disquieting shadow on public consciousness, tinging subsequent national endeavors with an unspeakable sadness.

Mourning the Nation follows the shifting traces of this specific historical event in Indian cinema of roughly the following five decades.[2] If that event occupies the status of a collective trauma in the psychobiography of the nation, these cinematic traces are indexical of acts of cultural mourning. I track the initial reticence in engaging with this traumatic experience, widely construed as an originary wound, and the subsequent emergence of a strong, at times obsessive, Partition discourse. These shifts are situated in relation to an evolving project of nation building, from the early decades when official policy centered on a secular imagination of the nation and a proud insistence on achieving economic self-sufficiency through state-sponsored capitalist development, to the current conjuncture marked by the simultaneous and seemingly irreconcilable movements toward globalization and religious nationalism. The central objective of this book is to advance an understanding of both the silence and the eventual "return of the repressed" as strands of one complex process. Since Partition cannot be isolated from larger historical processes, the book turns out a critical project of mourning, the experience of Indian modernity and nationhood through the lens of cinema. At stake is a theory of cinema as cultural mourning work.

Mourning the Nation is primarily a work of film history, specifically the history of Indian national cinema after 1947, organized around one historic event that puts to question the putatively natural unity of the nation. While such a transversal approach cannot provide a comprehensive account of Indian cinema, it brings into sharp focus the problematic of the national as a structuring principle of film historiography: what remains of the category of national cinema, when the national itself is in question? At the same time, this book is not a comprehensive account of every film that addresses Partition; indeed, it marks the impossibility of such an account, not only because there are simply too many "Partition films" by now, but more importantly because of the dispersal and displacement of the event in the course of its cinematic figuration.

To the extent that the book explores the entanglements of cinematic memory and history, it is also a work of history. Through its singular focus, it interrogates the historiographic nomenclature of the "event," exploring how one historic moment stretches in time, extending the spaces of experience and representation. It places Partition as a constitutive element within the biography of the nation, foregrounding the extent to which one event produces a refraction of various aspects of national life that seemingly have nothing to do with it. It identifies the rules, formal and implicit, that govern representations of national life and experience and tracks the uneven evolution of these conventions over the years. Thus, ultimately, the book engages the interrelations of history and film history: it is a book about the historicity of cinematic representations of Partition.

As its title suggests, *Mourning the Nation* is an investigation into the modern force field that we call nationalism and that, in recent years, has been at the center of much debate. Notwithstanding the remarkable emotional valence that nationalism continues to enjoy from Chile to Chechnya, scholars have sought to wean us off the mythopoesis of the nation as primordial, essential, natural. As a result, we now know that the nation is a cultural artifact: an "imagined community" that rests on the myth of "horizontal comradeship" among its members; an "ideological form" that presupposes the continuity of a national subject across centuries; one of many "invented traditions" that political elites have deployed to legitimize their power in the face of revolutionary and democratic challenges.[3] This epistemic weaning comes at the cost of a profound displacement, as we have to bracket some of the most cherished ideals of modern times, including a strong utopian belief in nationalism as a force promoting the expression and realization of popular will, the achievement of popular liberation and sovereignty, and the self-determination of collective destiny. Yet such dissection has become unavoidable. Nationhood leads to the inevitable erasure of difference, of alternative and equally salient poles of affiliation, in the service of a monolithic, and at times oppressive, identity. The proud and thunderous "we" that energizes and legitimizes many a national constitution—"We, the people"—remains, at best, a tenuous entity. Indeed, the very idea of *people* is ambiguous: does the word refer to an entire national collectivity, the "constitutive political subject," or does it invoke only the underprivileged, marginalized, faceless "masses"—Gramsci's subalterns, Fanon's *les damnés*—who remain the "objects" of nationalist strategies?[4] The modern state is widely charged with corruption and totalitarianism, administrative failures, myopic and unjust policies, and developmental programs gone awry; it is often at sharp variance with more romantically construed national communities, a chasm obscured in the hyphenated conflation *nation-state*.[5] In disavowing this structural absence of cohesion, nation-states vitiate vaunted doctrines of pluralism and emancipation. When the state itself is at the center of tension—the eye of the storm, as it were—and both the subject and object of violence, it can no longer claim to be an ethical agent of conflict resolution.

In addition to these ethicopolitical complications, the unprecedented spurt in the circulation of capital, astounding strides made in the fields of cybernetics and telecommunication, and the vertiginous mobilizations of various flows—of peoples, commodities, ideas, information—across territorial borders have fired our imagination, generated new modes of being and fostered supranational affiliations. Scholars point to the cognitive inadequacy of the national: for instance, Pheng Cheah stresses the increasingly spectral nature of nationality, and Arjun Appadurai argues for new ways of apprehending the spaces of modernity.[6] We are thus confronted with a double-edged historical loss: the sublation of the nation form by new spatial imaginations (effectively, the passing of an era), and the recognition of its inadequacies and illegitimacies (arising from a structural lack). I will submit that this sense of loss impels recent musings on nationalism: in its analytical explorations, this body of discourse is, in one sense, mourning the idea of the nation. The present book is a contribution to this discursive terrain: by training its focus on cinematic mediations of the truncation of a particular nation, it aims to complicate the history, and to advance a more nuanced understanding, of nationalism as a cultural-political force. Thus, for instance, one of the crucial insights of this book is that the idea of the nation was already being mourned in the heydays of decolonization and nationalism (the 1950s and 1960s), before antifoundational thought brought forms of community and politics under critical scrutiny.

This work is also an intervention in discussions of social trauma and mourning. It draws on the Indian case not simply to append yet another significant instance to international film history and to the growing archive of human catastrophes, but more crucially to tease out the implications such an inclusion has for these fields of knowledge in terms of redrawing their maps and boundaries. That is to say, I am interested in the mutually transformative articulation of trauma studies, area studies, and media studies. My project stems not only from a desire to say something about both the general question of mourning the nation and the particular instance of the Indian Partition, but also from a belief that such a juxtaposition of the general and the particular complicates and extends our understanding of both. How do frameworks of loss and mourning reframe Indian identity, history, and media? How does the Indian media world complicate film and television studies? In a similar vein, I hope to extend models of trauma, loss, and mourning beyond the contexts familiar to (Western) academia—namely, the Holocaust, slavery and the decimation of indigenous populations in the Americas, and the bombing of Hiroshima-Nagasaki.

This tension between the general and the particular animates the entire book. Here, the generalized idea of a structural lack—the absence of a natural national cohesion—is translated into a specific historical loss, the bifurcation of India.[7] Thus I move from a universal poststructuralist insight (that social formations are endowed with a gap or lack that refuses closure)[8] to a specific postcolonial experience (the fissures in Indian nationalism). Training a critical poststructuralist gaze onto a specific South Asian episode forces us to reevaluate historiographic "facts" and helps us grasp cultural memory and its political appropriations from the present moment; in turn, the particular experience puts pressure on universalized notions of structural lack (of unity) in the *socius*, in any *socius*, and enriches—thickens—the very idea of mourning work. I hope to tease out the correlation between the epistemological disruptions wrought by theories of nationalism and postcolonial criticism, and the uneasy, fraught, mournful experiences of modern times: working through such experiences cannot proceed without disrupting anchoring investments and certainties. South Asia, with its historical complexities and cartographic instabilities, is a prime example of what Irit Rogoff calls "geographies in crisis," a crisis that encompasses identities, affiliations, and rights as it undermines the "navigational principles" by means of which conflicts were decided just a few decades ago.[9]

I will argue that the Partition of India is a particularly harrowing moment within a larger trauma of the Indian modern, for what are the experiences of modernity and nationhood in the postcolonies if not largely traumatic? I engage in such polemics aware of several possible objections. One may question the usefulness of harping on the extraneous nature of the nation in non-Western societies. The nation form, imposed or not, cannot be simply wished away: once the idea gets introduced, it becomes the horizon of our collective imagination, the terrain of cultural fantasies and real struggles. As Partha Chatterjee has demonstrated so eloquently, Indian nationalism was not simply a derivative formation but involved significant practices of the imagination.[10] Indeed, one of the central concerns of this book is popular cinema's ambivalent and negotiatory role within India's project of nationhood. Second, one can argue that the experience of modernity, involving giant leaps that were both utopian and disruptive, was universally traumatic, and that European modernity was itself a differentiated affair. My claim that somehow modernity was more traumatic in non-European societies remains vulnerable to charges of a certain occidentalism. A reduction of the differentiated experiences of various parts of Europe, say Holland and Sicily, to a unitary modernity is equivalent to a typically Eurocentric epistemological condensation: a singular Europe as the self-same subject of History. Even in the West, as new structures and nationalist ideologies supplanted older political regimes and frameworks, modernity precipitated cataclysmic dislocations. Nevertheless, as the new frameworks emerged out of premodern European paradigms there was a semblance of continuity. For the postcolonies, in the absence of this gradual and rooted emergence of the assemblage of processes, attitudes, and institutions that we typically call modernity, modern nationhood wrought a form of violence—epistemic, material, and psychic.[11] Partition violence, and its mutation to the current specter of a South Asian nuclear blowup, happens to be a singular and extreme manifestation of this postcolonial predicament. Thus mourning in the truncated Indian context proceeds from a compounded sense of loss encompassing, among other things, an internalized sense of lack and inferiority, the loss of a familiar assumptive world, the loss of self-determination and of control over one's destiny.

The translation of the seemingly universal categories of traumatic loss and mourning to a historically contingent context presents multiple analytical challenges. The use of the "general" and "abstract" language of Euro-American theory in non-Western situations has generated much debate within, and spirited interventions from, postcolonial scholarship.[12] For instance, Dipesh Chakrabarty asserts that the rendering of particular experiences, frequently colored by "the religious, the supernatural, the divine, and the ghostly," in the disenchanted language of a universal, a "supervening general construction mediating between all the particulars on the ground," tendentiously erases "a field of differences."[13] I will add that since extant theories of trauma come with their own religious undertones, even the imputed "general" is deeply enchanted. Any postcolonial intervention in trauma studies must work through further complications arising from the blend of religious and structural-scientific idioms, the simultaneous pursuit of spiritual health and a rational restitution of social order.

Much of the language encountered in contemporary theories of social suffering is rooted in Western traditions; for instance, the dominant idea of witnessing comes from Judaic texts, while the possibility of redress is linked to civil society. Indeed, the contemporary sense of "trauma," which comes to us from German romanticism,[14] and which—in its stress on the precariousness, even impossibility, of the modern bourgeois self—involves something more than "injury to living tissue" and "psychic wound," has no adequate counterpart in the Indian vernaculars (*abhighat, chot, sadma*, and *manasik aghat* are partial translations). What factors might legitimize a reflexive transposition of the master code of trauma studies to South Asia? From its inception, Indian nationalism—at least in its hegemonic versions—has taken shape largely within an emergent bourgeois public sphere: modern Indian national subjectivity has had to negotiate its idealized and impossible extortions and the subsequent disenchantments. Partition marks a moment of rupture, a historical realization of the structural lack endemic to all bourgeois formations. As I argue below, the rupture has a more searing, corporeal dimension, experienced as the amputation of the national body, pillage and rape, physical injury and death. This sense of bodily harm, experienced both within and beyond the bourgeois realm, extends the sense of trauma to an entire national community. Freud himself had elaborated his theory of trauma after World War I to expand the scope of the experience from bourgeois psychosexual settings to the sheer biological level of the human corpus.[15]

Even if we accept this larger sense of trauma in late Freud, and the general Freudian premise that trauma unfolds over time as a delayed experience, it is reasonable to expect that the contours of trauma and the hermeneutics of mourning will be different in the South Asian context. The language of trauma, its frameworks, and the modalities of mourning remain culturally specific: "to mourn" a loss in India entails procedures and behaviors that are quite different from those in other cultures.[16] In most parts of India, white is the color of mourning, not black. The most common form of mourning, related to death, is imbricated with concerns about public hygiene, spiritual well-being, and rehabilitation of the mourners: local climate requires the quick disposal of the body; a period of ascetic restraint (dietary restrictions, sexual abstinence, meditation) is followed by rituals (religious offerings, charitable dispensations) aimed at the expiation of departed souls, and a feast marking the mourners' return to the normal flow of life. The analytical challenge, then, would be to delineate an "Indian paradigm of mourning" rather than simply inflect a Western paradigm to fit the Indian context (which produces, at best, a "paradigm of mourning in India"). A further complication arises from the fact that mourning modalities differ between religions and religious sects, between regions, between classes, and from one kind of loss to another. Within any one religious community, mourning rituals remain confoundingly heterodox; while mourning death frequently involves public expressions of grief, including loud wailing and bodily gestures, public mourning is far more muted in urban areas, especially among upper classes.[17] Ultimately, the grammar of mourning depends crucially on local philosophical and eschatological frameworks: in the Indian context, the Hindu-Buddhist notions of rebirth and *moksha* or nirvana constitute an imaginative approach to mortality; the concept of maya, which promotes a sense of the material world as illusion, enables a pragmatic approach to accepting loss. Similar frameworks from the Judeo-Christian traditions have been central to the formation of contemporary trauma studies around the question of the Jewish Holocaust: for instance, obscure versions of the Moses story that speak of his murder in the desert and the story of Abraham and Isaac have emerged as the urtexts for paradigms of loss, obligation, and witnessing.[18] To establish patterns of mourning that are singular to the postcolonial Indian context, one needs to delve into comparative ethics, religious studies, and ethnographies of mourning rituals— a task well beyond the scope of this book.[19] The contributions that I, as a media scholar, can hope to make to Indian trauma studies will remain necessarily circumscribed by these limitations.

The question about the specificity of Indian models of mourning gets transformed, within the contours of the present project, into a question about Indian forms of cinematic mourning. Not only do these cultural practices differ from external norms, but they are also variegated within the country—say, according to the conventions of various taste cultures and political perspectives: from the allegorical tales in Bombay films (chapter 2), to the studied mise-en-scène of the Indian New Wave (chapter 4), to the highly formalized melodramas of Ritwik Ghatak (chapter 5). Nevertheless, across the range of film cultures, mediations of loss frequently draw on what may be described as "civilizational" models of sacrifice, separation, and suffering available in the two epics *Ramayana* and *Mahabharata*, in classical literary texts like the Sanskrit play *Shakuntala*, and in shared legends of undying love, such as that of Emperor Shahjahan for Mumtaz Mahal. These familiar models of framing and making sense of experience provide shared rubrics for cultural mourning work. Thus the legend of King Harishchandra's grace in the face of adversity (the basis of the earliest known Indian feature film, 1913), Seeta's abduction and public suspicions about her chastity in the *Ramayana*, and questions of duty and a just war in the *Bhagavadgeeta*—all provide contexts for signification and ethical judgment to shell-shocked subjectivities and communities.

The point, ultimately, is not to understand all local differences as anthropological variations, thereby retaining the master categories of trauma and mourning, but to bring the categories into generative crisis. As I will demonstrate in the following pages, the culturally legible bundles of signification drawn from an epic imagination become the archetypal fragments in terms of which popular cinema allegorizes the trials of contemporary life and mourns loss through displacement and deferral. Such narrative deflections conjoin the overwrought mise-en-scène, the musical interludes, and modes of editing and sound-image relations emanating from vernacular practices, to consolidate (combining, in archaic terms, content and form)—at a *performative* level—a potent and singularly Indian idiolect for cinematic mourning. The singularity of this cinematic grammar inheres in the difficulty of subsuming it under any universal model of "cinematic mourning," just as the singularity of the Anglo-Saxon concept "trauma" is indexed by the difficulty of translating it into Hindi.

Memory, Trauma, and Partition Studies: Toward an Affective History

Speaking about 1947 remains a difficult task even after the passage of five decades: the corporeal, material, and psychic losses, the widespread sense of betrayal, the overwhelming dislocations—in short, the deep lacerations inflicted on one's sense of self and community—bring up intense and consuming passions. "How could this have happened *here*?" and "How could *they* do this to *us*?" are questions that keep recurring in oral reminiscences. Such incomprehension leaves one with the impression of a debilitating tragedy; the halting articulations reveal a reordering of notions like community and neighborhood, trust and interdependence, just as they keep redefining what or who is a Hindu, a Muslim, or a Sikh. Making sense of the crushing experiences and continuing public life require narrative operations that map "us" against "them," chronicle "our" helplessness against "their" duplicity, and locate the violence "elsewhere," away from a relatively tranquil "here." In many cases, a secular mythology is recovered in terms of accounts of valiant protectors who fought their own kind to save their neighbors belonging to another faith.[20]

It is not only at the level of the popular that such sentiments get unleashed: academic work can barely contain the underlying emotions. Not long ago, at a meeting of a prestigious South Asia Conference, the sober tenor of discussions during a plenary session devoted to Partition was interrupted by an upsurge of emotions: serious theoretical discourse simply could not contain the passions, the excessive other of objective, scholarly exegesis.[21] As participants' voices faltered, as their interlocutors became distraught, I realized that the lingering sense of loss, the fears and anxieties, individual desires and collective fantasies, were far too palpable and enduring to be relegated under the rubric of *excess*: indeed, in their multifarious verbal and corporeal expressions, they constituted nothing short of a psychosocial matrix—a structure of attitudes and sentiments. In this book, I hope to highlight the affective terrain of Partition discourse as a crucial and constitutive element of history.

An anecdote from my school days in the 1970s may help provide a sense of this wider matrix of attitudes and emotions. One day, when I was in the fifth grade, the mother of one of my classmates turned toward me and asked, more in the tone of a declaration than of an enquiry, "You are a *bangal*, aren't you!" At ten, I was old enough to know what or who a *bangal* was: someone who came from an East Bengali family. I was also old enough to know that both my father's and my mother's families had, indeed, migrated to the west from the eastern part of Bengal after that area had become East Pakistan in 1947. Older cousins had insisted that, as a true bangal, I had to support the East Bengal soccer team of Calcutta; without much thought, I happily complied, for the team in question often prevailed in the local soccer league over its archrival, Mohun Bagan, the *ghoti* or West Bengali team. This, bangal/ghoti, east/west feud was a source of entertainment, since it all took place within the metropolitan space of Calcutta and was an integral part of that city's vibrant cultural life. The abrupt interpellation by my friend's mother changed everything: as she went on to explain that I pronounced all my *r*s with a hard roll typical of east Bengalis, I felt as if I had been "found out." There was just that hint of accusation (or was it simply the triumph of detection?) in her voice that put me in my place, caused the irruption of a dormant bangal-ness in my self. Suddenly, the east/west tension had taken on a new significance: I, who was born and brought up in Calcutta, and had never even been to East Bengal, started feeling like an outsider, an uprooted refugee, in my hometown.[22] Such was the legacy of Partition: beyond sectarian feud, the truncation had spawned a complex web of loyalties and affiliations, transformed existing identities and created new ones, produced a rupture within national history, and set a new course for collective destiny. I had not lived in a united Bengal or through the upheaval, yet my acquired knowledge of the event and its repercussions—what may be called my postmemory of Partition— was strong enough to produce, at the slightest provocation, a range of confusing emotions. While aware of my obligations to the truth claims of history, I cannot claim for this book any level of objectivity, narrowly defined, that purports to elude or sidestep this affective terrain: what follows is, of necessity, an *interested* account, one that engages the emotional and the expressive as constitutive of the experience under scrutiny.[23]

This is not the occasion to chart the fascinating transformation of the academic conceptualization of memory from a faculty whose limitations were seen to constrain historical understanding to a form of knowledge that supplements and often outshines history as a portal to human experience; nevertheless, a few observations are in order to clarify my approach to the procedures and politics of memorialization.[24] By the early 1990s, the vicissitudes of memory—its partial, fragmentary, impressionistic, and transient nature—had become its source of strength. As critiques of humanism and its foundations dislodged essentialist notions of subjectivity and historical agency, memory, marked by its incompleteness and amenability to endless revisions, emerged as the favored narrative organization of human experience, a timely alternative to history. The polarization between history and memory gained potency through its metonymic links to other binary opposites: official/popular, elite/subaltern, objective/subjective, monolithic/polyvocal, truth/hearsay, Western/non-Western, oppressor/victim. Memory came to be construed as the domain of resistance: to remember was also to listen to oral testimonies, to recover forgotten traditions and worldviews, to bear witness to the experiences of the oppressed. The irruption of memory splintered History, *the* definitive, universalized, teleological account of human experience, into many competing and provisional *histories*.[25] In effect, the field of history was transformed: the emergent paradigm was contingent, malleable, multiple and more inclusive—a kinder, gentler history, if you will. In the more nuanced approaches, history and memory came to be regarded as supplementary rather than adversarial knowledge formations; in one celebrated characterization, they were inextricably *entangled*.[26]

This recuperation of the past on behalf of the subjugated and the marginalized produces its own aporia. The detractors of memory studies claim that its effect on analytical history has been transformative in rather insidious ways.[27] The attempt to hold onto experience through its memorialization frequently betrays a nostalgic yearning for a fading aura, a lost immediacy. Memory in these instances becomes a conduit for ontological reenchantment: it bears the promise of healing through the recovery of our connections to the real, to nature, to God, to the Other. If this attachment to a therapeutic project produces an attrition of memory's critical edge, does the postmodern recovery of premodern norms and practices, by way of a challenge to modern structures, resuscitate that edge? Once again, the memorial mission proves to be a dubious one, driven by an uncritical reverence for a supposedly authentic and self-evident premodern world. Here the invocation of the premodern reproduces the modernist equation of the savage with the sacred: if anything, memory undermines the cause it seeks to champion.

What sense can one make of the oscillations of memory studies between incisive analytics and nostalgic reenchantment?[28] I will submit that memory's resuscitation of ontology is dialectically related to the critical skepticism of recent intellectual enterprises. Memory has emerged as the interstitial term between critical thinking and affective attachment; by engaging human desires and fantasies, it promises to restore to life, and to politics, a lost sense of connection and purpose. Furthermore, contemporary invocations of memory signify a social realm far beyond the sense of an innate human faculty or experientiality; memory now consists of not just the fragmentary impressions in our minds, tinged with our fantasies, but also the myriad traces in archival documents, recorded testimonials, film footage. Through a decidedly structuralist understanding of its object, memory studies promises us a deconstructed essentialism: memory is not the same as unmediated experience, it stands in for experience. It thus becomes possible for us to invoke a mysterious experience qua memory and to analyze the workings of the latter, if only partially, in terms of its material articulations.

Traumatic incidents, with their radical erasure of experiential immediacy and subjective coherence, would seem to unhinge memory from essentialisms yet retain the charge of suffering. Indeed, social trauma emerges as the test case for thinking through the political functions of memorialization. The focus on traumatic memory, with its attendant interpretive impediments and uncertainties, sidesteps the problems associated with idealistic notions of identity and agency. It is then possible to conceive of a critical enterprise that upholds the reality of collective suffering and simultaneously interrogates and reveals the rhetorical aspects of its memory: shared memories of oppression, and not the actual experiences, become the grounds for moral claims and political mobilization. In recent years, memories of suffering—of slaves, colonized subjects, displaced tribes, queer groups, and, in some cases, of their descendants—have become the basis of collective empowerment. In place of liberal-humanist empirical suppositions, in place of essential ideals, we now espouse a critical pragmatism. This, then, is the new politics of trauma and memory that informs studies of various genocides and war atrocities, and claims of symbolic and material recompense made on behalf of the wronged of this earth.

And yet, the overwhelming nature of various traumas and the difficulty of their sublation in the fields of knowledge and representation give rise to claims of a transcendental status. This tendency finds its strongest expression in Holocaust studies: the impossibility of comprehending the horror of the concentration camps and gas chambers leads to the reframing of the Shoah as a sublime experience. The Final Solution emerges as the primary trauma of the modern era, an incomparably singular event that caused the train of progress to come to a grinding halt at Auschwitz. By implication, critical intellectual enterprise also reaches its limits in its encounter with this sacrosanct event. Within the subfield of Holocaust studies, this tendency has been subjected to critical interrogation—for instance, during the so-called Historians' Debate (*Historikerstreit*).[29] All the same, through sacralizing discourses, the Holocaust has come to be invested with a singular moral authority; this authority, in turn, generates what one commentator aptly calls "trauma envy."[30] When other wounded groups, from Native Americans to various populations in sub-Saharan Africa, make similar claims,[31] these assertions are important not because of their competing attempts to establish this population or that as the most victimized, but because their articulation challenges the very idea of a singular and transcendental trauma and exposes the power dynamics underlying global institutions, networks, and modalities of knowledge formation.[32]

I want to dwell on one particular tendency in the trauma literature focused on the Holocaust, the urge for sacralization, as it bears an interesting similarity to the ways in which Partition memories are construed. Jewish cultural and political identity is animated by memories of persecution that date back over two millennia. Invocations of the Final Solution place it in a single continuum with the massacre of Jews by Romans in 73 CE at Masada, the atrocities perpetrated by Egyptians many centuries ago are conflated with the 1967 war. Such a politics of commemoration produces a tendentious form of antihistory, a worldview in which Arabs menacingly blur into Nazis.[33] A similar process of metonymic displacements drives the Hindu fundamentalist rewriting of

South Asian history, and its current political projects: legends of Rajput and Marathi resistance to the Mughal emperors are invoked to rally anti-Muslim sentiments; the destruction of Hindu temples by marauding Muslim invaders a millennium ago becomes one with the defacement of ancient statues by the Taliban in Afghanistan; the recovery of a Hindu sacred space in Ayodhya—through the destruction of a medieval Muslim mosque that was allegedly built over a temple—emerges as the political cause around which a resurgent Hindu nationalism catapults itself into the mainstream of Indian political life. Memories of Partition, taken to be the ultimate instance of Muslim betrayal in the modern era, are woven into a threatening and cautionary discourse about Islamic duplicity and aggression. Meanwhile, parallel invocations of popular memory, focusing on Hindu transgressions, unfold in Pakistan.

History abounds in such pernicious acts of consecrating traumatic memories to the sublime, the sacred; hence, the continuing necessity of critically engaging with such reenchantments can hardly be overstressed. At the risk of playing into the hands of religious fundamentalists, scholars have to work through questions of religious faith and identity that remain central to recalls of Partition trauma. As the historian Shahid Amin has suggested recently, dismissing sectarian recollections of the past as simply regressive enchantments will not help in overcoming communal antagonisms; what is required is a nuanced understanding of "the relationship between the 'facts of history,' popular remembrance, and matters of belief." Harping on "inter-communal goodwill and harmony . . . leaves the field of sectarian strife as the special preserve of sectarian and 'communal' historians."[34] A more politically pragmatic approach would involve producing nonsectarian accounts of sectarian conflict. Given the absolute centrality of religion in Indian national life, it becomes imperative to move beyond secularism as a self-evident and secure social institution and to figure out what an actually existing Indian secularism might be like. While this is a task beyond the scope of this book, I hope to make a modest beginning in these pages by examining how post-1947 Indian cinema engages questions of religious identities and survival of communities in the wake of the trauma, pointing to representational strategies that might help us imagine a tenable secularism. As Cathy Caruth reminds us, "history, like trauma, is never simply one's own," for "one's trauma is [always] tied up with the trauma of another"; engaging with the trauma of Partition "may lead, therefore, to the encounter with another,"[35] producing the intersubjective and ethical conditions for a critical secularism.

To the extent that memories of 1947 continue to shape contemporary national experience, the event we call Partition stretches all the way to the present moment. In one important historical sense, the event also extends back in time to 1905, when the colonial administration decided to divide Bengal into two provinces. The professed reason for this truncation was administrative convenience: apparently, the large province, with a population of 79 million, had become ungovernable. However, the need to curb the rising tide of anticolonial nationalism in Bengal was at least as significant as the concern about governance. The plan envisioned a new province, comprising Eastern Bengal and Assam, in which Muslims would be a majority community. Thus, the cultural unity of Bengal on the basis of a shared language was undone through the introduction of religious nationalism. Nationalists were quick to recognize this ploy of "divide and rule," and the subsequent mass agitation led to the reversal of the partition in 1911. Nevertheless, the seeds of dissension had been planted within an incipient nationalist camp by pitting religious nationalism against linguistic nationalism: from then on, contesting aspirations and imaginings produced divergent ideals of the nation. An elastic conceptualization of Partition, extending backward and forward in time, highlights the way in which seemingly disparate historical moments congeal in the popular imagination around the fulcrum of 1947. Thus 1905, 1946, 1971, 1984, 1992, and 2002 fold into 1947; the Bangladesh War, the continuing civil war in Kashmir, the riots in Bhiwandi, Ahmedabad, Delhi, Bombay, and Godhra become elements of one single experiential chain that many place under the sign of "Partition."

If the precise historical demarcation of any event is, in general, a matter of contention, 1947 presents a particularly confounding case: in Kashmir, bloody skirmishes continued well into 1949; much of the violence associated with the bifurcation took place exactly one year before it, during the so-called Direct Action of August 1946, when pro-division political groups incited mass killings in Bengal to forestall attempts at maintaining unity and to make palpable the threat of continuing civil war if Muslims and Hindus were to share the same nation-space.[36] Popular understanding of a significant event, a palimpsest of impressions and emotions, takes us well beyond this historiographic problem of demarcation into the realm of fantasy. An appreciation of 1947 requires not just the objective accumulation and analysis of facts and figures but a great deal of interpretation and supplementation. It is simply not enough to blame the "large" forces of history: the machinations of the colonial administration, the denials and omissions instituted by the postcolonial state, the power games of the Congress Party and Muslim League in an earlier era, or the cynical invocations of religious antagonism by the Vishwa Hindu Parishad in the present. We also need to attend to the minutiae of the everyday: the local mentalities and micro-level actions, competing fantasies and disillusionments, and the fears and anxieties circulating before and after the national laceration.

A comparison of various national partitions of the twentieth century helps us map the roots of these enduring tensions. The event of 1947 is an instance of "colonial" partition, when a departing colonial power seizes the opportunity afforded by competing indigenous nationalisms to produce political and social chaos, to suggest—as a way of legitimizing its own colonial project, now largely denuded—that the colonized are not capable of self-rule. Cyprus, Palestine, and Ireland are instances of colonial partition, while the division of Germany resulted from Cold War tensions. Korea and Vietnam present composite cases: both former colonies, they were partitioned directly as a result of Cold War antagonisms. In Africa, as in the Balkans, the right to self-determination of various emerging nationalisms was flouted to carve out territories according to the whims and interests of the departing colonial powers; as a result, the independent dominions keep getting reconstituted through cyclical conflicts. Since the Cold War partitions in Germany and Vietnam have already been reversed, can we expect Korea to follow suit any time soon? What is it about the colonial partitions in Ireland, Palestine, and South Asia that renders them practically irreversible? How can interspersed and competing nationalisms find ways of coexisting within the same state, given the impossibility of redrawing state boundaries so that each territory corresponds to one sovereign community?

This last concern speaks to a paramount anxiety in partitioned territories: formal cartographic maneuvers simply fail to sort out populations according to the salient element of difference, be it race, faith, or political ideology. The fact of the truncation invests the difference with an aura of finality, yet fails to produce a clear resolution: the division becomes a festering wound, the continued presence of antagonistic groups in close proximity generates constant tension, and the multifarious intercommunity transactions of daily life become tricky. In places like Aligarh or Hyderabad, the daily call to prayer, often broadcast from the mosques on public loudspeakers, is also heard in Hindu neighborhoods and homes; in times of strife, this aural infiltration is experienced as annoying invasion. While many Muslims partake in the celebrations during Diwali, the Hindu festival of lights, and just as many Hindus join their Muslim friends in Eid festivities, these occasions can easily turn tense: local administrations have to plan carefully so that religious processions during Muharram, the Ganapati festival in Maharashtra, or the Pujas in Bengal, do not pass through areas that are populated mainly by the other community. Joe Cleary has drawn attention to this problem of interspersed communities, arguing convincingly that in places like Ireland, Palestine, and South Asia, it is the impossibility of separating belligerent communities, rather than the imputed strength or virulence of ethnic nationalism, that produces continuing tension. He points out that in such cases, the political settlements have failed to adequately address "the conflicting claims to self-determination asserted by the communities involved."[37] Indeed, attempts to produce ethnically or culturally homogeneous nation-states have taken the most disastrous forms, including ethnic cleansing (Africa, the Balkans), forced population transfers (Africa), and—what is becoming the favored mode in South Asia—the effective demotion of minorities to second-class citizenship. The strength of such an analysis lies in recognizing historical conditions, rather than an essential and naturalized element of ethnic rancor, as the primary cause of post-partition misery.

The presence of intermingled minorities produces anxieties about the future—not only minority Muslim fears of discrimination, pogroms, or forcible expulsion, but also majority Hindu fears of a future when Muslims may no longer be a minority in India. Recent trends in South Asia provide some justification for such trepidations: worried people often cite the eviction of tribal populations in northern and eastern Bangladesh, or the injunction of Islamic religious leaders and clerics to the Muslim population of the region to overcome their minority status through rapid biological reproduction. For some scholars, bringing up such fears entails playing into the hands of religious fundamentalists, as if the various fundamentalist groups, left to their own devices, would never think of exploiting these anxieties. I begin from another position: the need to track and interrogate the remarkable interpretive acrobatics involved in the cultural memorialization of Partition, so that we can confront the deep qualms and find ways of coexisting in a post-Partition state peopled with different communities, even different nationalisms.

Mourning the Nation shifts the spotlight from the high politics of the endgames of empire, and interrogates a set of mass cultural practices—the field of cinema—through which people remember and make sense of the experience from "below." This approach derives its force from the premise that nationalist and state-building projects involve substantial fabrications and contestations and cannot be thought of as grand "political" mechanisms isolated from a more diffuse cultural realm. In particular, an event widely experienced as the frustration of the fierce longing for independent nationhood, the betrayal of passionate sacrifices, cannot remain a matter of history or politics alone. Fantasy emerges as a way of elaborating and expressing the arcane emotions unleashed by the disillusionment: hence the need to attend to cultural narratives that advance popular, subjective understandings of the trauma. In this approach, fantasy is not a matter of private aspirations alone; rather, it crucially shapes the texture of political life.

The stress on the operation of collective fantasy has important methodological implications for my project. First, it puts pressure on the ways in which we generally think of history and politics. If these terms do not engage questions of fantasy and affect, they are not only too restrictive but also inadequate, even potentially debilitating, to the task of confronting social cataclysms. Second, elaborations of the historical beyond a narrow objectivity force us to reconsider the categories of experience and evidence. Indeed, *Mourning the Nation* marks a clear break from extant Partition scholarship in its distinctive approach to the question of what constitutes evidence for the historiographic charge of producing the "truth" about Partition. Historians draw primarily on official documents, newspaper reports, and writings of administrators and nationalist leaders, all of which comprise corroborative sources admissible within their discipline.[38] Edited collections of essays include pieces that focus on literary works, including novellas, short stories, poetry, and autobiographical writings; as written texts of some literary merit, these sources command a certain legitimacy.[39] More recent works in feminist historiography draw on oral testimonies of women who lived through the carnage of 1947; in engaging with popular sense-making practices, these accounts capture a heretofore hidden dimension of experience.[40] All along, and for all practical purposes, visual culture— especially popular cinema—has remained outside the purview of Partition scholarship.[41] If this neglect of the visual is not so pronounced in the case of other collective traumas such as the Holocaust, one still detects a disdain for the popular: academic studies that address visual representations limit themselves primarily to public archives of photographs, and to art cinema.[42] Popular visual forms such as commercial films and television series are ignored or summarily dismissed.[43] In contrast, I take on a range of cinematic representations, bringing to bear similar analytical frameworks and methods on both mainstream populist fare and more solemn critical work, undermining such polarities in the process. I examine not simply what is being narrated in these films, but how: I attend to the formal elements, the narrative flourishes and silences, the fabulations and equivocations. Why are the stories being told the way they are being told, and what are they trying to communicate in the process? How do they become mimetically plausible, even authoritative, in their reference to history? What kinds of social contracts do they hope to establish with their audiences, what affective matrix do they engage? This focus on the poetics and politics of Indian cinema compels us to acknowledge and catalog the materiality of vernacular lifeworlds, a singular materiality that refuses incorporation through abstraction into a universal or even a nationalist model of history.

Cinema and Mourning

Given this book's focus, it becomes important to address how cinema undertakes the representation of trauma and the task of mourning in ways that are distinct from, say, literature, oral history, or truth commission testimonials. For me, this is not simply a question about the medium specificity of film: one could surely take note of modes of narration and instances of camera movement, mise-en-scène, editing, or music that appear to take on the work of mourning, but these formal elements must be located within larger discursive strategies to establish the cinematic tropologies of trauma and mourning. In this book, I examine the ways in which institutions of cinema participate in the processes of collective mourning. I analyze not just the filmic texts, but also the roles of various groups such as producers, spectators, censors, and critics, and the intersubjective nature of such cultural negotiations. I also move across a range of analytical approaches (from institutional analysis in chapter 1 to auteur study in chapter 5), reading strategies (from allegorical reading in chapters 2 and 3 to close textual analysis in chapters 4 and 7), and archives (films, television series, industrial documents, legal records, popular press, personal interviews). Nevertheless, a few broad preliminary remarks about the relationship between cinema and mourning are in order.

It would seem that cinema is particularly suited to the task of mourning: after all, is not cinema—or, for that matter, its precursor, photography—always already mournful? As André Bazin, the trailblazing theorist of the medium, pointed out, one of the prime imperatives behind the plastic arts was the preservation of life traces in the face of their inevitable disintegration with time. He began his seminal essay "The Ontology of the Photographic Image" with the observation, "If the plastic arts were put under psychoanalysis, the practice of embalming the dead might turn out to be a fundamental factor in their creation. The process might reveal that at the origin of painting and sculpture there lies a mummy complex."[44] Bazin's references to "psychoanalysis" and "mummy complex," and his later invocation of "our obsession with realism"[45] point to the centrality of subjectivity in his theory of realism: for him, the ontology of the image has to be understood primarily in terms of the subject's needs in relation to temporality, and not in relation to an objective reality. For the human subject, photography becomes a way of staving off death because of its undeniable indexicality: the photograph is a distinct improvement over the painting not because it produces a stronger mimetic likeness but because it points to the presence of an actual referent in the past, now embalmed for posterity. As Roland Barthes was to declare later, "the referent adheres."[46] In the development of technologies of representation, cinema appears with its ability to record the passage of time: that is to say, cinema now adds to still photography's freezing of a single moment the capture of duration. In Bazin's consciously oxymoronic terms, "Now, for the first time, the image of things is likewise the image of their duration, *change mummified* as it were."[47]

In a less-known essay titled "Death Every Afternoon," Bazin notes that not only is cinema able to mummify the passing of time, it can also repeat it: "Art of time, cinema has the exorbitant privilege of repeating it." Yet it is distinct from the other arts, such as music, that also unfold in time. Musical time is "by definition aesthetic time," while cinematic time is of the same qualitative order as the time that we endure in our lives: "The cinema only attains and constructs its aesthetic time based on lived time, Bergsonian '*durée*.'" Bazin goes on to underscore the singularity of the cinematic medium in its ability to preserve and reproduce experience through his wistful observation: "I cannot repeat a single moment of my life, but cinema can repeat any one of these moments indefinitely before my eyes."[48] At issue here is the contingency of human experience and cinema's remarkable ability to record and repeat it at the subject's will. This medium, in its indexical referentiality, becomes a way of mourning the ephemeral nature of experience: for what a film depicts, what it points to, happened in the past and lives on only in a virtual sense, in the spectral images on screen.

Yet film is also subject to the vagaries of nature and time: it is vulnerable not only to accidents and natural disasters (fires, floods, earthquakes), but also to irreversible material degeneration. The medium that is supposed to help us forestall death and achieve an eternal luminescence is itself susceptible to erasure and decay. Cinema's failed promise of permanence ultimately serves to underscore, with great irony, the impermanence of everything in the face of the onslaught of time. The medium of cinema thus turns out to be one marked by profound loss. A materialist study of cinematic commemoration must be attentive to the institutions of archiving, preservation, and restoration, and to the disappearance of literally thousands of films within a matter of a few decades.[49]

Let us dwell a bit longer on the primacy accorded to the subject and to the notion of contingency in Bazin's account of realism. Recently, Philip Rosen has pointed out that Bazin's privileging of realism is associated with psychology rather than with aesthetics: it is more a matter of the phenomenological subject's obsession with the passage of time than a matter of physical likeness. Noting that Bazin consistently compared cinema to indexical signs for which the referent was present in the past (a mold, a fingerprint, a death mask, the Shroud of Turin), Rosen suggests that the photographic/cinematic image is, for Bazin, historical.[50] The subject is conscious of a temporal gap between the moment of the production of the image, and the moment of its viewing: in other words, the subject is aware of the historicity of the image. The indexicality of the image (the signifier) makes it credible, by pointing to the real existence of an actual place or object (the referent). This credibility is strengthened by the apparent lack of human agency in the photochemical process through which images are recorded. The aura of reliability leads to the spectator's investment and belief in the power of the image to represent contingent experience. The active imagination of the spectator, fueled by her desire and investment in the power of the cinematic image, bridges the temporal gap between the existence of the profilmic referent in front of the camera and the projected image.

I want to take Rosen's articulation a step further: if the spectator is aware of the passage of time since the filmic recording of a contingent event, yet accepts the image as a credible representation of it, then the cinematic image becomes a sublation of the now-lost moment. Recognition of a loss (the inevitable attrition of past experience with time), and the retention of what is lost in a sublated form (a filmic recording of that experience): from Sigmund Freud, we know that these are the essential steps in the work of mourning. Thus an impulse to mourn is inherent to cinema. If we acknowledge that, in a broad sense, the experience of modernity was traumatic (a characterization shored up by Marxian and Freudian notions of alienation, and by Walter Benjamin's idea of *shock*), then cinema, as *the* modern medium of representation, reveals from the very outset a preoccupation with the problematic of depicting trauma: thematically (Edwin Porter's *Life of an American Fireman* [1903]; D. G. Phalke's *Raja Harishchandra* [1913]), figuratively (Abel Gance's *J'accuse* [1919], in which the dead soldiers of the Great War arise and return home to see what their sacrifice has achieved, thus allegorically dealing with the loss and with the pressing problem of finding the dead and bringing their remains home to their families),[51] and formally (through the profilmic, as in the expressionist films of Weimar Germany, or through montage, as in revolutionary Soviet cinema).

Amid modernity's pervasive mournfulness, a contingent traumatic event unfolds with stupefying force: it remains largely inaccessible to our faculties, is partially "lost." A community's difficulties of understanding the experience, in placing it within a meaningful account, render it opaque: only fuzzy symptoms persist. No appropriate signifiers—words or images—are available for accessing such a tenuous encounter. The impasse produces a crisis of knowledge and representation: how does one apprehend, let alone depict, the unimaginable? Within Western aesthetic traditions, especially since the First World War, a consciously modernist response to such a crisis has been to foreground, to present, the crisis itself. In the history of cinema, German cinema's mediation of the problematic history of the Third Reich in general, and its horrific program of eliminating the European Jewry—the Final Solution—in particular, remains the most salient example of the medium having to grapple with collective trauma and responding in a decidedly reflexive fashion.[52] A schematic summary of this fraught history might provide a comparative framework for a better understanding of the Indian scenario. Given the record of the German film industry's complicity in the propagation and popularization of Fascist ideology through tantalizing aesthetics,[53] film images in general had become suspect: there was an ethical and political need for radically new representational strategies. Coupled with a semitheological proscription against pictorial representations of the unimaginable (*Bilderverboten*), this attrition of confidence in images instigated a powerful taboo against direct and realistic cinematic representations of the Holocaust. One should note that "realism," a loaded term, has had many iterations; here, I am referring to its most basic sense—a mimetic principle that offers its representations (carefully constructed in terms of commercially standardized techniques of verisimilitude that remain invisible or "transparent" to audiences) as "slices of real life." In contrast, the films of the New German Cinema of the 1970s, and most subsequent works dealing with memory at the personal and collective registers, adopt highly reflexive approaches.

By and large, media critics and theorists seem to have internalized this bias against realist cinematic representation. To come up with straightforward images of the atrocities requires profilmic situations recreating that which remains, in spite of its all-too-real incidence, unimaginable; in the process, an ethical line is crossed, traumatic situations are rehearsed, and the incomprehensible is both trivialized and sensationalized through its forced containment within standard procedures of reference and understanding. The most celebrated book-length studies on post-1945 West German cinema available in English, associated with the names of scholars such as Thomas Elsaesser, Anton Kaes, and Eric Santner, focus on modernist auteur films (*autorenfilme*).[54] In such accounts,

Alexander Kluge's *The Patriot* (1977), Hans Jürgen Syberberg's *Hitler: A Film from Germany* (1978), Helma Sanders-Brahms's *Germany, Pale Mother* (1980), and Claude Lanzmann's *Shoah* (1985), all markedly reflexive modernist texts, occupy pride of place.[55] So entrenched is the modernist bias within film scholarship that Joshua Hirsch can assert in his insightful 2004 book on Holocaust films: "As trauma is less a particular experiential content than a form of experience, so posttraumatic cinema is defined less by a particular image content—a documentary image of atrocity, a fictional image of atrocity, or the absence of an image of atrocity—than by *the attempt to discover a form for presenting* that content that mimics some aspects of posttraumatic consciousness itself, *the attempt to formally reproduce* for the spectator an experience of suddenly seeing the unthinkable" (emphasis added).[56] Hirsch is essentially arguing for a mode of representation that is more adequate to the charge of conveying a traumatic experience; in a sense, his is a hyperrealist quest for appropriate forms, given the task at hand. Writing about art in general, Dominick La Capra echoes Hirsch's validation of formalist experimentation—"At times art departs from ordinary reality to produce surrealistic situations or radically playful openings that seem to be sublimely irrelevant to ordinary reality but may uncannily provide . . . insight into that reality"—and of a "traumatic realism that differs from stereotypical conceptions of mimesis."[57] Needless to say, Hirsch explores mainly modernist films that consciously experiment with form. His attitude is indicative of the vexed relationship that many scholars continue to have with mass culture and with the various media publics, an interaction whose terms were thrown into sharp relief in the mid-1990s in the debate around *Schindler's List* (1995).

Interlocutors of Steven Spielberg's ambitious film on the Holocaust objected to the ways in which he turned a debilitating trauma into entertainment.[58] They argued that the Hollywood culture industry, with its reliance on neoclassical principles of linear narrative driven by character motivation, compositional unity, and eventual resolution of all enigmas, could not do justice in any sense to the subject at hand. They objected to the "sentimental optimism" at the heart of the film, which was completely at odds with the dire and desperate reality of the Nazi era, and to the way the weight of subjectivity was distributed between the various characters, so that spectators were encouraged to identify with an enigmatic, even attractive, Nazi oppressor, a Gentile businessman who became a savior by chance, and a mousy, stereotypical Jew.[59] Critics found a sinisterly fascist tendency in the film's totalizing quest for meaning, in the way it posed as a definitive master-narrative of the Holocaust by incorporating within its body all previous cinematic images and tropes, including the forced reality-effect of black and white imagery interrupted by the overtly presentational figure of the girl in a red dress. The filmmaker Claude Lanzmann, one of the most forceful critics of Spielberg, took him to task for the transgression of claiming to convey a horror that simply "cannot be transmitted."[60] As Miriam Hansen has argued, such high-modernist critiques of the film often reduce "the dialectics of the problem of representing the unrepresentable to a binary opposition of showing or not showing," rather than approaching it "as an issue of competing representations and competing modes of representation." She further argues that the binary formulation is predicated on a "modernist fixation on vision and the visual," thereby ignoring "the role of sound in the production of visuality" and in the mobilization of affect.[61]

Hansen goes on to locate in the entire debate around *Schindler's List*, and specifically in the way it is opposed to *Shoah*, the by-now hoary opposition between "art" and "kitsch," between "high" or elitist modernism and "low" or populist mass culture.[62] To this list of oppositional terms, one might add "high-minded" European philosophical investigation and "crass" American entertainment. What complicates this neat division are the circulation of these cultural texts within the same transnational public sphere and the history of their interactions: after all, it was an American television series, *Holocaust* (1979), that provided the immediate impetus for a cultural-discursive turn within Germany that resulted in the production of both Edgar Reitz's *Heimat* (1984) and Lanzmann's *Shoah*.

The debates reveal a continuing rootedness in the scopic regimes of post-Enlightenment modernity with their attendant epistemological and ethical preoccupations—including a cognate iconoclasm.[63] In general, these frameworks privilege a very particular notion of mimetic realism as an appropriate and adequate mode of apprehending reality; but in its confrontation with trauma, "mimesis" must also evolve so as to capture the shock and incomprehensibility of the experience. The shift from an obvious mimetic realism to a more tortuous modernist-reflexive mode signals an abiding investment in the image's evidentiary authority, its significance to modern subjectivity and agency, and its role in promoting social justice. The shift is commensurate with a bourgeois-liberal public sphere characterized by its institutions of aesthetic judgment and property rights, taste and social distinction, and its simultaneous entanglement in, and critique of, commodity relations. Of course, this ocularcentric epistemological-ethical horizon is predicated on certain polarizing distinctions (fact/fiction, subject/object, and so on), and on the marginalization of other perceptual faculties and the synaesthetic and the corporeal dimensions of experientiality—marginalizations that run counter to the ways in which real-life publics experience experience.

What if the hold of this post-Enlightenment regime on the Indian cultural field is, at best, tenuous? What if, as Kajri Jain argues,[64] this "epistemic bundle" has to contend with "other regimes of image value and efficacy" emanating from vernacular cultural circuits and practices that cherish a different set of image functions? That is to say, what if Indian image cultures derive their power from a different, even wider, set of social functions, beyond the narrowly juridical-ethical? Most significantly for my project, what if such a cultural field—unencumbered by the obsessive distinctions between fact and fiction, subjective and objective, direct address and reflexivity, creative novelty and archaism—is, in some ways, preternaturally equipped to deal with the bewildering challenges of traumatic situations?

International debates about modernism and mass culture surely inflected cinema in post-Partition India, but only to a limited extent, and more at the level of critical discourse than at the site of production. Ritwik Ghatak, industry personalities linked with the leftist Indian People's Theatre Association, and the directors of the so-called Indian New Wave of the 1970s, cited figures of the Soviet revolutionary cinema and polemicists associated with the Third Cinema paradigm (see chapters 4 and 5 of this book). In general, the filmmakers working in the Bombay or Calcutta industries operated largely unencumbered by the preoccupations marking the debates (although, as in the case of Mehboob Khan, they might harness stylistic elements from these movements). The more innovative among them, such as Raj Kapoor, Bimal Roy, or Guru Dutt, worked toward developing their own cinematic ideolects within the broad contours of a market-oriented culture industry. Their creative practices constituted what Hansen, among others, might describe as "popular modernism."[65] In the Indian context, popular modernism would signify an open and hybrid approach incorporating a range of artistic innovations alongside vernacular aesthetic norms: at stake was the fashioning of a vernacular film language at once accessible to an evolving national public and capable of mediating the mutations of national life, including the tectonic social and political shifts that were experienced as disruptions, even as trauma.

Popular modernism is not radically opposed to realism: in fact, the two overlap significantly. We must also remember that Indian notions of realism adhere to regimes of representability and social evaluation that are qualitatively different from their Western counterparts, so that what is considered credible, rational, or realistic in Indian cinema (to take the most obvious example, the ubiquitous "musical interruption") might appear as magical flights of fantasy or as critical reflexivity to audiences elsewhere. Indian cinema's tenuous espousal of Hollywood-style continuity is marked by the irruption of indigenous forms and motivations, such as frontal address, iconicity, and tableau formations (all potent and efficacious cultural shorthand that contribute to cinematic signification); an economy of looks and hierarchies informed by a *darshanic* mode (building upon the privilege of looking at a deity, or of an audience with the king); and expressive song sequences (drawing on the musical *raga*s [literally, mood or emotion] and the synaesthetic appeal of the *ragamala* paintings) with their lyric peformativity purveying an epistemic register in its own right.[66] These elements furnish the particularities of an Indian cine-poetics marked by the commingling of devotion and desire, commercial and aesthetic goals, ethical and ideological standards. Such a system of representation works with a model of "history" that is no rarefied master code, but one that thrives on the textures, rhythms, and contingencies of vernacular lifeworlds.

As I hope to demonstrate in the pages of this book, filmmakers responded to the trauma of Partition in multifarious ways. The troubled referentiality of trauma seldom led to modernist attempts at presenting the problem of representation; rather, filmmakers devised figurations for referencing the contingent experience by mining traditional cultural repertoires, including epics and religious texts, classical Sanskrit dramaturgy, folk theater, and oral traditions. I will argue that, in comparison to their German counterparts, Indian films that bore traces of historical loss were able to hold onto a largely realist mode because of three important reasons. In sharp contrast to the German context, there had been no marked assault on public confidence in the cinematic image, due to its sinister, even lethal, manipulation by the ruling bloc against minority interests; hence there was no compulsion to evade mainstream visual idioms.[67] Nor was there any prohibition on imagining the unimaginable; in fact Hinduism, which boasts 330 million gods and goddesses, is a singularly iconophilic religion, underwriting a veritable empire of images rooted in the materiality of quotidian life. Furthermore, vernacular narrative traditions work through frequent repetitions, detours, and deflections—strategies that are all well suited to the tasks of fashioning figurations of trauma and mourning. That is to say, popular Indian aesthetic traditions work with formal tropes that can perform the gaps, confusions, and compulsions of traumatic memory without self-consciousness in the Western modernist sense, yet produce engagingly reflexive discourse. In such departures, prompted by the interplay of anthropological *and* historical factors, we begin to evince the singularity of an Indian paradigm of cinematic mourning.

In general, in the Indian context, the absence of conscious and overt mediations, the use of standard images and idioms, and the penchant for displaced figurations, all lead to a deceptively simple and "realist" representational field which is, nevertheless, replete with indirect allusions, performative and expressive fragments, and submerged narratives: we are alerted to the need for a particular kind of *reading strategy*, one that is able to move beyond the explication of manifest modernist interventions, and itself intervene forcefully to uncover and make visible the spectral traces of trauma (chapters 2 and 3). I adopt such a "reading" strategy, remembering that the context is irrefutably one in which not only is affect as significant as reflection, but also the two are possibly inseparable. For the institutions of cinema engender a participatory and performative public space in which sensory experience and discursive contestation come together. Knowing through cinema involves not only the visual dimension, which may expunge referential images of trauma, but also the other bodily senses—usually marginalized but now mobilized synaesthetically through image, words, performance, and sound, troubling mnemonic traces like image or sound flashes, and psychic processes echoed in formal elements like expressive frames, deliberate camera movements, and editing rhythms.

The Temporality of Trauma

The shattering nature of the event, which precludes easy processing while it is still too recent and raw, also calls for such an interpretive strategy. Traumatized subjects require a certain amount of time to work through their experience. Theirs is not a simple problem of remembering, as they do not suffer from amnesia; on the contrary, they are frequently overwhelmed by incoherent and incomprehensible recollections that they cannot place within a cogent experiential narrative. Such assimilation occurs slowly over time, and only then does the experience begin to make sense: through its retroactive incorporation into an anecdote, the experience is finally "experienced." Thus a certain belatedness (what Freud referred to as *nachträglich*) is constitutive of every trauma.[68]

Testimonies of survivors of Partition violence—focusing on the general looting, mutilation, and killing, the abduction and rape of women— reveal a measure of numbness and incredulity: the experience, in its incomprehensibility, takes on the attributes of a trauma.[69] The tumultuous event emerges in these accounts as a time when everyone became temporarily insane: reason took a leave of absence, as human beings turned into violent, unthinking, instinctive savages. The shell-shocked accounts convey the difficulty of incorporating the episode within a sensible narrative, a difficulty that introduces an element of latency into the collective experience. Several commentators have recognized precisely such a temporality of deferral with respect to the collective readiness to engage with Partition; historian Gyan Pandey, for one, talks about something like a "collective amnesia" for almost four decades after the event.[70] This is not to imply that earlier historical scholarship avoided the event *tout court*, or that no literary works or films dealt with the experience; nor was it a matter of simple forgetting. In fact, in the northern provinces, in everyday parlance, there was a surfeit of memory; however, it was mostly disturbing memory that stretched the limits of credibility and haunted people in inchoate ways. In mainstream historical accounts, as in the cultural arena, there was a willful forgetting or, rather, a subtle reframing of the episode as an anomalous chapter in the nation's career. As I demonstrate in chapters 1 and 2, such amnesia/reframing had much to do with the exigencies facing an infant postcolonial nation-state. Nevertheless, this kind of disconnection from the past condemned the nation to compulsive reenactments of social violence. Haunting took the form of both disquieting memory traces and tragic repetition.

It is possible to construct a rough timeline for the cultural process of working through Partition trauma; indeed, such historical reconstruction is an important part of this book's project of mourning. For the first twenty-five years after independence, concerted attempts at nation building led to the containment of the scission as a one-time disruption of harmony. The creation of Bangladesh in 1971 through another violent truncation revived memories of 1947. The very next year, the twenty-fifth anniversary of national independence became an occasion for extensive soul-searching: a pervasive disillusionment with achievements in the postcolonial era allowed for widespread critique of nationalist agendas. The entire project of nationhood under the aegis of the Congress Party, with its socialist rhetoric and insistence on secular democratic pluralism, suffered a crushing blow in 1975 when Prime Minister Indira Gandhi declared a State of Emergency, suspending various constitutional rights of the citizenry to consolidate and extend her increasingly autocratic rule. This extreme delegitimation of political institutions and ideologies created a vacuum, ushering in an era of uncertainty and change. With a beleaguered polity and a weakened central administration, marginalized regional forces came to the fore: separatist movements gathered steam in Punjab, Kashmir, and the northeastern provinces. The centrifugal tendencies were not limited to India alone: a bloody civil war in Sri Lanka extended to the Indian state of Tamil

Nadu; in Pakistan, bitter feuds raged over the socioeconomic status of the *mohajirs* (refugees). With the specter of 1947 multiplying on various fronts as demands for further secessions, South Asia witnessed a forceful return of the repressed. The decisive turn came in the mid-1980s, when the assassination of Indira Gandhi by her Sikh bodyguards led to a pogrom against the Sikh community in North India. The violence, allegedly sponsored by functionaries of the ruling Congress Party in some areas, was particularly devastating in Delhi, the nation's capital. The rude jolt of 1984 revealed the shocking extent and depth of communal malevolence in Indian society—a veritable heart of darkness, as it were; it destroyed the feasibility and unquestioned sanctity of institutions such as secularism and civil society. Taking advantage of the waning popular confidence in the political platform and leadership of the Congress Party, the Hindu right wing was able to mobilize support around the notion of an essential Hindu identity (*hindutva*) as the bedrock of a resurgent Indian nationalism; the Bharatiya Janata Party or BJP, the more centrist face of the hindutva movement, managed to lead a broad coalition to power in the mid-1990s. On the economic front, the official rhetoric of socialist development and self-sufficiency rang hollow as India fell far behind various Asian countries. After the fall of the Communist Bloc in Eastern Europe, and with the intensification of the forces of globalization, economic liberalization became the new mantra, the emergent official policy. The resurrection of national pride and purpose in terms of Hindu chauvinism and the opening up of the national economy are not isolated developments: the former serves to deflect attention from the latter's dubious effects, namely a compromised economic sovereignty and burgeoning disparity across various income groups. In sum, wide-ranging ideological and policy shifts on various fronts produced a social space in flux; this atmosphere provided the opportunity for and fostered a collective willingness toward a reappraisal of the nation's past. The surge in Partition discourse in the last two decades is best understood as an overdetermined phenomenon, aided by the emerging structures and reflexive tendencies of a society in transition, and by the sheer passage of time.

While the above timeline is, like any other heuristic, a sweeping simplification,[71] it manages to capture an important mechanism of cultural memorialization. It foregrounds moments of national crisis, moments that have been indexed as occasions for mourning; thus 1947, 1975, and 1984, in marking conjunctures when the nation experienced the loss of something it cherished, echo each other and get linked in popular memory as salient stages of one long ordeal. This ordeal encompasses other seemingly iterable violent reenactments, moments of palpable haunting referred to as communal riots. Every time violence breaks out, previous massacres are cited and connections between them established—in the media and in everyday conversation alike—as a way of framing and understanding the latest atrocity.[72] Nevertheless, this schematic history misses one vital and fascinating aspect of cultural mourning work. When I spoke with various writers, artists, and filmmakers, most agreed with me that the post-independence popular cinema of the 1950s and 1960s had largely steered clear of Partition, deeming the episode to be too brutal and upsetting to be brought alive on screen. Once in a while, however, someone would counter this standard perception with the claim that cinema had, indeed, dealt with the experience substantially, only to disappoint by failing to name any title beyond the handful I already knew of. In spite of the virtual absence of "Partition films," I was sufficiently intrigued by this contrary albeit marginal impression to begin looking more carefully at a wider range of films from the period. In particular, I searched for signs of indirect or implicit mediations of the trauma that might have resonated with contemporary experiences, providing a sense of broad cultural engagement. As I demonstrate in chapters 2 and 3, Indian cinema of the first two decades after 1947 abounds in narratives in which Partition appears in displaced, allegorical forms, intimating a kind of melancholic obsession.

While reflecting on the temporality of trauma, I came to realize that the latency of such an experience does not always imply delay: latency can also take on a submerged manifestation, existing in parallel time. Put another way, a traumatic experience need not unfold at a lag: it can generate a temporality all its own, one that runs alongside and yet is out of sync with the present. Thus cultural mediations do not always wait for the passage of time to blunt the shock: rather, they produce their own mitigations through figural sublimations and displacements. We often describe such representations as having a "haunting" quality, without being able to articulate successfully what it is about them that haunts us. Meanwhile, the description itself subconsciously alludes to the indirect trace of trauma: underlying the main diegesis, beyond the time of the narrative, we sense another ghostly subtext, a second temporality. The recognition of this spectral or negative presence has implications for Partition studies, in that the particular structure of "Partition experience" assumes greater significance than the experience itself.[73] This structure is marked by deferral, gaps, and uncertainties, providing no guarantee of the eventual assimilation of the experience within a coherent history, or of therapeutic closure.

Coming to terms with a trauma requires thinking through the unthinkable, speaking about the unspeakable: it is a task that is neither routine nor transparent but which places unusual demands on our cognitive and psychic resources.[74] That is to say, dealing with trauma is a critical—analytical *and* pressing—project. Translating these concerns to the Indian context, we can say that working through Partition requires, first, acknowledging the difficulty of integration in the field of knowledge and representation; and second, recognizing how, because of this difficulty, social resistance simultaneously elides the trauma (through deliberate forgetting and the reiteration of a fantasy of unity), *and* exposes it (through the intensification of communal prejudice and violent acting out). Such contingencies suggest a trajectory of interpretation and mourning that, in engaging the buried nuances, split temporalities, and spectral traces, must be, of necessity, nonlinear and multilayered. Thus, we can broadly construe the project of *Mourning the Nation* as one of listening to the post-Partition silence for its own disquieting articulations and situating the silence as both a portent and a precondition for the subsequent discursive eruption.

A Hermeneutic of Mourning

My aim here is to construct, from a dispersed cultural terrain, a *hermeneutic of mourning*. In effect, I am attempting to provide an interpretation of the cinematic interpretations of the lived experience of a loss. My point of departure is the following hypothesis: while any experience of loss gives rise to a need for some form of mourning, there is no certainty as to how such a process will unfold. Mourning can be explicit or subterranean, direct or displaced; it can help us come to terms with and to move beyond the experience, or it can protract, even compound, the sense of loss. Subsequent events, often unrelated to the original loss, frame and transmute the compulsions and progressions of mourning.[75] Drawing on cinematic engagements with a historically specific experience of collective loss, this book demonstrates that mourning work—the task of understanding, memorializing, and overcoming loss—does, indeed, proceed in dispersed and unexpected ways. How, then, can one even propose to chart a hermeneutic of mourning? Since common understandings of "hermeneutics" often presuppose a determinate, teleological, and totalizing trajectory for acts of interpretation, what is the point of engaging in an invocation that seems oxymoronic? My intent is to bring back a particular hermeneutic dimension to the understanding of history, a utopian dimension already present in the Hegelian understanding of historical interpretation as the exploration of the past and the present with an eye to the future. Keeping in mind contemporary critiques of immanent meaning, immediacy of experience, coherent subjectivity and agency, and foundational politics, I still want to hold onto the utopian impulse that was central to romantic hermeneutics, one that enables us to apprehend the multiple and textured denouements of loss and mourning. While Hegel's idealism finally locks us into a teleological model, certain moments in the German romantic hermeneutical tradition of the early nineteenth century—most notably Friedrich Schleiermacher's references to the "secondary," "underlying," "digressive," and "collateral" strands of thought in a text[76]—convey a more nuanced and open-ended notion of hermeneutics. These elements were subsequently overlooked but have now been resuscitated and developed in contemporary philosophy and cultural theory following disparate thinkers like Walter Benjamin, Hans-Georg Gadamer, Jacques Derrida, Reinhart Koselleck, and Fredric Jameson to complicate questions of textual meaning, authorial legacy, and the mapping of history.[77] These questions become particularly complex with respect to the postcolonies, where multiple, irreconcilable time horizons and lifeworlds jostle as so many spectral presences in the dense time of the now. Dipesh Chakrabarty, Walter Mignolo, and Elizabeth Povinelli have been particularly eloquent in theorizing this density of postcolonial imagination and experience from a materialist perspective.[78] Others, like Ackbar Abbas, Achille Mbembe, and Ashis Nandy, have evoked loss, disappearance, and mourning as the defining moments of contemporary postcolonial life.[79] While my invocation of a hermeneutic conjures up a historical denouement of cultural mourning work, it is a historicity that remains fundamentally shot through with the unsettling complications of postcolonial temporalities.

The kind of ambivalence/uncertainty that I have in mind is productively harnessed in an essayistic documentary by Amar Kanwar, *A Season Outside* (1998), produced around the time of the fiftieth anniversary of independence and Partition. Even as the two sibling nation-states celebrated the golden jubilee of their sovereign existence, the animosity in South Asia hit a new peak as both India and Pakistan flexed their nuclear muscles by conducting tests in rapid succession in 1998. Emerging out of this tense atmosphere, *A Season Outside* is a wistful look at the complex ties that bind the two peoples, and at the deep sense of loss that pervades popular consciousness in the region. The film chronicles a strange ritual marking loss and longing daily at sundown at the Wagah checkpost on the India-Pakistan border: every evening, scores of people assemble on both sides of the border, staring silently at each other across the fences, as members of the two armed forces go through equivalent ceremonial exercises.[80] What sense can we make of this haunting exchange of looks across the international border, the formal signpost of the rift, overlaying the matching official rites? Is it simply a fascination with the other, a fascination that can also turn into abhorrence and aggression, or is it also indexical of a deep wound, an abiding sense of loss, that confounds the self/other binary? I will argue that footage of the twilight ritual intimates a melancholic ambivalence, an ambivalence that retains a possibility for working through—even transforming—the prejudices and expressions of belligerence to something more affirmative. Through its contemplative look at the ties that simultaneously alienate and bind, the film underscores a need to mourn not only what transpired, but also what could have been.

Mourning the Nation speaks to a contemporary ethical turn in philosophy and cultural theory. The ethical charge of mourning work springs from the very uncertainty at the heart of it: there is no guarantee of any preordained, preferred solution. In the following pages, I explore an entire field of discrete—empirical as opposed to idealized—mourning practices that entail not only rational strategies of overcoming loss but also the more ambiguous modes of obsessing and acting out. In a fundamental sense, I am assembling an archive of commemorative practices: hence, an archivist's discriminating gaze comes into play. What epistemic and ethical spaces do cinematic representations of 1947 occupy? Do these invocations always work through troubling experiences in a principled way, fostering an enduring critical relationship to the past, or do they promote mere sensationalism and the nostalgic production of kitsch and spectacle? An ethical approach does not evacuate questions about a politics of mourning, and so we must also ask: what futures do these mediations envision for social life in South Asia? I make distinctions between aesthetic strategies that reiterate structures of hate and reproduce acts of aggression, and those that dislodge these patterns and look to a more utopian future. In short, what kind of politics these representations inspire, and how they fit in with evolving relations of power, remain crucial concerns. Here, the historicity of representations is key to my critical project. Depictions of trauma, dispersed as they are over the years and across film genres, do comprise a before/after temporality, an early phase tentatively demarcated from a later one, in which similar modes of representation take on very different functions in relation to the tasks of memorialization and mourning. Chapters 1 through 3, which focus on the early years after 1947, adopt a sympathetic approach to mainstream commercial films. In contrast, the concluding chapter on the sharp rise in the incidence of Partition films in recent years takes a more critical stance, denouncing an overarching and banal historicist mode that paradoxically promotes forgetfulness, and whose continuing lack of self-consciousness now has disquieting political implications.

A Melancholic Nationalism

Until the mid-1980s, much of the sadness in public discourse centered on the actual territorial truncation—the *batwara*, the *bibhajan*, the *deshbhag*; there was far less mention of the murderous riots, while the incidence of abduction and rape was practically expunged from conversation.[81] The violence done to the land came to be construed as the main form of Partition violence, perhaps because the link between territoriality and violence could be more readily acknowledged than the more troubling relation between violence and community, or the more sinister question of sexual violence. Nevertheless, the implicit linkages and wounds could not be elided: the investments had already been established in the charged iconicity of *Bharatmata*, Mother India, produced through the articulation of the cartographic and the corpothetic. As Sumathi Ramaswamy points out,[82] two distinct modalities of imagining the national body of India—a "disenchanted geographic" gaze that maps the territory, and a more romantic, "enchanted somaticism" that invokes the nation-as-mother—mobilized a seductive idealization and, one might add, produced the conditions for a more affecting disillusionment.

The focus on territorial attrition as the main form of loss was largely determined by the particular history of Indian nationalism. Colonialism triggered a cataclysmic rupture with the past, since colonial settlement proceeded at the cost of previous forms of life and community. At the same time, colonialism helped produce a sense of territorial unity in the subcontinent, introduced in large measure through modern technologies of communication and travel (railways, telegraph, national highways). In effect, colonialism compensated for the disruption of temporal continuity by establishing spatial contiguity—a substitution that had implications for a nascent Indian national consciousness. Anticolonial nationalism congealed around a modern spatial imagination of an undivided India—*Akhand Bharat*—whose imagined unity, as well as maternalization, was counted on to make up for, and to heal the wounds from, the temporal rupture. The decolonizing project was crucially linked up with this substitutive fantasy of plenitude. In thwarting that collective fantasy, the geopolitical truncation tainted the euphoria of freedom with a profound sense of loss. The exigencies of nation building required a collective disavowal of this loss, leading to an inability to mourn.[83] As I hope to show in part I of this book, such disavowal involved not so much procedures of forgetting as mechanisms of reframing.

The inability to mourn produced a widespread feeling of despondence—a national condition of melancholy whose symptoms mark

Indian cinema of the 1950s. Freud theorizes this condition in relation to mourning in his classic work "Mourning and Melancholia."[84] Mourning is induced by the loss of a love object that one clearly recognizes to be separate from oneself. Such loving is informed by the awareness of distinct boundaries between "I" and "you," and an acceptance of the potential for misunderstanding, disillusionment, even betrayal. When "reality-testing" indicates that "the loved object no longer exists," a directive is issued to withdraw "all libido" from the agent's "attachments to that object." However, the process takes some time, during which "each single one of the memories and expectations in which the libido is bound to the object is brought up and hyper-cathected, and detachment of the libido is accomplished in respect of it."[85] Once the process of *Trauerarbeit* or mourning work is completed, the subject's ego becomes free and available for cathexis to new loved objects. Melancholy, on the other hand, is a reaction to the loss of an object that is loved not as an entity distinct and separate from oneself, but as a reflection of one's self-worth. This is a more narcissistic form of love, as the loved object is loved precisely for its supposed oneness with the subject, through a disavowal of its otherness. When loss occurs, there is a debilitating sense of self-impoverishment. The first step required for mourning involves the establishment of clear boundaries between "I" and "you," the recognition that the lost object is an entity separate from the subject. After this primitive level of mourning is accomplished, the usual mourning work can proceed. This clear distinction is later complicated by Freud: in *The Ego and the Id*, he explains melancholia as a psychic process that is *constitutive* of the ego, in that the object or ideal which is lost is internalized and substituted for the ego, i.e., the abandoned object is preserved by and as the ego.[86] Freud further claims: "the object-loss is withdrawn from consciousness," or as Judith Butler puts it, "the object is not only lost, but that loss itself is lost, withdrawn and preserved in the suspended time of psychic life. In other words, according to the melancholic, I have lost nothing."[87]

In the aftermath of national independence, the project of nationhood required a dismissal of Partition as a one-time aberration in an otherwise continuous tradition of secular unity. Cultural practitioners participated in such a project as melancholic subjects: the post-Partition Indian ego was constituted by the experience of loss, and the lost secularist ideal was placed at its core. The unspeakability and unrepresentability of the loss was governed by "forms of social power" that, according to Butler, "regulate what losses will and will not be grieved." The mourning of the loss due to Partition was governed by the Nehruvian nation-state, intent on carrying out its rationalist project of modern nation building through a "social foreclosure of grief."[88] But this refusal of loss was achieved at a tremendous psychic cost: the ego was marked by a deep ambivalence, absorbing both love for and rage against the lost object.[89]

The post-independence secular Indian subject, marked by a strong desire for modernity, held onto certain cherished, if thorny, ideals. At least five major sets of others emerged: the departing British as the racial other (the object of nostalgia, and grudging respect born of two centuries of colonial indoctrination); the Anglo-Indian (the embodiment of miscegenation, hence an object of condescension); the fundamentalist Hindu as the atavistic other (disavowed in the name of secularism, a disavowal that was politically facilitated when Gandhi—the "Father of the Nation"—was assassinated by such a figure); the Pakistani Musalman (a figure whose very existence destabilized the myth of secular unity, and who thus emerged as the main focus of rage and abhorrence); and the Indian Musalman (a vexing category, simultaneously marking the triumph of secular national community and emerging as the locus of endless suspicion, specially in periods of heightened Indo-Pakistani animosity).

Such a narrative of psychic ambivalence helps explain why even avowed secularists can harbor such strong misgivings about the secularist ideal and often display deeply entrenched fear and suspicion of other religious communities. It shows us how Indians are able to downplay Partition and simultaneously harbor hostility toward the breakaway nation-state of Pakistan. Its most alarming expression is the nuclear arms race between India and Pakistan—a melancholic inversion of the parts of a fractured national body against each other, in a mad rush toward mutual annihilation. The ambivalence also helps us understand the specific dynamics of mourning work in the early years after Partition in response to tangible, concrete historical loss rather than to abstruse structural absence. The indirect and often unconscious mediations of the national bifurcation—compounded by the largely traumatic experience of modernity—constituted, in effect, a form of preliminary mourning work that paved the way for more explicit mourning later on in the 1980s and 1990s.

Mourning and Transformation

The central query driving this book is: what cultural mechanisms does mourning entail in a scenario of collective trauma? By focusing on cinematic mediations of Partition, I hope to identify a range of discursive tactics and psychosocial procedures in terms of which cultural mourning work has unfolded in India, reworking conceptions of nation, national history, and national subjectivity all along.

From a Freudian perspective, mourning technically involves the recognition of the loss of an object or ideal, and the gradual reduction of one's investment in, or attachment to, this lost entity. As one influential formulation defines Trauerarbeit, the work of mourning: "Intrapsychic process, occurring after the loss of a loved object, whereby the subject gradually manages to detach himself from the object."[90] At a social level, mourning becomes a more complex and messy affair, involving intersubjective transactions and mutual accommodations. For Theodor Adorno, such a task of collective mourning requires "working through" traumatic history and understanding and moving beyond the "objective conditions" which produced that history to begin with.[91] I recognize the value of Adorno's insistence on overcoming the objective conditions so that a society does not keep reproducing or acting out the trauma: clearly, the transformatory potential of mourning work is of paramount interest to him. This notion of "objective conditions" must also include psychic processes and their material articulations: cultural expressions of the preconceptions, anxieties, and fantasies regarding self and community. In short, we have to work with a capacious sense of objective conditions that takes into account the extant structures of feeling. Mourning work in a riven social formation would involve the gradual divestment or *decathexis* from a lost ideal of unity, and the subsequent mitigation of communal distrust and antagonism.

It is one thing to hope and strive for such a trajectory; its realization remains altogether another matter. If a social trauma, in its incomprehensibility and ineffability, takes on the aura of a *negative sublime*, then collective mourning turns out to be a particularly enigmatic process. While the psychic expenditures and adjustments involved in mourning are already demanding on an individual subject, such operations become far more tortuous at the social level: the multifarious allure of that which could have been, the lost object or ideal, proves particularly enduring for segments of society, often congealing into startling yearnings and regrets. In the South Asian context, memories of social and economic losses still rankle; the counterfactual—that which never was, a free and united India—continues to beguile, producing a deep sense of betrayal and bereavement. At a social level, vitriolic invocations and political mobilizations of such sentiments frequently appropriate the process of mourning to disastrous ends.

For all that, one can hardly overstate the promise of transformation at the heart of any act of mourning, a promise that lives on because personal or collective history is not beholden to some preordained teleology. The very unresolved nature of collective understanding, which often leads to recidivist flare-ups, also presents a productive opening: the possibility of overcoming—moving beyond—exhausted and exhausting sentiments of resentment and loathing, and prospects for greater empathy and tolerance among communities. This continuing trace of an untapped potential, a flickering optimism that will not die, takes on a particular poignancy in the South Asian context, where communal riots have persisted in the postcolonial era; another bloody truncation has led to the birth of a third sovereign state (Bangladesh); the scuffle over Kashmir continues largely in terms of religious affiliation; after three major wars and countless skirmishes, India and Pakistan have pushed each other to the brink of a nuclear holocaust. While it is entirely possible to explain the recent nuclearization of the Indo-Pakistani feud in terms of other contingent factors—one could argue, for instance, that India's nuclear program is prompted more by the need to counterbalance China, and by a desire to stake out a greater role in world affairs, including a permanent seat on the United Nations Security Council, than by its sibling rivalry with Pakistan—prevalent memories of Partition and subsequent bilateral tensions have ensured that Pakistan remain the focal point of national anxieties and military aspirations. Clearly, whatever shifts have occurred in objective conditions have not brought about the kinds of transformation one would hope for: in fact, the acute politicization of religious difference all over South Asia has exacerbated communal tension and effectively jettisoned an earlier nationalist commitment to secularism in India. In this bleak scenario, tapping the transformatory potential of mourning work has gathered the force of a political imperative.

No other factor has compounded this urgency more than the triumphant revival of religious nationalism, the long repressed other of mainstream Indian nationalism. In recent decades, faith-based identities are being stringently redefined, and communities are becoming antagonistically positioned with a fervor not seen since the mid-1940s. The champions of hindutva are militantly promoting the notion that India is for Hindus, and that various religious minorities are welcome within the space of the nation-state as long as they accept this claim. Meanwhile, Islamic fundamentalists in India, as also across the borders in Bangladesh and Pakistan, are staking out their own claims and forging long-term plans to overcome their minority status in this part of the world.[92] Now, each self-righteous assertion is answered with a counterclaim, and each incendiary act provokes a more bellicose reaction. We have witnessed the most horrific instance of such heightened combativeness in recent times at Godhra in the province of Gujarat: in early 2002, an alleged act of violence against Hindus, now adjudicated to have been the result of an accidental conflagration on a crowded train, provided the excuse for a prolonged pogrom directed against Muslims and effectively endorsed by the local government through its inaction; a year later, the suspects arrested in connection with the detonation of car bombs in two crowded Gujarati neighborhoods of Mumbai—explosions which killed around sixty people in August 2003—declared that theirs was an act of revenge, in retaliation for the Godhra massacres. Other recent instances of violence range from the killing of Kashmiri Brahmins by Islamic terrorists, to bomb blasts on Mumbai trains and at the Malegaon cemetery in 2006—local acts that increasingly are linked to global terrorist organizations. In this atmosphere of intensified belligerence, looking back at Partition involves what may be described as "doing history from the present"—that is, studying the past in order to learn from it and to understand the contemporary historical conjuncture, and to transform our relationship to the past in order to envision a better future.

Historiography, Mourning, and the National Subject

What are the possible pitfalls of such anachronism? One could argue that in my attempt to counter the forgetting that erases Partition from historical accounts or shrinks it practically to a vanishing point, I run the risk of reducing an entire social matrix and its evolution to this one event. I could end up claiming that Partition is the root cause of all our national woes, just as I could reach the implausible conclusion that every post-1947 film narrative is an allegory of the truncation. What I hope to accomplish in the following pages, though, is provide a sense of the extent to which Partition is constitutive of subsequent national life by presenting diachronic processes alongside synchronic relations: how the experience of Partition interacts with, and modulates, other aspects of collective existence, and how that experience itself gets reframed and rearticulated in popular culture over the decades to fit evolving needs.

A related question, posed after a talk I presented at a conference, gave me pause: it pressed me to examine my assumption that Partition was essential to post-1947 Indian identity, and my transparent conviction that Indians needed to come to terms with the experience. Was it necessary, or even pragmatic, to accord such a centrality to the event? Was I not, in a sense, allowing the ordeal to hijack crucial procedures of identity and community formation, to commandeer the denouement of history? When my interlocutor identified himself as someone who was born and brought up in the southern state of Kerala, I realized that "southerners" did not have to live directly with the violence and multifarious fallouts of 1947, such as the material and psychic displacement of refugees and the tribulations of déclassé populations. The exchange pointed to the range of differentiated experiences and evaluations that make up the legacy of Partition.

The simultaneous invocation of historiography and mourning in these pages presents the possibility of a practical impasse. My project of excavating cultural mediations of Partition, which is part of a current, pervasive impetus toward the historiographic recovery of Partition memories, does raise justified concerns about probable social repercussions. Several commentators have argued that such acts of remembering are imprudent, as painful memories of an originary wound might rekindle communal fury and generate further strife.[93] One remains suspicious of most such contentions, homologous as they are to a general official tendency to bury the truth in the name of law and order, thereby negating the possibility of social accountability or of affective restitution. A particularly macabre incidence of official cover-up comes from the March 2002 pogroms in Gujarat. When twenty-six people were killed in one village, the police quickly buried their bodies in a nearby garbage dump. When relatives of the victims went to the local police station to claim the bodies, they were turned away. In the absence of a clear closure, many relatives kept hoping that their loved ones would return, until bones and skulls were stumbled upon four years later in March 2006. At that point, the police complained that "the people who dug up the remains conducted *illegal exhumations intended to disturb the peace.*"[94] In this particular case, the hasty burial might have been motivated by the widely alleged police complicity in the pogroms; nevertheless, the police action shares with the rhetoric of forgetting a predisposition to conceal in the service of an imputed social order.

Historiographic retrieval would then seem, at first glance, to be in direct conflict with the task of mourning, which requires the gradual depletion of our investment in the lost object, a waning of passions. Hence, the juxtaposition of the two paradigms—historiography and mourning—would appear to be methodologically untenable. Yet as a range of traumatic experiences from diverse places such as China, Argentina, Germany, and South Africa have demonstrated, the skeletons do keep surfacing. A willed cultural amnesia cannot obliterate hurtful memories, nor can it block the mechanisms of mourning: both memorialization and mourning work proceed in spite of all kinds of proscriptions. Since the outcomes of such surreptitious cultural practices are frequently distressing, more active and frank engagement emerges as a reasonable and vital course of action. Indeed, I will argue that remembering and mourning are interdependent processes: the vivification of memories and emotional attachments is a precondition for mourning work, for it is the renewed and temporarily intensified experience of loss (hypercathexis) that allows the pent-up emotion to finally exhaust itself, leading to the attrition of attachment. As long as unanticipated roadblocks do not thwart the process (for collective mourning, political manipulation proves to be a common impediment), what we are finally left with—what we remember—is a distilled sublation of the original object, its decathected trace. Such memories help us bear witness to the social suffering, without necessarily setting off the mechanisms of tragic repetition.

Nonetheless, the menace of social hurdles, of which political interference is one familiar instance, calls attention to the limits of the mourning paradigm. When we speak of collective mourning, we face an intractable question: *who is it that mourns?* Are we not assuming a unified and coherent national subject who undertakes the task of mourning? This book does invoke the idea of a singular national subjectivity, but only as a heuristic; one of its main objectives is to establish the absolute impossibility of sustaining such a construct. Beginning precisely with the moment of its demise, the book proceeds to track the constant dispersal, scripted or subliminal, of the national subject in cinema. We could say that it is the mourner who is being mourned here as a chimeral projection. This introversion captures the sense of partial erasure, and of simultaneous retention in a modified form, implied in the invocations of a "beyond" in the phrases "working through," "coming to terms with" and, of course, "moving beyond." Mourning, then, emerges as a process of bracketing, of putting under erasure concepts that are inherently vexing, but which continue to have for us a heuristic utility, even—dare I say—an enduring appeal. It is in this sense that *Mourning the Nation* constitutes an intervention in film historiography in terms of the interrogation of one of its structuring categories—the national.

Writing as Mourning Work

The writing of this book also emerges as an act of mourning. Mourning here entails both a movement beyond loss and its retention as a sublated trace. The specific contours of this mourning work are shaped by my own experiences, my life in the realm of the exilic—between "now" and "then," between a "here" and an "elsewhere." While I come from a family of Partition refugees (my prehistory), I now live in the USA, in what is referred to as the Indian diaspora. The history of my subjectivity—my subjective location—comprises two forms of exile, forms that are captured by the two tropes of partition and diaspora. If the nation is the hegemonic form of modern collective life, then both partition and diaspora constitute radical dispersions of that community, putting into question the inevitability and legitimacy of the nation form. If the nation is the ground of an imagined yet felt wholeness, then both kinds of dispersion rend that ground, divide our selves, exile us to a horizon of loss. Indeed, partition and diaspora, both significant moments in the evolution of the nation, define and locate the experience of nationality in relation to, and within, the larger experiences of modernity and globalization. The link between the two terms was already apparent to filmmaker Ritwik Ghatak in the early 1960s, if we go by the evidence of his 1961 film, *Komal Gandhar* (discussed in chapter 5). In mourning the national partition, I also mourn, with Ghatak, the national dispersion in the diaspora: in effect, I mourn the nation in relation to the modern-cosmopolitan-global.

Melancholia remains the substance of Indian modernity, after independence as before. The poet Faiz Ahmed Faiz captured this melancholia when he lamented the onset of a "dawn" that was mottled by the night and expressed his sense of disillusionment:

> This leprous daybreak, this night-bitten dawn,
> this is not the dawn we awaited with longing sighs:
> this is not the dawn that drew our friends on
> believing that, somewhere in the desert of these skies,
> they would find the resting place of the stars,
> the coast where night's sluggish tides reach the shore,
> somewhere find the boat of heartache and drop anchor.[95]

The poet's anguish was caused by the death of a collective dream at the precise moment of the birth of the nation-state. Such a dream was a necessary national enchantment that fueled the struggle for freedom in the colonial era, and which was to propel an independent people onto new collective glories. With the truncation of the nation, its hopes and aspirations were blighted forever.

Faiz was mourning not just the loss of some world and life that South Asians once possibly had, but also the loss of a future. Such an affective horizon comes into play every time South Asian cricket fans wonder wistfully what a joint cricket team might have achieved in international competition.[96] The poignancy of this affective position, which involves a structure of feeling that may be described as proleptic melancholia, arises from a loss of futures and possibilities, a loss of idealism. A very specific temporality is in evidence here, one that assumes that the past once had several futures. Such a temporality (I shall call it the temporality of the anterior future)[97] sets us free of the force of necessity that drives totalizing models of history. It is in such mourning work that we begin to glimpse lost, perhaps forgotten possibilities: melancholia here is not simply about holding onto what never was to begin with (a unified India); rather, melancholia becomes a mode of resuscitating that which could have been. If, in the South Asian context, that does not translate exactly into a fantasmatic reunification of Bangladesh, India, and Pakistan, it may at least point to a peaceful future in which the splintered states, and the religious communities within each state, are not endlessly threatening to obliterate each other. In a global context, such affective engagement with the unspent, unrealized potentialities of collective organization at sub- and supranational levels may help us transcend the tyranny of the nation form: a kind of mourning work that helps us dream about futures and communities.

I.

A Resonant Silence

CHAPTER ONE

Cinema's Project of Nationhood

IN THE MONTHS I SPENT at the National Film Archives in Pune, scouring films for traces of the Partition, the image of a child on the back of a donkey captured my attention. I was certain that I had seen this image before, yet this was the first time I was viewing the particular film—the megahit *Shabnam* (1948), whose success at the box office helped consolidate Filmistan studio's reputation in the late 1940s as the producer of rollicking entertainment. Soon enough, I came across the same shot in an official documentary, *The Agony of the Partition*, produced by Films Division in 1985. This led me to think that I had also seen the image reproduced in print media, although I was not sure of it: after all, the representation echoed a familiar iconographic trope of capturing social suffering (famines and earthquakes, wars and genocides) through singular images of children.[1] My *punctum*, a personal affinity, had penetrated a referential opacity to disclose an entire *studium*, a shared cultural field.[2] More than the veracity of my memories, at issue was the existence and disjunctive circulation of photographic/filmic images of Partition.

This serendipitous detection of stock footage of Partition in a popular narrative film of the time marks an interesting juncture in my research. It is not surprising that footage of refugees from 1947 found its way into a commercial film made in the next couple of years; after all, such

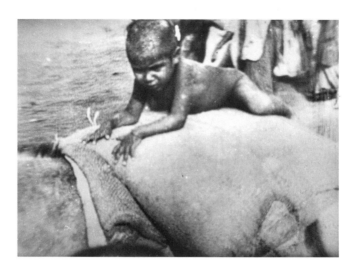

Shabnam: Child on donkey. Courtesy of NFAI.

insertion is standard practice for genres like war films and biopics. This "discovery" is remarkable because it indexes the existence of film footage of Partition/independence and of surrounding events (for example, the 1946 riots in Calcutta; refugees on the road, on the roofs of trains, and in camps; Nehru's famous midnight speech in Parliament; and Gandhi's cremation in 1948). After all, there were armies of film crew—associated with the pre-independence government agency Information Films of India, private film-producing bodies like Wadia Movietone and Motwane Company, and international news agencies like Agence France-Presse and Reuters—ready to document the historic end of the British Raj and the birth of an independent nation-state. So the paucity of Partition documentaries turns out to be a beguiling paradox. Only in 1985 did the Films Division release *The Agony of the Partition* as part of a series on India's struggle for freedom. Even in that short piece, the focus shifts quickly to Gandhi's assassination: the trauma of Partition is deflected onto the shocking death of "the Father of the Nation."

The narrative of *Shabnam* has no apparent connection to 1947. The film is about Indian refugees fleeing Burma in the wake of the Japanese bombing of Rangoon in 1942. If we categorize the incorporation of footage of Partition refugees as just an instance of a standard cinematic convention, we overlook one significant fact: commercial cinema's representation of the plight of refugees in 1942, using images of refugees from 1947, constitutes a conscious, anachronistic displacement. In 1949, mainstream films would not take on the subject of Partition, yet they would tap into experiences and anxieties of the day by narrating a tale of refugees from 1942, emphasizing filmic traces from 1947 to establish verisimilitude.

Shabnam takes a tale of bewildering dislocation and privation on the road and turns it into an entertaining romantic caper, peppered with colorful characters (a fiendish feudal prince, a tribal ingenue, snake charmers) and engrossing, if highly improbable, situations. It is one of those Filmistan products in which we discern the gradual crystallization of genres in terms of themes, iconography, characters, and settings—cinematic codes whose influence continues to this day. It is also a text whose metaphoric displacements and allegorization—oblique narrative mechanisms that are important to the formation of genres and consolidation of audiences—reveal its fraught ideological labors. One realizes, for instance, that the iconic substitution of refugees allows the film to circumvent the immediate shock while engaging contemporary structures of feeling. The very iconicity of the shot of the child on a donkey ruptures the narrative about refugees from Burma and points indexically to Partition refugees: the traumatic event—an originary wound, as it were—persists in its photographic trace.

The esemplastic maneuvers from *Shabnam* draw our attention not only to the goals that were being pursued in commercial films in roughly the first decade[3] in the career of the nation-state, but also to what was being left out to achieve these goals. I start by posing the following question: if contemporary films did not represent what was clearly the most momentous event in modern South Asian history, what were they doing instead? The objective of this circuitous approach is an understanding of both cinematic expressions *and* silences as intertwined figurations constituting an overarching discourse. The present chapter examines the specific expediencies that shaped cinema in spite of the general indirection and opacity of a traumatized cultural field; chapter two explores what the films, unable to depict directly, registered in implicit ways. The first two chapters, then, are of one piece: while this chapter delineates some modes in which popular films attempted to carve out a role for cinema in a project of nation building, chapter 2 undertakes an excavation of "hidden" narratives of Partition, revealing the ambivalences of Indian nationalism at its presumed pinnacle.

The balance of this chapter (1) situates popular cinema of the first decade in relation to a hegemonic nationalist project and an official national culture, (2) tracks cinema's agonistic relationship to the postcolonial state in the course of salient controversies (the bastardization of culture; the moral corruption of women, children and the masses; regulation and censorship), (3) documents industrial initiatives, including the formation of genres and the consolidation of audiences, and

(4) explores popular cinema's dexterous and creative negotiation of the contingencies of that period by focusing on two key films.

Nationhood

In the years immediately following independence, Indian cinema was caught up in a collective endeavor of nation building, offering narratives that negotiated the challenges and choices facing its publics. In that sense, popular cinema participated in what the great Mexican writer Octavio Paz referred to as India's "project of nationhood."[4] While such an undertaking is common to, and remains crucial for, all modern nation-states, it becomes particularly daunting in the case of India, given the diversity that characterizes its social field and the deep laceration that marks its birth. But as Paz points out, it is not just a matter of negotiating the plurality of languages (around eighteen official languages, hundreds of dialects), races, ethnicities, religions, castes, regional lifestyles: India is "a living museum, one in which the most modern modernity coexists with archaisms that have survived for millennia."[5] Thus, for Paz, India—like Mexico, his homeland—constitutes "an enormous historical contradiction."[6]

I take Paz's invocation of "historical contradictions" as shorthand for the multiple textures and fissured temporalities of postcolonial modernities, which trouble historicist assumptions about the gradual subsumption of all local difference by a teleological and unitary history. Recent critiques of historicism[7] are directed not just at Western histories of "peripheral" nation-states, but also at hegemonic nationalist accounts that follow "universal" paradigms of modernization—an influential instance of which is to be found in the writings of Jawaharlal Nehru,[8] India's first head of state. There is a fundamental tension in Nehru's evocation of the past and his articulation of a future for the nation: a tension between wanting to exalt national heritage as a source of collective pride and wanting to break with it, to move beyond traditional obstacles into a modern future.

The central contention of this chapter is that popular Hindi cinema of the late 1940s and the 1950s was involved in negotiating the contradictions of an incipient nation-state and was often able, both thematically and formally, to imagine and narrativize parallel, even immiscible, notions of time and being. In the course of such negotiations and imaginings, this body of films evinced an ambiguous relationship to official discourses: its frequent undermining of Nehruvian ideals of secular modernization and techno-rationalist development complicated its assimilation within a hegemonizing nationalist project. The chapter provides an admittedly selective sense of the cultural-ideological transactions, sketching a few of the debates that throw into sharp relief the epistemological and moral paradigms, rhetorical strategies and affective frames in terms of which popular cinema realized a nuanced, often equivocal, sense of nationality. In establishing these intricacies of popular cinema's narration of the nation, the chapter advances an understanding of "India" not as a prerealized and frozen entity, but as perennially in a state of becoming, in difference from and in contention with alternative sociopolitical formations. It also cues us in to what is elided: the subterranean impulses of national life, comprising what one might call a collective unconscious.

Hindi cinema is by no means exceptional in its dialogic participation in, and recalibration of, a project of nationhood: one can cite Italian neorealism's rearticulation of nationhood through a shift from the operatic bases of fascist cinema to the more quotidian world of the folk commedia dell'arte,[9] or recent Hollywood cinema's multiculturalist renegotiations of American identity.[10] However, what is striking is the extent to which Bombay films have been able to capture the dilemmas of the lived world of the masses, engage them at the level of their desires and fears, and generate a palpable realm of belonging that has emerged as the strongest realization of an imagined collectivity—more compelling than state-sponsored nationalism. Ashish Rajadhyaksha draws our attention to the ritualistic and performative realm of the "national" conjured up in Indian popular cinema in terms of a cinephile "insiderism" involving "a buddy-culture of speech and body-language" further elaborated in print media ("reviews, gossip columns and magazines, publicity materials, novelisations") and, one might add, on television and the Internet.[11] He argues that "the dynamic of these idioms" does not readily coincide with "that of official, 'national' India in any predictable fashion": in this respect, the Indian industry remains distinct from Hollywood, whose projections of the national remain closer to official versions. While Rajadhyaksha does not theorize the differences between the Indian and American contexts, an explanation will probably have to start with the distinctive relations, real and imagined, between culture and the state in the two countries, and the underlying phenomenological and philosophical assumptions about the loaded question of representation. In Europe and North America, theories of the modern state and theories of culture evince a striking convergence, with modern "Culture" increasingly conceptualized as supplementary to the state: the overarching stress is on the pedagogical responsibility of culture in producing modern citizen-subjects. Nevertheless, culture's "civilizing" mission as an appendage of state governance remains sharply contested, a contestation palpable in the long history of proletarian resistance to the very idea of cultural education.[12] This pedagogical role has a far more vexed history in postcolonies like India where class difference is compounded by factors such as difficulties in adopting the imported values and institutions of civil society,[13] and the coexistence of irreconcilable lifeworlds.[14]

Notwithstanding the differences, popular culture plays an important role in both India and the United States in establishing a space where desire and politics intersect. In her study of the libidinal politics of the American nation, Lauren Berlant observes that Americans are bound together because they "inhabit the 'political' space of the nation, which is not merely juridical, territorial (*jus soli*), genetic (*jus sanguinis*), linguistic, or experiential, but some tangled cluster of these."[15] Berlant calls this space the National Symbolic. It not only provides the technical definitions of the citizen's rights, duties, and obligations, but also aims "to link regulation to desire" by infusing desire into political life. Thus the National Symbolic harnesses people's libidinal investments and channelizes them. Citizens' rights, duties, and responsibilities are made to matter in affective terms through the production of "national fantasy": national culture comes to be imbued with local, more personal desire, "through the images, narratives, monuments, and sites that circulate through personal/collective consciousness." Berlant asserts that "America" emerges as an amalgam of "ongoing collective practices," and its national subjects share "not just a history, or a political allegiance, but *a set of forms and the affect that make these forms meaningful.*"[16]

The concept of the National Symbolic is useful in understanding Indian popular cinema's promotion of a negotiated national subjectivity capable of projecting its Indian-ness, and being a citizen of a modern nation-state. The concept draws our attention to the two-fold necessity for both a set of cultural forms and the affect that makes these forms meaningful. In this respect, popular films of the period in question can be seen productively as cultural forms that sought to make transformations of national life (to a bourgeois, capitalist, democratic, secular polity) emotionally intelligible to the people. Debates surrounding these transactions, and efforts toward the consolidation of genres and their publics, are the focus of this chapter. In foregrounding collective fantasy, the concept also enables an analytic aperture onto the obscure, often subliminal, emotions and drives that course through the socializing rituals of cinema, producing unforeseen involutions in the nationalist script. That optic is the concern of chapter 2.

Cinema as National Culture:
Art or Mass Communication?

To situate Indian popular cinema within a postcolonial national culture, we first need to map the ambiguous, at times contentious, truck between the film industry and official nationalism. What positions did the state and the cultural establishment adopt toward cinema as a mobilizer of national fantasy? How was it perceived in relation to time-honored cultural fields, such as literature and the fine arts? What kinds of assumptions about national spirit and creativity shaped such divergent attitudes about the place of various aesthetic domains in national life, producing, in effect, a hierarchy of the arts? In what ways did such predispositions influence public stance and official policy? I begin with a detour through the field of "national art" to identify the expectations that were brought to bear upon culture in the early years after independence.

Art history emerged as an important arena for the post-independence construal of national culture and heritage, its discourses and practices seeking to form an aesthetic canon. Nineteenth- and twentieth-century nationalist leaders had posited, following orientalist constructions of India, an "essential" spirituality of national being as a way of asserting the superiority of Indian civilization over the West.[17] Within an ideological-institutional context provided by the Nehruvian state apparatus, the modern formation of "Indian Art" retained the transcendental as an essential and constitutive category. Focusing on the grandiose *Exhibition of Indian Art* put together in 1948 in the halls of the Government House in New Delhi, Tapati Guha-Thakurta charts the specific operations through which "ideas of nation and history were represented/fabricated within the body of an art display."[18] The exhibition, the catalogue, and the lectures together constituted "a rich allegory of history and nationhood,"[19] amassing artifacts "salvaged" from various dispersed, at times obscure, regional locations and "elevated" to the status of "masterpieces," aiming to provide a "visual enactment of the grand theme of a national art history, running through the whole sequence of great schools and ages."[20] The production of an aesthetic tradition, defined by a profound, timeless spirituality, was a thoroughly modern move, yoked as it was to the consolidation of a modern nation-state. The spiritual itself emerged as a "secular designation," as works of art were emptied of "all prior religious meanings and cult values" and framed in terms of their historical and aesthetic lineage.

As Guha-Thakurta points out, the narrative of "national art" embodied in the 1948 exhibition was developed around a "resounding absence . . . of the 'modern.'"[21] An antecedent exhibition of "typical master-pieces of Indian art," organized in London by the Royal Academy of Arts between November 1947 and February 1948 to mark the transfer of power, served both as a repository and as a model for the Delhi event to draw upon. However, artistic achievements of the colonial era included in the London exhibit were left out from the nationalistically inflected Delhi show. The permanent collection at the National Museum in the nation's capital, which adopted the singular focus of the 1948 exhibit on ancient and medieval art heritage as its curatorial logic, objectified and memorialized art history "in sharp dissociation from the present."[22] This move ties in with a shift in urban art centers in the 1940s, which Guha-Thakurta identifies as the "passing of the age of nationalism in modern Indian art, and the disengagement of artists from the demands of na-tion, history and tradition."[23] While Guha-Thakurta appears to equate "nationalism" with a monolithic and official version of it, overlooking the myriad negotiations of such "demands" in the arts, her insight that, by and large, modern artists were left alone by official institutions to pursue their own interests remains useful: engagements with past forms and styles—with "nation, history and tradition"—were developed out-side of the statist art historical establishment.

In contrast, cinema had to contend with the state on very different terms. A new medium of representation, it offered no large body of past achievements that could be edified in the service of a frozen, roman-ticized "heritage" encapsulating all that India had stood for through the ages. While Indian cinema frequently drew on a civilizational ar-chive of ideas and forms, the representations reverberated with quo-tidian foment. Cinema was by nature embroiled in the maelstrom of contemporary political life; its potentialities could not be harnessed easily. Official doublespeak transmitted anxieties about the medium's mercurial attributes: even as the state derided and denounced cinema for pandering to base instincts and promoting values and lifestyles that conflicted with an "authentic" Indian ethos, it called upon the industry to play a significant role in nation building. The terms of such interpel-lations were intrinsically contradictory; for instance, the industry was expected both to uphold tradition and to promote progressive social reforms. The central government's institutional policies also reflected similar tensions: while the Ministry of Culture was in charge of litera-ture and the fine arts, cinema was placed under the purview of the Min-istry of Information and Broadcasting; while the Sahitya Academy and the Lalit Kala Academy were set up to promote literature and the fine arts respectively, there never was a Chalachchitra Academy for the ad-vancement of cinema. Such distinctions were made, no doubt, on the basis of cinema's wide reach and potential influence: it was perceived as a medium of mass communication—primarily of commercial and ideological, rather than aesthetic, significance. Not surprisingly, the state adopted a predominantly regulatory stance toward cinema.

Besides censorship, which I address below, the official regulation of cinema was executed through regimes of licensing and taxation. The first category entailed the issue of import licenses to procure technical equipment (cameras and raw film stock, editing and sound machinery), and licenses to construct cinema theaters (in response to the scarcity of building materials like steel and cement). Taxation, administered by the provincial governments, was fervently disputed.[24] Given the huge annual turnover of the film industry, entertainment tax was a significant source of revenue for the regional governments. But the tax structures differed across the states, and over time in the same state, reflecting the particular predilections of the local power blocs toward the industry. Arbitrariness marked the administration of taxes as various films were granted a tax-free status on the basis of their purported espousal of ideals of national integration or a progressive social consciousness. In many cases, tax exemptions became a way of rewarding producers who were close to the ruling blocs and who had helped the winning parties in the elections. Nevertheless, such a practice created a space for the local contestation of a national hegemonic order, as some of the provincial governments (e.g., West Bengal, Kerala, Tamil Nadu) represented—or were compelled to accommodate—political views that were at variance with the policies of the Congress Party and its union government.

This dispersion of official regulation indicates the deeply contested nature of the very ideals and institutions that such control sought to protect and promote. Moving away from a unitary view of regulation, we start to glimpse the ideological battles and dialogic accommodations that came to constitute the deeply ambivalent relation between Indian cinema and the Indian nation-state. The state itself vacillated between curbing cinema as a social vice ("The Indian film industry is mostly composed of pimps and prostitutes and we can't think of it in terms of a national industry!")[25] and engaging the industry as one of its ideological apparatuses (as exemplified in the 1949 official proposal that film theaters were to screen approximately 2,000 feet of newsreels and documentaries before each feature presentation and to pay rental for the privilege). A 1953 editorial in a Bengali film magazine criticized the Information and Broadcasting Minister for his doublespeak on the film industry: first he declared in Calcutta that the government had "no special authority" over the industry, and then he asserted within days in Parliament that regulation was necessary.[26]

State indecisiveness led to half-hearted initiatives of extending institutional support to the industry. A Film Enquiry Committee headed by S. K. Patil was set up in 1949, with representatives from the film industry, to assess the state of the industry and look into possible official assistance to help cinema develop into "an effective instrument for the promotion of national culture, education and healthy entertainment."[27] In its report, submitted in 1951, the committee was critical of recent developments, particularly the emergence of a mass-cultural idiom and the star system, and the dominance of black market money. Its recommendations upheld many of the concerns and demands of the industry people: setting up a Film Council, government investment in film production, extension of institutional credit through a film finance corporation, establishment of a film institute and a film archive. Unfortunately, the report became yet another document gathering dust on the ledges of bureaucracy: the idea of the Film Council was scuttled, and it took decades to implement some of its other recommendations, leading to charges of indifference, callousness, even outright discrimination. Official recognition of Indian cinema as an industry with significant contributions to the GNP came only in 1998, fifty-one years after independence.

Cultural Deracination and Moral Panic

The ambiguity that marked official attitudes was echoed and amplified by public discourses outside government circles. When *Filmindia*, the popular magazine from Bombay, hailed cinema in 1948 as "a medium that can, and should, be the eyes and ears of the nation,"[28] it was claiming for cinema a paramount role in national life. A reader wrote in about the "need to present to the masses excellent designs and resources of living in a Free India." She called upon cinema to uphold "subjects as may espouse feelings of nationality, patriotism, bravery, self sacrifice, self-reliance and strict discipline in us," such as "strong powerful pictures of the lives" of heroes from the nation's past.[29] But these were ideals neither unanimously espoused nor easily achieved; issue after issue, *Filmindia* lambasted the Bombay film industry for its failure to live up to such expectations, calling for greater control of the industry to ensure the production of "cleaner" films.[30]

The increasing standardization of mass cultural forms according to emerging global norms and the centralization of their (re)production mark them out from folk forms, which enjoy a comparative aura of organicity and authenticity. For a new nation-state, industrial standardization provided one significant reason for a general suspicion of mass culture: when the stress was on promoting cultural forms that appeared to reflect the "true" mindset of the Indian people, mass culture appeared corrupted and corrupting in its homogenizing hybridity. Public suspicion of Bombay cinema found frequent expression around the issue of the import of Western "immorality" into film narratives. At stake was the preservation of Indian culture and ways of life, infused with their characteristic and supposedly unassailable spirituality. Polemics about "clean," "moral" and "truly Indian" culture came together in two controversies of the 1950s, relating to the alleged bastardization of Indian music and the prurient nature of cinema. These moments intimated a mounting sense of crisis in spite of—or, perhaps, because of—the neurotic attempts to fix cultural categories and to provide a stable basis of national identity.

Cultural purists were angered by the film industry's practice of interweaving classical music and dance forms with elements from folk traditions, low-brow popular stage, and Western sources. They decreed the "vulgarization" of *bharatnatyam* and *odissi*, classical dance forms developed in temples, through the incorporation of movements drawn from more vivacious folk dance forms of northern and western India; they covered their ears hearing Latin horns blast through a sublime raga. Conservative circles were particularly threatened by the rising popularity of "bastard" film songs across the nation. This incipient "culture war" over the hybridization of national high art forms came to a head when Dr. B. V. Keskar, the new minister of information and broadcasting, announced new policies for the All India Radio (AIR) in July 1952, drastically reducing the broadcast time allotted to film songs and dropping the custom of announcing the name of the film. Enraged at this loss of free advertisement opportunity for their films, the producers, in their capacity as copyright owners, took away AIR's licenses for broadcasting film songs. As film music disappeared from AIR stations and was replaced by classical music, its audience shrank rapidly. Meanwhile, Radio Ceylon started broadcasting Indian film songs on its new commercial shortwave service, capturing a large section of the Indian audience. Ultimately AIR came to a compromise with the producers and started playing film songs again in 1957.[31]

The controversy drew much attention to the field of popular film music, which had emerged as one of the strongest locations of "national culture" in the most dynamic and lived sense of the term. Declaring "a living culture is not afraid of foreign influences," popular music director Salil Chowdhury historicized the very idea of Indian music, tracking how the classical forms developed out of folk music. For Chowdhury, it was important for a composer to move with his times, to respond to the inspirations of his own milieu, and to find forms adequate for expressing emergent sensibilities.[32] Madan Mohan, another major music director, argued that it made no sense to hold on to archaic oppositions between popular and classical music, as film music had actually helped to popularize classical music among the masses. Moreover, he claimed for popular film music the status of the "first really *national* music we ever had," since it had "broken through linguistic and provincial barriers."[33] Indeed, film songs captured the national imagination like no other art form—more than the films of which they were parts. Even today, songs from films of the 1950s remain cherished objects: beyond nostalgia, they enter everyday parlance as readily available utterances, their shared meanings enabling expressive, idiomatic usage. Meanwhile, classical music and dance continue to flourish in contemporary India. Film music has confounded all instrumentalist arguments for a protected and institutionalized national culture and emerged, ironically, as a vital force of cultural integration.

Armed with the stock physical/spiritual and West/East polarizations, critics of commercial cinema directed their ire at onscreen sexuality, reductively tracing it to the influence of Hollywood, alleged propagator of degenerate Western values. The desire to establish a transcendental national character blinded this "moral police" to the vibrant eroticism of Indian aesthetic traditions. Not only was cinematic eroticism considered antithetical to Indian sensibilities, but it also was deemed vulgar and in bad taste. Such invocations of taste revealed the class dimension of the denigration of popular films: only children and the infantalized "masses," and not the educated elites, were seen at risk of contamination. In 1954, in a vital show of civic mobilization, 13,000 women of Delhi signed the Petition against Prurience, addressed to Prime Minister Nehru and alleging that cinema was having pernicious effects on their children, enticing them to stay away from schools, leading to a premature development of sexual interests, and inculcating delinquent tendencies in general. They called for necessary measures to curb this evil influence, perhaps going to the extent of a constitutional amendment.[34] One report stressed the wide support for the petition, claiming that it was backed by an equal number of illiterate women who could not sign their names.[35] The petition drive was a striking popular attempt at lobbying the state's cultural policies, which was seen to have significant ramifications for the future of the nation. The fact that the appeal came from mothers (subjects interpellated to ensure the continuity of the nation and its ethos), on behalf of the children (the future of the nation), generated a charged response: the debates that followed in public forums were characterized by strong emotions. One editorial described the Bombay film industry's response as delirious and incoherent, citing matinee idol Ashok Kumar's fear of an anti-industry conspiracy.[36] Indeed, incoherence marked all sides of the controversy, signaling basic confusions in public opinion on the subject of cinema, concerning the relation between representation and social behavior, the medium's social role as both entertainment and education, and the status of movie stars, seen as both good role models and bad influences.

Female Sexuality and Censorship

Much of the objection to cinematic delinquency targeted the representation of female sexuality, the source of perpetual vexation for colonialists and nationalists alike (with male sexuality remaining largely beyond discursive contestation). Earlier, nationalist narratives of art history had sought to contain the sensuality of erotically charged classical female forms by linking these representations, as Guha-Thakurta notes, to "nature and fertility cults of the past" and "vegetal motifs of flowering and reproduction."[37] The full-bodied female figures were transformed into signifiers of collective meaning, a stress on social iconographic functions playing down their considerable erotic appeal and disavowing the possibility of primarily individual and carnal appreciation. In the course of such nationalist reinscriptions, the feminine image emerged as a crucial ground of mediation between the spiritual and the sensual. Figurations of the woman in early modern Indian art followed similar patterns of idealization and allegorization. Whether in the increasingly kitschy neoclassical works of Raja Ravi Varma from the late nineteenth century,[38] or in the mystical idealism of the Bengal School in the early decades of the twentieth,[39] we find a preoccupation with working out an "authentic" or "essential" Indian aesthetic style through the representation of female figures. Recent estimations of modern Indian art have located one of its important populist strands in the realm of calendar art which, as an indigenous "culture industry," incorporates and develops earlier traditions.[40] Kajri Jain identifies in calendar art "the fine, florid lines and sinuous romantic *nayikas* [heroines] with elongated Ajantaesque fingertips"[41] and the idealized, spiritualized women from "Abanindranath's Mughal miniature-style illustrations of the *Rubay'yat*."[42] But calendar art also emphasizes the sensuality of female figures,[43] an emphasis that draws on Ravi Varma's ample bodies in repose and is elaborated in terms of twentieth-century low-brow "bazaar" idioms[44] involving scanty, albeit decidedly Indian costumes.[45]

In cinema, sensualized depictions of women were accepted so long as their professed intent was the negotiation of collective dilemmas and so long as a moral-spiritual dimension prevailed. But charges of Western influence and un-Indian excess arose whenever a female character's sexuality, as primarily an expression of personal desire, threatened patriarchal prohibitions crucial to modern state formations. Since the "true" core of an Indian self was supposedly impervious to external influences, Westernized expressions of individuated sexuality were considered deviant and perverse. Conventions of acceptability based on the opposition of purity and contagion led to all kinds of arbitrary criteria: thus the image of a woman singing in the rain wearing a wet—hence revealing—cotton sari was less likely to offend nationalist critics than the image of an Indian woman in a skirt dancing to Western music in a bar.[46]

Purporting to protect indigenous mores from the assault of alien influences, the institutions of censorship in independent India paradoxically retained, with a few modifications, the colonial censorship codes.[47] This continuity does not seem so surprising when we remember that Indian nationalist and British colonial interests had converged even in the heydays of the struggle for freedom to produce codes eliminating sexual situations. As Madhava Prasad points out:

> British censorship policy in India was partly determined by the anxiety to protect the privacy of the ruling race, to restrict native spectators' access to the white zenana [woman]. Indigenous patriarchies which fiercely defended their domestic space against the reformist intrusions of the alien rulers, also fought for the same privilege of guarding the view, resulting in a social compromise that was reflected in the effective exclusion of all representations of the private in Indian cinema. Censors relentlessly tracked down the minutest instances of vulgarity, obscenity, suggestiveness, etc.[48]

Prasad goes on to argue that censorship cannot be reduced to the mere imposition of restrictions by the state on a filmmaker's freedom of expression; following Noel Burch, he offers a civilizational understanding of censorship as the official codification of attempts by a people to resist external threats to their culture.[49] Here, we should extend the very idea of the "external" to include the pressures that the nation experienced internally at the time, indicated by the wide range of responses of social groups to the state's internalization of "external" models in its ambitious program of modernization. This chapter presumes a broad, sociopolitical notion of censorship as an institution that was the outcome of certain "ideological compromises," reflecting the relative authority of conflicting social forces.

One social force to reckon with was cinema's ancillary press, which expressed much anxiety and ire over filmic representations of the woman. An editorial in the January 1950 issue of *Filmindia* titled "Slandering the Nation" took issue with the exaggerated and stereotypical representation of village girls in typical romances. The shrill, vitriolic tone of the following quote underscores the writer's indignation:

> Evidently our village belles lack even the primary modesty that keeps a "dopatta" [veil or scarf] in its place covering her bosoms . . . She must be a completely shameless wench to do what she is always shown doing with her costume. . . . At the village well all the young village belles almost invariably sing a sexy song which tells us that they are all in terrific heat with the season irritating them in the wrong parts and that they are waiting either for a "sajan," a "balam," a "sainya," or a "piya" which all mean a mate for their youth. And they sigh and twist in the agony of youth in tune with the soft and suggestive words of the song. If you hear one such song near the village well, you must come to the painful conclusion that all our village girls are sex-starved . . . And as soon as the song ends, there comes the inevitable "pardesi babu" (the young boy from the distant city) all thirsty, looking out for a drink of water.[50]

The commentator failed to recognize the possibility that these generic tales were expressing the apprehensions of a largely rural nation confronting the unsettling transformations collectively referred to as "modernization"; that perhaps these narratives were negotiating the conflicts between the (gendered) rural and the urban worlds; that romantic love was being proposed as the common ground on which all such conflicts could be symbolically resolved. He did have a point in his criticism of the stereotypical, exoticized depiction of village women meant to titillate audiences. But titillation was not the only function that these representations performed; as I argue below, they were also related to the production of the village as an idyllic space by urban filmmakers who were responding to a compound affect of culpability and loss. The editorial started from the Gandhian presupposition that the "real" India was to be found in its 700,000 villages, then it obsessed about the damage done to the "image" of the nation by Indian popular cinema's depiction of village life: "A thousand other things which our film producers continuously show on the screen about our village girls and our village life only contribute to prove conclusively that we are a nation of immoral men, virgin[51] mothers and heartless scoundrels without any national character, culture or tradition."[52] But who occupied the vantage point from which such conclusions were apparent? Clearly, the commentator was speaking from an urban bourgeois position with a distinctly Anglophone Indian inflection, and he was addressing Indians such as himself.

He presumed unproblematic, consensual forms of "national character," "culture" and "tradition," without pausing to consider the possibility that aspects of what he found deplorable in the representation of villages might, in fact, be constitutive of rural life; that the representations appeared overtly sexualized partly because of his own urban morality tinged with Victorian sensibilities.

These are double-edged arguments that require further elaboration and unpacking. The issues became particularly convoluted as the nationalist culture police sought to weed out Western influence, yet its own terms of reference were often imported from the West. This aporia at the heart of Indian modernity rendered necessary the constant ideological fabrication of inherently Indian entities defined by immutable, timeless qualities. The ruling classes enacted discursive and performative rituals of "preserving" Indianness by seizing certain signifiers like "woman," "rural life," and "the masses"—which named the others of an elitist, patriarchal and often urban hegemonic ruling bloc—and petrifying them outside time, history, and politics.

A letter from a reader of *Filmfare* magazine, written in response to the 1954 petition against prurience, points to one deleterious effect of excessive priggishness: "The censors see vulgarity where there is none, and with sex, in any form or context, completely taboo in our films, it is more likely that the younger generation is in danger of growing up to be narrow-minded bigots to whom sex will signify something that lurks in dark corners and only to be talked about in horrified whispers."[53] A similar view was expressed a few years earlier by Pandit Indra, a Bombay scriptwriter, in a spirited defense of eroticism and sexuality in Indian films, penned in response to the self-righteous diatribes in *Filmindia* editorials. He quoted from classical Sanskrit literature to question the Indianness of modern formulations of national character, implying that eroticism was a healthy aspect of Indian lifeworlds, and that the contemporary urban Indian bourgeoisie had inherited its aversion to sex and sexuality from a Victorian moral horizon. Indra addressed "the editor and the ministers," in a direct plea to those groups who wielded a great deal of influence in shaping national cultural policies: "The editor and the ministers will please change their view of life otherwise a day may come when will make the whole country a sex-starved one. The tragic result of such sex starvation will be terrible and really that thing will be vulgar for which they will be responsible."[54] Just as vernacular syntax inflects his English, Indra's take on eroticism complicates hegemonic views of a "clean" modern national identity with roots in a "noble" and "transcendental" past. From the vantage point of the present, his pronouncement takes on a prophetic ring; but that is another terrifying story.[55]

Industrial Initiatives

If the state was in two minds about the film industry, the latter's attitude toward the state manifests corresponding vacillations. While there was palpable excitement about a sovereign indigenous government, there also was deep resentment against its vexing policies, especially high taxes and the continuation of colonial censorship laws. Existing business practices were seen to favor distributors (money lenders charging as much as fifty percent interest rates) and exhibitors (whose bargaining powers were enhanced by the restrictions on building new theaters), leaving film producers at their mercy. One of the persistent demands of the industry was the consolidation of an incomplete capital market through the establishment of financial institutions; it was met finally in 1960, with the inception of the Film Finance Corporation.[56] The Film Council, recommended by the Film Enquiry Committee Report of 1951 as a forum for sustained interaction between the state and the industry, remained only an idea.

On closer inspection, the history of the abortive idea of the Film Council shows considerable division within the industry. Madhava Prasad points out that while the Council was meant to *regulate* the affairs of the industry—by improving organizational efficiency, eliminating the influence of black money and adventurers with little commitment to the industry, promoting professionalism and discipline, regularizing wages and hiring policies, and encouraging quality through the careful planning of film projects including development of film scripts—its detractors worried about the potential for arbitrary state control.[57] Prasad records how the "fragmented industry would always put up a show of internal unity" whenever the Film Council was poised to become a reality: "Rumours about government plans to nationalize the industry and to introduce licensing for producers surfaced to strengthen the resistance to the proposal."[58] Given the general preponderance of licensing and controls (a stifling regime disparagingly referred to as "Licensing Raj") in independent India, such fears were not altogether unfounded.

The industry took some initiatives on its own to redress its problems. The formation of the Film Federation of India in 1951, with representation from various sections of the industry, was a major step toward self-organization. The executive of the FFI was to be the industry's spokesperson, and to act as a liaison officer with the government and the public, to promote industrial interests. Attempts were also made to establish a financing body under the Indian Motion Picture Producers Association, given the official apathy. However, the industry had to depend on the whims of the state in other respects, including protection from foreign competition, license to import technologies of filmmaking and projection, and license to build new theaters.

In spite of the industry's distrust and the state's antipathy, the former accepted, with some trepidation, the inescapable truth of the latter's overarching authority, while the state recognized, if grudgingly, the tremendous power of this mass medium. The gradual official recognition of cinema's importance in national life took various forms: from the institution of national awards and financing, to compulsory screenings in all theaters of newsreels and documentaries fostering national integration and promoting official programs. For its part, the industry complemented its demands for official recognition and infrastructural assistance with a pledge to serve national interests. It sought social legitimacy by taking on a pedagogical role: inculcating a strong sense of belonging, negotiating differences to establish a consensual ground, promoting relevant sociopolitical ideals and values in attractive narrative packages, developing a common aesthetic characteristic of a national cinema. As onetime information and broadcasting minister I. K. Gujral put it retrospectively, the film industry had "to pay a 'social tax' in the form of socially relevant, progressive themes and messages."[59] It seems reasonable to surmise that something more than a cynical calculation of business interests was involved in such a pledge: that in the first flush of independence, many in the industry harbored a genuine desire to become a part of the grand adventure of transforming India into a sovereign and modern democracy. It seems equally plausible that the strained state-industry relations contributed to self-censorship on the part of the industry—including its silence on Partition.

Creating a National Audience/Creating Genres

These dual motivations—business concerns and an avowed commitment to collective development and emancipation—were articulated in the popular genres. The history of the Bombay Talkies, the preeminent studio of the mid-1940s, and of Filmistan, a studio set up by a group that broke away from the former, reveals concerted efforts at fashioning cinematic genres for a national audience, drawing on the codes of successful Hollywood and British films and the vast repertoire comprising Indian epics, folk performative traditions, Sanskrit dramaturgy, and modern vernacular stage and literature. Already in 1943, audiences had been offered such a hybrid narrative in Bombay Talkies' *Kismet*, which combined elements of Warner Bros. gangster flicks and crime thrillers with a coincidental structure that invoked the agency of fate. The film became the biggest box-office hit of the pre-independence period, enjoying a continuous run of three years in a Calcutta theater.[60] Buoyed by such successes, studios in the forties and the fifties worked to establish popular generic conventions, crystallizing and consolidating successful patterns as industry codes. Recognizing the potential of a vast national market, studios harnessed a range of cultural and social references, creating modes of address that could engage various sections of a national audience.

In adopting such strategies, Bombay filmmakers displayed a keen understanding of a "national audience" as a differentiated and evolving entity, in marked contrast to official notions of a preconstituted, selfsame, and inert national collectivity. They created their "audience" by entering into a dialogic relationship with the spectators: training them to respond to the industry's emerging language while fine-tuning that language in response to popular feedback. Not surprisingly, commercial Hindi films produced in Bombay, along with their ancillary world of gossip magazines and fan activities, came to constitute over the years a more compelling ground of national belonging than any state-sponsored institution. The emergence of Bombay in the late forties as the primary center of Indian cinema was no coincidence either.[61]

Filmistan emerged as the first major studio in the course of Bombay's ascent within the sphere of national mass culture.[62] Riding the crest of a sudden spurt in film-producing activities after World War II and taking advantage of the lifting of various licensing requirements and restrictions on the use of raw film stock, Filmistan was instrumental in systematically mobilizing the processes of codification and marketing. The studio was often referred to as a "film factory"; its generic film narratives—usually light, escapist fare—evinced an appreciation of the exigencies of mass cultural production for an increasingly widening market, driven as they were by the logic of "an all-encompassing entertainment formula designed to overcome regional and linguistic boundaries."[63] These generic narratives, and their subsequent elaborations, came to provide the empirical basis for a model of an indigenous, national film form, the so-called All-India film.[64] While the contextual terms in discussions of this model have generated much dissension among critics, the invocation of a collective national register has found wide acceptance.[65] The very name "Filmistan" conjures up a utopian, unified realm of belonging, away from the contentious sectarian invocations of *Hindustan* (the vernacular term for India, signifying the land of the Hindus) and *Pakistan* (the land of the Muslims), and transcending official boundaries.

A quick run through Filmistan's hit productions gives us a sense of the emerging themes and tropes, a number of which are combined in the typical plot. Popular genres included romantic comedy (*Eight Days* [1946], *Shabnam* [1949], *Paying Guest* [1957]), tales of patriotic sacrifice (*Shaheed* [1948], *Samadhi* [1950], *Anandmath* [1952]), historical romance (*Anarkali* [1953]), primitivist romance (*Shabnam*, *Nagin* [1954]), crime thriller (*Munimji* [1955], *Paying Guest*), and social melodrama (*Shehnai* [1947], *Sindoor* [1947]). Doubles, masquerades, cross-dressing, confusion over lineage, and coincidental structures were among the recurrent devices, adding intriguing twists and hilarity to the narrative denouement. Song-and-dance numbers were incorporated in a variety of forms: as staged performances, as romantic interludes, as commentary by a minstrel or a group of singers. Other production companies followed in the footsteps of Filmistan: Navketan produced films like *Taxidriver* (1954), *House Number 44* (1955) and *Nau Do Gyarah* (1957), combining elements of romance, crime, proletarian life, caper, comedy, and masquerade; Bombay Talkies juxtaposed crime, romantic obsession, and rebirth within the structure of a ghost story in *Mahal* (1949), and crime with family melodrama in *Sangram* (1950). B. R. Chopra's debut film *Afsana* (1951) was a crime thriller with "double" protagonists; Raj Kapoor, another newcomer, created a stir with the compelling films *Aag* (1948), *Barsaat* (1949), and *Awara* (1951), spanning family melodrama, romantic idealism, class antagonisms, and crime and justice.

By far the most important cinematic development of this period was the emergence of a fluid master genre, the social film. The lack of specificity of this pervasive form, bordering on the vacuous, enabled it to accommodate competing demands on the industry. Ravi Vasudevan quotes contemporary industry commentators on the class-specific appeal of various pre-independence genres; according to these sources, plebeian audiences reveled in the visceral attractions and moral imperatives of the stunt, mythological, and costume films, while the devotional and social films were more popular with the middle classes.[66] With the collapse of the older major studios (New Theatres, Prabhat, Bombay Talkies) after the war, a new species of speculative producers focused on making a quick buck became the dominant force in Indian cinema. In an attempt to expand the audience, the more sensational elements of spectacle, action, and dance were brought into social films; at the same time, a suspiciously large number of films (as many as fifty-one in 1949) was being pushed as "socials," possibly as a way of bringing some credibility to "slapdash" concoctions. A review of Raj Kapoor's *Barsaat* reveals a clear understanding of this process, declaring that the film is "a box-office hit and it deserves to be so because it . . . satisfies the demands of the better classes while meeting all the needs of the masses."[67]

As Vasudevan argues, these films consolidated "a redefinition of social identity for the spectator," as the mass audiences that were seen once to appreciate mainly sensational and moral tales "were now being solicited by an *omnibus form* which also included a rationalist discourse as part of its 'attractions.'"[68]

The so-called social film followed the reform-minded literary traditions, whose roots can be traced back to the articulation of the need for social reforms in India by Raja Rammohan Roy in the early nineteenth century. Roy represented an educated elite class that aspired to be the conscience and vanguard of a nascent national collectivity. Inspired by liberal Western ideals of equality, fairness, and justice, he challenged the oppression of women and the lower castes by a Brahmanical hegemony, seeking to undermine the authority of the current religious orthodoxy by invoking ancient Hindu religious texts. Such maneuvers became the modus operandi of early nationalists, who invoked differentiated conceptions of the traditional, battling bigotry in terms of a resurrected, "ideal" national heritage. Novelists in the twentieth century elaborated on this reformist impulse.[69] Taking its cue from vernacular literatures—which it drew upon both to establish its own credentials as a national art form and to capitalize on existing narrative resources—cinema became involved in the projection of a modern Indian self dedicated to the ideal of a reformed society, now cast in the light of rational-liberal values. But in such narratives of a rite of passage into modernity, the nation seemed to emerge "more as an evolutionary trace in the consciousness" and less as a hegemonic process of endless negotiations.[70] While such an idealized conception of an inherent, timeless Indianness rested on the elision of all conflicting energies, these disavowed impulses found expression via the melodramatic structures that became integral to the social genre.

Melodrama, which comprises thematic and formal resources proficient at intimating the complex arbitrations occasioned by sociopolitical change, frequently emerges as the predominant narrative genre in transitional societies. Public drama is acted out in the private sphere of the family: collective trepidation is externalized as the disarray of familial structures of kinship, intensity of affect projected through hysterical bodies. How is the family invested with such significance? Far from displacing the social dimension with the personal, melodrama claims the body and the familial domain as the very sites of sociopolitical conflicts. In Peter Brooks's celebrated formulation, melodrama seeks to recover the security of divinely sanctioned meaning and hierarchical authority that has dissipated in a postsacred world: meaning comes to inhere in the personality, as characters are invested with the constitutive psychic elements of family identities.[71] A typical scenario involves the placement of key characters within an Oedipal triangle, and the working out of problematic tensions through the play of forbidden desires. Manichean oppositions (polar moral values and choices), interpersonal triangulations, coincidental structures, and expressive stylistics set up situations of heightened crises and then proceed to resolve them in contrived and banal ways. Many commentators see such exercises as attempts to impose order on what is irreparably anarchic—attempts marked by self-consciousness about their feasibility being limited to the symbolic dimension.[72] Such an intriguing awareness brings a critical edge to the genre; even when it is absent, melodrama's wistful, subversive longing for utopian change points to an implicit social-critical function.

But melodrama has to be understood in terms of its specific historical formation; modern India is not quite the disenchanted world that Brooks claims for post-Enlightenment Europe, nor is it so crucially predicated on individualism. No universal modernity can fully subsume the desires and fantasies driving Indian subjectivities, or supplant the granular nature of local lifeworlds. This incongruence gives rise to the singularity of Indian melodramatic forms. Even seemingly standardized expressions take on distinctive inflections: the triangulations and coincidences draw on vernacular paradigms, the core tensions are played out within a locally salient moral space. Broadly speaking, in Hindi films of the first decade, melodrama is yoked to reformist socials to intimate the disorientations wrought by capitalist modernization and to project the demands of nationhood in an affective register. For instance, melodrama in the early films of Raj Kapoor takes on a somber tone reminiscent of film-noir: overwhelmed by the flux of life, their protagonists lurch between noble autonomy and abject criminality, their struggles setting the stage for the transfiguration of quasi-feudal patriarchal institutions in modern legislative-juridical terms. My focus on Partition will underscore a further topicality of melodramatic tropes: their ability to engage apprehensions about the futures of community and to register the anguish regarding the suffering of women, at a point when memories of recent violations are fresh in the collective psyche but repressed in public discourse. In the post-1947 context, melodrama's ornamentality indexes the subterranean scene of loss.

Realism, a concept closely associated with social reformism but frequently opposed to melodrama, shifted in mid-twentieth-century Indian popular cinema—away from its empiricist dimension, toward the performance of social contradictions and idealist projections. Another populist strand of Indian realism—naturalism—was predicated on faith in a mystical correspondence between reality and its representation. Bracketing both empiricism and naturalism, modern Indian realism became a matter not of representing accurately what the nation was, but of imagining what it should be, keeping faith in that imagination, and working toward that ideal: a moral and utopian realism, as it were. In a public address reproduced in *Filmindia*, the Bengali director and producer Debaki Bose asked audiences to "beware" of films that take them away from "actual life" by creating "a synthetic hunger." Appearing to anticipate subsequent psychoanalytic film theory, Bose declared that cinema works by "creating desires, partly satisfying them; creating fresh desires again, partly satisfying them again; leaving a void always to want more and finally creating a habit."[73] He went on to explain how "the daydream of the cinema makes wakeful hours of life almost unbearable":

> These films tell us lies about sex life. They tempt the poor honest farmer and the labourer into thinking of the feminine star as a possible star of his daydreams, while his poor wife is at the time toiling and preparing bread for him. . . . the charm of the just ordinary wife seems too little to him, in comparison with the glamour of the "IT" girl on the screen who makes love to the audience straight through an invitingly alluring close-up of either her made-up eyes, . . . her bare legs or her whole body with costumes and gestures that emphasise nudeness more than they hide it. . . . And apart from this question of sex, there is another. . . . In our entertainment films, every set, with its articles of furniture, is becoming too rich and too loud. . . . Our little fortunes, our ordinary dresses, our mere living appears very common-place and repulsive in comparison.[74]

Displaying a deep understanding of the gendered address of film images, their promotion of consumerist culture, and the inscription of the spectator in perpetual lack, Bose advocated films that would help audiences appreciate their own lives, "to accept our lot with a better grace." In effect, he proposed a kind of cinematic realism that would ground films in the lived experiences of the Indian people and help them in their daily struggles. While that might sound like an empiricist call to represent existing objective conditions truthfully, there was also an idealistic component to Bose's appeal: his rhetorical alignment with the real experiences of the masses had clear prescriptive implications for the contentious category of the national. By emphasizing the need for the cinematic depiction of an "actual, satisfying home life" (as opposed to fantasy-oriented escapism), he was underscoring the need for the projection of an idealized national life for an imputed national audience.

The realism advocated in the first decade has to be understood in relation to the ideological project of securing a modern Indian nation, and the need for a national cinema differentiated from Hollywood. Italian cinema of the late 1940s and early 1950s provides the paradigmatic film historical instance of nationalist rearticulations of realism: imagining a new kind of nation through its celebration of the lives of decent, hardworking people, effectively divesting them of any responsibility for fascism and simultaneously providing a model for cinema in the wake of a war-ravaged Europe. In the Indian postcolonial context, policy makers had to choose between alternative patterns of socioeconomic development defined in terms of the polarized axes capitalism/socialism, urban/rural, industrial/artisanal, individual interests/community values. The adopted path of capitalist industrial development, which did not coincide with any of these extreme poles, was a hybrid compromise involving a complex bureaucratic licensing regime and Soviet-style central planning. Nevertheless, the predilections of the ruling elite were heavily geared toward industrialization, urbanization, and higher education—forces and institutions that were intimately aligned to the interests of the urban bourgeoisie. Likewise, the cultural field was molded through endless balancing acts between competing aesthetics and ideologies. One such strand was a leftist cultural movement, led by the Progressive Writer's Association (PWA) and the Indian People's Theatre Association (IPTA), with ties to the Communist Party of India. It promoted realism in the arts as a means of initiating social change. The objective representation of reality was expected to reveal existing contradictions in social relations and pave the way for revolutionary change. The influence of these politicized cultural initiatives was felt throughout the industry: K. A. Abbas, Chetan Anand, and Bimal Roy made films that clearly signaled their faith in the transformatory potential of cinema. However, the progressive rhetoric of Nehruvian ideology largely preempted sustained leftist cultural-political critique and mobilization, effectively taming such impulses through their incorporation within a mainstream nationalist agenda. Realism in Indian cinema evolved as a highly contested and differentiated category both in its conception and practice, yet hegemonic discourses on the issue betrayed a moralizing, middle-class lilt.

In practice, an Indian realism was driven more by a sense of social culpability than by a desire for social justice. Sudipta Kaviraj argues that change in traditional social formations has to occur "within a governing rhetoric of continuity. Historical change is accomplished surreptitiously, without declaration or trace, often shamefacedly, with something like a sense of guilt."[75] The remorse brought on by modernity's sweeping changes, coupled with the guilt about the specific biases of official programs, produced an obsession with "authentic" Indian mores. Cinema, just like modern Indian politics, had to mediate what Kaviraj calls "the meeting of two histories": the "shamefaced, subterranean change of traditional Indian society" and "the dramatic, overt changes brought in by modernity."[76] Cinema was expected to represent the "real" India, uphold its "timeless" traditions and ways of life, and simultaneously project the blueprint for a modern, democratic national life. Films that did not meet these requirements were moralistically denounced as "escapist," "senseless," and even "sick." The stress on realism evolved out of a double-edged fear that Indian cinema would lose its cultural moorings or, worse still, project a lumpen, undisciplined, irrational national character that would be embarrassing to the ruling bloc and compromise the nation's place in the sun. While Indian cinematic realism comprised multiple forms (the socialist realist stylistics of Mehboob Khan, the realist melodramas of Bimal Roy, the neorealist inflections of early Satyajit Ray films), these variations all shared a basic melodramatic modality that, in both its moralizing and expressive capacities, accommodated the strains of continual negotiations.

To sum up, films of the first decade after independence constituted practices of the imagination that, with varying degrees of success, participated in a collective endeavor to create the space of the National Symbolic by interweaving multiple—often contradictory—strands: a realism that engaged with the vernacular and the quotidian, even as it sought to subsume these levels within a modern, national mainstream; a social reformist impulse that resuscitated the trace of a timeless tradition and recast it in rational-liberal terms; a melodramatic mode that enabled the pressures of conflicting demands on cinema to be inscribed on the cinematic body and subverted hegemonic structures and narratives through the oblique articulation of suppressed anxieties and energies. In the balance of this chapter, I will explore the entanglements of and exchanges between these strands by focusing on two films: one was a box-office flop, the other a smash hit. My interest is in establishing Hindi cinema's overarching symbolic economy that extends well beyond box-office metrics. In each film, the narrative and the mise-en-scène purvey the spaces, institutions, actions, fashions, values, and relationships that might constitute a blueprint for better living. Yet both films intimate profound misgivings about the core drives animating a contemporary project of nation building, thus significantly recalibrating that very project and making the stakes legible to their publics.

A Disquieting Flop

Mehboob Khan's *Amar* (1954) was a failure at the box office, a fact that, by itself, is not very interesting. But the film was a product of the most successful phase of the producer-director's career, flanked as it was chronologically by three of his legendary works: *Andaz* (1949), *Aan* (1952), and *Mother India* (1957). It had the ingredients of a hit: three of the most popular stars of that, or any, period (Dilip Kumar, Madhubala, Nimmi) in a romantic triangle, and a plot that developed around topical oppositions between the city and the countryside, between the rational-juridical and the religious domains, and more sensational fare such as crime, courtroom scenes, and a sexual seduction bordering on rape. Yet *Amar* failed to draw audiences, largely because the public could not accept matinee idol Dilip Kumar in the ambivalent role of an opportunistic lawyer unwilling to own up to his actions. There is more to be said about this atypical casting; but first, I want to explore the film's negotiation of a putative national agenda.

Khan's films routinely focus on the tribulations of a transitional society. The rural milieus of *Aurat* (1942), *Amar*, and *Mother India* are domains of archaic practices and values, involving honor, kinship structures, and blood feuds. While the modern state apparatus is credited as the purveyor of progressive alternatives (juridical laws protecting property, life, and community interests; modern technologies, including dams and tractors for mechanized cultivation), the films register a palpable trepidation about it. The female protagonists are fraught icons negotiating social contradictions: in *Andaz*, the new urban woman's subjectivity emerges from the articulation of traditional family values with modern individualist sensibilities.[77] The earth mother of *Mother India* (a remake of *Aurat*, now developed into an explicit nationalist allegory) embodies conflicting energies and ideals: at once nurturing and threatening, she fights against nature and circumstance to protect her family, then kills her errant son to uphold community values. Mythologized as an anchor of continuity and social reproduction, she has the honor—at the end of the narrative—of ceremonially inaugurating a modern dam, echoing newsreels featuring leaders engaged in techno-modernist rituals.[78]

In *Amar*, the dualities are exteriorized by splitting the woman in two: the urbane, educated Anju, and the rustic, illiterate Sonia. Both are stunningly beautiful, and both are in love with the hero Amar. Sonia expresses her feelings and desires mainly through her gestures and looks; her most cogent verbal communication takes the form of songs sung to the birds and animals. She inhabits stylized pastoral settings reminiscent of the sylvan hermitage of Kalidasa's classical Sanskrit play *Shakuntala*, and its populist renditions in calendar art—with fluttering pigeons and playful fawns and light streaming through blossoming vines. In contrast, Anju is a modern subject of civil society: she is ratio-

Lobbycard for *Amar*: Sonia and Anju. Courtesy of Parimal Roy.

nal and fair, articulate and self-possessed; her habitat bears the trappings of modern, urban living. She comes to the helpless Sonia's defense when the latter is discovered to be pregnant on her wedding night and is about to be ostracized by her family and community. Anju also embodies the arbitration between rational-secular discourses and religious faith: she extols the virtues of modernization and stresses the need for social agency, but she retains her faith in Hindu divinities. When she realizes that it is her fiancé Amar who has impregnated Sonia, she does not allow her emotions to cloud her reason. Instead of any hysterical outburst, she calmly sacrifices her love to uphold social order and to serve a sense of justice.

The film projects a paternalist reformism by underscoring a need for the urban citizenry to take on the cause of rural India: it interpellates those with a better understanding of the workings of administrative institutions to assist others who are unfamiliar with modern practices and values. Amar, the hero, is an apathetic lawyer until he meets Anju; she is able to instill a greater sense of social responsibility in him, inspiring him to fight a lawsuit on behalf of the village community. But when Sonia comes running to him one stormy night, pursued by a murderous village goon, he gives in to carnal passions and takes advantage of her panic and disorientation (not to mention her infatuation with him). Indeed, Sonia's ordeal in the narrative indexes a broader dimension: the trauma of traditional rural societies ravaged by the experiences of modernity and nationalist centralization. As her pregnancy—more a sign of loss than of fecundity—becomes visible, and the entire village taunts her, she refuses to divulge the identity of her child's father out of her love for Amar. In a pivotal scene that firmly establishes his cowardice and villainy, Amar joins her tormentors to ensure her silence. It is the point at which Anju comes to Sonia's rescue, in a compassionate overture that bespeaks both social and feminist concerns. The village goon also speaks up for Sonia, in a show of sympathy that springs from their shared social evisceration, his qualms about modern legal institutions, and personal suspicions about the lawyer.

Amar is by no means the only film from the 1950s to express misgivings about the processes of modernization. B. R. Chopra's *Naya Daur* (1957) pits traditional technology against modern machinery, dramatizing the opposition in a race between a horse-drawn carriage and a bus. An older father figure opposes increasing mechanization, championing classless community values in a humanist vein; the younger hero takes a more pragmatic stand on the impending transformations, advocating the collective management of emerging technologies by the people. Interestingly, the narrative makes the villain the chief proponent of modernization, thus revealing doubts about nationalist programs of industrial development. An earlier film, *Gaon* (*The Village*, 1948), adopted a more militant stance toward the encroachment of modern industries in the sylvan countryside: it depicted villagers as being vehemently opposed to the construction of mills and factories on their land, and going to the extreme measure of burning down industrialists' camps. One commentator criticized the producers of the film for being "totally ignorant of the fundamental principles of the national economy," alleging that they were propagating "dangerously anti-national" ideas and making "a mockery of Nehru's cries for more industries and more production."[79]

Mehboob Khan, a devout Muslim, also considered himself a dedicated Indian. His religious difference from India's majority Hindu population was a large part of his identity, forcing him to acknowledge the centrality of religion in any conception of an Indian self. With *Amar*, he went against the grain of ascendant ideological dispositions, offering a critique of the secular pretenses of the new nation-state. The temple, which various characters keep running back to, assumes a singular significance as the setting for important revelations, the site of legitimation. Anju is disturbed by Amar's resistance to prayer, staged in his halting steps in the temple compound; she learns the truth about Sonia and Amar as Sonia prays to god; in the end, Amar and Sonia become a sanctified couple in front of the deity, and Anju comes down the stairs with a beatific expression on her face; the film concludes with a long shot of the temple. Privileging the temple as a locus of personal and public life and upholding the authority of the spiritual domain over rational juridical regimes, Khan effectively asserts that there can be no Indian modernity sans religion.

Religion remains a vexing question for state apparatuses. Religious interests cannot be reconciled easily with the disenchanted demographic categories in terms of which the post-enlightenment state constitutes its population as an object of biopolitical intervention. Modern governmentality requires the reduction of the reality of religious demographics (e.g., the fact that one religious group may be in a clear majority, its interests poised to have a decisive influence on all contentious official policy) into an innocuous cultural phenomenon of minimal relevance in a secular nation-state. Yet the political salience of religious affiliations continues to be reaffirmed through the cynical manipulation of faith-based electorates, and the eruptions of sectarian violence in Central Europe and in South and West Asia. Since the 1990s, a wide range of scholarship has attempted to come to terms with the contradictions that have beset the self-avowedly secular Indian state. Commentators argue that the problems with Western secularism in India point not to a failure of political will, but to the need for a different formulation of the concept.[80] The officially embraced notion of secularism, underwritten by a middle class with its strong desire for a cosmopolitan modernity, cannot be imposed and operationalized in the Indian context; it leads to an "impasse" in which the state ends up discriminating between religions in its attempts to defend personal civil rights (upholding the religious freedom of minority communities, yet overruling it for the majority Hindus, whenever there are conflicts between religious tenets and civil liberty issues—so that there is no uniform civil code).[81]

Several films of the 1950s contest the desacralization of Indian identity even more vigorously than *Amar*. Religious faith, the repressed other of Indian modernity, returns with a far more disquieting force in *Nastik* (which, like *Amar*, is released in 1954)—an intensity accentuated by the film's direct invocation of Partition violence. The protagonist Anil loses his parents in the carnage, and then his two siblings during the subsequent dislocations. Out of shock, he becomes a staunch atheist (the literal meaning of the film's title) and a cynical sociopath. His rage is directed at one priest, who refuses to help his dying brother because they are penniless. Looking for revenge, he ends up following the priest around the country, visiting various Hindu pilgrim centers. In the course of this elaborate chase, Anil has, ironically, undertaken his own pilgrimage. A dormant spirituality, the trace of an integral inner life, is resuscitated in him, underscoring the impossibility of a self without religious conviction. Like *Amar*, this film asserts the importance of religion in Indian life. It appends a reformist critique of organized religion, exposing its mercenary focus on wealth. But *Nastik*, in following its protagonist across Hindu shrines spread all over the country (Dwarka, Rameshwar, Puri, Varanasi, Brindavan), also conjures up for its audiences the vision of an essentially Hindu nation-space: a "realistic" trail produces an ideological cartography. If Anil loses his faith because of the horror of the Partition, he regains it partly in the course of his pilgrimage: by implication, the narrative locates his troubles in a time and space that is tainted with undesirable religious presence (Muslims) and delivers him into the wholeness of a Hindu nation (India after the Partition).[82]

Both heroes are redeemed by religion at the end of the two films, but Amar remains a far more complex character than Anil: while the latter evinces a whole-hearted belief in divine powers, the former is, at best, deferential. After a series of miracles restores his faith, Anil joins other ecstatic worshippers in a devotional song. The entire scene is composed like a tableau, intercut with close-ups of rapturous faces. Hearing the repeated chanting of "Om Hari Om," Anil's traumatized wife Rama comes out of her stupor, and he falls at the feet of the deity in thanksgiving. In contrast to this delirious mise-en-scène, *Amar* ends on a far more subdued note. While the lawyer acknowledges divine authority by accepting Sonia as his wife in front of the temple deity, the narrative makes it clear that his action is prompted in large measure by his sense of social justice: he assumes responsibility for his actions, marking himself out from predatory feudalist males. Thus Amar's dual acquiescence to divine authority and social responsibility articulates a more multifaceted modern Indian self.

Audience sympathy rests squarely with Anju, Amar's fiancée, whom he wrongs and who acquires a saintly aura through her selfless actions. Anju embodies both the nurturing and accepting qualities expected of a heteronormative Indian woman and the democratic, reform-minded spirit necessary for a modern (perhaps protofeminist) citizen. While Radha of *Mother India* must turn violent to achieve justice, Anju resorts to the modalities of civil society (although inflected by religious faith): the latter's public persona remains reasonable, calm, and collected. The fact that Anju is played by the angelic Madhubala further enhances the character's appeal. In contrast, Amar is deeply flawed; the atypical casting of Dilip Kumar, one of the most popular and enduring stars of Bombay cinema, as the vacillating lawyer only aggravates spectatorial discomfort. What do we make of Mehboob Khan's intriguing hero? Does this baffling choice point to a deep sense of crisis in national identity, to the impossibility of real heroes at that conjuncture? Perhaps the auteur had wanted, consciously or unconsciously, to engage his audiences in a collective recognition of their own implication in contemporary national events, so that they could not continue to blame others for all collective afflictions. Writing about Partition violence, scholars such as Gyan Pandey and Sudhir Kakar have noted the common practice of narrativizing violence by pitting "us" against "them."[83] As Pandey notes, violence marks the limits of community: hence it is always seen to happen "not here" but "out there." "They" are always the aggressors, the perpetrators, while "we" are the victims who retaliate only to save "ourselves." If some violence happens in "our" area, it is explained away as being necessary to protect "ourselves," to maintain "our" honor. Even when "our" people rape and plunder, these deplorable acts are normalized as arbitrary, isolated happenings commensurate with the social frenzy. Thus the blame for all atrocities rests on "them," while "our" community remains righteous and honorable. Could it be that Khan's problematic casting of a popular star, who commanded cultural valence as a cathectic locus of identification, in the role of a cad muddied precisely these convenient separations between "perpetrators" and "victims," between "us" and "them," which enabled various communities to continue blaming other groups for all collective woes? Could it have forced spectators to confront their own accountability in the violent conflagration, by presenting the other at the center of fantasies through which ideas of self and community were forged?

Of course, the star Dilip Kumar already embodied a crisis of identity: born Yusuf Khan, he was a Muslim actor who took on a Hindu screen name to ensure his marketability in Hindu-majority India at a time of heightened communal strife.[84] Contemporary audiences seemed oblivious to this detail, or they accepted him as a screen idol on the basis of his histrionic abilities and his gesture of assuming a Hindu alias. If Yusuf Khan's transformation marked one of the ways in which deep communal tensions worked themselves into the operations of the film industry, then Dilip Kumar's emergence as one of the main stars of Indian cinema, through a series of on- and offscreen masquerades, profoundly called into question all claims to naturalized religious identities, Hindu or Muslim. The political and military histories of South Asia, and strong transborder cultural affiliations in the region, further complicate an account of this revered thespian's career. In the mid-sixties, when India and Pakistan went to war, the actor was subjected to official intelligence investigations: there were rumors that he was a Pakistani agent. More recently, in the late 1990s, the actor was the center of a controversy when the government of Pakistan bestowed on him that country's highest civilian award (Nishan-e-Imtiaz), raising fresh questions about his loyalties.[85] The ontologizing designation of Dilip Kumar as a *mussal-*

man at certain historical flash points undercuts the figural potentialities of the star: he remains a split icon, forever the object of nationalist scrutiny.

More than casting, it is the surreal mise-en-scène of *Amar*—captured in the coruscant black-and-white cinematography of the longtime Mehboob collaborator Faredoon Irani—that captures the tortured political unconscious of the 1950s. One intense, hallucinatory sequence vividly exemplifies this contextual undertow: the "chase" scene, in which Sonia is running from the village goon Sankat, leading up to her seduction in Amar's chamber. It is a storm-swept night, with the customary gusty winds and thunderbolts that make for much audiovisual drama. But Mehboob takes the scene to another level of expressive saturation: as Sonia hides in a shallow pool, the camera goes underwater to show her holding her breath as Sankat's legs trudge past her crouching figure. The sexual encounter between Sonia and Amar is made to seem like a rape, although we know that she is completely infatuated with the lawyer: when a rain-drenched Sonia rushes in looking for refuge, a predatory Amar stares at her, getting aroused by her fear; Sonia looks disheveled and terrified in the flickering light of the lamp; the lamp falls and shatters; lightning flashes through the window; a bit later, we see a catatonic Sonia stumbling away into the night. The sequence conveys a sense of betrayal and outrage, indexing the constant violation of the feminized rural world by an intrusive and conniving urban sector. While this melancholy perspicuity alternates with a hopeful, celebratory impulse throughout the film, a series of haunting songs—set to melody by the composer Naushad, and sung mainly in female voices—accentuate these tonal modulations.

A Morbid Hit

The material and ideological chasm between a paternalistic elite and the vast population under its rule was not the only factor producing a burgeoning sense of crisis in the 1950s. The euphoria of independence soon gave away to sobering thoughts about the enormity of the tasks at hand. The contradictions haunting the social and cultural fields (a commitment to uphold official programs of national development, while harboring reservations about them; a desire to move beyond recent losses, without being able to mourn them) found expression in the overwrought narratives and a fantasmatic, baroque-noir style. Notable among such films were the ones directed by Raj Kapoor (specially *Aag*, *Barsaat*, and *Awara*), evincing a dark cinematic vision often at odds

Amar: Sonia's fear arouses Amar. Courtesy of NFAI.

with the optimism of a newly independent society. At the same time, *Aag* and *Awara*—like Satyajit Ray's *Apu Trilogy* (1955–59)—were powerful instances of cinematic bildungsromans that braided together narratives of the self with those of the nation.

Awara (aka *The Vagabond*) opens as a courtroom drama, with the lumpen Raju being tried for the attempted murder of Judge Raghunath. Raju's childhood sweetheart Rita, who also happens to be the daughter of Raghunath's deceased friend, and currently his ward, takes on his defense and proceeds to uncover his "true identity" as the estranged son of the judge. As such, the bulk of the narrative unfolds in flashback. The film establishes its social-reformist credentials early on, when young Raghunath marries a widow against his family's wishes. But he displays a more conservative attitude toward criminal behavior, holding that one's *khandan* (blood lineage) crucially determines one's life, and that a person cannot escape his forebears' past. A long meditation on this "nature versus nurture" debate in a melodramatic mode, the film marks a modernist tendency within popular cinema toward the interrogation of various normalized components of identity, including class, caste, and religious affiliations; it also performs the limits of an emergent bourgeois liberalism. Believing that a criminal's son can only be a criminal, a young Raghunath finds Jagga, the son of a bandit, guilty of a crime he did not commit. This ruling turns Jagga into a hardcore criminal; upon his escape from prison, he kidnaps the judge's wife as an act of vengeance. Realizing she is pregnant, Jagga releases her, anticipating her family to suspect the paternity of the child. His ploy works: people speculate that she may be carrying the bandit's son. Raghunath gives in to social pressures and to his own jealous suspicions, and throws his wife out.

A close analysis of the mise-en-scène of the wife's eviction brings to light a distinctly Indian sensibility, clarifying the ways in which melodrama, realism, and social concerns were harnessed together and worked out in popular Hindi cinema of the first decade. The sequence is framed in mythic terms, with multiple references to the epic *Ramayana*. In this well-known tale, the demon king Ravana abducts Seeta, wife of the virtuous demigod King Rama. When Rama gets back his wife after a tumultuous battle and Seeta appears to be pregnant, his subjects question her chastity, as she has been at the mercy of her abductor. Seeta proves her purity by entering a blazing pyre and emerging unscathed. But after she gives birth to twin sons, rumors persist, and Rama asks her to prove her innocence once more. Humiliated by this lack of trust, she calls upon Mother Earth for shelter in her fertile bosom. According to legend, the earth parts to shield Seeta from the merciless, toxic gaze of social patriarchs.

In the film, Raghunath's (one of Rama's many names—literally, "master of the Raghu dynasty") sister-in-law angrily taunts him: does he consider himself greater than the virtuous Rama, that he dares to ignore social indignation over the four nights that his wife spent at Jagga's? Raghunath enters his bedchamber to find his wife in great agony. It is a Gothic setting with grandiose furnishing: the baroque bed appears sepulchral; the ornate clock and the cherub statue take on the force of fate or *mahakal*, eternal time of Hindu-Buddhist eschatology, so that Raghunath seems stuck in a preordained stream of events. As he stands against the doorframe, towering over her, she implores him to ignore the gossip. His own dilemma is established through a montage of high- and low-angle shots; low-key lighting, swinging chandeliers and ominous shadows convey emotional intensity. A storm rages outside, lightning flashes through the window, drapes billowing with every gust of wind add to the eerie atmosphere. As he is overtaken with bilious suspicion, Raghunath turns around and stands with his back to his wife in a low-angle shot; she gets up from the bed, supporting herself by clinging to his back. At that point, he bursts out denouncing her, shoves her aside, and asks her to get out. Denied his support, both physical and emotional, she falls to the floor, then drags herself away into the stormy night. As she lies on the street in pouring rain, we hear a song on the soundtrack, reminding us of Seeta's plight from the *Ramayana*. The as-yet invisible singer asks rhetorically: why does not the earth part, and the sky split in two? A shot of dark rain clouds follows: the jagged silvery edges appear like a crack in the sky, an iconographic echoing of the part-ing earth that had sheltered Seeta. The sequence addresses spectators in terms of an all too familiar narrative scenario, inviting them to relive Seeta's woe. Soon, the song turns diegetic: we see the singer and a rapt audience that joins in singing the refrain. Drawing on folk traditions of oral-musical narration (*kathakata*) and of enacting scenes from the epic (*Ramlila* performances), the sequence turns itself into a collective experience: audiences have an entry point into the narrative and a sense of active participation. Invoking cultural memory, at the levels of both content and form, the narrative establishes its verisimilitude; "realism" in this instance encompasses nothing short of an epic tradition.

The abandoned wife brings up her son, Raj, on her own: theirs is a dif-ficult life, lived in slums in abject poverty. As the boy grows up, he comes under the influence of the criminal Jagga and gets initiated into a life of crime. Jagga takes the ultimate revenge on Raghunath, proving that the offspring of a decent, righteous family can fall into crime. Countering Raghunath's belief, the film asserts that environmental circumstances foster criminal behavior and underscores the need for social interven-tion. This collective concern is reiterated in the course of the court hear-ings. Rita, in her capacity as defense counsel, reminds Raghunath that his heartless actions caused his wife to migrate from Lucknow to Bom-bay, where their child grew up in the slums. In the film's penultimate sequence, Raj elaborates on the wider social implications of this family drama: as he makes an impassioned reformist plea about the need to save innocent children from society's gutters, the camera pans across the courtroom and tilts upward, coming to rest on the plebeian gal-leries.

Awara resorts to the melodramatic ploy of obfuscating the protago-nist's ancestry, only to have his real blood identity revealed in the end. By staging Raj's interim proletarianization, the narrative appears to shift away from archaic notions of bloodline and to participate in a cele-bration of egalitarian values, in consonance with modern democratic institutions. Even if the hero is slated to return eventually to a position of privilege, the narrative offers points of identification for a wide range

1

2

5

3

6

4

Awara: Raghunath throws his
wife out. Courtesy of NFAI.

7

8

of audiences. When Raj sings cheerfully about the pleasures of being a street-smart vagabond ("Awara Hoon"), he strikes a chord in audiences from various classes and backgrounds all over India and beyond: in China, in the Soviet Union, in the Middle East.[86] If the masses can relate to his plebeian lifestyle, the upper and middle classes sympathize with him in his temporary fall and enjoy voyeuristically the guilty pleasures of a life lived on the edge.

Within the parameters of a family melodrama, *Awara* works out the trepidations of a fragmented body politic and a rapidly changing society through the complication and dissolution of kinship ties. Multiple Oedipal configurations and conflicts involving a wronged mother, punitive but righteous father (the judge), evil surrogate father (the bandit), girlfriend/mother figure (Rita), and a fallen son capture wider social tensions. In her book-length study of the film, Gayatri Chatterjee brings out some of these far-ranging significations; for instance, she calls attention to the complex relationship between Judge Raghunath and his ward Rita, set up through repetitive shot structures (for example, similar shots of Raghunath returning home from work to his wife, and later to Rita) and a strong sense of competition between the judge and his estranged son for Rita's affections and loyalties.[87] These interpretations in terms of entangled relations are not just a matter of retrospective reading: contemporaneous commentaries talk euphemistically about the dark tenor of the film; anxious rumors about its incestuous underpinnings predate its release.[88] These speculations were intensified by the casting: Prithviraj Kapoor, Raj Kapoor's real-life father, acts in the role of Judge Raghunath; Nargis, whose romantic affair with the married Raj Kapoor was an open secret at the time, plays Rita.

In many ways, the film shows us why, more than any state-sponsored institution, the realm of popular cinema has been so successful in consolidating an emotionally compelling sense of community. An overall melodramatic mode, moving song sequences, sympathetic protagonists, and appeals to the spectators' hearts and minds in terms of familial and familiar situations, enable *Awara* to weave an irresistible web of affective investments and identifications and simultaneously refigure feudal, patriarchal authority in statist, juridical terms. Judge Raghunath embodies the Law, shown here to make possible the continuation of a nexus of quasi-feudal and colonial structures and attitudes within the framework of a postcolonial state. It is this impersonal edifice that he privileges over matters of the heart early in the narrative (e.g., in conversation with Rita over dinner). But at the end, while talking to Raj in prison, he reveals a change of attitude. Through his transformation, the film upholds a palpably emotional register over the rationalist notion of

justice embraced by the state: the heart is celebrated as the site of compelling alternative claims. Of course, the very fact that Raj is serving a
prison term for his crimes constitutes an acknowledgment of the state's
legal-juridical mandate.

Kapoor wrote, produced, and acted in his directorial debut, *Aag*, at
the age of twenty-three, and he immediately caught the attention of
the industry and the media as someone with a "brilliant future."[89] But
by the time *Barsaat*, his second directorial venture, was released, his
work was being termed "morbid" and "frightening."[90] One review stated
flatly: "It is a pity that this youthful, vivacious lad at the age of 25 should
allow him-self to drift into the morbid regions of the human mind and
leaving alone the sunshine of life flirt with its deep shadows to create a
screen drama, which, however *successful at the box office*, still remains
poor entertainment. . . . And how badly the world needs entertainment
in *these tragic days* need hardly be emphasized here!"[91] The baffled commentator recognizes Kapoor's times to be "tragic" yet cannot accept the
"morbid" undertone of his early films. There is a disavowal of contemporary imperatives and a stress on some preconceived, dissociated notion
of cinematic entertainment. The commentator even acknowledges the
commercial success of Kapoor's films but fails to make a connection between this success and the films' engagement, at some level, with spectators' experiences and anxieties. Could it be that Kapoor's dark sensibility—his "morbid" style—was not at odds with the optimism coursing
through a newly independent society but, rather, was indexical of the
deep melancholia that characterized Indian cultural consciousness in
the wake of the national truncation that came at the end of nearly two
centuries of foreign occupation, a melancholia that even the euphoria
of independence could not dispel?

Modernity, National Imagination, Historical Difference

Awara remains an acme in popular Hindi cinema's accomplishments, a
skillful orchestration of diverse elements made to resonate with the experiences of, and thus engage, a differentiated audience: folk music and
theater, indigenous epic narratives are combined with melodramatic
flourishes reminiscent of early Orson Welles works, and the social concerns of Frank Capra and late-1930s Warner Bros. gangster films. The
point here is not to trace Hollywood's influences but rather to think of
cinema as an essentially modern and global cultural form. Indian popular cinema has always been in dialog with other film industries, incorporating—without much worry about originality—aesthetic elements

ranging from Soviet socialist realist iconography to Latin jazz-funk. The nine-minute-long dream sequence in *Awara*, which might remind some of the "Broadway Steps" segment from *Singing in the Rain* (released in 1952, a year behind *Awara*), combines art deco–inspired sets with giant statues that reflect mass-produced, "bazaar" appropriations of classical Indian sculptures. Yet the final product remains discernibly Indian.

The affectionate designation of *masala films*—spicy and formulaic—alludes to this unmistakably Indian nature. However, such a categorization is, ultimately, dismissive: it implies that commercial Indian films never get the techniques "right," and at best they are derivative. The problem lies in the tendency to judge Indian films in terms of standards salient to (Western) film criticism. In relation to European modernism, masala films seem hopelessly unself-conscious, being neither a cinema of negation nor one of metaphysical angst; although, as the preceding discussion suggests, one can recognize entirely different orders of reflexivity and intertexuality in these works. Compared to classical Hollywood cinema, these films appear primitive in their inconsistent use of continuity editing techniques, their recourse to frontal tableaux, their frequent use of song and dance sequences; yet, as critical work on Indian popular cinema demonstrates, such "departures" have to be appreciated as well-thought-out formal strategies dictated by local norms.[92]

To underscore what is at stake here, I would like to invoke a rather striking example from another film, *Afsana* (1951), released the same year as *Awara*. When the long-lost lovers finally unite at the end of the film, they end up looking ecstatically—not at each other, but at some point off screen to the right. This seemingly idiosyncratic joint look in the film's concluding shot needs to be understood as a gesture of deference to a higher authority—perhaps a religious icon outside the frame, or invisible but omniscient fate. Here the particular organization of looks is motivated by, and hence makes sense in the context of, decidedly Indian codes: for instance, a darshanic or devotional mode.[93] Similarly, the frequent references to mythic structures constitute attempts to recast beguiling problems in collectively shared and legible terms. This strategy is noticed also in other parts of the world, for instance in Hong Kong martial arts (*wu xia*) films, or in biblical references in Hollywood films. However, nowhere else does the epic remain such a significant part of contemporary life and culture as in India. The two epics *Ramayana* and *Mahabharata* persist as vital reservoirs of civilizational conventions, beliefs and values, which Indians continue to draw upon in their daily lives.[94] If we fast-forward momentarily to the late 1980s, we find that the epics have infiltrated mass culture: serial adaptations of the two epics, each lasting well over a year, remain the

Dream sequence from *Awara*: Raj and Rita dance in front of a giant Shiva statue

most popular programs ever on national television cutting across religious affiliations; by early 2008, new television productions are in the works. But beyond such remakes, the epics continue to purvey a kind of cognitive framework that structures the understanding of historical experience; that is to say, experience becomes a contextual iteration of the epic. This continuing influence of the epics raises an interesting conundrum; if films are an essentially modern cultural form, then this persistence of the premodern epic marks out Indian cinema as a rather idiosyncratic phenomenon by Western standards—but only according to such standards.[95] Furthermore, it alerts us to the possibility that the social formation of which this cinema is a constitutive part, will never fit readily into Western teleological models of history or modernization. This is not so much a claim about Indian society or cinema's "exceptional" status, which would only bracket the Indian situation as a marginal curiosity to the Western-masquerading-as-universal norm; rather, it is an argument about the need for more accommodating theories of modernity and cinema that are concomitantly attentive to the specific historicities of local experiences.[96]

A popular film like *Awara* shows a remarkably creative engagement with its context. That film's invocation of the epics, or the challenge to statist notions of a secular Indian self in films like *Amar* and *Nastik*, comprises complex incorporations and accommodations. One of Benedict Anderson's most salutary insights is that "all evolutionary/progressive styles of thought" remain limited in comparison to religion in one fundamental sense: they respond to pervasive questions about human vulnerability and fatality "with impatient silence."[97] However, Anderson's presumption of a planetary process of desacralization leads him to posit the emergence of nationalism as a modern religion, one that undertakes "a secular transformation of fatality into continuity, contingency into meaning."[98] The evidence of Indian popular cinema suggests that such a "secular transformation" is anything but a done deal. As Partha Chatterjee points out in his compelling critique of Anderson, Indian society has never imported modern Western political and cultural forms passively; these forms have been creatively transformed and fused with indigenous structures.[99] Our close attention to situated cultural texts, which serve as sites for the discursive production and continual reinscription of Indian modernity and nationhood, offset claims about the inevitable demise of local lifeworlds in the face of a universal History.

If our discussion of *Amar* and *Awara* point to such situated recalibrations in the domain of cinema, it also begins to register the profound collective apprehensions about that historical conjuncture. Confusions about paternity, suspicions about illicit pregnancy, undercurrents of incestuous longings—these are dramatic elements that destabilize the comfort zone of a secure and acceptable moral universe and threaten to compromise the plausibility of the narratives. But these vexing plot twists were to find their way into one film after another, placing troubling demands on the spectators. What historical hauntings were being projected in these dark melancholic tales, complicating a hegemonic cultural nationalism? This query is the focus of the next chapter.

CHAPTER TWO

Runes of Laceration

THE MELANCHOLIC MOOD that pervades *Awara* is even more pal-pable in *Aag*, Raj Kapoor's directorial debut, released in 1948. While this earlier film includes fleeting references to the truncation, its haunting allegorical allusions to the brutalities and blighted aspirations leave a far more vivid impression. I begin with a discussion of *Aag* to elucidate this chapter's focus: the intersecting and constitutive functions of mel-ancholia and allegory in early cinematic mediations of Partition.

Scarred Idealism

Aag, like *Awara*, enacts the maturation of its protagonist into an au-tonomous subject. Kewal (who, like Raj in the later film, is played by the director himself) refuses to follow in his forefather's footsteps to become a public prosecutor. He questions the education system that the country has inherited from the colonial British regime: after all, how does it help Indians to know how many wives Henry VIII had? Spurning conventional avenues of power and privilege, Kewal leaves home to pursue his interest in theater, an artistic endeavor of dubious repute, and finally proves his mettle with help from the wealthy theater owner and painter Rajan.[1] The stage—and, by extension, cinema—provides a domain for breaking with the past and undertaking novel acts of the imagination. Kewal goes to extremes to exert his creative independence, resisting any kind of interference from Rajan and spurning an old stagehand's experience ("I want a fresh approach," he declares). Theater, whose live performativity vivifies experience, is counterposed to painting and sculpture, which freeze beauty into inert representations but cannot capture life or the "soul" of its subject.

In a pivotal sequence, the homeless Kewal wanders into an empty theater; delirious with fatigue and hunger, he proceeds to reenact his histrionic exit from the family fold. Facing the camera in a medium shot, Kewal relives his forceful declaration of independence from his father and his tearful adieu to his mother. Objects, images, and aural slivers pulsate and come together in the magical space of the theater's backstage. As Kewal picks up an old flute from the dusty floor, a high-pitched but tender melody on the soundtrack mobilizes an entire weave of cultural associations—most notably, tales of love and loss, and the desperate yearnings of separated lovers. A female mannequin, an inert theatrical prop, moves him to tears: it is not clear whether he remembers his mother or his beloved—or, perhaps, an unattainable ideal. The scene encapsulates the iterability of the central woman figure whose loss constitutes the originary trauma in Kewal's life, and whose replacement becomes his constitutive obsession; simultaneously, it conveys the appositeness of the performing arts as a medium for working through wrenching experiences, for mourning loss.

After all, the primary motivation in this narrative of personal growth comes from the pursuit of a compound ideal: art and love. Kewal keeps searching for Nimmi, his long-lost childhood sweetheart and partner in his youthful creative endeavors. The moment of their separation is invested with a haunting intensity: hearing that Nimmi is leaving town with her family, the young Kewal (played by Raj's younger brother, Shashi Kapoor) rushes to the bus station, just as the bus is pulling out; we see him running after the vehicle, through its rear window (as if from the point of view of its passengers, who remain offscreen). The shot continues as he gradually falls far behind, a desperate and desolate figure at the far end of a fast-expanding, empty stretch of road. On the soundtrack, we hear the voice of a grown-up Kewal, overcome with emotion: "But Nimmi left; I saw my dream die before my eyes. And I could do nothing. I was so helpless. Man is so helpless. There I stood, as my life sped away from me. Life, like the road, appeared long, dark and desolate . . ." The scene sets a despondent tone for the entire film, as we accompany the protagonist on his mission of reclaiming a lost plenitude. This mood is very much in evidence in the moonlit scene on the sea beach, which begins with Kewal and his college sweetheart Nirmala. Oddly, Nirmala soon disappears from view without any explanation; a couple from a local fishing community sings rapturously about the moon ("Dekh chand ki ore," look at the moon), as if to underscore Kewal's loneliness. This scene presages another: when Nirmala abandons him and their production of the play *Shakuntala* to marry a man chosen by her parents,[2] Kewal finds himself alone on the beach once again. Framed by sand dunes, palm branches, and fishing nets, he sings a mournful song ("Zindah hoon is tarah"). The poignant lyrics ("I am alive, but lifeless, like a burning lamp that gives no light") and melody imbue the already dense, chiaroscuro mise-en-scène with an unearthly aura. Later in the film, Nargis as the idealized Nimmi sings yet another song ("Na ankhon mein ansoo, na hoto pe") whose lyrics describe melancholic absorption: "No tears come to my eyes, nor a sigh escapes my lips, yet I have not smiled in ages." Then she goes on to wonder about the one teardrop that wells up in her eyes: "Will it, too, be wasted?" There is recognition here of the potential productivity of loss, the productivity that springs from an endless search and leads to an aesthetic representation of the search itself—that is, to a film like *Aag*.

In pursuing his lost love and his artistic ideal, Kewal conflates the two: the theater increasingly turns into the recompense for a missing presence. While selecting a heroine for his show, he keeps looking for someone who can live up to his beloved Nimmi. Finally, when he finds someone close to his imagination, the camera dollies in on her face in a swooping gesture. The woman says that she has lost her family, her name, and her honor in the hell-fire that now engulfs Punjab. Pleading Kewal not to ask her any more questions, she hides her face in distress. In trying to regain his lost love, his ideal, Kewal only finds a woman whose sense of being is fraught with her unspeakable experiences. Within the narrative of *Aag*, she represents thousands of tormented women and is a synecdochic figure for the idealized nation, one that indexes both national honor and shame.[3]

The recovery of love, of a lost ideal, proves to be a tortuous process. Kewal provides the woman with a fresh identity, calling her Nimmi: she starts life anew as the female lead in his show. They fall in love, and it appears as if our hero has found his muse. But on the night of the premiere, he realizes that his friend and benefactor Rajan is also in love with "Nimmi." In a stunning sequence, constructed as a series of intercuts between offstage action and the show onstage, Kewal is united with his estranged parents; he decides to sacrifice his love for the sake of his friend; finally, he burns his face and sets the theater on fire. His "failure" to achieve his dreams gets etched onto his body in the form of a disfigured face.

The film begins on Kewal's wedding night, as he approaches the new bride and unveils her in a gesture of romantic anticipation. But the returned gaze amounts to abject disappointment: the bride shrieks in horror at his burned visage. His search for a woman who will look beyond surface beauty into his soul seems interminable; in a sense, he awaits his own unveiling. He counters helplessness—being *bebas*, being out of control—by retaining the power of narration: the story unfolds as a long flashback from his subjective point of view, and he gets to put his various heroines to the test. When the ultimate embodiment of his ideal woman declares her love for him, especially his handsome face, his hair, his blue eyes, Kewal disfigures his face, then asks if she still loves him. This play between veiling and unveiling, extended in terms of corporeal mutilation, dramatizes the misrecognition between the physical and the transcendental, the real and the mythic. But his desperate attempt to register the triumph of his soul over his corporeal being (an idealist polarity that drives the narrative) also mimics, I will argue, the desperation and the ultimate mutilation of a social body in search of a sovereign statehood. Through his despairing act, the narrative appears to challenge an idealized and unproblematic citizenship that involves the negation of social contradictions and the integration of amnesiac individuals in a network of activities instituted by the state on behalf of the nation.[4] The frustrations of a quixotic subject point to analogous distortions in the realization of a nationalist utopia, and the disfigured self presents an allegory for the dismembered nation.

While Kewal's disillusionment leads to self-mutilation, Rajan's frustrated desire for the idealized woman figure propels him to turn on his own creations: in a fit of jealousy, he tears up all his paintings. This frenzied defacement echoes the malevolent attacks on the idealized woman-as-community in the wake of the national truncation: in both situations, disillusionment with the ideal precipitates aggression against it. Kapoor appears to be making a comparative point about the nature of mourning across various aesthetic media. Painting requires a distance between the painter and his subject: thus the object of his gaze, and of his desire, remains crucially external, and other, to him. In contrast, Kewal's obsession with the theater, an essentially performative art form, allows him a more fluid subject-position that is more amenable to masquerade and capable of mustering greater empathy for others, including women. While Rajan's frustration is expressed outward, Kewal's disenchantment undergoes a melancholic introjection and turns against his own self.

Although the narrative ends with a contrived union between the original Nimmi and a disfigured Kewal and a sense of fulfillment is restored, the scar remains as a reminder of loss. What sense can we make

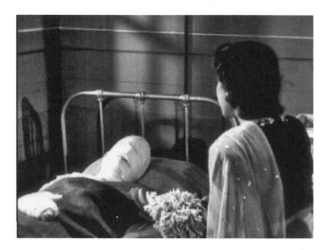

Aag: Nimmi visits a bandaged Kewal in hospital.
Courtesy of NFAI.

of this dual strategy? Since the narrative works within a commercial mode, it is under pressure to provide affective closure; at the same time, it resonates with an unfathomable pessimism. Kapoor's first film, released in 1948, cannot ignore the deep wound inflicted by the national amputation and the accompanying violence; the tone of the film, which casts a shadow over its youthful idealism, intimates the shock more eloquently than the narrative's single direct reference to Partition. *Aag* cues us in to the cryptic ways in which Indian popular cinema engaged with a portentous historical horizon inescapably constituted by the trauma of Partition. An array of indirect, tacit figurations come into play: conscious displacements; subconscious, even unintended allusions; indexical citations; accidental traces; evocations of broad, analogous sentiments. While allegory remains the standard way of thinking about such implicit mediations, what would be an adequate conceptualization of allegory that captures such a range of strategies in this singular cultural context?

Allegory: A Form of Expression

At one level, allegory appears to be an inherently logocentric mode, always pointing to some deeper kernel of truth; yet its potency rests on a deferral of meaning, decentering notions of truth and being. The concept of allegory that I invoke here is different from the signification of abstract meanings through illustrative images or writings; rather, I follow Walter Benjamin's explication of allegory as "a form of expression" in relation to the baroque world of German *Trauerspiel* (tragic drama),[5] and Paul de Man's discussions of an allegorizing tendency in European romantic literature from the second half of the eighteenth century.[6] Both Benjamin and de Man want to restitute to allegory a status more significant than a baroque or romantic curiosity, a mere "playful illustrative technique."[7] Both authors compare allegory to the much-exalted symbol to bring out the former's potential for a radical hermeneutics.

As de Man argues, allegory's literal meaning deconstructs the figural meaning and vice versa; this in-built mechanism of dispersal creates the potential for an allegorical mode of reading as a critical, often subversive, sense-making practice.[8] The symbol implies a simultaneous, spatial relationship between image and object, which can therefore coincide; in contrast, "time is the originary constitutive category" for allegory, since "it remains necessary, if there is to be allegory, that the allegorical sign refer to another sign that precedes it." The meaning of an allegorical sign emerges from the "*repetition . . . of a previous sign with which it can never coincide, since it is the essence of this previous sign to be pure anteriority.*"[9] Thus de Man poses allegory as promoting "a conception of *the self seen in its authentically temporal predicament,*" against the symbol as part of "a defensive strategy that tries to hide from this negative self-knowledge."[10] The insight I glean from de Man is that allegory inaugurates a reflexivity on the part of the subject, a reflexivity that proves crucial to the precarious hermeneutic of a traumatized self.

Benjamin coaxes out the temporal distinction between symbol and allegory through his discussion of nature and history. His conception of "nature" involves not so much the world in its ontological materiality as the revelatory moment of danger that disrupts homogeneous historical time, in which deep contradictions become visible as the habitual or "natural" social condition. The reconciliation implied by the symbol is revealed to be equally evanescent; it holds only for an accidental, lyrical moment as a utopian possibility: "In the symbol destruction is idealized and the transfigured face of nature is fleetingly revealed in the light of redemption."[11] From a Benjaminian perspective, Partition is one of those critical historical conjunctures at which social frictions, usually elided by naturalized symbols of national unity (the map, the flag, the anthem), come into view.

Likewise, history is unhinged from the idealism of a Hegelian actualization of time and reinterpreted as a random series of transitory, fragmented experiences. Allegory, which is born "by virtue of a strange combination of nature and history,"[12] confronts us with "the *facies hip-*

pocratica of history as a petrified, primordial landscape. Everything about history that, from the beginning, has been untimely, sorrowful, unsuccessful, is expressed in a face—or in a death's head."[13] A form that reveals "man's subjection to nature," the essence of allegorical signification is the reformulation of history as a narrative of suffering, and its success resides in the intensity with which it captures the sense of death, decay and dispersal.[14]

In Benjamin's reading, the melancholic content of baroque tragedy undergoes a transformation: melancholy becomes a matter of *form*.[15] In particular, melancholy fuels an allegorizing impulse: "The only pleasure the melancholic permits himself, and it is a powerful one, is allegory."[16] Benjamin stresses the revelatory potential of the allegorical intuition: it turns the image into "a fragment," thus extinguishing "the false appearance of totality." The image now emerges as "a rune," intimating all that classicism is not allowed to reveal: "the lack of freedom, the imperfection, the collapse of the physical, beautiful, nature."[17] Such revelations take on a subversive force, underscoring the political potential of the allegorical form and of a strategy of allegorical reading. This possibility is taken up by theories of twentieth-century avant-garde art, which draw on Benjaminian notions of allegory and the fragment.[18] Extending this Benjaminian intuition to the realm of the popular, I will claim that an allegorical mode of reading can also help us reclaim mainstream films as creative engagements with their overdetermined contexts, as cultural texts that express social contradictions in their own clumsy and provisional ways. Benjamin himself recognizes, and stresses, that it is the allegorical structure of the Trauerspiel that allows it to "assimilate as its content the subjects which contemporary conditions provide it."[19] Thus allegory in his estimation operates as an omnibus form that maps social space in its visible and covert dimensions.

Two clarifications are necessary. First, to say that the allegory is an omnibus form is not to push for a totalizing figuration: in terms of the concerns of this book, reading popular films as allegories of Partition need not imply their reduction to this one moment.[20] Put another way, allegory's assimilation of contextual elements as its "content" never takes on a totalizing function: rather, the dispersion that characterizes the social space is retained—indeed, foregrounded—through allegorical representation. The runes, the fragments present the always inchoate and abstruse aspects of social life.

Second, the idea is not only to look for allegorical significations that are produced consciously by the authors, but also to dissociate the text from such intentionality and to look for submerged patterns that can be read as unintended, inadvertent allegories. Such a strategy of allegorical reading becomes particularly interesting in the case of genre films produced by a commercial film industry, films that primarily purport to exploit formulas successful at the box office but which, nevertheless, allegorize social conditions and tendencies without much, or even any, thought. As Ella Shohat points out in her discussion of Israeli genre films: "The classical definition of allegory has always privileged intention as well as the complementary activities of an author who hides and hints and a reader who discovers and completes. But it is possible to detach allegory from any originary intentionality in order to discern implicit, unconscious and even inadvertent allegories. Here, the allegory lies less in the intention than in the reading, as well as inhering in the context from which the films emerge."[21] Shohat's critical model of "reading" places the sociopolitical context of the films in the foreground. I want to draw attention to two distinct, if closely linked, specificities that also qualify allegorical reading: the first pertains to the cinematic medium, while the second relates to a cinema's cultural context.

One crucial dimension of film spectatorship, the phenomenological, takes us beyond the literary trope of "reading." Through compelling in-vocations of temporal and spatial configurations, films engage viewers in a virtual sensorium of perceptual impressions and emotions. Haptic and physiological sensations induced through the nature of the film stock (grainy or saturated), color (bold or washed out, warm or cold), framing of shots (centered or askew; suspenseful, even sinister, off-screen space; high- or low-angle shots), camera movement (deliberate tracking, or jerky handheld camera), rhythms of editing (slow, dreamy dissolves or jarring jump cuts, fast edits or very long shots), music (tonal or dissonant, minor or major key), sound perspective and dynamics (on- or offscreen, loud or muted) influence our understanding of film narra-tives, and such influence is not limited to what Linda Williams evoca-tively categorizes as the "body genres" of horror, porn, science fiction, and melodrama.[22] Indeed, if one thinks of melodrama as a mode that overlays various other film genres, then cinematic "meaning" becomes a remarkably complex event. Synaesthetic sensations expand film viewing to an experience far beyond one focused on the literal meaning of the narrative. These subliminal mechanisms of signification that come into play paradigmatically, around the syntagmatic progression of the plot, are of a different order than those involved in acts of reading. Indeed, viewing films involves a performativity on the part of the spectator: he not only experiences strong emotions and sensations but also exults, cowers, laughs, cries, shouts out, trembles, covers his eyes or ears, and even walks out in disgust. In what follows, I use the term *reading* in an extended sense, to include the complex webs of fantasy and desire, identification and alienation that constitute the contract between a film and its audience.

This social contract, which is historically and culturally negotiated, points to a second level of specificity that motivates allegorical reading: it has to do with vernacular regimes of representation. Modern Indian aesthetics has emerged along uneven and disjunctive trajectories, through convoluted transactions between seemingly inconsonant aesthetic realms, political claims, and social practices (e.g., consumerist entertainment and reformist pedagogy, Western naturalism and vernacular ritualist idolatry).[23] Traces of these contradictions inhere in the specific aesthetic forms and modalities: in an allegorical imperative (as opposed to a naturalist iconography or a linear narrative); in a proclivity toward epic dispersion (in contrast to the focused teleology of the modern novel); in a penchant for the acutely melodramatic (driven by pleasures and anxieties only partially tempered by bourgeois-liberal moral codes). Thus, in the epics and the *Puranas*, as one story inaugurates another before it, voices and temporalities collide and coalesce; interminable deflection and dispersion compose vertiginously nested narratives.[24] Intriguingly, there is tremendous self-consciousness about these structures and logics—not only within the texts, but also at the level of their popular dissemination. This epic mode constitutes a vernacular historical consciousness: continual narration and reinterpretation become ways of apprehending and imagining history.[25]

The convergence of these layered, polysemic modes has produced capacious and ingenious aesthetic formations that can engage the pluralities and contradictions of contemporary India. In modern Indian art, epic and allegory combine to take on the problematic of the nation in both its empirical and utopian dimensions. Thus Ravi Varma presents "a range of regional, feminine, and classical figure-types, each purposefully posed as 'Indian'";[26] Abanindranath Tagore, doyen of the Bengal School, invested his works with a "mystical and sublime idealism"[27] most evident in his allegorical creation *Bharata-mata* (*Mother India*, 1905), with its "dual impression of intimate familiarity and divine transcendence."[28] When we get to Mehboob Khan's 1957 film *Mother India*, the epic and the allegorical conjoin the melodramatic to produce a contemporary discourse of great emotive and political potency.

An allegorical reading practice sensitive to the specificities of Indian cinema must be alert to the potential for signification beyond the storyline, signification that might inhere not only in the formal elements and the collective reception of the medium but also in the historical context, and that might be conjured up forcefully or as the most obscure hint. In these pages, I hope to capture the ways in which the trauma of Partition litters an entire cultural landscape with its melancholy insinuations:

from actual photographic trace (the boy on the donkey in *Shabnam*), to the tormented characters and pregnant mise-en-scènes of 1950s films; from the angry diatribes against Muslim artists and technicians in the trade magazines to the anemic, one-dimensional cinematic characterizations of Muslims; from the cursory references to sectarian violence to the profound sadness of song lyrics, displaced allusions, and narrative/iconographic deflections. The task at hand is not one of hermeneutic completion: it is, rather, one of hermeneutic association. Our challenge is to recognize the multifarious cinematic fragments and to "read" them as runes intimating the deep wounds of a traumatized social formation otherwise invested in an ideological itinerary of forgetting.[29]

Such a reading practice is motivated largely by a retrospective constitution of the experience of Partition as a collective trauma, a frame suggested by the curious trajectory of the experience itself—the initial disorientation and silence, the gradual return of the repressed, and the recent outpouring of memories and representations. My point, further, is that an allegorical reading strategy is dictated by the confrontation of cinema and trauma. There is something about the medium of cinema that renders representations of traumatic experiences particularly problematic: its power to "bring to life" ontological reality threatens to make such experiences uncomfortably palpable, its ability to revivify events that resist referentiality and intelligibility rends the time of the now and induces existential crisis, overwhelming the fragile subjectivities of the traumatized. As veteran producer-director B. R. Chopra put it with reference to the *bibhajan*, or bifurcation: "It was such an experience that those who had lived through it, could not go on living if they were made to endure it a second time [on screen]."[30]

Before we move on, one particular point merits further reiteration. Allegory becomes significant to post-Partition Indian cinema not only because of its traumatized context, but also because of a vernacular aesthetic system that has congealed over centuries and that defies easy translation to other cultural traditions. Thus it is not possible to establish equivalence between allegorical structures from various troubled cinematic formations (say, German, Indian, and Japanese) simply in terms of a structure of delay and deferral, ignoring the singularities of their aesthetic histories.

The "silence" that is induced by social trauma is of a perplexing nature and invites substantial framing and interpretation. Silence itself need not amount simply to an absence of discourse: rather, following Michel Foucault, we can think of silence as yet another form of discourse, as "an element that functions alongside the things said, with them and in relation to them within overall strategies."[31] Just as a crushing experience cannot be erased from memory but keeps surfacing involuntarily and unexpectedly with an incomprehensible urgency, so also the silence over Partition has been far from complete. The stray references are highly dispersed, charged and, often, incoherent: when discovered, they present themselves as fragments that are not readily legible. How, then, are we to read the silence over the Partition "in relation to" the "things said" in cinema? How are we to recognize the "overall strategies" of signification?

Stray Articulations

In the early years after 1947, Partition entered films mainly as a point of reference, establishing characters' backgrounds and coordinates. There were passing allusions to a character's orphan or refugee status, or origins in provinces (Sind, Baluchistan, West Punjab) that were now parts of Pakistan (e.g., in *Namoona* [1949], popular star Dev Anand plays a refugee). Many films depicted North India in economic doldrums, its social fabric under tremendous stress from the tumult and dislocations (*Garam Coat* [1955]). Only a handful of Hindi/Hindustani films addressed the experience of Partition directly and at length: they included *Lahore* (1949), *Nastik* (1954), and *Chhalia* (1960). In chapter 4, I will turn to these exceptional texts to explore how they undertook a subtle reframing of cultural memory to uphold particular versions of identity, community, and nationality. For now, to appreciate just how rare these cinematic engagements were, consider the following estimate: over a period of fifteen years (1947–62), during which the average annual production of Hindi films stood around 120, fewer than a dozen films featured notably explicit representations of the Partition.[32]

The press, in particular, obsessed about Partition, the handover of power, and the riots.[33] By early 1947, the division of the country was imminent; in the months leading up to the event, cinema's ancillary press called for restraint and calm. But the tone changed after August: once Pakistan became a reality, animosity mounted steadily, reaching a peak during the 1948 incursion of Pakistani paratroopers in Kashmir. Thus in April 1947, *Filmindia* magazine declared: "The Hindus are to blame for the present communal orgies. They are reaping what they sowed with their hyper-religiosity." It singled out the intolerance of upper-caste Hindus—who "banned even the shadow of a Muslim on their door step"—as the root cause of communal strife in the country.[34] Two months later, the editor ascribed the riots to "the ever-increasing number of have-nots," claiming that politics and communalism were "merely a camouflage under which the hungry stomachs" were "fast marching towards a communistic goal." In a utopian vein, he concluded that the nation was heading not "for a civil war but a social revolution" in which the "golden crowns" of Indian capitalists would "lick the dust in abject submission."[35] From such attempts to reinterpret the communal crisis in socialist utopian terms, the magazine veered into increasingly shrill and blatantly partisan rhetoric after the eventful month of August. It employed strong, graphic language to provide its spin on recent developments, signaling a general atmosphere of hysteria and animosity; for instance, the October issue stated that "the Muslim slogan of 'Love me and love my religion'" had been "thrust down the cold throats of thousands of dead Hindus all over India and Pakistan."[36] There were several editorials and reports on anti-Indian sentiments and continuing victimization of Hindus, and on demonstrations at screenings of Indian films in Pakistan.[37] Soon after Partition, political events came to be reported and commented upon in manifestly nationalist ways, pitting India against Pakistan. An editorial from early 1950 claimed: "In a thousand and one ways the Muslims in Pakistan have been provoking a war between India and Pakistan during the last thirty-two months since the ill-fated partition." Pointing to the atrocities against Hindus, including women and children, and the looting of Hindu property in Pakistan, it criticized the Indian government's inaction: "And yet our secular State has borne these misfortunes with a cool and philosophic resignation which has been mistaken as weakness and impotence on our part." Reducing the avowed secularity of the state to national impotence, the editorial went on to pose a sinister and loaded question: "But how long will the masses listen to this wise advice of our leaders in the midst of the ever-mounting list of outrages and provocations?"[38] Another editorial from 1952 summarized the content of a Pakistani documentary from a purportedly Muslim perspective: "Those whom we have ruled for 900 years and from whom was wrested this country of ours by the sacrifice of countless Muslims, that enemy is poised at our frontiers."[39] It reported that Pakistani audiences were hailing the documentary *Josh-e-Jehad* with cries of "Allah-ho-Akbar" ("Allah is Great"), and that the Pakistani press was exhorting the *mujahids* (crusaders) to slaughter Indians, fly the flag of Islam over Delhi's Red Fort (an icon of the Mughal Empire), and propagate Islam by conquest and conversion. Citing extremely belligerent examples of anti-Indian discourse from Pakistan, the editorial questioned the Indian government's attitude of appeasement: "Pakistan is too virile and aggressive a nation to heed the gentle cooing of a peace pigeon" like Prime Minister Nehru. It charged that Nehru had "gaged" [*sic*] the entire nation, subjected it to the "silent bondage" of secularism and peace.[40] The most notorious instance of *Filmindia*'s sectarian journalism came in the form of yet another editorial in March 1952: titled "The Crescent over India," it claimed that the "common Islamic ritual of blood, rape, plunder, religious tolerance and fanaticism" could be traced back all the way to the Prophet Mohammed.[41] Reiterating what was a widely held view of the Islamic invasion and rule of India, the piece tapped into sectarian popular memory to mobilize a Hindu-Indian national identity and to whip up hostility toward Islamic Pakistan.

Admittedly, *Filmindia* remains an extreme example: as Sumita Chakravarty points out, Baburao Patel, the editor of the magazine, frequently used it as a forum to promote his own partisan politics.[42] However, in focusing her attention primarily on *Filmfare*—another English-language film magazine that came to challenge the older publication's market soon after being launched in 1952—Chakravarty confines her analysis to discourses that more or less concurred with a hegemonic nationalist project. She loses track of a significant alternative voice, whose existence further complicates the notion of a unified Indian nationality. It is not enough to dismiss such views as fanatically communal, hence undesirable: they cannot be made simply to disappear. I believe it is absolutely necessary to chart the evolution of factional rhetoric: to understand how people came to despise other communities to the point of wanting to eliminate them, how such rabid religious sentiments continued to be nurtured among large sections of the population, and how official secularism came to be regarded as a sign of weakness and thus widely disparaged. Otherwise, public discourse is impoverished over time: what is unthinkable from a hegemonic perspective comes to constitute the troubling, subterranean unthought of society.[43] By tracing the gradual and sustained development of politicized religious identities since independence as the unheeded other of an authoritative secular Indian identity, we stand to gain a better comprehension of the recent emergence of Hindu nationalism as a hegemonic force.

If readers' letters are any index, then the whereabouts of Muslim stars and celebrities emerged as a major source of popular anxiety. Throughout 1948, readers of *Filmindia* kept inquiring about Muslim industry figures; as it turned out, many of them, like singer-actresses Khursheed and Noor Jehan, and the composer Ghulam Haider, had migrated to Pakistan.[44] Much of the editorial ire was directed against Muslim producers and writers suspected of vacillation in their nationalist affiliations, even of stronger "spiritual allegiance" to Pakistan. They were described as "Pakistani paratroopers, dropped without the parachutes," who needed to be watched constantly, lest they use the powerful medium of cinema to "propagate the glories of the Mughal empire" and "the numerous blessings of Islam" to convert Hindu untouchables into Muslims.[45] There was a palpable bitterness in invectives such as the following: "When Pakistan was in the debating stages, these producers had moved heaven and earth to contribute their money, mite and malice to attain it and with a passion that had made them unnecessarily odious to their Hindu friends. Today that passion has become a dead weight on their conscience."[46] Endless snide comments were made about Muslim producers who chose to live in India but kept their financial assets in Pakistan.[47] One report charged that some Muslim filmmakers were selling duplicate negatives of their films to kinsfolk and business associates in Pakistan at nominal prices; as a result, the government of India was losing export taxes on these films.[48] Film reviews took Bombay's Muslim directors and writers to task for their alleged misrepresentation of Hindu life. Shahid Lateef and Ismat Chugtai, the director and the writer respectively of *Arzoo* (1950), were criticized for their lack of understanding of the institution of Hindu marriage.[49] Similarly, Shums Lucknavi, the writer of *Rakhi* (1949), was chided for suggesting an illicit sexual relationship between a brother and a sister; the reviewer suggested that the Muslim writer could not appreciate the "sanctity" of the Hindu brother-sister tie, since Islam permitted marriage between first cousins.[50] In harping on essential and immutable Hindu traditions and stressing Muslim inability to capture their essence, the reviews overlooked the possibility that the films in question could be interrogating extant social structures and their pathological mutations.

Even *Filmindia* could not keep up its sectarian diatribe unequivocally. When a reader asked what would happen to the Indian film industry if all Muslim producers left for Pakistan, the editor replied: "The screen would lose its vigor, imagination and enterprise."[51] This wistful admission, uncharacteristic as it was, does complicate our understanding of the decidedly biased viewpoints in the magazine's pages. It reveals the level of confusion, the mixed emotions and extreme reactions generated by an exceedingly painful phase in Indian national history.

Kashmir emerged as the focus of the most vituperative popular debate of the time. The dispute over Kashmir, the occasion for the first armed confrontation between the independent sibling-states, sprung from the fact that the inhabitants of the province were predominantly Muslim, but they were ruled by a Hindu royal family that decided to join India. A film titled *Kashmir* (1950) extolled a virulent brand of Indian nationalism to counter the dispute over the province. A print advertisement promoting the film referred to the "saffron earth" of Kashmir, claiming a naturalized Hinduness for the province on the basis of chromatic association. Kashmir was celebrated as "Paradise on Earth," a gift of bountiful nature; but human greed created all kinds of problems:

> Once again savage in man woke up; greed growled and barbarous passion wanted to burn the sober beauty. . . . Neighbors became dishonest

and tensions got rot. Raiders came in torrents, devastation pervaded and the greatest havoc was wrought [sic] in the name of religion. Uncultured, uncivilized and inhuman raiders were paid and fed to fight a Holy War— What a Shame; they were hired to kill their own kith and kin and to wipe out their own religion in the name of Religion.[52]

Through such over-the-top rhetoric, contemporary politico-religious struggles were recast in grand historical terms: military skirmishes between the two infant nation-states were interpreted anachronistically, juxtaposing incursions of Pakistani paratroopers with medieval Islamic invasions, thus reiterating the archaic "barbarian outsider" status of Muslims. At the same time, Pakistani Muslims were pitted against Indian Muslims: the former were described as mercenary raiders "hired to kill their own kith and kin." The advertisement called Muslims external raiders and simultaneously solicited their loyalty to the Indian nation-state. It was a typical attestation to the problematic position of Indian Muslims: with the realization of Pakistan, they became the internal other of an Indian national self. Another advertisement for the same film proclaimed: "We'll nail *Old Glory* to the Top of the Pole."[53] This strange reference to the Confederate flag reveals a profound anxiety about Kashmir. The odd slippage, through its invocation of the American analogy, recognizes the "holy war" over Kashmir as a civil war, not just an alien invasion. Moreover, by equating the Indian flag to the banner of the vanquished Confederate forces, the seemingly resolute proclamation unwittingly betrays a deep apprehension about the outcome of the struggle in Muslim-majority Kashmir.

After 1950, discourses in film media became increasingly preoccupied with cinema's role in the project of building a modern nation. Discussions of the aftermath of the division remained focused on political tensions between the two states and the impasse over trade relations and cultural exchange. But there was a distinct silence about the carnage: as if everyone had reached a consensus that there was no point in dwelling on it, that public discussions of the experience would be of no use.

Reading the Runes

An allegorical reading strategy promises to take us beyond the apparent erasure of the Partition in films of the first decade, helping us discover oblique, even serendipitous, traces of the trauma. It involves the identification of recurring themes and motifs that carry the burden of displaced anxieties, and formal structures that intimate hidden conflicts. In revealing the subterranean fissures in national life and the shocking dimensions of human suffering, such an approach poses a threat to received narratives of national history. Through such analytical maneuvers, we can reclaim these popular fabulations as pragmatic and imaginative mediations of an arduous historical conjuncture. At stake is an appreciation of the cultural reluctance to acknowledge the immediate past as something of a historical necessity.

Before turning to thematic displacements, I will address the more intractable problematic of film form as allegory. The difficulty of locating an allegorical imperative in cinematic form is compounded by its frequently aleatoric and implicit nature: that is to say, the formal elements emerge as allegories quite inadvertently, and only in the most diffuse ways. Take one formal structure widely employed to represent memory and its vicissitudes: the narrative device of the flashback that typically returns us to a time before the current moment in a narrative. Maureen Turim, who provides us with the most sustained investigation of the film flashback as both a formal device and as a microcosm of film temporality, establishes a clear connection between trauma and the temporal disjunction of the flashback in the works of modernist auteurs such as Ingmar Bergman, Akira Kurosawa, and Alain Resnais.[54] It is more difficult to establish such a relation for popular commercial films that, as a rule, eschew reflexive formalist maneuvers. I want to return briefly to Raj Kapoor's *Aag*, in the hope that this exegetical flashback will help elucidate the abstruse nature of the task at hand.

Partition returns as recognizable flashbacks in *Nastik*, discussed in the previous chapter, and in *Alo Amar Alo* (1972), discussed in the next. *Aag* presents a more interesting case of the film flashback at the moment when Kewal and Rajan encounter the nameless, homeless woman played by Nargis for the first time: as she verbally alludes to her suffering in the Punjab carnage, the camera rushes toward her face from a medium shot to a close up—held in profile, first looking down, then tilting up. Complementing the verbal narration, the framing and the camera movement do the work—usually performed by a dissolve—of allowing another time to interrupt the story time. The film presents at least three more enigmatic instances that, one way or another, act as flashbacks in the body of the narrative and that, in alluding to larger social processes, take on a strong allegorical function. The first instance comprises a sequence discussed above, with Kewal reliving the moment of his ostracization from the family in an empty auditorium. While the soundtrack reproduces his parents' remonstrations and entreaties, we see our hero talking passionately to an inert statue. At one point, there is loud applause at his powerful histrionics: the narrative engages in a sound flashforward, presaging his eventual success at the bleakest mo-

Aag: Kewal discovers "Nimmi." Courtesy of NFAI.

ment of his life. Past, present, and future come together in this hallucinatory scene that becomes a metacommentary on the capacity of theater—and, by extrapolation, of cinema—to engage human experience in its temporal fullness and fragility. The youthful Raj Kapoor, in his directorial debut, alludes to the creative and affective potency of cinema's social address in tapping into a collective structure of feeling oscillating between loss and optimism. The second instance, also mentioned before, has to do with two song sequences on the moonlit beach. Again, as Nirmala is already out of our sight during the first song, the scene becomes an effective flashforward. The loss, already foreshadowed in the first sequence, is made concrete in the second with intercuts of Nirmala in her bridal regalia getting married to somebody else. Once again, loss and the subsequent melancholy are framed as the very conditions of creativity. During the first song ("Look at the moon"), Kewal ignores the full moon in the sky and looks intently at a lamplight. The flickering flame is the fire—the *aag*—of creativity that propels him, and that always threatens to consume him when it turns into uncontrollable passion. Partition, the underside of independence, the originary vio-

Aag: Projecting the "ideal woman"

lence that makes nationhood possible, is alluded to in terms of the fine balance that artists must negotiate. The third instance follows Kewal's "discovery" of the new Nimmi as the embodiment of his fantasy of the perfect woman, a fantasy articulated in virtually impossible terms: "As innocent as dewdrop, as frolicsome as a mountain spring, with tears that could move oceans, with a smile that makes the world smile with her—a girl with wine in her eyes, music in her voice, and magic in her movements." Not to mention a woman who can look beyond the surface and appreciate Kewal's soul! A self-conscious production of the ideal woman follows in a surreal setting that harks back to the classical Indian antiquity of Kalidasa's dramaturgy, refracted through the lens of late-nineteenth-century chromolithographs and twentieth-century calendar art: Nargis, dressed in traditional *ghagra-choli* and carrying an earthen pot on her head, sways to music in front of a set of pillars. The shadows cast by the pillars, which she must pass through, capture visually the play between revelation and obfuscation at the heart of any enchanting fantasy. At one point, as she turns on her heels, she drops the pot and it crashes to the ground: the music turns discordant, as if a string has snapped, and Kewal is jolted out of his fantasy. History seems to intervene in the shape of the broken vessel, underscoring the impossibility of holding onto a fantasy of the "ideal woman" in the face of the untold sufferings of real women alluded to, if all too briefly, in the very previous scene. Incorporating such bungling missteps, temporal miscues and stroboscopic moodswings, and a stunningly expressive mise-en-scène, *Aag* captures in its very form something of the tensions coursing through an entire cultural landscape. Allegory provides a way of registering the melancholia that results from a desire to make sense of an abjectly meaningless situation; it also opens up a fragile space for action in the face of a sheer abrogation of historical agency.

Home/Body: Fantasy, Loss, Figuration

A set of beguiling thematic displacements enabled popular cinema to simultaneously deflect and present, as enigmatic runes, the ordeal of the Partition. The loss of a unified community and of territorial integrity thwarted the dream of a national family—the compelling ideological edifice that anchors many a modern nationalist movement. Not surprisingly, in the post-1947 era, the inversion of this foundational allegory became a primary source of registering the widely felt disillusionment. The sense of dislocation was played out as the disruption of familial structures within sentimental family melodramas. Tellingly, the 1940s and 1950s saw a remarkably large number of films with the word *ghar* (home/family) in their titles, including *Ghar* (1945), *Ghar Ghar Ki Kahani* (1947), *Ghar Ki Bahu* (1947), *Ghar Ki Izzat* (1948), *Gharana* (1949), *Hamara Ghar* (1950), *Gharbar* (1953), *Ghar Ghar Mein Diwali* (1955), *Ghar Grihasthi* (1958), *Ghar Sansar* (1958), and *Ghar Ki Laaj* (1960).[55] The dissipation of a stable, familiar world—once the basis of a coherent, centered subjectivity—was mediated in terms of the gradual disintegration of Indian homes: the films referred explicitly to the breakdown of the extended family and the shift to more individualistic values, and more obliquely to the fragmentation of the nation.

To take one example, *Hamara Ghar* (*Our Home*) invokes a well-known diegetic frame from the epic *Mahabharata* in a story of a close-knit family of five brothers and their mother. When a relative instigates fraternal disharmony, the mother reminds her five sons of the need to be united in terms of the structure of a room, which requires four walls and a roof. She also extends her metaphor from the level of the room/home/family to the collectivity, asserting that integrated families are the basis of a strong, unified nation-state ("Sangathit gharonse hi sangathit rashtra banta hai"). Commenting on this allegorical dimension, a contemporary review stated that Durga Khote, the actress playing the mother, was a perfect personification of "the mental picture of Mother India," while the actors playing the brothers "display[ed] various attitudes and temperaments and thus vividly portray[ed] the colourful contrasts obtained in the country."[56]

Doubles   Many films narrate the tale of two siblings (usually brothers) accidentally getting separated and growing up into radically different people—one good (often a policeman), and the other evil (a criminal). These Manichean figures usually fall in love with the same woman. In a final showdown that brings the entire family together, the good brother triumphs and the bad one gets reformed or killed, the melodramatic closure "resolving" a range of moral and/or social conflicts.

In Western narrative traditions, conflicting values are usually incorporated within the same character; it is mainly in comedies that the conflicts get embodied in two separate figures. In the Indian context, the contradictions are exteriorized by being projected outward as two sociological types and then worked through as their conflicts. As Ashis Nandy points out, an important clue to the place of popular films in contemporary Indian consciousness is provided by

> the integrative role the double has in relation to self-concepts fragmented by uprooting and deculturation. . . . The double here dramatizes the discontinuities introduced into Indian society by new social and political forces and simultaneously neutralizes them "ritually," in terms of available cultural categories. So the ultra-modern, arrogant, super-competent, western-educated professional has ultimately to turn to his twin—a rustic, good-hearted, spirited but nevertheless oppressed body from the backwaters of village India—to defeat the hard-hearted smuggler or black-marketeer who in turn is a negative model of modernity and negative mix of the East and the West.[57]

According to this view, then, narrative doubling emerges as a way of negotiating the trauma of modernity and nationhood. Such an approach helps explain why doubles have been one of the most enduring features of Indian popular cinema.[58]

Partition was a particularly wrenching moment within the broader trauma that Nandy writes about. In the following decade, there was a plethora of doubles in Bombay films in the strict sense of the term: a single actor playing two characters. *Filmfare* magazine noted "a new vogue in the industry—double roles," following the success of *Nishan* (1949) and *Afsana* (1951).[59] While the consolidation of successful generic elements was a major factor behind the sudden spurt in the number of cinematic doublings, I will argue that the trend also marked the exteriorization of deep anxieties regarding national identity.

Accidents and Natural Disasters   While maintaining a general silence on Partition, cinema conjured up the visceral dimensions of analogous experiences through the depiction of accidents and natural disasters: a boat accident in *Milan* (1947), a train accident in *Anokhi Ada* (1948), a staircase fall in *Paras* (1949), an automobile accident in *Jaan Pehchan*

(1950), a horse-riding accident in *Deedar* (1951), a sudden storm in *Afsana*. Each of these aleatoric moments was no doubt seen as a credible narrative ruse because of the crucial role accorded to *bhagya*, or destiny, in Indian hermeneutical systems. It also seems plausible to think that the sudden catastrophes in so many films were allusions to the social tumult. Indeed, the historical event was so cataclysmic in its effects that it prompted a cultural reformulation of history as natural disaster: human history took on the force of furious nature and, by implication, an air of inevitability. One of the most striking instances of such cultural reinscription is the earthquake that rends the happy family apart in the landmark film *Waqt* (1965), discussed later in this chapter. This equation of Partition with natural disasters could not always erase the thorny issue of human agency and accountability, nor could it assuage guilt. Characters in films of the period frequently suffered physical wounds, leading to defacement or dismemberment: they became flawed subjects, whose wounds could be read metonymically as marks of a collective laceration. It was not just a matter of the characters having to bear the signs of national trauma; the trope suggested that they could participate in a project of nationhood only as irredeemably split agents. The scorched face of the idealistic protagonist in *Aag* was emblematic of such a deeply impaired national subjectivity. In a sense, these damaged figures emerged as the ravaged subjects of a national history projected as a "landscape of ruins."[60]

Jaan Pehchan, starring the same lead actors as in *Aag*, also stages the defacement of its hero Anil—this time through a car accident. Anil keeps stroking his disfigured face, saying that an ugly person has no home; his shame about his scar keeps him from returning to his wife Asha. Homelessness is here related to bodily damage, producing an echo of the dislocations that accompanied territorial truncation. An earlier sequence comments on the production of an idealistic world through the elision of daily experiences. Anil is a city sculptor who comes to the village and finds his muse in the beautiful Asha. He makes her pose like a "typical village belle" with a water pot, so he can capture it in marble: he even wants her to be "life-like," as if she has just frozen for a moment in the act of skipping around joyously. By calling attention to such tropes of cultural fabrication,[61] the film reveals Anil's predominantly idealistic investment in Asha—a revelation that upsets her greatly. Refusing to be frozen as an abstraction, she attacks her statue: once again, this act of "self-mutilation" registers a refusal to be made a part of a model transaction that erases palpable experiences.

Accident, disfigurement, and self-mutilation comprise, yet again, the narrative pivot in *Deedar*. The protagonist Shamu (Dilip Kumar) loses his eyesight in a horse-riding accident in his adolescent years. He grows up pining for Mala (Nargis), his lost childhood sweetheart. Years later, he regains his eyesight through a complicated operation, only to find out that Mala is happily married to his eye surgeon: just as in *Aag*, the protagonist's benefactor turns out to be his competitor in matters of the heart. Unable to face the unbearable present with its conflicting emotions and loyalties, Shamu blinds himself again. Self-mutilation becomes a way of holding on to an ideal and a lost innocence, even as it marks the acknowledgment of the impossibility of their realization or recovery.

Amnesia   The decade also saw a preponderance of amnesiac protagonists, whose condition dramatized the vicissitudes of memory under trying conditions (*Anokhi Ada, Shabnam*, and *Bhaisaheb* [1954]). The female protagonist in Mehboob Khan's *Anokhi Ada* loses her memory in a train accident and keeps having involuntary, incomprehensible flashes of recollection. She is torn between two men who inhabit the two distinct spaces of her bifurcated memory: the first, who ironically calls himself Laatsaheb (the viceroy), is of upper-class origin but chooses to be a proletarian adventurer in protest of his capitalist father's exploitative ways;[62] the second is a middle-class professor who rescues the amnesiac woman and looks after her. The narrative enacts her quandary in terms of coincidental situations and melodramatic exteriorization. The professor declares his love for the heroine in exactly the same words as Laatsaheb had used earlier in the film, the semantic recurrence producing an unaccountable turmoil in her memory. In a scene remarkable for its virtuoso lighting, the lid of a grand piano forms a sharp V pattern with the staircase as she climbs it—caught between an open pair of scissors, as it were—absorbed in her disconcerting thoughts and retrospections. The amnesiac's predicament makes us wonder if, when, and how she will be allowed to regain her memory and her sense of a coherent self. In the end, a frustrated Laatsaheb, despairing of ever winning back her affection, throws a stone at her, hitting her on the head. This blow restores her memory; the amnesiac phase is reduced to a temporary disorder. Nevertheless, the recovery of a unified self is ruled out, because the interim cannot be expunged from memory. This narrative obliquely enacts the kind of cognitive violence—the reduction of the Partition to an anomalous disruption—that enables the nation to hold on to a precarious sense of spatial and temporal unity. That the national dimension is indexed by the figure of the woman is actually made explicit in the film by another woman, who resorts to a "land equals woman" paradigm to explain to Laatsaheb that his beloved now belongs to another man: "Just as this land belonged to the British before, and is ours now."

In *Shabnam*, the heroine Shanti has a breakdown when her father dies from snakebite, and she is told that her lover Manoj has also been killed. In a long take, she stumbles around a palace room lashing out at the feudal prince she holds responsible for the death of her loved ones, finally collapsing on the steps leading to a door. The camera tracks back, passing the palace pillars at a sharp angle, and comes to rest with the two characters against the door frame, now held in a long shot. The next shot shows Shanti lying in bed: she cannot remember anything, not even who she is. Taking advantage of her amnesia, the prince tells her that she is Shabnam, and that she fainted from happiness at their wedding. Interestingly, *Shabnam* is an Islamic name with Persian roots, while *Shanti* is of decidedly Hindu, Sanskrit origin. The play on religious affiliation through this obfuscation of identity takes on a greater charge in light of the fact that Shanti is a refugee traveling from Burma to India in the early 1940s: thus the prince is likely to be a local overlord somewhere in Muslim-majority East Bengal which, in 1947, becomes East Pakistan. Through such complex invocations of spatial and religious geographies, the film invests a tale of personal trauma with strong social and historical resonance.

Homelessness: Migrants, Refugees, and Orphans   Mass uprooting and separation, resulting not only from Partition but also from industrialization and urbanization, turned the tenuous moorings of a national citizenry into a fecund source of drama. Films like *Naukri* (1954) and *New Delhi* (1956), focusing on migrant workers, charted a passage from a local sense of "place" to a national "space" (usually presented in terms of a journey from the countryside to urban centers), mourning the loss of an "authentic" self, an "original" location, and simultaneously recording an excitement about new possibilities. While certain films featured Partition refugees (*Aag, Namoona, Manzoor* [1949], *Nastik*), drawing on contemporary experience to establish their characters and conflicts, their singular hardships were quickly transformed into generic struggles involving romance, family honor, class mobility, and social responsibility.

Orphans constituted a common representation of homelessness in the mid-1950s, although films such as *Baadbaan, Boot Polish, Ferry, Munna*, and *Pamposh*, all released in 1954, displayed a range of approaches. The orphan hero of *Baadbaan* is brought up by a rich judge and educated abroad; but learning that his biological parents are fisherfolk, he returns and dedicates his life to his "true" community, thus recovering his "original" identity and location. Raj Kapoor's *Boot Polish* allegorizes the need for honest, hard work in the infant nation-state in terms of its young orphan protagonists, who give up begging and take to polishing shoes.[63] In contrast to the social concerns of these films, *Pamposh* projects a fairytale universe of picturesque landscapes and costumes. A review at the time of its release comments on its packaging of exotic Kashmir locations, perhaps with an eye on the foreign market.[64] It is also possible to read the film as both a recognition (as orphan) and disavowal (through the integration of the child's life within a serene, beautiful world) of the embattled status of Kashmir.

Thus the dramatic loss of national unity in 1947, which derailed the normative narrative of the nation as one happy family, found implicit representation in films of the late 1940s and 1950s in terms of inverted allegories about broken families, separated siblings, accidents, and disasters; the ideologically loaded notion of home was put to question in countless films about refugees, migrant workers, bastards, and foundlings. Forms of duality and deception, already in evidence in many of these narratives, point to another festering crisis—a crisis of recognition, of identity—that takes center stage in films involving masquerade, suspicious paternity, and the woman's body.

Masquerade and Crossdressing   In developing "imperso-nation" as a strategy that enables popular Hindi cinema to mediate social difference and to promote subject positions offering broad, permeable terms of identification, Sumita Chakravarty (1993) situates the mechanism of masquerade as constitutive of a cinematic project of nationhood. I want to underscore the simultaneous critical function of masquerade: in enacting the heterogeneous impulses that constitute national life, masquerade provides a corrective to the totalizing tendencies of self-evident statist discourses. In the first decade, double roles and crossdressing were two common forms of masquerade, particularly in films produced by Filmistan studios. In their wild, wacky comedies like *Shabnam*, *Munimji* (1955), and *Paying Guest* (1957), constant switches between identities transported audiences to a vertiginous, liminal space, which was distinct from the actual, agonistic social domain with its polarizing definitions and demarcations. It is possible to read the films as willful parodies of various boundary concepts, countering collateral mobilizations of such demarcations to fragment the body politic. One might detect in the middle of all the generic hilarity a strong intent to transgress symbolically the new jagged frontiers whose imposition drove a wedge through a people and resulted in widespread suffering. Such a conjecture is strengthened by traces of contemporary experience in these plots: for, instance, the female protagonist of *Shabnam* disguises herself in men's clothes, emulating a strategy adopted by women refugees to protect themselves during Partition riots.

Unwed Mothers, Illegitimate Births   The conception of children by unwed women constitutes a sensational subversion of family and marriage, and of the social order that is sustained by these institutions. If
the woman is valued and integrated within a heteropatriarchal economy
primarily on the basis of her reproductive labor, then illegitimate births,
in undermining these normative grids, ultimately threaten the overarching structure, the state. Fear of social retribution turns pregnancy out of
wedlock into a personal predicament; such pregnancy also becomes an
index of social degeneration, a source of collective shame. In traditional
Indian narratives, the unwed mother has to disown her newborn child
in order to maintain the sanctity of social institutions: the paradigmatic
figure here is Princess Kunti, a character in the epic *Mahabharata*, who
is impregnated by the sun god and subsequently abandons her son
Karna to uphold the social order. The child is brought up in a family of
chariot drivers: his royal origin remains a secret to him. Years later, as
Karna is about to join a bloody feud against her other five sons, his half
brothers, Kunti meets Karna and divulges his true lineage in order to
dissuade him from fighting. This mother-son drama has proved to be
something of an urnarrative for Indian cinema, providing the emotional
ingredients for allegorizing larger disruptions of the social scene within
a well-known plot structure. Yash Chopra's directorial debut *Dhool Ka
Phool* (1959) remains one of the most interesting instances from such
a subgenre centered around bastards/foundlings. Mahesh and Meena
are in love, but Mahesh gives in to family pressures and marries a rich
heiress, while Meena finds herself pregnant. To avoid social stigma, the
unwed mother abandons her son; sometime later, she gets married to
a lawyer. A kind old man brings up the child, but his foundling status
leads to his social ostracization and eventual criminality. The drama of
his tangled identity comes a full circle when he is produced on charges
of theft in a court presided over by his biological father, Mahesh; by coincidence, his mother's lawyer husband takes up his defense. Finally the
truth is revealed when Meena herself takes the witness stand.

   In *Adalat* (1958), Rajinder and Nirmala do tie the knot, but while the
former is away on business, his rich parents disown his pregnant wife.
She comes under the influence of the villainous Kedarnath, becomes
a singer in a bordello, and gives up her son for adoption. Years later,
Kedarnath brings the couple together in the bordello, with the intent of
blackmailing Rajinder. A scuffle follows; fearing for Rajinder's life, Nirmala kills the villain. In a courtroom finale, Rajinder jeopardizes his social status to defend his wife. When the young public prosecutor Ratan-
lal challenges Rajinder's account, the former's foster mother divulges
that he is actually Nirmala and Rajinder's son. Even as the estranged

family members reunite, Nirmala dies of heartbreak. *Adalat* recounts the story of a family separated by suspicions of illegitimacy—suspicions that prove fatally oppressive for the woman. Similar stories of distrust and separation, echoing the two epics, recur in a large number of films, among which *Awara* remains paradigmatic.

Through their complex interweaving of epic allusions, contemporary class dynamics, obfuscation of identity and lineage, social production of criminality, and the subjugation of women under quasi-feudal and rational-juridical systems, these films conjure up a strained social order; more significantly, they offer symbolic resolutions to the underlying contradictions and quandaries. The old man who brings up the foundling in *Dhool Ka Phool* is a Muslim who keeps advocating communal harmony. He sees the boy's lack of background as a possibility to overcome narrow religious affinities and develop into a human being with a secular, all-embracing identity (a prospect articulated in the optimistic song "Tu Hindu banega na Musalman banega": "You will grow up neither a Hindu nor a Muslim"). Here, cinema appropriates the figure of the foundling in a bid to go beyond the collective wound and to invoke a new order of identity.

Gendered Violence: Tales of Honor and Shame

In the chaotic months surrounding Partition, as reason and civility were held in abeyance, communal antagonism took a sinister turn and targeted women. The gendered nature of violence was not simply the expression of unbridled male power and lust: it found its rationale in the cultural equation of woman with community. Cultural procedures of desecration are closely linked to the seemingly opposite gestures of sacralization: what is sanctified is also set up for vandalization. The figure of the woman is put on a pedestal so that it can be controlled and, when necessary, brought down: either way, it remains an object of patriarchal dispensation. Such maneuvers, incisively interrogated by feminist critics,[65] were in motion in South Asia circa 1947. The yoking of a community's dignity to the purity of its women was normalized in terms of cultural memories of the violation of Indian women by alien invaders in the early fourteenth century. Circulating legends about desperate forms of resistance put up by women to avoid collective ignominy construed the "woman" as the ultimate site of a community's spiritual invincibility. Thus Chittor might have fallen to Muslim invaders, but Queen Padmini and her female companions were credited with the preservation of their people's honor through self-immolation. By way of such legends, bodies of women were turned into signs in cultural transactions producing memories and paradigms for future behavior. In times of sectarian violence, both property and women of other communities were targeted for vandalization, to bring about their material devastation and cultural-psychic humiliation.

In the turmoil of 1947, a frustrated desire for the wholeness of the national body mutated into corporeal brutalities against women, as thousands of them were terrorized, abducted, and raped, supposedly by members of other communities.[66] The collective response to their plight took two extreme forms. At the levels of community and family, there was silence: violations of women were covered up locally, in a bid to avoid shame and scandal. Women were not allowed to engage with and work through their ordeals; instead, they were expected to repress their experiences, act as if they had not been subjected to the worst kinds of abuse, and carry on with their "normal" lives. However, the official response went to the other extreme, adopting an incredibly interventionist stance. Both the Indian and Pakistani governments decided to exchange abducted women, apparently in a bid to restore national honor.[67] As Veena Das observes, in discourses about the exchange of women from the two sides, "it was assumed that once the nation had claimed back its women, its honor would have been restored. It was as if you could wipe the slate clean and leave the horrendous events behind."[68] The actual experience was far more complicated.[69] Many of these women had been forced to undergo religious conversion; in the months in captivity, some had managed to figure out a new, if precarious, life for themselves. Now they were yanked away from that life through intrusive official policies, as impassive pawns of interstate exchange: no one asked them what they wanted. Many families that had originally filed reports of missing people and urged the government to undertake rescue missions were now unwilling to take back their "sullied" women: they were more ready to abandon them and forget they ever existed. Thus many recovered women were consigned to a kind of social death, while others were "sacrificed" by their fathers, brothers, and husbands to "save" them from the ignominy of a "tainted" life.[70]

If this dark chapter in national history was largely omitted from official accounts through orchestrated procedures of institutional forgetting, it could not be excised from popular consciousness. Shame and grief about the harrowing experiences found indirect, yet emotionally resonant experience in popular cultural texts. While women's experiences were largely shrouded in silence, a ghostly pall enveloped the cultural field. In chapter 1, I noted the morbidity that seeped into films like *Awara* and *Amar*. The invocation in *Awara* of Sita's plight after her rescue from abduction takes on a direct historical valence in light of the fact that government pamphlets, issued with appeals to reluctant families to take the rescued women back, used the same epic story to argue that women could remain pure despite being away from their families.[71]

I will argue that the preponderance of film narratives focusing on the drama surrounding illegitimate births in the 1950s was yet another index of the widespread shame underlying the public secrecy. Depending on the plot focus, there are at least three possible variations of this subgenre, leading to three different but related tropes: (1) the shame associated with illegitimate pregnancies, seen in films like *Dhool ka Phool* and *Dharamputra* (1961); (2) suspicions around paternity, which eventually prove to be unfounded—examples include *Awara* and *Adalat*; and (3) the social marginality of bastards and foundlings, as in *Dhool ka Phool*. As already noted, these elements can be traced back to well-known episodes in the two epics, the *Ramayana* and the *Mahabharata*. Through the transgression, real or imagined, of the revered institution of marriage, and the resulting destabilization of the family structure, these texts were negotiating a disgraceful juncture in national history whose excesses put to question the legitimacy of all patriarchal institutions and structures, and the basic tenets of community. Other films, like *Dastaan* (1950), expressed their agony through a sublimation of the trauma, and a more generalized critique of women's oppression within an archaic heteropatriarchal system that showed practically no sign of reform under the new regime.

Even the genre of patriotic films, riding the crest of a nationalist upsurge in the wake of independence, found it difficult to dispel the deep collective anguish. Two of Filmistan's box-office hits, *Shaheed* (1948) and *Samadhi* (1950), and Bimal Roy's *Pahela Admi* (1950), are set in the heydays of India's freedom struggle: they all privilege the public over the private. In each case, the drama is set in motion with the hero's enlistment in the anticolonial struggle in response to a nationalist call for personal sacrifice. The two latter films, released in 1950, record their heroines' initial distance from, and their eventual espousal of, the nationalist cause. In *Samadhi*, Lily overcomes her initial qualms, seen as personal, petty, and selfish, and becomes fully integrated into the nationalist movement. She joins her beloved Shekhar on the battlefield in Burma; they cross the border onto Indian soil, but are shot down soon after. Their joint sacrifice transforms them into an idealized national couple: noble, dutiful citizens held up as the basis of an ideal family and hence, metonymically, of an ideal nation. A poster for the film depicts them in a gilded frame: a portrait of the archetypal national couple,

Poster for *Samadhi*: model national couple.
Courtesy of NFAI.

worthy of emulation. Lata, the female protagonist of *Pahela Admi*, becomes suicidal when she finds out that her fiancé Kumar died in serving the motherland; eventually, she overcomes her despondency and joins the revolutionary Indian National Army in a bid to carry on Kumar's legacy. Thus, the two films from 1950 chart the triumph of collective interests over individual desires and the evolution of politicized female subjectivities.

Sheela, the heroine of *Shaheed*, presents a very different picture. As Ram, the hero, leaves home and becomes a freedom fighter, Sheela pines away at home. Her tortured attempts to put up a brave face (especially when she forces herself to smile at Ram's request) and her failure in developing a full-fledged patriotic self indicate the narrative's inability to project an unproblematic national female subjectivity in 1948, just a year after the trauma. The growing rift in the romance and the couple's diverging expectations are conveyed through the skewed placement of the characters in relation to each other. In certain scenes where one would expect them to be intimate, Ram stands facing the camera in medium close-up with his back to Sheela and expounds on the need for self-sacrifice in response to the call of the nation, while she comes apart in the background. At other points, a forlorn Sheela leans against a window or a door frame, or lies in bed, remembering Ram talking or singing to her. Through the stylized use of props, low-key lighting, canted framing, deliberately paced camera movements, music and voice-overs, the film stages its heroine's psychic and physical unraveling. Wittingly or not, it violates standard editing norms in expressive ways, as if such standards are not adequate to the representational needs of the narrative. As Ashish Rajadhyaksha observes, "You can actually see Hollywood-derived continuities of action literally fall apart when the placement of the love story shifts away from the couple and takes on its supreme role of endorsing male honour."[72] Time and again, the narrative positions "the hero's nationalism and the heroine's endorsing of his commitment" in such a way as to "provide her with a subjective view, and then remove this, replacing it as a view of the Nation, as she is then (literally) sacrificed at the altar of her own symbolised, 'national' self."[73]

Both *Shaheed* and *Samadhi* were directed by Ramesh Saigal under the Filmistan banner, and their two male protagonists were not significantly different. However, the passage from the gradually disintegrating Sheela of 1948 to the bold Lily of 1950 was a significant one, marking popular cinema's deepening implication in a project of nationhood. The 1948 film does remind us that the transition was neither easy nor assured, that the suffering of the previous year could not be simply wiped away without any lingering trace.

Allegory as Historical Necessity

The discussion in chapter 1 situates commercial Hindi cinema of the immediate post-1947 period as having a strong sense of engagement with its context, an engagement that is profoundly dialectical in its confrontation of the pressing questions of the day: how to participate in a hegemonic project of nationhood, and simultaneously explore underlying contradictions and alternative visions for the future? Via such arbitrations, popular cinema becomes a site for working out the contours of an Indian modernity in which capitalist processes of development championed by the state can proceed alongside habitual precapitalist social relations.

In this chapter, popular Hindi cinema emerges as a commemorative site in which memories of the Partition live on in indirect ways. Notwithstanding the multiple pressures toward reducing the experience to a historical anomaly and focusing on the task of nation building, the exploration of various thematic and formal elements reveals the persistence of traumatic memories in oblique and fragmented forms. These are the runes that lead us to another strand in the narrative of the nation, a strand whose implicitness may have to do as much with civilizational modes of remembering tribulations, as with a desire to repress them. Indian narrative traditions speak of perplexing experiences in oblique terms, often in intertextual and allegorical forms. Mythic structures and familiar tropes become useful ways of framing and making sense of painful memories, especially when they resist easy comprehension and assimilation. Implicit mediations of Partition in Hindi films should be appreciated for what they are: culturally specific ways of dealing with collective trauma.

The methodology of allegorical reading is beset with a tendency for forced hermeneutic fulfillment—which would involve, in this case, linking all kinds of unrelated cultural fragments to Partition. This problem of telescopically falling into trauma arises from the very nature of trauma as an event that must be construed, and thus experienced, retroactively. Of course, the obverse of this problem is a certain obviousness, even redundancy, in locating the cultural traces of trauma: once the links are revealed through careful analysis, they appear too banal to merit so much attention. It is a problem inherent to psychoanalysis: when the hidden scenes are revealed, the painstaking work of detection and recovery are rendered transparent, invisible. Operating between these two poles of reductionism and redundancy, I am arguing for an allegorical reading practice that will allow us to put together, from cinematic fragments, the post-Partition cultural terrain as a traumatized landscape—a Benjaminian "landscape of ruins." The fragments are comprised not only of the images, dialogue, music, story events, characters, and settings, but also of the biographies of personnel, public impressions, and discourses—in other words, an entire cultural archive of tangible documents and felt sensations.

One could ask, for instance: why are the famous songs from the late 1940s and 1950s—a period that is celebrated as the golden era of Hindi film music—so achingly sad?[74] Are the melancholy lyrics and lilting melodies of the Mukesh song "Bhoolne Waale Yaad Na Aa" ("I do not want to remember the one who has forgotten me"), from Mehboob Khan's *Anokhi Ada*, expressing the torment of one who is in love with an amnesiac? Is the Mohammed Rafi number "Yeh Kooche Yeh Nilaam

Ghar Dilkashi Ke" ("These By-Lanes, These Auction Houses of Pleasure") from Guru Dutt's *Pyaasa* (1957), articulating the disillusionment of nationalist idealism ("Jinhe naaz hai hind par wo kahaan hain," Where are those who are proud of Hind?), simply capturing the sentiments of a national audience overcome by modernity? Or do these haunting songs perform a further affective labor on behalf of a national public sunk in a deep stupor of loss and longing? The veiled connections to the turmoil of 1947 become more manifest in other cases, as when Radha, the iconic *Mother India*, calls upon villagers not to abandon their land following a devastating flood, but to join in the task of reconstruction and rehabilitation: "O jaane waale jaao na ghar apnaa chhor ke / Mata bulaa rahi hai tumhen haath jor ke" (O village-folk, please do not abandon your own home, Mother [here, also connoting community or nation] is entreating you with joined hands). Is it far-fetched to assume that the song would speak to 1950s audiences in terms of a contemporary experiential horizon replete with memories of refugees fleeing from their own homeland in the wake of events that unfolded with the numbing force of natural disasters?

Personal backgrounds of Bombay film industry "insiders" came to inflect commercial films with subtle specters of the schism. A large number of producers, directors, writers, technicians, and actors hailed from the Punjab, Sind and Bengal provinces, parts or all of which went to Pakistan. Some were actual refugees; others, who had already migrated to Bombay, were faced with a sudden loss of an originary home. In both cases, there was a deep sense of dislocation stemming from the impossibility of returning to one's own village or town, which now lay on the other side of an artificially imposed border. The bifurcation generated feelings of loss, nostalgia, melancholy, bitterness, resentment, even anger: emotions that informed the careers of the Kapoors, the Chopras, the Anands, Balraj Sahni, Bimal Roy, Ramanand Sagar, and a host of others who shaped Bombay cinema as we know it.[75]

Ravi Vasudevan suggests that Hindi cinema of the 1950s was "constructing itself as a 'national space' . . . founded on loss and displacement." He identifies certain narrative elements—the tropes of renunciation and theft, the use of reputed Bengali literary texts as sources—that together constitute something like "an act of mourning whereby the loss of a now physically and symbolically distant identity is internalized" in narratives that evince a desire for an original self and mark its impossibility.[76] For instance, the renouncer hero, typified by the protagonist of Bimal Roy's *Devdas* (1955), "circulates within the space of loss, a trajectory which culminates in regression and death but can also carry a more critical inflection."[77] Theft takes on the "narrative function" of addressing "the past, the realm of lost status and property" in films like *Kismet* (1943) and *Awara* (and later, in *Waqt* [1965]). It is "the mark of obsession with a past plenitude" which "cannot solve present quandaries"; it denotes "the last vestiges of a desire for a past which must be left behind."[78] Vasudevan provides a valuable insight about the insertion of the regional into the national, referring to the iconic presence of Bengal and Bengali literature in the Bombay cinema of the 1950s. He claims that even as the regional was "suppressed or bracketed within the imaginary formation of the nation," Bombay auteurs had to draw on established "regional and non-cinematic texts as markers of cultural desire and authority." Through such invocations, "traces of a lost ideality"—that is, the cultural preeminence of undivided Bengal—got "memorialized and sublimated."[79] A very different process of iconization of the regional was at work around the same time, one that drew attention to the very loss of ideality and turned Punjab into an icon of national disfigurement (as in *Aag*).

The displacement from Punjab around 1947 continues to influence the lives of many industry stalwarts. An April 1997 reunion in Bombay of transplants from Lahore allowed a group of them to "take a trip down memory lane" on the occasion of the fiftieth anniversary of Partition. The high level of nostalgia was evident from the reminiscences, and the elaborate arrangements to have "authentic Lahori food and drinks" flown in.[80] The mood was reflected in the repeated recitation of a saying from the late 1940s that expressed the feelings of loss and longing: "Bahut ghumi hain Dilli aur Indore ki galiyan / Na bhule hain, na bhulenge, Lahore ki galiyan" (I have often roamed the lanes of Delhi and Indore / But I haven't forgotten, I can never forget, the lanes of Lahore).[81] While the producers and directors who hailed from Punjab or Sind readily acknowledge the deep impact Partition had on their lives, they are less enthusiastic about detecting unconscious traces of the experience in their works. They were possibly intent on overcoming the pull of the painful past and establishing successful careers within the post-independence industry. Their disavowal partially explains both the productive emergence of Punjab as a protonational imagination, and its deracinated, reified nature.

From my conversations with Bombay's commercial filmmakers, I got the distinct sense that they privileged authorial intention and did not care much for allegorical reading strategies. Thus director Yash Chopra recognized his second film *Dharamputra* (1961) as a cinematic engagement with Partition and communal violence but saw no such connection with the trauma in his first and third films, *Dhool Ka Phool* and *Waqt* (1965). B. R. Chopra, who produced the three films and happens to be the director's elder brother, corroborated his view. Nevertheless, these conversations produced a conundrum. Yash Chopra thought that a significant number of Hindi films dealt with the trauma of the Partition; however, he could remember the names of only about five such films. He referred me to his elder brother, known for his detailed knowledge of the industry. Intriguingly, B. R. Chopra seemed to believe that by and large, the film industry steered clear of the experience.[82] Thus he confirmed my hunch about the paucity of films about the Partition; at the same time, he agreed with his brother in discounting allegorical interpretations of popular films. Be as it may, I was still left with the question: why was Yash Chopra convinced that the Partition had often been the explicit subject of Hindi films?[83] The most probable explanation I could come up with was, ironically, in terms of the oblique depictions of the experience.

Popular cinema did undertake considerable, if indirect, mediation of the trauma: viewed contextually, the emotional stories pointed to a larger social narrative. The displaced anxieties surrounding the bifurcation seeped into the films, usually in ways that remained obscure even to the filmmakers. These traces, however implicit and unconscious, did resonate with audiences whose experiential universe constituted an eminently primed reception context. Thus, circumventing authorial intent, the repressed returned repeatedly to popular cinema, generating an overarching impression that the Partition had already been dealt with. That impression could have crystallized over several decades—as it seemed to have for Yash Chopra—into a clear recollection of ample and explicit representations. In other words, the memory of oblique cultural mediations had evolved, over the years, into a belief about extensive cinematic memorialization.

Yash Chopra's debut film *Dhool Ka Phool* was a big commercial success. As I pointed out before, it incorporates a strong secular message in the figure of an old Muslim: he brings up a boy abandoned by his unwed mother, exhorting him to transcend religious boundaries. The film incorporates several popular generic elements: family melodrama centering on pregnancy outside wedlock, blurred lineage and slide into criminality, courtroom drama resulting in the reunion of estranged family members, a strong secularist plea for social healing. Chopra sees the narrative as a poignant retelling of the Karna–Kunti story in a contemporary setting, but he does not recognize any oblique connection between the Partition and the separation of family members or the references to communal relations.

Two years later Chopra made *Dharamputra*, a deliberate exploration of the Hindu–Muslim strife, with evocations of the Partition (in terms of a bridge between two neighboring houses) and the violence accompanying it (scenes depicting Hindu rioters beating up Muslims and setting their properties on fire). When an unwed Muslim woman gets pregnant, she gives up her son to be brought up by her Hindu neighbors. Dilip, the son, grows up to be a fanatic Hindu (much to the consternation of his liberal foster parents) and rushes to kill his Muslim neighbor during the riots of 1947, not knowing she is his biological mother. At this point, his foster mother divulges the truth about his origin: a close up of Dilip's stunned face is followed by a series of rapid cuts showing debris falling in an earthquake, waves crashing on rocks, riot scenes, dead bodies, streams of blood coming together in a pool, refugees. While bringing out the imbrication of the personal and the social in this bravura display of Eisensteinian montage, Chopra retains the focus on Dilip's psychic disintegration: his selfhood, his beliefs, his universe fall apart. Calling into question orthodox conceptions of religious identity, the film ends with an impassioned plea for communal harmony within an independent nation-state. The final sequence includes live footage of Nehru addressing vast congregations. Upon its release, the prime minister praised the film profusely; however, audiences stayed away, in spite of the moving story about illegitimate birth and abandonment. Apparently, people were still not ready to face cinematic representations of communal violence: memories of 1947 were too fresh in their minds, too debilitating to be relived on-screen.

Chopra and his team at B. R. Films regrouped and came back four years later with the smash hit *Waqt*. Ostensibly a film about time and destiny, it is yet another story of a family getting separated accidentally and reuniting years later in a courtroom. This time around, the separation is caused by a devastating earthquake, which, seen in isolation, is just an unfortunate natural disaster, with an actual historic referent in the terrible Qetta earthquake of 1935. However, if we consider this earthquake in relation to the shot of falling debris in *Dharamputra*, intimating Dilip's unraveling identity, other hermeneutic possibilities emerge. Since Chopra invokes natural calamities metaphorically, the juxtaposition allows us to read the earthquake in *Waqt* as a figure for another order of cataclysms, namely social disasters precipitated by communal strife. It helps us recognize that the story about the breakup of the family might inscribe a larger story—that of the severance of a people by artificially imposed boundaries.[84]

The commercial failure of *Dharamputra* prompts Chopra to allegorize his concerns in *Waqt*. In his passage from the explicit representation of communal violence to its allegorization, Chopra enacts a further allegory of cultural praxis: of the processes through which Parti-

Dharamputra: Dilip's world disintegrates. Courtesy of NFAI.

tion comes to be repressed and sublimated in popular cinema. In other words, his flight to an allegorical mode of expression itself allegorizes a general trend in popular cinema, made imperative by that specific historical conjuncture. This meta-allegorical dimension is crucial to our understanding of popular cinema's constitutive role in the National Symbolic *and* its political unconscious. Insofar as this shift remains a largely unconscious move on Chopra's—and the film industry's—part, there is a disavowal of its ideological operation, namely the elision of the Partition through repression and sublimation; a unified nationality, projected through the displacement of the single most traumatic collective experience in the *bios* or political life of the modern nation, emerges as a "sublime object of ideology."[85] This apparent lack of consciousness facilitates the cinematic equivocation whereby the national rift is simultaneously repressed and represented; it also helps maintain the fiction of the industry's unfaltering faith in an official project of nationhood.

The central contention of this chapter is that popular Hindi cinema of the 1940s and 1950s mediated its traumatized horizon by shifting to an allegorical mode. The explanations for this cultural metadispersal are multiple: the exigencies of promoting the concept of a unified nation, ensuring communal harmony, the task of creating a modern postcolonial democracy and its citizenry; the need to harness support for a program of capitalist industrialization under the aegis of a centrally planned economy; the pressure of expectations on a national cultural endeavor, specially regarding its mediation of national history and its projection of a national identity; indigenous paradigms of narration, which privilege oblique modes; the difficulties of narrativizing a recent traumatic experience, still raw in people's memory; the dangers of inciting communal animosity and producing psychic breakdown; the social desire for symbolic resolutions to as yet irreconcilable conflicts; and considerations of genre formation and box-office returns. The question at hand is, without doubt, thoroughly overdetermined. But this complex contingency does underscore one distinct fact: popular cinema's reticence in engaging directly with the experience of the Partition was shaped by historical forces. By way of a conclusion to this chapter, I will propose that popular cinema confronted a problematic that emerged from its immediate material, social, and political context, and it came up with its own cultural-ideological solutions. Indeed, its allegorical mediation of the collective experience of truncated nationhood, when viewed in relation to that particular conjuncture, takes on the aura of a historical necessity. Hence, popular cinema's deflection of contemporary history in the realm of allegory—what some might call escapism—demands to be understood as a thoroughly historical intervention.

CHAPTER THREE

Bengali Cinema

A Spectral Subnationality

FOCUSING ON THE BENGALI FILM INDUSTRY based in Calcutta, this chapter examines the local involutions that complicate a regional cinema's participation in a project of nationhood. The central question that I seek to answer here is: How are nationalist fantasies transmuted within the singularity of a traumatized local?

Why Bengal? Because it was one of the two provinces to be actually split up, and its inhabitants experienced the worst kinds of violence and dislocation with long-term consequences; because Bengal's unique position in the evolution of modern Indian nationalism created strong regional aspirations that were to brush against, and inflect the truncated province's integration within, post-independence nationhood; and because the events of the late 1940s ushered in drastic changes that transformed the national film market, ending the primacy of the Calcutta industry. Once a vibrant protonational formation, Bengal after 1947—in the west, as in the east—was reduced to its own spectral shadow.[1]

The First Partition of Bengal

Bengal occupies a premier position in South Asia's encounter with colonial modernity. British colonialism established a foothold in Bengal, then extended its power over the rest of the subcontinent. It was in this eastern region that a nascent Indian national consciousness took shape, first as a negative locus of reactions against colonial power (Why is it that we cannot enjoy the very political ideals and civil rights that the British extol and teach us?), and then as a positive sense of collective identity (We too have a rich heritage and a glorious history, and therefore the basis of a national self). As Sudipta Kaviraj points out, the structure of consciousness that germinated among a Western-educated, predominantly upper class and Hindu Bengali intelligentsia, was extended to include other classes, to posit a Bengali community (*bangali jati*).[2] Over time, the boundaries of the collective "we" were further broken down, and Bengalis extended the scope of the "narrative contract" through which nation-ness is produced to draw in "communities who had nothing really to do with them in the past, constantly gerrymandering the boundaries of their national collective self."[3]

By the end of the nineteenth century, the colonial administrators came to recognize the rising political consciousness of the Bengalis as an emerging threat. As a preemptive measure, aimed at scuttling anticolonial mobilization, the British authorities decided to bifurcate the province in 1905. Although the official explanation for the partition ran in terms of administrative facilitation, the underlying political agenda (of inciting communal tension by carving out a Hindu-majority western part and a Muslim-majority eastern part) was not lost on the colonized subjects. Indeed, Lord Curzon, the viceroy of British India, clearly expressed the colonial intention:

> The *Bengalis*, who *like to think themselves a nation*, and who dream of a future when the English will have been turned out, and a Bengali Babu [gentleman] will be instilled in Government House, Calcutta, of course bitterly resent any disruption that will be likely to interfere with the realisation of this dream. If we are weak enough to yield to their clamour now, we shall not be able to dismember or reduce Bengal again; and you will be cementing and solidifying, on the eastern flank of India, *a force already formidable*, and certain to be a source of increasing trouble in the future.[4]

Recognizing the nationalist consciousness of the Bengalis as a "force already formidable," Curzon called for the immediate implementation of a "divide and rule" strategy. Another colonial administrator brought home this exigency: "Bengal united is a power; Bengal divided will pull in different ways."[5]

It is true that the subsequent Swadeshi (indigenous self-sufficiency) movement,[6] possibly the first mass nationalist mobilization in India, succeeded in forcing the government to annul the partition of Bengal in 1911. It is also true that the movement had lasting influences on subsequent nationalist politics: most importantly, by reiterating a natural and historical integrity of the culture and territory of Bengal, it established, through metonymic extension, a similar congruence for all of India in the nationalist imaginary. At the same time, the short-lived partition drove a permanent wedge through such imagined collectivities. The extant balance of power within Bengal's nationalist political leadership was revealed to be hopelessly lopsided in favor of upper-caste Hindus; not surprisingly, the bulk of the nationalist rhetoric construed the nation-space as an inherently Hindu realm. While this manifest bias did not stand in the way of strong and effective articulations of Hindu–Muslim unity at the time—in direct retaliation of the thinly veiled colonial attempt to produce a chasm between the two communities—it did feed into the divisive tendencies that came to plague the nationalist movement from the 1930s.

If Bengal was restored to its undiminished state, the capital of British India was transferred simultaneously from Calcutta to New Delhi. The year 1911 thus marked a turning point in the intranational distribution of power: it inaugurated an era of North India's ascendancy and a steady decline in Bengal's influence. In the 1920s, mass nationalist agitations spread all over the country, and the prestige of the Bengali *bhadra-lok*[7] contingent, consisting of leaders from elite backgrounds (landed gentry and urban professionals), dwindled significantly with the rise of alternative power blocs (most notably in the form of Gandhi and his followers). The Bengali leaders found themselves increasingly marginalized within the Indian National Congress; some of them broke away to form oppositional nationalist parties. By the 1940s, when the truncation of the country had emerged as a distinct possibility, the fate of Bengal seemed to have slipped away from its own leaders: it rested largely in the hands of an all-Indian leadership, whose concerns were not necessarily in alignment with the specific interests of the local population.

This diminution of Bengal's influence was not confined to the political field. By the early twentieth century, Bombay had become the undisputed commercial capital of India. In the mid-forties, it also emerged as the primary center of commercial Indian cinema, eclipsing the national prominence of the Calcutta studios. How the film industry of Bengal responded to this challenge in the post-Partition era is one of the central concerns of this chapter. But first, the developments leading up to Partition need to be sketched for a fuller understanding of the political, social, and cultural ramifications of the event as they came to inflect Bengali cinema.

Mounting Communalism

The passage from the strong show of nationalist unity in retaliation of the first administrative partition of Bengal to the gradual rise and intensification of communal antagonism that contributed to the second, widely demanded and more permanent bifurcation of the province, was a complicated process.[8] While earlier historiography tends to produce the shift as an inevitable development, recent accounts have questioned this teleological element, pointing to the contingent, aleatory nature of local politics pertaining to spatial institutions (involving not only land ownership and tenancy but, as P. K. Datta demonstrates, also spatialized social relations—including altercations over markets and burial sites, and the playing of music near mosques)[9] and legislative actions, one instance of which was the significance accorded to religious affiliation as a demographic category in the constitutional reforms of 1935.[10] Some broad historical trends and crucial junctures can, nevertheless, be isolated within the cataclysmic denouement without reducing its complexities.

One significant development between the two partitions was the crystallization of a strong peasant awareness, specially among the predominantly Muslim agrarian population in the eastern districts of the province.[11] Given the intransigence of the Indian National Congress about not entering into a coalition with the populist peasant movement, and the constant efforts on the part of the colonial administration to disperse all attempts at transcommunity alliances, the developing rural consciousness could not be harnessed to mobilize an effective, progressive political bloc. Instead, the peasant movement of Bengal, centered on Islam as the basis of a utopian world of agrarian unity and egalitarianism, came into gradual alignment with the increasingly sectarian politics of the Muslim League. By 1943, the League was in a position to take control of the provincial government.

In the last few years leading up to the Partition, the establishment of Pakistan appeared imminent: fearing that Muslim-majority Bengal would go to Pakistan, the Hindu leadership of Calcutta campaigned for the division of the province, and the inclusion of its western districts within India.[12] On the other hand, in stark contrast to its call for the bifurcation of the country, the Muslim League opposed the partition of Bengal; it wanted the inclusion of an undivided Bengal in Pakistan. Yet another small group of leaders, led by Sarat Bose, proposed a fundamental negation of communal politics and affirmation of regional aspirations: a united and *sovereign* Bengal, based on a cultural-linguistic integrity and insulated from the convoluted all-India political imperatives.[13] Thus there was a radical discursive transformation of "United Bengal" since 1905. These regional twists to partition politics took a violent turn, partly as a result of the desperate and cynical attempts that were afoot to influence ongoing negotiations: in August 1946, deadly riots broke out in various parts of the province, most notably in Noakhali district and in Calcutta. The experiences of those turbulent years generated an entire order of impressions and feelings, traces of which persist to this day. A significant part of the conflagration was the rumors of widespread brutality that circulated throughout Bengal, and that were rendered credible by more localized violence. Hindus in the east were particularly paranoid about the possible Muslim desecration of their temples and idols and disruption of their religious practices if and when Bengal became a part of Pakistan. Both communities were fearful about the safety of their wives, sisters, and daughters, given the predilection to target women.[14]

If the rumors of violence and victimization were not wholly unfounded, the level of apprehension was exacerbated by long-standing bigoted perceptions. The Hindu leadership of Bengal failed to understand or accept the budding political awareness among the rural Muslim population, thereby contributing to the widening chasm.[15] The rising apprehension was part of a general, self-fulfilling process whereby the population of Bengal was gearing up for the impending vivisection. Once prospects of the political separation took on an ineluctable force, the polarization of communities escalated through mechanisms of othering and demonizing: suddenly, familiar networks of trust and cooperation collapsed, as one's neighbors belonging to another faith became one's most feared enemies. The air of distrust, the spiraling hatred, the felt vulnerability of minority communities in specific locations—provided the affective justification for as drastic a measure as the geopolitical severance.

The Second Partition of Bengal

The historical facts about the event—escalating Muslim *and* Hindu separatism leading up to Partition, the horse-trading over districts, how many thousands were killed, how many millions got uprooted—while subject to debate, are readily available. Recent research has begun to turn its attention to memory, thus bringing within historiography the localized, subjective dimensions of the experience. Studies and anthologies on the Partition are focusing increasingly on oral and written testimonies, stressing differential factors—such as gender, religion, and region—in the cultural construction of memory.[16] Thus, for instance, historian Dipesh Chakrabarty examines reminiscences of people who lived through the Partition to discover "the structure of sentiments" that may be used as a frame or "grid" for reading "the irrevocable fact of Hindu–Muslim separation in Bengali history and the trauma surrounding the event."[17] My project, with its focus on the cinematic mediations of Partition, enjoys a certain affinity with such historiographic attempts at understanding the entanglement of history and memory. Before turning to Bengali cinema's take on the events circa 1947, I want to outline a few salient points that emerge from noncinematic popular accounts.

Testimonies dwell on two main aspects: the wrenching dislocation, and the shocking violence. The bifurcation of the province on the basis of religious influence and the fear of persecution of religious minorities caused large masses of people to migrate between the two Bengals. They were by no means foreigners, yet their experiences had something in common with the plight of exiles. While forced by circumstances to abandon their hearth and home, they found themselves in surroundings that were somewhat unfamiliar, yet tantalizingly similar to their old milieu: their geographical displacement amounted to no more than a few hundred miles, and often much less. This strange proximity of the abandoned homeland, and the simultaneous sense of cultural-linguistic contiguity *and* difference, produced precarious subjectivities suspended between the past and the present, between the putative plenitude of a lost home and the current contingent existence in temporary camps and refugee colonies. Hindu East Bengali refugees in West Bengal, widely regarded as a liability that would hold up postcolonial development, faced reactions ranging from cold indifference to outright hostility. Often objects of ridicule on account of differences of customs and dialects, they were charged with cultural miscegenation for tainting the elite culture and way of life in Calcutta.[18]

Violence, while as salient as the bifurcation in survivor testimonies, remains incomprehensible.[19] It is precisely this inexplicability that keeps the brutality so vivid in memory but also leads to its marginalization in teleological accounts of history. Even in the face of wild rumors, many had kept their hopes alive, banking on the humanity of the other community. When violence broke out in one's own neighborhood, when one's home was looted and burned down, one's family victimized, all hope was finally abandoned. A large part of the trauma involved experiences that one could not foresee: neighbors turning into tormentors, friends attacking each other, the familiar world becoming sinister. To ensure the continuation of private lives and communities, survivors had to resort to the art of forgetting—not in the simple sense of the term, but as subtle reorientations of memory. Since extreme violence throws community life into radical disarray, vicious acts were remembered to have occurred outside one's own neighborhood, perpetrated by members of other communities.[20] Notwithstanding these mnemonic acrobatics, the experience of Partition acquired a traumatic structure: people who lived through it were scarred permanently by what they had to endure, the shattering of their assumptive worlds taking a long-term toll.

For the balance of this chapter, I shall limit my analysis to West Bengal, for East Bengal and Bangladesh's experience has been somewhat different.[21] Through the experience of Partition, (West) Bengal becomes a world inscribed in loss: loss of corporeal wholeness, of (sub)nationalist unity, of political leadership, of cultural ascendancy, of a sense of belonging, of neighborly harmony. Bengal's hopes of coming out of the shadow of colonialism and staking out its place in the sun as a constituent of a new international order are dashed to the ground: instead, it is made to feel like "a hapless pawn in the endgames of empire."[22] Sapped of its former political energy and cultural vitality, Bengal is reduced to one of many middling provinces within India. Indeed, through such devaluation, midcentury Bengal comes to embody Benjamin's description of history as a landscape in ruins.

How did Bengalis mourn their losses, and what were the terms of their grieving? In his analyses of autobiographical essays of Hindu refugees from East Bengal, Dipesh Chakrabarty detects the deployment of

> a particular kind of language, one that combines the sacred with the secular idea of beauty to produce, ultimately, *a discourse about value*. These are narratives that have to demonstrate that *something of value to Bengali culture as a whole had been destroyed* by the violence of the partition. The "native village" is pictured as both sacred and beautiful, and it is this that makes communal violence an act of both violation and defilement, an act of sacrilege against everything that stood for sacredness and beauty in Hindu–Bengali understanding of what home was.[23]

At stake was the production of an ideal that could serve as a condensed signifier of all that had been lost by Bengalis. The "native village" as "home" emerged as that privileged concept in the post-1947 Bengali imaginary.

Moving beyond the scope of standard social migration studies, Chakrabarty identifies "four narrative elements" that achieved this ideal.[24] The sanctity of the native village derived from a patrilinear connection: through the veneration of the home of one's male ancestors, one effectively worshipped them.[25] Three other elements worked to secure the "secular idea of beauty." The first of these looked back in time to establish certain continuities from antiquity, often conjuring up the relics of a "glorious past"; the second strand invoked the role of the village in recent nationalist history. Thus, the memoirs resorted to the decidedly modern strategy of appropriating the sign of history in creating an ideal of homeland: the "remembered village . . . derive[d] some of its value from the associations it could claim with the nation's antiquity and anti-colonial struggle."[26] The last component drew on established literary traditions to conjure up an idyllic present for the native village: the model was the "powerfully nostalgic and pastoral"—and ultimately kitschy—"image of the generic Bengali village" that had been developed since the late 1800s "for and on behalf of the urban middle classes."[27] For instance, Rabindranath Tagore immortalized an eternal "sonar Bangla" (golden Bengal, the "golden" appellation referring both to the beloved status of the land, and to its harvest, and hence to value), which took on an iconic value for the long struggle that culminated in Bangladesh in 1971.

Focusing on this literary influence, Chakrabarty provides a genealogy of "the Bengali village as a modern cultural value," explicating why and how the figure becomes so crucial for Bengalis in the aftermath of Partition. If the "riverine landscape of East Bengal" was central to this ideal, equally important were what Chakrabarty calls "the new ways of seeing that landscape," framed by the influences on "the Bengali imaginative eye" of Sanskrit literature, classical Indian music, "European writings, paintings and the technology of the camera."[28] Nationalist Bengali literature had mapped the Bengali countryside as the realm of the Bengali "folk"—the site of the "true Bengali heart"—positing it against the "artificiality" of the city of Calcutta. According to such romantic formulations, the (urban) Bengali could discover his innate spiritual self only in the verdant rural landscape: "A place, true, marked by suffering, poverty and sometimes a meanness of spirit but yet the abode of some very tender sentiments of intimacy, innocence and kinship."[29] This modern idyll was being evoked in the wake of the Partition by refugees, many of whom had left their rural homes for the concrete jungle of Calcutta, and by Bengalis in general as a way of capturing what it was that had been violated, shattered, lost.

The Bengal Famine of 1943

What the historiography of the truncation frequently overlooks, even when it is attentive to popular memory, is the complexity the experience takes on in the context of Bengal: in the popular imagination, the anguish over Partition merges with the trauma of the devastating famine of 1943 that killed about 3 million people, one-third of the province's population. The fact of this fundamental overdetermination sheds light on the specific iconographic elements and collective obsessions that characterize Partition memories; it goes a long way in explaining the deep melancholia that has plagued Bengali life since the forties.

The official explanation for the catastrophe ran in terms of a shortage in the availability of food: the Famine Inquiry Commission pointed to a poor harvest, caused by cyclone, flooding, and fungus breakouts, and to disruption caused by the war (supplies diverted for feeding the British army, and the termination of the import of Burmese rice after the Japanese occupation of Burma). But as economist Amartya Sen has demonstrated convincingly, the shortage was not that drastic: in fact, a more severe crop failure in 1941 had not led to a famine.[30] The real reason was sharp movements in relative terms of trade and exchange entitlements, precipitated by official policies and attendant public responses: the inflationary pressures from the deficit financing of war expenditures; uneven increases in incomes and purchasing powers; prohibition on interprovince food trade; speculative hoardings and panic purchase, significantly intensified by administrative chaos. In short, the famine was no natural disaster: it was manmade. Sen also concludes that the "famine was essentially a rural phenomenon"; the main urban areas, specially Calcutta, were "insulated from rising food prices by subsidized distribution schemes" and experienced the trauma "mainly in the form of an influx of rural destitutes."[31]

The reality of the Bengali countryside, strewn with corpses, threatened the collective pastoral fantasy, thereby accentuating the fetishistic preoccupation: the memory of this deathscape compounded the abiding sense of social death a few years later. The earlier stream of starving destitutes who abandoned their rural homes and made their way to the big cities (mainly Calcutta and Dhaka), seemed to merge seamlessly with the refugees fleeing real or dreaded communal persecution. The sense of an emaciated Bengali body (which the rest of India evokes to this day in the figure of the *bhukha Bangali*, the famished Bengali)[32] was rendered more acutely poignant by the drastic amputation of the body politic.

The famine and the bifurcation, as experienced by the people of Bengal, were fused into a single historical conjuncture, whose enduring affect was a debilitating loss of plenitude. Mother Bengal, once a golden, bountiful, and nurturing land of possibilities, had become a fragmented dystopia; the Bengalis, once a gentle, creative people, had been brutalized, torn asunder, impoverished. From now on, Bengal would be sunk in a deep, melancholic reverie about its glorious past: for several generations, all visions of its future would be compromised by this nostalgia and found lacking. It was on this problematic ground that West Bengal struggled to keep up with programs of securing a postcolonial Indian nation-state.

A Regional "National" Cinema:
Audiences and Taste Cultures

Reduced in size and stature, and saddled with a staggering refugee rehabilitation problem, West Bengal was a faltering participant in a modernist agenda of capitalist development. Indian Bengalis also suffered from an ideological vacillation between their own residual sense of a Bengali nationality, and a broader Indian identity, which was now being mobilized aggressively by a centralized, statist power structure to consolidate its own legitimacy and to supersede such regionalisms decisively.

This, then, is the sociopolitical backdrop in relation to which I attempt to understand Bengali cinema's mediation of nationhood and contemporary national history in roughly the first decade after independence. What was the state of the Calcutta film industry in this period? In spite of a seemingly drastic reduction in the size of the market for Bengali films, there was a sudden spurt in the number of annual productions: it more than doubled in a year, from fifteen in 1946 to thirty-three in 1947, the year of Partition. The number peaked at sixty-two in 1949, indicating an "artificial boom"[33] resulting primarily from the inflow of black money from the profiteering activities of the war years. The influence of the "fly-by-night producers," who were interested in making a quick buck, was apparent from a greater stress on generic formulae and marketability, and a decline in concerns about quality and taste.[34] Yet the 1950s are widely recognized as the "golden age" of Bengali cinema: it was a period that saw a corpus of immensely popular films whose influence can be felt to this day; it was also a decade in which the industry stabilized, with the average annual production standing around forty-seven.

Two significant impulses stand out in the discourse around Bengali cinema. First, there was the general recognition of a national imperative to develop a vital cultural field, including a representative cinema, as part of wider attempts to consolidate nationhood—an awareness complicated by tremendous local anxieties about the rapid emergence of Bombay as the primary center of cinema in the country, and the future place of Bengali cinema within a putative national cinema. Second, the cultural healing of the composite wound of the forties, often through generic fantasies of love, unity, and plenitude, emerged as an overarching concern.

The editorial in the inaugural issue (October 1948) of the Bengali cinema journal *Chitrabani*[35] expressed the desire to provide a public forum, which could take an active part in building a strong culture industry (including stage, screen, and radio) by fostering dialogue and cooperation among the audience, producers, and the government. Lamenting the anarchy unleashed by the sudden influx of the nouveau riche in film production, the editorial stressed the need to promote quality, which was absolutely necessary for "the progress of a long-dormant nation."[36] Imbibing a rhetoric of reformist development, the piece called for a clean and healthy film culture.[37] Interestingly, the journal evinced a clear understanding of cinema as a commercial industry: hence, it argued for a balance between the pedagogical and entertaining functions of films. Thus, a review of the Hindi film *Neechanagar* (1946)—which was acclaimed by leftists and audiences at international film festivals—complained about the dour, unrelenting documentary realism of the film. Proposing a realism that was more imaginative and more emotionally compelling, it declared that a harmonious blend of truth and fantasy made for a more successful film.[38] Here, the journal shifted from its usual tirade against Hindi films, displaying a pragmatic approach to a socially relevant yet affectively engaging cinema.

Chitrabani also printed an article titled "The Responsibility of the Audience," by the famous Marathi producer/director V. Shantaram, in which he berated the educated middle-class critics and viewers for dismissing popular Indian cinema as light, obscene, and harmful, yet lapping up "third rate Hollywood releases."[39] He called upon both critics and audiences to take an active interest in the development of Indian cinema. Arguing that producers would make decent films only if there was an audience for them, he underscored the need for responsible criticism, and for film clubs and organizations. While declaring in a nationalist vein that he preferred the illiterate proletarian audiences who patronized Indian films to the educated classes with their predilection for Western cinema, Shantaram reverted back to a decidedly elitist position: in spite of his professed dislike of the educated elite, he called upon them to help develop better cultural taste among the masses.

The journal itself was, indeed, blatantly elitist in its tone; when it emphasized the entertainment value of films, it spoke from a middle-class perspective. The editorial in the annual number (published in September) of each year reiterated a kind of "mission statement," resorting to highly romantic prose to represent the journal as a resolute voice of reason and discriminating taste, fighting to protect a crisis-prone cultural field from the onslaught of degenerate influences and the endless demands of capital. Various contributors typically characterized the "masses" as being "backward in their intellectual capacity," implying they were capable of appreciating only the most sensational plots and spectacles, the basest of emotions.[40] The editor's attitude was so condescending at times that it riled at least one reader into writing a letter of protest: he remarked that the editor's lack of civility and tolerance was shocking for a publication in a free country.[41] Apparently, the editor had responded to another reader's mail by declaring that "people like him" should not bother to pick up "this" magazine, implying that the publication was meant for a more cultivated readership.

Hemen Gupta, a well-known director, expressed a different view of the "masses" in a piece on cinema and censorship. He argued that the common viewers were quite capable of appreciating quality films: they patronized bad films only for a lack of good ones. For Gupta, audiences were the only censors necessary, and the market mechanisms of demand and supply were enough to eliminate bad films over time. He did envision the gradual emergence of a more responsible and discriminating audience: thus, in spite of his professed faith in the "masses," Gupta betrayed his developmentalist expectation of an ideal national audience whose ideality was to be determined in relation to a preconceived notion of "good taste."

In such discussions of audience, a monolithic conception of the "masses" was pitted against an equally undifferentiated idea of a discriminating, educated middle-class audience. Underlying the various arguments was a common element: an understanding of "taste" as an absolute and preordained standard of cultural judgment, and not as a highly contingent and shifting indicator of upbringing, education, and social origin—in short, of class. As Pierre Bourdieu has argued so convincingly, taste is never an innocent category: it "fulfill[s] a social function of legitimating social difference."[42] In the context of discourses about Bengali cinema of the fifties, invocations of taste originated from an essentially middle-class bhadralok position, with its obsessive privileging of education and bourgeois refinement. The contingency of this particular fixation with taste becomes apparent if we connect it to the widely felt anxiety of falling into a déclassé situation in a world marked by the very real experiences of property loss, penury, and homelessness. As I shall demonstrate in my discussions of individual films, being *bhadra*—that is, being of upper-class or middle-class origin, and proving one's distinguished background through one's refined behavior—became a way of resisting the ignominy of a decline in socioeconomic status.

Taste brings up the issue of censorship, since entertaining without offending refined sensibilities requires "a sense of limits."[43] In general, discussion of Bengali cinema privileged nongovernment initiatives—by film clubs, cinema organizations, the press, critics, and film enthusiasts—to develop a discerning audience; not surprisingly, a strong tradition of cinephilia and film-club culture developed in Calcutta from the late forties. Meanwhile, censorship by the government came under frequent criticism. For instance, Hemen Gupta launched a scathing attack on the official censor board, calling for its disbandment or a radical overhaul. He argued that the board was composed mainly of bureaucrats and army personnel, who had very little understanding of the film medium; as a result, popular cinema was forced to fall in line with and promote an official point of view.

Film Censorship and the Fear of Popular Dissension

Gupta's ire was fueled, in part, by personal experience: two of his films had difficulty getting clearances from local censor authorities. The controversy over these two films—*Bhuli Nai* (1948) and *Biallish* (1949)—generated a heated debate about the role of film censorship in relation to cinema publics, a national political-cultural hegemony, and local popular movements. When the West Bengal Censor Board refused to grant an exhibition certificate to *Biallish*, it also took the unusual step of releasing a public explanation. This document provides fascinating insights into the workings of a bureaucratic mentality. It states that the film "cannot be certified for exhibition in the Province of West Bengal as it is at present likely to excite passion and encourage disorder."[44] The apprehension about public passions stemmed from the film's vivid depiction of police and military brutality against freedom fighters during the anti-British Quit India movement of 1942. Oddly, the film seemed to have upset the censor authorities in independent India as much as the original uprising bothered the colonial rulers. Was this reaction indicative of a general bureaucratic fear of popular anger and mass movements? Perhaps so, but the objection had much to do with possible repercussions on popular perceptions of the army and the police system: there always exists the possibility of excessive use of force, whether in the colonial or in the post-independence era, and representations of historical repression reiterate this potential for brutality. In the Indian case, this possibility seemed even stronger, since the colonial administrative, police, and military structures had been more or less retained by the postcolonial government: since "the system" was not that different, it was probably capable of similar excesses.

Perhaps more significant was the quirky political dynamics between the center and the province. As one commentator pointed out, the Censor Board—in stating that representations of official repression in 1942 would incite mass agitation—appeared to suggest that the people of Bengal did not differentiate between the colonial government and the Congress Party's government, that they did not have much confidence in the post-1947 sovereign state.[45] While this particular commentator found such a suggestion to be preposterous and illogical, I find it rather interesting in the light of recent subaltern historiography and the political history of West Bengal over the last six decades. Notwithstanding Nehru's espousal of a Fabian socialism, his Congress Party formed a central government that clearly assigned highest priority to a program of national development through industrialization. While such a policy was marked by an obvious urban bias, the Congress Party could marshal wide support in regions where it enjoyed overwhelming support (e.g., the northern states). Given the strong presence of leftist political forces in Bengal, the province's incorporation within a Congress-led hegemony was, at best, tenuous. If peasant movements in the preindependence years could be thwarted in the name of a nationalist cause, by raising the specter of a common enemy in the British Raj, now the simmering discontent in the rural areas—and even among the urban unemployed—started to coalesce against the nationalist government. The tremendous popularity of Dr. Bidhan Roy, the first head of the province after independence, enabled the Congress Party to maintain its hold on West Bengal;[46] but there was always a strong, if marginalized, undercurrent of antistate (and anti-Congress) sentiments. Leftist cultural politics, initiated by the Indian Peoples Theatre Association (IPTA), petered out in most parts of the country, but it continued to thrive in West Bengal. Not surprisingly, after the initial nationalist euphoria was over (especially with the humiliation of the Chinese invasion in 1962), and after Dr. Roy's death in 1961, the leftist forces gradually gained momentum throughout the sixties, culminating first in the extremist Naxalite movement (crushed only through the most outrageous police and military repression), and then in a moderate left-coalition provincial government in 1977, which has been in power ever since. Therefore, in retrospect, the idea that the Censor Board was still worried, after independence, about the possible fallout from representations of state-sponsored violence does not seem that far-fetched.

The Censor Board further declared that there were "many indecent scenes"[47] in *Biallish*, without any elaboration as to which specific scenes crossed the limits of decency, and in what ways. It charged the film with "many factual errors" and distortions that served to "cheapen and debase" a "historic episode in India's struggle for independence."[48] The film was about events from the very recent past, and "factual errors" could easily be rectified; yet, instead of asking for necessary corrections, the board refused a certificate outright. This stifling approach has been typical of official positions: it is, after all, much easier to ban a cultural intervention than to actually confront contentious history.

My claims about the link between the political atmosphere of West Bengal and the local Censor Board's fear of popular emotions are supported by the fact that the film was cleared in most places outside Bengal. Having seen *Biallish* in the adjoining province of Bihar, a viewer was perplexed by the intransigence of censorship authorities. In a letter written to the editor of *Chitrabani*, he wondered: Must cinema limit itself to romantic tomfoolery, to flowers, the moon, and the stars? If it cannot move with the times, if it cannot engage with society and politics, what is its purpose?[49] These pointed questions indicate the intense nature of the debate raging in popular discourses of the time regarding the role of cinema in postcolonial India.

Building a National Culture

The question of taste, with its precept of a "sense of limits," frequently masks an ideological tension about what can be represented and what must be left out. This process of selection became critical in establishing the parameters of a "national culture." The Bengali film *Diner Por Din* (1949) was a reflexive meditation on the contentious cultural field: it focused on a (fictitious) attempt to institute a National Theater. The central narrative conflict sprung from the selection of the first play to be staged at the theater: most members of the selection committee displayed a preference for a "safe" play that would not "offend" the sensibilities of the patrons by questioning their privileged and sophisticated lifestyles. Thus the film attempted to reveal how ambitious and well-meaning cultural projects could be hijacked by, and incorporated into, an ideological hegemony for its own reproduction, engendering an insipid national culture in the process.

The director and the writer of the film, Jyotirmoy Roy, had also written the story for Bimal Roy's celebrated film *Udayer Pathey* (1944), credited with working out a new romantic-realist aesthetic within a melodramatic mode. The earlier film portrayed an emergent form of political and cultural awareness: the protagonist was an impoverished novelist deeply involved in the workers' movement. *Diner Por Din* focused on an educated, middle-class youth—now mired in poverty and trying to make a living through sundry tutorial assignments—with a strong desire to serve the cause of social emancipation. The romanticism associated with cultural production was now informed by a social awareness and a sense of commitment. This politicized subject came out of a midcentury Bengali cultural scene profoundly influenced by the IPTA—the premier body of progressive cultural politics that counted both Bimal Roy and Jyotirmoy Roy as its associates.[50]

In *Diner Por Din*, the "establishment" is split into a villainous schemer, the rich industrialist Nidhiranjan, and an enlightened, benevolent figure, the (former) landlord Shibshankar. The nouveau riche industrialist and his cronies, who control the theater's planning committee, want to barter away all social concerns and usurp the cultural field for their own personal aggrandizement. In critiquing these new cutthroat capitalists, the film sides with the feudal landlord—the "old" money. This may seem like a strange tactic for a narrative with manifest leftist leanings, but it makes sense in the Bengali context. The landed aristocracy largely spearheaded the so-called Bengal renaissance in the nineteenth century; the intellectual and social contributions of this class became the very basis of Bengal's preeminence within modern Indian history. In the dog days of the 1940s and 1950s, a strong, palpable nostalgia about Bengal's recent past turned the accomplishments of the enlightened landlord class into cultural capital: hence the film counts on a representative of that class, in alliance with the educated middle-class hero, to provide leadership in shaping a vital national culture.

Ajin, the protagonist, opposes the cynical power-mongering and sides with the more conscientious and caring Shibshankar. He finds another ally in Samata, the daughter of a neighboring refugee family, struggling to find a foothold in their new surroundings. Her name literally means "equality"—an allusion to the democratic ideals always in danger of being corrupted. Samata and her educated, if indigent, neighbor come together with an elite but enlightened citizen to build a cultural institution that is able to stave off attempts to appropriate and adulterate its utopian intent, at least for the time being. The film offers an optimistic, if cautionary, vision of the task of fostering a national culture: it portrays a new social consciousness arising from the fusion of residual and emergent idealistic forces to challenge a narrowly instrumentalist paradigm of capitalist development and to keep alive a critical impulse within cultural praxis.

Bombay vs. Calcutta

Discussions of national culture were marked by a discernible anxiety about the declining influence of Bengal in the pan-Indian cultural sphere; this anxiety was most pronounced with regards to cinema, as the forties witnessed the rapid ascension of the Bombay industry. The very first issue of *Chitrabani* featured an article on Bengali contributions to Indian cinema, prefaced by an editorial note asking readers not to misjudge this emphasis as *pradeshikata*, or provincialism.[51] Nevertheless, precisely such a parochial thrust emerges as the crux of cultural discourses from the endless reiteration of "genuine" reasons for Bengali pride.

A subsequent report on the first international film festival in India in 1952—which was spread over the four metropolitan centers of Bombay, Calcutta, Delhi, and Madras—criticized the central government for discriminating against West Bengal: while the other cities received 20,000 to 30,000 rupees for putting up the festival, Calcutta was allotted only 500. Moreover, festival films screened in Bombay and Calcutta were not exempted from entertainment tax: thus the "festival" was really so only in Delhi and Madras. Nevertheless, as the report triumphantly stated, returns from the sale of festival tickets in Calcutta were greater than the combined returns from the rest of the country. The writer congratulated Bengal for its superior taste, love of culture, and appreciation of international art, stressing wistfully that such attributes were signs of the continuing vitality of the fragmented, doubt-ridden region.[52] The report revealed a tension between loyalties generated by two different kinds of geopolitical imagination, characterized by Marsha Kinder as microregionalism and macroregionalism.[53] On the one hand, it intended to confirm Bengal's vanguard position within the nation by placing it as a keen player in a global cultural field: thus the cosmopolitan interests of a subnational entity (a microregion) were being evoked to challenge the supremacy of the nation. On the other hand, the report—in a nationalist vein—touted the Indian film festival as the first of its kind in Asia, thus claiming a certain cultural ascendancy for the nation within the macroregion.

As the Bombay film industry established its iron hold on the national market, the Bengali press mounted a tirade against Hindi films for their alleged indecency and exploitative sexual fixation, and their senseless aping of Hollywood products. Such criticism, while not entirely unfounded, was frequently accompanied by rather hyperbolic claims: that the Bombay industry was facing a crisis;[54] that it was being kept alive by gifted Bengali artists and technicians;[55] that only Bengali cinema could save all of Indian culture from the vulgar morass into which Bombay was dragging it.[56] Simultaneously, there was a constant apprehension of contagion—that Bombay-style excess would corrupt Bengali cinema.[57]

The Bengali censure of the Bombay industry finds a particularly sensitive node in the controversy surrounding the depiction of Netaji Subhas Bose,[58] the militant Bengali hero, in the Hindi film *Samadhi* (1949). Until his presumed death in a plane crash, Netaji—as Bose was known popularly (the apellation means "revered leader")—was seen as the one nationalist figure that could challenge Nehru for the leadership of independent India.[59] For a long time after 1947, many a Bengali refused to believe that he was dead and continued to pray for his return, driven by a wistful belief that he would never have allowed Bengal to disintegrate, and that he alone could revive Bengali eminence. This desire for a hero's resurrection was fueled by the heartbreak of the forties and Bengali insecurities about emerging power equations in national affairs. Deified as an icon with composite affective valence, Netaji and his legacy had to be guarded zealously against all forms of perceived violations. Not surprisingly, all cinematic depictions of the hero came under intense scrutiny. Various commentators criticized *Samadhi*, a product of the Filmistan studios, for trivializing a glorious chapter in the history of the freedom struggle by reducing patriotism to the formulaic ingredients of a typical Hindi film.[60] It was judged in comparison to *Pahela Admi* (1950), another Hindi film that was produced by New Theatres, the revered Calcutta studio, and directed by Bimal Roy, a Bengali. Both films were set against the backdrop of the heroic anti-British military exploits of Netaji's Indian National Army (INA) in southeast Asia. According to one review, *Pahela Admi* evinced a certain dedication to upholding nationalist sensibilities, while *Samadhi* reflected a commercial attitude in closely following a generic recipe, so that patriotism became yet another crowd-pulling element.[61] In the former film, the focus was on the activities and the noble sacrifice of the members of the INA; the romantic narrative remained secondary. *Samadhi*, on the other hand, focused on the romance and the spy intrigue: the INA and its supreme commander were peripheral plot components.

Much of the controversy stemmed from the actual mode of representing Netaji, raising fundamental questions about the authenticity of photographs and cultural proscriptions on visual representations of deified historical figures. In *Pahela Admi*, the leader appeared only in documentary footage, while *Samadhi* turned him into a diegetic character; thus they were seen respectively to uphold and violate a widely held realist sensibility whose crux is a belief in an indelibly indexical association between the photograph and its referent.[62] One commentator was offended by the *Bombaywallah*'s depiction of Netaji, using an actor.[63] His indignation was surprising, as the Hindu Indian scene was suffused with visual representations of gods and deified heroes, and there was a long tradition of actors pretending to be divinities on stage and, more recently, on screen. The commentator was, perhaps, influenced by the general Hollywood norm of avoiding frontal representations of Jesus in the mid-twentieth century.[64] His irritation revealed his own tangled investments in, and his distrust of all non-Bengali representations of, the idealized Bengali icon. The regional angle becomes apparent from the commentator's sense of shock at the fact that a Bengali actor had portrayed Netaji in *Samadhi*: one did not expect any better from the Bombay producers, but how could a Bengali be part of such a travesty? Of course, all such discussions conveniently overlooked the fact that Bombay's Filmistan studio, which produced the film in question, was founded and owned by Bengalis. From the fifties' bourgeois Bengali perspective, it would probably become yet another proof of Bombay's corrupting influence.

Trends in Genre Formation

Given this relational determination of Bengali cinema, what broad trends in the Calcutta film industry were discernible in its first decade after independence? What anxieties and aspirations marked the attempts to move beyond the collective anguish of the forties? As I have indicated above, post-Partition West Bengal was stuck in a melancholic stupor—without any immediate possibility of progress, revolution, or redemption, without any vision of a secure future. Bengali cinema's response to the demands of modernization and development was profoundly equivocal, more so than in the case of Hindi films. Thus, while patriotic films celebrating nationalist ideals emerged as an important genre, their intense representations of revolutionary activities intimated a populist militancy that rattled the institutions of official power. By invoking nationalist ideals that were widely felt to have been vitiated in the process of securing independence, and in commemorating the tremendous sacrifices that had not been allowed to bear full effect, the films participated in local popular resentment that extended across the temporal watershed of 1947, raising fears of mass agitation against the nascent nationalist government. Films such as *Bhuli Nai*, *Biallish*, *Jaijatra* (1948), *Chattagram Astragar Lunthan* (1949), and *Biplabi Kshudiram* (1950) revealed a dimension of popular anger that was absent from patriotic Hindi films, that could scarcely be contained within an overarching rhetoric of nation building.

Another popular genre of the period was the modern crime thriller with its detective figure as an embodiment of rationalist discourse. Interestingly, the films in this genre often appeared in hybridized form, incorporating aspects of horror and supernatural narratives. Thus, in films like *Kalochhaya* (1948), *Kankal* (1950), *Hanabari* (1951), and *Maraner Porey* (1954), crime was complicated by gothic elements such as ghosts and haunted houses, and by romantic beliefs in such paranormal phenomena as reincarnation and clairvoyance. By staging an enigmatic and contentious return of the irrational within a rationalist paradigm, these cinematic fabulations clearly undertook a negotiation between premodern and modern universes. However, in most cases, the gothic or supernatural element would turn out to be a hoax, thus reinstating the validity of logical discourse and indicating a desire for modernity.

Comedy, which had already proved to be as popular on Bengali screen as on stage, became particularly successful in the 1950s. Starting with the runaway hit *Barjatri* (1951), there was a series of films with enduring appeal: *Pasher Bari* (1952), *Patri Chai* (1952), *Sharey Chuattar* (1953), *Griha Prabesh* (1954), and *Chatujjey Barujjey* (1955). Featuring neighbors, prospective couples, and in-laws, these films found humor in both everyday interaction and more formal situations like matrimonial negotiations. One commentator linked this surging popularity of comedies to an audience that was tired of maudlin cinematic fare portraying the travails of a bleak, quotidian life; instead, these light entertainers offered spectators a respite from everyday drudgery in the form of clean, simple diversion. At the same time, the commentator chastised instances of crude and crass humor, alleging that sometimes comedies tended to trivialize and degrade events and characters to a point that became offensive.[65] These observations registered a need for some kind of cultural panacea—both to overcome contemporary social despondence and to stave off cultural regression.

Nevertheless, mushy tearjerkers abounded as melodrama, along with its hybrid subgenres (family melodrama, social melodrama, romantic melodrama), continued to be the master genre of Bengali cinema.[66] Overtly sentimental tales of misery became a way of engaging history—not as much working through as wallowing in collective grief.

For instance, the 1951 film *Babla*, named after and revolving around the struggles of its young protagonist, paints an unrelentingly dismal view of life, in which the occasional signs of hope are overwhelmed by an enveloping sense of doom. The narrative charts the gradual disintegration of a lower-middle-class family through a series of catastrophes. Babla's father, who works away from his family in Calcutta, dies in a road accident on the day his wife and child finally arrive in the big city. Mother and son end up in the city slums: Babla goes to school, as his mother toils day and night to make a living. Just as he establishes himself as a brilliant student and gets admitted to a good school on scholarship, his mother contracts tuberculosis. The young Babla struggles on all fronts and repeatedly proves his worth as a person; still, he cannot save his mother. Through its coincidental and recurrent structure, the narrative captures a milieu whose desolation is so extreme that it takes on an aura of inevitability, as if all the misery is ordained by fate. Such an excessive, melancholic immersion was, of course, only one of several cultural responses to the collective Bengali experience. As one viewer pointed out, *Babla* was representative of a genre of mawkish films whose manipulative sentimentality was starting to wear down audiences;[67] he seemed to imply that spectators were eager for a break from narratives of despair. While the strong show of comedies corroborated such an estimation of audience expectations, a more convincing confirmation was provided by the popularity of an altogether new breed of romantic narratives that helped an enervated population dream again.

Flight to Fantasy

I am referring to a cluster of romantic melodramas, the most celebrated of which featured superstars Uttam Kumar and Suchitra Sen. This idolized screen couple acted in some thirty films, from 1953's *Sharey Chuattar* to 1975's *Priya Bandhabi*; as many as twenty of these were released in a five-year period between 1954 and 1958, widely acknowledged to be the golden years of commercial Bengali cinema.[68] Together, the stars cast a magical spell on audiences and became the locus of their collective fantasies, offering symbolic restitution for something of value that had been lost to Bengali society as a whole.

Given the rapid and far-reaching social transformations under way in the 1950s, the preeminence of the melodramatic mode is not surprising. As we noted in chapter 1 above, melodrama seeks to make sense of social upheaval by mediating it within the private context of the home, and eventually to impose order through the resolution of crisis and the reconstitution of the family.[69] If the accentuated social flux leaves people confounded, melodrama mirrors the felt disorientation through the characters' behavior, which is often strikingly at odds with their actual objectives: a protracted series of tentative actions obfuscates causality and motivation, and the goal is reached only after much delay. In the Uttam-Suchitra films, the star-crossed lovers unite eventually, but only after surmounting great uncertainty and obstacles. One title, *Pathey Holo Deri* (1957), which translates literally as "delayed on the way," actually alludes to this structure of deferral and eventual resolution. The lovers are separated either by circumstances beyond their control, or by misunderstandings that generate a complex emotion designated as the untranslatable *abhiman* ("hurt pride" is a feeble approximation), rendered potent by underlying sexual tension. Formal elements—languid song sequences, low-angle soft focus shots, mannered speech and body language, tensile proxemic patterns and fluid transitions—capture the ambiguous state of simultaneously holding back *and* yearning.[70] The romantic affect of separation is always the displaced manifestation of other, more social contradictions—class conflicts, the pressures of capitalist modernization, the ratiocination of the "joint" or extended family. It is precisely the attenuation and dispersal of narrative logic—the intervening complications often conveyed through a mise-en-scène of excess—that mediate the social ferment.

The middle-class espousal of a capitalist paradigm of development required an attendant shift away from community values to a decidedly more individualist calculus. Extended families started breaking up into nuclear units, leading to much debate over the very notion of family. Films such as *Punarmilan* (1959) and *Sashibabur Sansar* (1959) addressed the dissolution of the extended family, providing a public forum for the expression of anxieties over the disappearance of a familiar world. Such a concern informed many of the Uttam-Suchitra films; at least one of these, *Sadanander Mela* (1954), explicitly countered the new-sprung individualism and the concomitant dissipation of community life by promoting cooperative living among squatters on the property of an industrialist whose pecuniary interests had alienated his own family. In the end, the capitalist proprietor was convinced by his rebellious daughter to join this tenuous community on egalitarian terms, as just another member. While upholding the utopian democratic aspirations of the postcolonial polity, the film also denounced the more self-seeking tendencies of capitalist modernism.

Both egalitarianism and the pressures of an emerging capitalist market required transformations in gender relations, transformations that threatened to unhinge traditional power structures within the family.

Commercial Bengali cinema's response conformed to a broad pattern observed in cultural mediations from various parts of the world: it sought to safeguard existing gender hierarchies through a reconstitution of (feudal) patriarchy in line with (modern) capitalist values. Thus, in film after film, Chhabi Biswas and Pahari Sanyal[71]—two revered thespians of the Bengali stage and screen—played father figures (father, uncle, avuncular neighbor, professor, doctor, employer, wealthy benefactor) who were, essentially, enlightened despots. As patriarchs who articulated their apprehension about the rapid changes and their eventual appreciation of the forces of modernization, they served a dual function: as a critical voice, and simultaneously as a legitimating, normalizing authority. If a clash between their imperious, intransigent ways and the attitudes of the younger generation introduced tension in the family, it was finally the expansive, liberal, and affectionate embrace of these patriarchs that ensured cheerful, fairy-tale closures. Eccentric, wise, and incurably romantic, they would frequently resolve the very conflicts they had initiated and bring the feuding lovers back together. If their eventual sanction of modern values signified the refiguration of patriarchy in tune with the demands of an emerging social formation under a modern nation-state, the same move also ensured their retention of ultimate control, both narrative and historical.

Theorists of melodrama have drawn attention to its ability to foreground certain contradictions experienced by the bourgeoisie in capitalist societies. Chuck Kleinhans, for instance, writes about the alienating experience of the capitalist workplace, and the expectation that domestic life—carefully tended by the women—will somehow make up for it.[72] Thus a split between "productive work" and "personal life" (with its attendant notion of personal identity and happiness) leads to a fundamental contradiction: peoples' (i.e., men's) needs, while arising from their experience outside the family, are supposed to be alleviated within the family by women (traditionally excluded from the sphere of production). Melodrama calls attention to the contradiction, articulating it in excessive, hysterical ways; yet, ultimately, it does not work to change the situation. The gendered expectations that require endless sacrifice and self-effacement on the part of women are bolstered by an arsenal of culture-specific myths and structures: in the case of Bengali cinema, such reiteration was achieved through references to mythic female role models (Sita, Sabitri, Sati, Behula) and invocations of traditional values (e.g., the unquestioning respect to be accorded to husbands and elders).

In the 1950s, the sheer economic necessities of a post-Partition Bengal with its destitute refugee families forced many women to take on jobs ranging from the home-based production of paper bags to secretarial and stenographers' positions in corporate offices; educated Bengali women also started entering the labor force in large numbers, specially as educators. This development exacerbated the contradiction: while the elderly patriarchs registered initial consternation (who will look after the domestic sphere?), they were quick to realize the positive effects both in private and public terms (greater family income and national product). The melodramas of the 1950s and 1960s recognized women as a productive force of economic growth and simultaneously reiterated women's role as homemakers. The fundamental operation they carried out was that of bringing the categories of patriarchy, capitalism, and the modern nation-state into a new alignment, thus recasting existing gender hierarchies in rational-functionalist terms that were more acceptable in a modernizing society. In his film *Mahanagar* (*The Big City*, 1963), Satyajit Ray presents the dilemmas of an *adhunika*, a contemporary woman, who is ready to join the workforce. When her husband is laid off and she takes on the job of selling sewing machines from door to door in order to support her family (which includes her retired in-laws and young sister-in-law), her father-in-law is outraged; soon, however, he is pressing for a new pair of glasses. Her son is upset with his "bad mother" for abandoning him for long hours; later, he comes around when she buys him toys with her earnings. Ray skillfully brings out the conflicts that plague the modern woman trying to realize her productive agency, balancing it with her traditional role of homemaker. He portrays the shifting dynamics within a lower-middle-class bourgeois family, reflecting wider changes in Bengali society at a time when the problem of unemployment was becoming more acute even as new career opportunities were opening up for women in corporate offices and retail business. The protagonist of *Mahanagar* learns to take on, even transgress, many of the structural limits imposed on a middle-class Bengali wife and mother. In contrast, Ritwik Ghatak's films from the early 1960s derive their critical edge precisely from the hypermelodramatic depiction of women's ongoing oppression: in these bleak tales, modernity and its attendant processes do not liberate the woman as much as they ruin her. While this last point is developed at length in chapter 5, I bring up these modernist auteurs' works here to underscore that their concerns were quite similar to those of commercial Bengali films. Where they parted ways was, of course, in their political intent.

If melodrama eventually reproduces the bourgeois family and the subordination of women, if it settles for a closure that upholds the status quo, can we really claim for it a transgressive potential? Several theorists, developing on Laura Mulvey's lead, have shown us that the genre, by focusing on the material and cultural conditions of women's lives and by explicitly playing out the contradictions they face daily in the domestic sphere, provide great satisfaction to female audiences.[73] The screening of ideological contradictions that arise mainly from sexual difference, provide women spectators with a mise-en-scène of their own experiences. More important, certain melodramas allow for the expression of female desire through subversive excess and even place the woman's point of view at the center of the narrative. Suchitra Sen's screen persona provided such a point of identification for Bengali women in the 1950s. Parameters of that persona were established in her very first film, *Sharey Chuattar*: beautiful, young, educated, self-possessed, proud, strong-willed, and yet nurturing. She emerged as the embodiment of the adhunika, whom audiences desired and looked up to. It did not matter that she was somewhat stiff in her bearings, a bit artificial in the way she delivered her lines: her allure as an idol was only enhanced by these traits. In fact, Sen's challenge to hegemonic structures was less in terms of her characters' actions in the narrative, and more in terms of her appearance and style. In other words, whereas the protagonist of Ray's *Mahanagar* gradually found her agency through her actions, the characters that Sen played exuded a poise that was essentially iconographic. In this respect, Sen's characterizations were rather similar: they were all smart, active, gorgeous creatures who nevertheless remained curiously frozen through the narratives, rarely posing a serious challenge to the status quo. Indeed, her purported agency was couched mainly in terms of anxieties about class mobility and an emerging consumerism—connections I shall get to presently. Nevertheless, Sen's iconic agency dovetailed nicely with melodrama's formal and stylistic predilections and provided audiences with the satisfaction of watching familial and sexual contradictions unfold on screen. Her coupling with Uttam Kumar, undisputedly the most popular star of the Bengali screen, allowed for the projection of a certain fantasy: the adhunika could now desire, and even express that desire within limits imposed by the narrative. Of course, the heroine's passion for one particular star-hero across so many narratives served to rein in feminine desire, domesticating it within a monogamous ambit, even de-eroticizing it by investing it with the aura of "true love." Sen as heroine often had to pay a price for her (transgressive) desiring: her masochistic characters suffered endlessly from forbidden longings (*Saptapadi* [1961]), renunciation (*Sagarika* [1965]), symptomatic illnesses (*Pathey Holo Deri*). However, Uttam Kumar as hero had his own vulnerable moments: for instance, he was blinded in *Sagarika* and became an amnesiac in *Harano Sur*. In these narratives, the handsome matinee idol, in his infirm glory, came to depend on women: if

Agnipareeksha:
cover art
for publicity
pamphlet.
Courtesy of
Parimal Roy.

the heroine took on a nurturing role, she also witnessed instances of male crisis. Thus, when considered intertextually, the Uttam-Suchitra films transported audiences to an intensely romantic space where the two leads seemed destined for each other.[74] Gender roles were somewhat blurred in this quixotic realm, until the permissible resolutions to various contradictions, social and sexual, reestablished the structural boundaries. A detailed discussion of one particular film may help elucidate this strange dynamic of transgression and perpetuation.

Agnipareeksha: What Does a
Modern Bengali Woman Want?

A print advertisement for *Agnipareeksha* (1954)—one of the most beloved films starring our star couple—depicts Suchitra Sen with tousled hair and a garland in hand, standing in front of a road sign with two empty boards, perpendicular to each other: these cues suggest that she is at a crossroads, she is looking for her mate, and she is bewildered.[75] Above this picture appears a question in bold lettering: "Which way?" The ad speaks to the readers directly: "A disoriented adhunika's anxious query to you . . ." Posing a series of polarities that reflect the most contentious issues of its day, and internalizing them as a modern Bengali woman's personal dilemmas, *Agnipareeksha* attempts to work through them within a melodramatic framework. Based on a popular novel by the celebrated woman writer Ashapurna Devi, scripted by a man named Nitai Bhattacharya, and directed by a male collective known as Agradoot, the film echoes the curious vacillations of its female protagonist: it wants to be a reformist film with a feminine perspective but remains very much the product of a heteropatriarchal culture industry.

Tapasi, the heroine, finds herself shuttled between two very different universes. Her parents are upwardly mobile urban folks with decidedly modern aspirations; her grandmother, who still resides in their ancestral mansion in Kusumpur village, holds on to more archaic values. The confrontation between modern-capitalist, individualist-rationalist attitudes on one side, and premodern community-based, duty-bound outlook on another, is staged here as a generational conflict, with the youngsters caught in between. The traditional-modern polarity is further overlaid with the rural-urban dichotomy: in such a Manichean depiction, the countryside is the realm of kind, nurturing, and trustworthy people, although it is ruled by superstitions and is socially and economically stagnant; the city is dynamic and exciting, but is inhabited by artificial, duplicitous, opportunistic people. At stake is the very character of the future citizenry, which is to come into being through moral and cultural transactions between the various poles.

The teenaged Tapasi is close to her grandmother and enjoys visiting her in Kusumpur. On one of these trips, the grandmother accedes to her dying friend's request and marries Tapasi off to his grandson Bulu. The young bridegroom seems quite unremarkable, appearing timid and shy; the marriage is never consummated, and soon the bride's enraged parents whisk her off to Calcutta. Over time, the experience seems surreal: Tapasi remembers it mainly as a game in which she was a puppet. Her mother wants her to dismiss the entire episode as a farce and focus on all the great prospects that life has to offer. But in her heart, Tapasi cannot discount the experience, as she had exchanged vows with Bulu, if only mechanically, in a sacred ritual with the fire god (*Agni*) as witness. Eventually she meets and falls in love with Kiriti, a dashing young doctor. He is suave and handsome (all of Tapasi's peers desire him), with multiple foreign degrees (animating a characteristic Bengali middle-class obsession with higher, preferably Western, education), and with both inherited assets and prospects of a considerable future income stream (an attribute that Tapasi's mother takes to). As their intimacy develops, Tapasi becomes increasingly agitated: she cannot decide whether she is married, unmarried, or a widow. Her subjectivity and her fulfillment are determined primarily in terms of her relation to a male mate—current, future, or past. Her female friends are, likewise, caught in a web of constant anticipation: even as educated, cultured, and socially adept young women, they are forever waiting to be discovered and claimed by some man.

The audience is given enough clues to figure out that Kiriti *is* Bulu, her husband, now transformed into a self-possessed, modern, cosmopolitan subject. But Tapasi does not realize this until the very end: through her misrecognition, the narrative dramatizes the confrontation between tradition and modernity as the conflict between the "double" Bulu and Kiriti. Although much of the film unfolds from her point of view, ultimately she remains a pawn in the hands of the primary male subject. Since the audience realizes the truth before the protagonist does, the transgressive potential of her desire for "another" man is contained: it is her masochistic struggles that become the primary locus of spectatorial pleasure. The film abounds in instances of her suffering: out on a date with Kiriti, Tapasi sees a newly married couple, which brings back memories of her own marriage and makes her feel guilty. In a quasi-flashback, which occurs with a traumatic intensity, she sees her face transposed over the young bride's. Indeed, the film depicts Tapasi's experience of her wedding as a trauma, further underscoring the melodramatic displacement, onto more private terrain, of larger social ordeals originating from discontinuities introduced in the name of modernity. As Tapasi's grandmother leads her to the ritual, her bewildered incomprehension is conveyed through a subjective camera and sound montage: an out-of-focus glimpse of Bulu's dying grandfather lying on a bed in the background; tilted close-ups of the chandelier above and the *alpona*[76] on the floor; snatches of the priest's chants and music on the soundtrack. At the end of the film, when Tapasi returns to this ritual space with her old grandmother, close-ups of the chandelier, the (now empty) bed, and the alpona recur. This time, the camera keeps panning with a tilted frame in an accelerating, circular motion, as Tapasi is overwhelmed by her memories. As she is about to collapse to the ground, Kiriti springs forward to her rescue and finally reveals himself as Bulu: the trauma is finally assuaged at the site of its origin.

Ultimately, *Agnipareeksha* implies that there is no real contradic-

Agnipareeksha: Tapasi's trauma

tion, that all conflicts are mere misrecognitions; the ground on which
it makes such a claim is a set of eternal values and behavioral norms
that will enable Bengali society of its time—and, by implication, of all
times—to weather change and emerge unscathed, secure in its essential
qualities. The narrative is able to uphold such a transcendental immuta-
bility through an ideological sleight of hand: the traditional, rural Bulu
(the feudal representative) gets magically reformed into the rational
professional (an agent of modernization). There are no signs of his own
conflicts, no traces of his material and psychic struggles: patriarchy gets
surreptitiously refigured, without ever becoming a contentious category. This cover-up is also the source of the woman's confusion; yet remarkably, it is precisely her misrecognition of Kiriti/Bulu, the narrative
element which should draw attention to the ideological obfuscation,
that deflects attention from it by turning the confusion into a motor of

melodramatic masochism. Therefore, I will argue that *Agnipareeksha*, like most other Uttam-Suchitra films, presents a rather limited vision of the modern woman: her "liberation" is achieved in primarily consumerist mass cultural terms, heavily inflected by upper-class tastes (fashionable clothing, cars, jewelry, houses, pianos and organs, parties, drinking, dancing, Western music). This iconographically modern woman is made to suffer the contradictions, without much promise of transformation. On the one hand, Tapasi's grandmother reiterates that dharma is far more important than one's desires, that love (*priya*) is secondary to what is morally desirable (*shreya*); on the other hand, her mother constantly harangues her about the imperative of finding an accomplished mate. The title of the film, which translates as *Trial by Fire*, alludes to an episode in the epic *Ramayana*, which provides a framework for the subordination of Indian women: Sita's subjection to a test of her purity, after her return from captivity, by entering a blazing fire. The reference does not challenge the subjection so much as it reiterates Sita as a model of Indian womanhood. The name *Tapasi* also refers back to Indian antiquity, to women who would undertake vows and meditate steadfastly to achieve a goal that, frequently, would be an ideal husband.

Discourses around the two stars also reveal a certain gendered differentiation. An early piece on the couple commented on their acting competencies, and on their good looks; while it lauded Suchitra Sen's graceful demeanor, sweet speaking style, and felicity of expressions, it pointed to Uttam Kumar's natural flair for broad-minded, unselfconscious, and lively characters.[77] The focus, clearly, was on Sen's feminine grace, and on Uttam's self-assured masculinity. Their offscreen mythologies, elaborated upon in fanzine hagiographic accounts, further strengthened such impressions. Uttam Kumar became the most influential persona in the Bengali film industry: for a major part of the sixties and the seventies, he was a virtual one-man industry, as the fortunes of Bengali cinema became crucially dependent on his box-office draw. Meanwhile, Suchitra Sen left acting after bouts of illness, which apparently affected her looks. Even at the peak of her career, she was constantly worried about how she would look on-screen, trying to be photographed from her "better side," thus belying popular impressions about her self-possessed nature.

One significant moment in the film explores masculinity in relation to class. When Kiriti throws a garden party, some lower-class goons peep over the wall to watch *deshi mem*s (Indian women who act like Westerners) dance. They like what they see, and try to crash the party; as one of them remarks, "We are now citizens of an independent country." Invoking the democratic ideals of the incipient nation-state ironically, the film draws attention to the distance that exists between political democracy, already institutionalized through universal adult franchise, and social and economic egalitarianism, which remain a dream. Furthermore, the film performs a fundamental tension between populism and elitism: it capitalizes on the lifestyle of the upper-class socialites and recognizes the vicarious pleasure derived by mass audiences from watching high society at play; it also makes fun of the leisure class through the sarcastic comments of the lumpen intruders, and through stereotypical representations of the nouveau riche (Tapasi's mother, her mannered friends, the effete and clownish Mr. Lahiri). Thus, the film develops an array of identificatory entry points for a segmented audience, playing on sameness and difference, simultaneously promoting a desirable hegemony and trangressive pleasures.

If the cultured members of the gathering are all cowering and helpless in the face of aggressive lumpen behavior, Kiriti is of a different mettle. He is the outsider who has made his way in; he is also the more conscientious face of elite society, who does not look down upon the masses but will not put up with anarchy either. Rejecting some of his guests' suggestion that they call the police for the protection of the women, Kiriti takes on the intruders and beats them up. Having incorporated a critical class commentary, the narrative restitutes authority to the extant elite patriarchal order, with one significant modification. This is Kiriti's pivotal scene, in which he emerges as the scion of a reformed patriarchy. He does not have to depend on the state, and proves to be an able protector of the law, property, and propriety on his own. However, his act is not the macho bravado of an oppressive feudal despot: he acts rationally to punish some goons for their reprehensible behavior. His feudal, traditional background, his rootedness in inherited values, and his training in modern, rationalist thought, mark him out as the perfect citizen of a new national order. Transcending the tradition/modernity divide, embodied here in the Bulu/Kiriti doubling, he emerges as the reconstituted patriarchal subject who can spearhead the modernization of society and simultaneously safeguard time-honored structures.

What, then, can one say in retrospect about the historical-cultural value of *Agnipareeksha*, and of Uttam–Suchitra films in general? As the above discussion demonstrates, these romantic tales circulated as national fantasies within a local context, promoting specific social transformations and recalibration of self-concepts that were deemed essential to a project of nationhood. In the ravaged world of Bengal, they undertook the more primary, if onerous, task of extricating an entire population from a deep melancholy through the restitution of a sense of plenitude in terms of the recurrent narrative union of the romantic

Agnipareeksha: The pleasures of bourgeois life

stars. The connection between the two leads, continuing across roles in multiple films, took on the aura of destiny: they appeared to belong to each other forever, across various lives. In the imagination of countless fans, if Uttam Kumar was as desirable as Krishna, the love god, then Suchitra Sen was the mortal incarnation of Lakshmi, one of Krishna's consorts: the fact that people close to Sen called her Rama, which is another name for Lakshmi, only strengthened this joint deification. Sacral legend blended with pop-cultural hagiography to produce star mythology, generating secular cultural value. But it was not just the eventual union of the lovers that produced a sense of fulfillment. These melodramas frequently depicted a plush life in upper-class settings: restaurants and bars in luxury hotels, where cabaret performers entertained the rich; social clubs where the urban elite threw parties to celebrate yet another achievement, or to commemorate yet another anniversary; plush living rooms (often with a majestic, arced staircase in one corner, on which the heroine would make her grand appearance) where the leads played on the grand piano and sang mellifluous songs.[78] The fantasies afforded a kind of vicarious pleasure that was a welcome respite for mass audiences reeling from the hardships of quotidian life in post-Partition, postfamine Bengal. By exposing them to postwar consumerism and painting alluring pictures of the good life, these films sought to bring audiences out of melancholic pessimism and enjoin them to the task of national development within a state-regulated capitalist framework.

Tenacious Specters

If the trauma of Partition was, by and large, excised from Bengali films of the late forties and the fifties, it still left its oblique traces. The most obvious and common way in which the ordeal insinuated itself back into films was, perhaps, as an overarching sense of economic doom, concretized in the figures of refugees, orphans, the homeless, and the unemployed. Even when these characters remained marginalized in the narrative, they would hover persistently in the background, as signposts indexing the depleted social matrix. If a rare film managed to eliminate these abject figures altogether, it could not erase an anxious undercurrent that coursed through the cultural sphere. Bengali society, with its bruised, famished, and uprooted multitudes, was spiraling into an abyss: former middle-class families from the east were now beggars on the streets, markets, and railway platforms of Calcutta, while people in the western districts were facing difficulties from the tremendous strain on local resources. This rampant déclassé drift generated intense anxiety in the Bengali psyche, across all classes: it was the fear of slipping economically, of not being able to hold onto accustomed lifestyles, of becoming proles or, worse still, destitutes. As native inhabitants of West Bengal struggled to maintain their position, and the eastern refugees fought to regain a modicum of their dignity, there was a curious displacement of a host of socioeconomic concerns onto one single category: one's *bhadralok* (gentry) origins assumed a new significance as a way of marking oneself out from riffraff. Even if a family was out on the pavement or living in a slum, it could assert its entitlement to respect, if it could prove to be from a background of some distinction. Being bhadra implied being cultured, educated, of some means; if the economic resources were lost now due to historical forces beyond individual control, a bhadralok still had his refined breeding and could therefore expect some consideration from his more fortunate social peers. This expectation, while based on a rather tenuous premise, gathered some social force. People bought into it partly due to a modern Bengali obsession with the niceties of bourgeois middle-class life. Perhaps more important was the sheer shock of seeing so many people, not very different from oneself, in such a predicament, and experiencing the double-edged sensation of empathy mixed with apprehension about one's future.

The poignant anxiety of the déclassé bhadralok, which seeped over to other segments of the population, provided the dramatic charge in many a melodrama of the period. Its presence is most evident in romantic narratives in which the lovers come from disparate economic backgrounds; even when there is no gap in economic status and the narrative tension derives from some other difference (education levels; old money vs. the nouveau riche; a lovers' tiff due to some misunderstanding), the friction is often presented as deriving from one party's lack of social refinement—being *abhadra*. My point here is that the sociocultural obsession with being bhadra that runs through Bengali film narratives of the fifties in general, and the Uttam–Suchitra vehicles in particular, reveals a widespread apprehension about the economic and social decline of Bengal and thus hearkens back, ultimately, to the dual trauma of the 1943 famine and the 1947 bifurcation.

Signs of Laceration: Two Kinds of Bengalis

There is more concrete cultural evidence to support my reading of the collective stress on respectability as an expression of anxieties surrounding Partition. In post-1947 West Bengal, the refugees from the eastern districts of undivided Bengal are referred to as *bangal*s; the native inhabitants of the western districts are known as *ghoti*s. As I noted in the introduction, the two groups differ in terms of dialects, social customs, rituals, and culinary habits. As Calcutta was the main center of culture and commerce in undivided Bengal, the official Bengali language developed around that city in southwest Bengal; the western part was more urbanized, while the eastern part remained primarily agrarian. Since the onset of modernity in the nineteenth century, West Bengalis or ghotis from the Calcutta area, who are generally Hindu, have enjoyed a certain cultural ascendancy within Bengal:[79] they consider themselves more modern, more culturally refined, and more progressive than the bangals, who are dismissed as comparatively backward country bumpkins.

With the influx of impoverished *bangal* refugees after 1947, the rural/urban, backward/modern polarization took on another layer of signification: the have-nots and the haves. Now, as West Bengal (and particularly Calcutta) teetered with thousands of homeless refugees, as infrastructural facilities began to collapse, and social problems took on staggering proportions, ghoti condescension turned into rancor. The bangals, already thought to be coarse, illiterate and uncouth, were now blamed for the economic decline and the social woes of the province; they were found to be abhadra in every sense. The entire discourse of respectability and refinement, which was such a major element in fifties' Bengali cinema, masked deeply ambiguous sentiments—and often outright animosity—toward the bangal refugees. In this sense, the anxiety about bhadralok status was a transfigured expression of apprehension about socioeconomic uncertainties.

Several comedies sought to accommodate and diffuse accentuated bangal–ghoti tensions within humorous settings.[80] The differences between the two groups were exploited to produce farcical situations that became occasions for conducting complex negotiations in a light vein. The most common strategy was to introduce a stereotypically bangal character in the proceedings, to produce good-natured conflict and a few laughs. By the end, of course, all dispute would be settled, and general camaraderie would prevail: audiences would feel secure in the knowledge that in spite of their difference, the bangal refugees could be assimilated within the mainstream population of West Bengal. As with all stereotypical representations, the minority was depicted as being different from the norm, and turned into objects of ridicule: on grounds of their accent, their deportment, their customs and food habits, even their disorientation in new surroundings. And ridicule, even when framed as amiable teasing, is still ridicule: it proceeds from an assumption of cultural inferiority.

Of course, the majority group is never fully confident in its presumed superiority and must work at securing it through constant reiteration. Underlying the jovial teasing is a thinly veiled animosity that surfaces at the slightest threat to the established cultural hierarchy. Consider, for instance, the caricatural character of Kedar in *Sharey Chuattar* (the first film starring the Uttam and Suchitra pair), a rollicking comedy set in a boarding house. Kedar embodies the stereotypical concept of a loud-mouthed, crass, and ultimately absurd bangal who seems forever famished: as soon as his friend returns from home after a vacation, he hastens to see if he brought back homemade ghee; he frequently visits people who serve good quality tea; smelling freshly made dessert, he runs around looking for the source. He is the jocular friend of the hero Rampriti (played by Uttam Kumar); but once they start wooing the same girl, Ramala (Suchitra Sen in her screen debut), he turns into a scheming fiend. Of course he is too inept to cause any serious damage: his pathetic attempts at winning Ramala's affections produce mere hilarity. Failing both in romance and in villainy, the bangal is reduced to a harmless clown—a comic plot device.

Bhanu Bandyopadhyay, who played Kedar, was a real-life bangal who made an entire career out of his bangalness, on stage, screen, radio, and comedy recordings.[81] In spite of all the stereotyping, he managed to infuse his early comic roles with a certain pathos that confronted audiences with a sense of the real contradictions of post-Partition West Bengal: his characterizations, marked by a poignant excess, obliged spectators to bear witness to the material and psychic tribulations of the displaced. Over time, this urgency and intensity was lost: Bandyopadhyay's bangal characters became forced and hackneyed. Indeed, it would be an interesting exercise to study the trajectory of this popular comedian's acting career as a way of understanding the gradual cultural assimilation of East Bengali refugees over the years, and the complete reification of the bangal as a comical archetype.

Bandyopadhyay also appeared in *Ora Thake Odhare* (1954), another comedy featuring Uttam Kumar and Suchitra Sen, which could well be the most explicit comic depiction of the ghoti–bangal rift. The film is exemplary in its refusal to project one group's cultural superiority over the other; instead, it engages the quirks of both groups, allows a great deal of name-calling on both sides, and finally comes across as a strong plea for mutual understanding and coexistence. While the film is about the interactions of two families, one ghoti, the other bangal, that happen to be neighbors, the title—which translates as "They live on the other side"—clearly alludes to the other Bengal across the new political border; it engages contemporary social sentiments, locating the comedy as a microcosm of a larger reality. If the narrative thrives on humorous confrontations arising from differences between the two families (expressed in absurd bickering and ricocheting snubs[82] involving education, upbringing, sophistication, and so on), it also stresses the commonalities: both families have similar material needs (they share one iron, one radio, one sewing machine); they depend on each other in their daily lives (the ghoti wife sends the bangal daughter on an errand; the ghoti father borrows money to help out the bangal patriarch). There is significant intermingling of tastes, crossing of cultural boundaries: for instance, while the bangal head of the family keeps buying *hilsa* fish (a decidedly bangal culinary obsession), the ghoti patriarch happens to crave hilsa in hot mustard sauce (a typical bangal preparation).

As East Bengali refugees settled down in their new surroundings and faced partial, but inevitable, assimilation, they came to focus on certain practices and attributes as the fulcrums of their distinctive cultural identity. Supporting the soccer team East Bengal emerged as one of the pivotal rituals defining a bangal identity in West Bengal. The team's rivalry with its ghoti counterpart, Mohun Bagan, spilled out of the sports arena into every corner of the province. *Ora Thake Odhare* portrays this sports rivalry in a hilarious scene, when the two families assemble in one room to listen to the radio coverage of a soccer game. A series of short takes, often in close-up and medium close-up, capture the shifting excitement as the game proceeds. The scene ends with a rather theatrical long take, in which the entire group is held in a frontal long shot, fighting loudly with wild gesticulations: what we get is something like a tableau, allowing us to "hear" the linguistic differences and "see" the idiosyncratic mannerisms. The radio reception is rather poor: it crackles and fades out from time to time, as the two families strain their ears over their own voices. The scene leaves audiences with a distinct feeling that in spite of all their differences, the ghoti and the bangal families are in a similar predicament: that the faulty radio reception signifies larger historical problems, beyond individual agency, that all inhabitants of 1950s West Bengal have to face together. Interestingly, it is the men who initiate fights between the two families, while the women try to get along. The film reiterates a gendered conception of public and private spheres, according to which the men operate in a rational, competitive domain of commerce, politics, and law and cannot help carrying over some of their workplace aggression into their homes; the women, who primarily tend to the domestic space, are more nurturing and accommodating. The men in this diegetic world want to rehearse social antagonisms even with their close neighbors; in contrast, the women want to get along, to build community with the new people in their surroundings. The more caring, "feminine" traits find their purest expression in the character of a middle-aged aunt who arrives fresh from a village in East Bengal. She does not understand the hardened, world-weary attitudes of the big city, nor does she get the tension between the two types of Bengalis; in her rustic simplicity, she wants to embrace her new neighbors as her kith and kin. In her figure, the film celebrates, and also mourns, what seems to have been lost to Bengalis as a result of the political severance.

Violence, Terror, Shame

Communal violence remained one component of the Partition experience that could not be easily sublimated by fantasy or by comedy. Violence terrorizes; it hurts, humiliates, and leaves deep scars both on the body and the psyche. The emotions that violence mobilizes—fear, anger, hatred, shame—are experienced with an undeniable intensity; they refuse to be domesticated by textual processes. Violence in cinema, unfolding with a mimetic potency, raises particularly charged ethico-political questions.[83] Not surprisingly, much like its Hindi counterpart, popular Bengali cinema of the 1950s shied away from direct representations of the trauma. And yet, as with Hindi films of the period, it is possible to locate indices of communal aggression and victimization in Bengali films. But do we see instances of explicit engagement in, say, the Uttam and Suchitra melodramas? Given their preoccupation with the woman's suffering, do they venture to address the rampant abduction and rape?

In many ways, the violation of women became the focal center of the entire experience: it was the source of misbegotten triumph, and of the most abject humiliation. Since members of both Hindu and Muslim communities were involved in the brutalities, and since the victimized women were not the only ones to be tormented by their memories, a sense of shame transcended all facile distinctions between aggressor and victim to engulf the entire Bengali society. Thus the rare reference to the atrocities comes in passing, as a shameful acknowledgment of an experience that did occur (a realist gesture, aimed at establishing a historical milieu), but is too painful to be dwelled upon. Thus, in the film *Sabar Uparey* (1955), the heroine, Rita (Suchitra Sen), tells the hero, Shankar (Uttam Kumar), that she is a "tormented" (*nigrihita*) woman from East Bengal. But the admission becomes a romantic gesture, occurring in the narrative at a point where the two are getting closer. When Shankar expresses his amazement at Rita's willingness to associate with him even after knowing that his father is a jailbird, she reassures him by referring to her own sullied past. Partition trauma figures all too briefly in order to establish a strong bond between two individuals of dubious origins.

As far as I can tell, it was only in the early 1970s that the gendered aspect of Partition violence found substantial representation in a commercial Bengali film. The 1971 civil war in East Pakistan, which resulted in the birth of Bangladesh, created another historical situation that reproduced many of the conditions of 1947. With the genocide of the Bengali population of East Pakistan by the Pakistani army, waves of refugees poured into West Bengal; the violence and dislocation revealed the chronic sociopolitical contradictions in the region and brought back intense memories of past sufferings. Twenty-five years after the end of colonial rule in South Asia, the region's ambitious experiments with modernity and nationhood appeared to be hanging in a precarious balance. An introspective, self-critical tone emerged in certain popular films of this period; for instance *Alo Amar Alo* (1972), which turned out to be Uttam and Suchitra's penultimate film together, evoked painful memories of Partition violence to establish the persistence of certain conflicts and structures of exploitation. Sen plays Atashi, the eldest daughter of a poor family[84] living in an illegal refugee settlement called *Nabajiban Colony*: the name, which signifies a "new life," registers the optimism of these displaced people. The community's women make paper bags and garments and sell them through a cooperative union; the state does not condone the endeavors of these squatters and discourages a nascent leftist consciousness by arresting the guy who tries to organize the folks politically; the people worry about possible eviction by the police; in spite of all the difficulties, the refugees believe they are better off here than the people who stayed on in East Pakistan (a blatantly nationalist position, strengthened by the 1971 carnage in East Pakistan).

Through a series of flashbacks, the film conveys the pleasures of a prosperous past life, and the subsequent turn to madness and mayhem. On Atashi's birthday, her mother makes *payesh*;[85] the dessert brings back her father's fond memories of the pomp with which they celebrated her first birthday in East Bengal. His flashback starts with a shot of fireworks in the night sky; baby Atashi, adorned in flower ornaments, sits on the lap of a Muslim family friend, who expresses his wonder at the lavish arrangements; finally, the film cuts back to the father's smiling face in the present, lost in his nostalgia. Atashi, while cooking in the kitchen, has her own flashback triggered by a mention of Pakistan: there is a transition from the oven fire to a shot of rioters' torches. In a long shot, we see the family running away from their home (a brick and concrete structure, as opposed to the thatched roofs and mud walls of their present quarters) under cover of the night. The flashback ends with a medium shot of Atashi lost in reverie, the oven fire burning high.

This menacing memory forebodes the agony that Atashi will have to endure soon. Trouble comes in the shape of Nilendra (Uttam Kumar), a young industrialist with a deeply ambiguous character. On the one hand, he is highly educated, cultured, and altruistic: declaring that the state already has too much on its hand (and thus making a case for both the social preeminence and the social responsibility of private capital), he provides generous financial aid to the refugees; on the other hand, he uses his class position and clout to exploit women sexually. Holding his loveless upbringing responsible for his pathological inability to love someone (the film carefully humanizes him with his own childhood flashbacks), he goes about satisfying his carnal needs with impunity, without much consideration for his victims' psychological fallouts. While on a tour of the colony, he sees Atashi, likes what he sees, and when her father refuses to sell her to him for money, sends a goon to pick her up forcibly. As Atashi runs to the doctor's chamber to get medical assistance for her ailing mother, she gets abducted. Having been hardened by life's struggles, Atashi does not give in: during the tussle that follows, she gets hit on the head, and loses consciousness. When she comes around, she has lost all her memory, except for the idea that she is looking for a doctor. She mistakes Nilendra for a doctor; he, in turn, feels contrite about the injury she has suffered (as if the abduction, by itself, is not violent) and takes care of her. As an amnesiac, Atashi is plagued by unaccountable flashes of violence, incorporated in the film as rapidly cut shots in negative. Her confusion and bewilderment turn her into a little girl; she comes to trust, and depend completely on, her "doctor."

In the end, maintaining the tradition of uniting the two stars in their films, Nilendra wins over Atashi, but not before she comes out of her amnesiac stupor and takes him to court, mainly to clear her own name. Since the rich industrialist is made to face the law, the film upholds the democratic ideals and institutions of the state. However, the possibility of punishment is enough, as the romantic hero cannot be punished: in court, Atashi admits voluntarily that Nilendra never forced himself on her and actually took care of her in captivity. This admission implicates her with her tormentor, much to the consternation of her family. Here, the narrative clearly plays on the confusing experiences of women abducted during Partition: in captivity, many of them formed tender attachments with their abductors; when the Indian and Pakistani governments arranged for mass exchange of these women, many were unwilling to go back to their original families. The families also harbored mixed feelings about their "tainted" women. By placing the generic union of the romantic leads under the cloud of familial and social disapproval, the film unambiguously commiserates with those unfortunate women and restitutes to them a certain dignity.

Alo Amar Alo resuscitates memories of violence from the Partition era and reframes them in two important ways. By presenting the riots as part of the female protagonist's disquieting memories, the film alludes to the extensive abuse of women during Partition—a connection that is reinforced by her own subsequent torment. At the same time, the film launches a criticism of the state-supported program of capitalist development in the postcolonial era: it implies that the state and the capitalists have collaborated to exploit the poorest sections of the population. These two critical connections jointly lead to a further social allegation: that women are as vulnerable to victimization in the seventies as they were during the maniacal days of the late forties. On what basis, then, can Indians claim that they are a free country, a civil society, a modern nation? Implicitly posing this question in 1972, the year marking the twenty-fifth anniversary of the nation's independence, the film reveals an introspective mood in the cultural field. This self-conscious gesture is not so surprising, as a major anniversary usually becomes an occasion for stock taking. The film's more radical implication relates to Partition historiography: it appears to suggest that perhaps Partition violence is not the exceptional, one-time aberration that it has been made out to be, but rather a particularly flagrant instance of festering problems that are integral parts of the Indian social matrix.

I present these arguments to track the evolution of a particular body of generic romantic melodramas over the years, and to demonstrate how a fantasy of plenitude associated with a pair of stars, once invoked as an antidote to Partition blues, is refigured for subsequent critical purposes. Thus the same discursive trope gets deployed over time for the very divergent purposes of both obfuscating and interrogating conflicts. This shift shows us, once again, that a genre or a mode does not, by itself, constitute an ideological cover-up or an act of revelation, that its function changes with the context in which it is mobilized. The context itself may be more ready to handle certain issues, as is clearly the case with the early 1970s in relation to Partition trauma. In that sense, *Alo Amar Alo* operates more or less within a cultural mainstream, participating in general trends characterizing its contemporaneous politico-cultural hegemony.[86] Nevertheless, with this film, we are clearly in the realm of candid explorations of the collective anguish. In chapter 4, I turn to certain "Partition films" widely celebrated for their thoughtful mediation and their bold political vision.

The Return of the Repressed

CHAPTER FOUR

Dispersed Nodes of Articulation

IN THE THREE DECADES following Partition, explicit representations of the trauma materialized in cinema every once in a while to rend the conformist silence. While these rare films cluster together at certain points in time (1949–50, 1953–54, the early 1960s, and 1973), any straightforward temporal schema is complicated by considerations of modes of production, ideological proclivities, formal and stylistic approaches, and segmented publics. The films fall into four approximate groups: (1) commercial Hindi films of the 1950s and early 1960s; (2) leftist Bengali films of the 1950s; (3) Ritwik Ghatak's films from the early 1960s;[1] and (4) M. S. Sathyu's landmark film *Garam Hawa* (1973), which constitutes a category in and of itself. The Ghatak films are the focus of the next chapter. Among the few commercial Hindi films that address the trauma (*Lahore* [1949], *Apna Desh* [1949], *Firdaus* [1953], *Nastik* [1954], *Chhalia* [1960], *Amar Rahe Yeh Pyar* [1961] and *Dharamputra* [1961]), as many as three revolve around abducted women. The two Bengali films, *Chhinnamul* (1950) and *Natun Yahudi* (1953), have their roots in a leftist cultural scene: produced by people with strong political convictions, these texts adopt an explicitly polemical stance in addressing the dislocation and subsequent problem of rehabilitation of the East Bengali refugees. Sathyu's *Garam Hawa*, while influenced by earlier political works, belongs to a different moment circumscribed by two major historical currents: the rekindling of Partition memories during the 1971 Bangladesh War, and the onset of a period of national reflection whose cinematic signpost was the so-called New Indian Cinema.

The films originate from very different locations and persuasions (politicized cinema self-consciously situated against mainstream cinema and its pursuit of surplus value; regional Bengali cinema as opposed to Hindi and Urdu films aimed at an "All-India" market), and they pose, work through, and resolve the crucial problems of the day in distinctive ways. Nevertheless, they evince remarkable congruencies, engaging similar concerns (statehood and its legitimacy, future of community life, religious difference, autonomous subjectivity, women's agency, mass displacement, and rehabilitation), employing common formal strategies (stock documentary footage, montage of newspaper headlines, voice-of-god commentaries, acute angular shots, realist melodrama) and generic characters (righteous but crisis-prone patriarchs, unwed mothers, disoriented refugees), settings (trains and railway stations, mosques and temples, refugee colonies, alienating urban spaces) and mythologies (narratives of purity and contagion, tales of neighborly benevolence and cynical opportunism, religious fanaticism vs. class politics). Thus, in spite of the temporal and spatial dispersion, certain elements congeal into recognizable tropes.

These equivalences across discrete film theoretic categories—mainstream and oppositional, regional and national, art and commercial—put pressure on their autonomy and exclusivity. When commercial films are as effective as more reflexively political texts in expressing their misgivings about the imposition of artificial and arbitrary political boundaries across a population, and in challenging the postcolonial state's policies with regard to displaced people, how important is it to insist on their mutual alterity? It seems more productive to think of the films as a range of cultural responses, differentially politicized, to a single event, differentially experienced: together, they comprise an emergent discursive configuration about Partition. All the same, the categories remain efficacious not just as convenient heuristics, but also as terms of contestation within a particular cultural modernity which, through their implication in institutional rituals of legitimation and negation, emerge as decisive material forces. Thus the "commercial" film *Apna Desh*, directed by the celebrated social reformist filmmaker V. Shantaram and distributed nationally, is, for all practical purposes, lost: even the National Film Archives in Pune does not have a copy of the film in its collection. Yet the Bengali film *Chhinnamul*, which was seen more widely in the Soviet Union than in Bengal, was preserved by leftist cultural institutions and kept in very limited circulation by alternative channels of distribution. Because the polarized categories spawn their own genealogies, with concrete ramifications, they continue to be useful for film historiography.

Notwithstanding their commonalities, these sporadic moments do not constitute a coherent corpus. Nor does a clear causal chain come into focus from the array of catalytic imperatives (the refugee "problem," recurring riots, Indo-Pakistani face-offs, civil war in East Pakistan, filmmakers' personal sense of loss) behind these films. No one cultural group or movement can claim authorship of these interventions, no such formation can be deduced retrospectively from them. Bearing no fixed or predictable relationship to hegemonic structures, these contingent and unsutured articulations burst through the general silence; unable to dispel that silence, they remain stranded in it. All the same, as manifest expressions of the inchoate sadness coursing through post-1947 public life, these films stand out as defiant signposts of early mourning work—the visible shards of a larger, more "complete" history that remains inaccessible. The precarious and elliptical nature of the hermeneutic that emerges from these scattered articulations underscores the impossibility of grasping the discursive field surrounding Partition in its totality.[2] Thus this chapter, in its structure and feel, stages *en abyme* the central problematic of my project.

Partition Violence in Commercial Hindi Films

In the first thirty years after independence, only a very few Bombay films openly took on the tumult of 1947. While I know of seven such works, I have been able to track down prints or copies of only four: *Lahore, Nastik, Dharamputra,* and *Chhalia*; the rest—*Apna Desh, Firdaus,* and *Amar Rahe Yeh Pyar*—remains frustratingly elusive.[3] Recall the brief discussions of *Nastik* and *Dharamputra* in chapters 1 and 2 above: in the former, the recovery of the hero's religious faith, eroded from the trauma of Partition, takes a trajectory that ultimately regenerates the politically charged notion of an inherently Hindu national space. In contrast, *Dharamputra* upholds a secularist ideal, presenting religious identity as a matter of culture and not of blood. Nonetheless, the precise ways in which these films mediate questions of community and violence merit further attention.

Both films present communal violence in brief, stylized scenes, the shift from a realist to a consciously presentational mode sidestepping ethical problems associated with screen representations of brutality still raw in popular memory. In an early sequence of *Nastik*, shots of the

Nastik: Spectral violence—rioters in silhouette

film's protagonist on a train and documentary footage of refugees are intercut with opaque silhouette shots of homicidal rioters. This montage, accompanied by a song addressed to god and bemoaning the state of the world and the drastic transformation of human beings, expressively conveys the hero's anguish against a backdrop of social mayhem and portends his imminent loss of faith. *Dharamputra* introduces communal tension about midway into its narrative: a middle-aged Muslim couple sadly looks upon angry demonstrators, demanding the bifurcation of the country and the separate state of Pakistan, under the very window from which they once proudly watched anticolonial marchers. Alternating skillfully between shots of public turmoil and disconcerted individual characters, a subsequent sequence builds up to the actual riots: conflicting processions demand *akhand Bharat* (undivided India) or sovereign Pakistan; leaders address huge, restive crowds; Dilip, the protagonist, incites his fanatical, torch-bearing Hindu associates; his secularist brother blames religion for the current impasse. A matted shot of a crowd forms a map of India; the borders of the map burn, until the two extremes fall off, denoting the severing of East and West Pakistan. This cartographic evocation is followed by a collision montage, further accentuating the truncation of the body politic: lightning strikes a tree, whose branches burn down; waves crash onto rocks; scenes of rioting and arson follow. Next comes a scene in which Dilip gets to learn he is actually Muslim by birth; again the film shifts seamlessly from this private melodrama (whose subjective dimension is projected in terms of another montage of an earthquake and falling debris), back to riot scenes. These metonymic chains produce a gripping subjective impression of the madness individuals and social groups were caught up in during the months surrounding Partition. The expressive is yoked here to a rhetorical register: blood from three dead bodies lying on the street flow into one single stream, as a singer—perhaps *vivek*, a personification of conscience—asks, "Whose blood is it? Who are the dead?" Note that in both films, such rhetorical questions are posed in songs that are either nondiegetic or sung by itinerant figures that have no other role in the narrative. Moving away from the individuated drama propelling much of the film, the songs comment on the social carnage: they reframe the violence as aberrant behavior on the part of people who have temporarily lost their sanity and relented to brute instincts, thereby disavowing entrenched social antagonisms and keeping alive the possibility of a national community.

If *Nastik* and *Dharamputra* employ strategies of visual estrangement and aural commentary,[4] *Lahore* goes a step further, acknowledging the difficulties of representing violence formally in terms of a blank screen. Released within two years of the truncation, this film shifts away from the brutality to focus on the subjective dimensions of human suffering. It opens with a strong invocation of an exile's nostalgia; shots of the city of Lahore, taken from a moving vehicle, are accompanied by a man's wistful voice-over declaration: "I have wandered the streets of Indore and Delhi, but they are not the same as the streets of Lahore." Who is the subject of enunciation, this "I" who mourns his banishment from his hometown, who refuses to let other urban sites replace the beloved cityscape that still saturates his memories? As the reminiscing continues, we realize that the voice belongs to thousands of nameless, faceless exiles, forced by the turn of events to abandon their homes. "Thinking of Lahore, my heart beats faster": this accelerating heartbeat has a strong resonance not just for the refugees from Lahore, who have particularly vivid memories of the city, but also for others with similar experiences. The sheer nostalgia and longing that infuse the text (enhanced by simple, nearly imperceptible devices, such as the recurrent use of smoke as a transitional motif between sequences) draw differentiated audiences into the narrative.

Even before the upheaval, the two lovers—the diligent Chaman and his beautiful neighbor Lilo—encounter a series of detours in their romance, which presages their impending separation. While Chaman is away studying in Bombay, Lilo breaks into a forlorn song: the camera begins a slow pan from a street lamp, eventually coming to rest on her in a long shot through a window. The rest of the scene is put together combining medium shots and close-ups, all gorgeously lit to showcase the actress Nargis's striking features. The unbearable intensity of loss and yearning is captured in several similar musical sequences constructed around the lovelorn figure of Lilo.[5] Just as she is about to reunite with Chaman, history intervenes: the nation is truncated, riots erupt, and Lilo gets "lost" in the melee. As Chaman returns to Lahore, with fond plans of moving his family to Bombay, all hell breaks loose. As the family escapes via the back door following an explosion in front of their ancestral home, the screen cuts to a series of newspaper headlines, announcing the Partition.

At this point, the screen fades to blankness for about a minute, registering the impossibility of visually representing the still-raw trauma. As in the opening sequence, an invisible commentator returns on the soundtrack: "And after that, the light receded into darkness. The devil came to rule over the followers of Ram, Krishna, Mohammed and Nanak . . . Human soul had died . . . Refugees, homeless in their own homeland, went towards an unknown destination. Who knows where this journey, started in hatred, was to end." A song following this explication declares the absence of god, as actual footage of refugees is crosscut with shots of various diegetic characters trudging along dusty roads. After much suffering (including the death of Chaman's younger brother), the family reaches the refugee camps of Amritsar in the Indian part of Punjab, the poignancy of these scenes enhanced by mournful *sarengi* music.[6]

The balance of the film centers on Chaman's attempts to locate Lilo in Lahore and reinforces the main narrative strand with subplots about two other abducted women—one a Hindu and the other a Muslim— to make an enlightened plea for the rehabilitation of women who had already suffered enough pain and ignominy.[7] When he realizes that a Muslim man has Lilo captive in her own family home, Chaman refuses to give up on her; putting his life on the line, he disguises himself as a Muslim vendor and eventually rescues her. Even as the film audaciously brings up the socially sensitive issue of women kidnapped by men of another faith, it has to reassure audiences constantly that Lilo has not lost her sense of honor—that, indeed, no Hindu woman would ever come to accept such a debasing situation of her own free will (she is described as a "walking corpse" with "vacant eyes"). Taken to an extreme, this obsession with honor requires an abducted Hindu woman to kill herself; alternatively, Hindu kinsmen are expected to kill these sullied women, to protect the community's honor. It is precisely this kind of fanatical reasoning, which puts the lives of these women in peril, that

Lahore sets out to counter, but it stutters and ultimately falls in line with the patriarchal construal of "woman" as primarily a node of symbolic exchange.

Anil, the protagonist of *Nastik*, reveals a similar mindset. Enraged on learning that his younger sister Kamla has been turned into a "singer" by a rich man, he blames her, turns a deaf ear to her tearful entreaties, and leaves in a huff. The film works hard to consolidate the impression that Kamla is still pure and unsullied, since this happens to be the night of her "debut."[8] But the brother's scorn has a devastating effect: feeling abandoned by her only living kin, Kamla dies of heartbreak. In a sense, it is the brother who kills her, indirectly upholding the tradition of "honor killings." Kamla is cleared of suspicions only posthumously: a contrite Anil rushes back to find her lying dead. Such plot twists mark the film's endemic vacillation regarding abducted women: it punishes the woman for her probable violation even as it confirms her chastity, expresses deep anguish over her predicament, and argues, with great difficulty, for a more sympathetic attitude. Sadly, this "progressive" appeal must still be embedded within a hoary discourse of purity and contagion.

Apna Desh and *Chhalia* present more flesh-and-blood, and hence more conflicted, women protagonists who, in sharp contrast to Lilo, form some kind of bond with their Muslim abductor (*Apna Desh*) or benefactor (*Chhalia*). When they try to return to their families, they face troubled resistance, even outright rejection. Caught between two antagonistic worlds, the women experience a deep crisis of identity: homeless and abandoned in a most profound sense, they belong nowhere. The protagonist of *Chhalia* finds refuge with two underworld criminals— one Muslim, the other Hindu—on both sides of the new border. The film appears to suggest that compared to the state or the bourgeoisie, the lumpen classes are more compassionate, and more equipped from their daily struggles to negotiate social anarchy. Eventually the family and the national community are held up as a woman's proper refuge: she is united with her husband, mainly through the efforts of her two underworld benefactors.

Apna Desh (the title translates as "One's Own Land" or "Homeland") is more radical in its intent. Raped in Pakistan, Mohini, the film's Hindu protagonist, arrives in India as a refugee, only to be ostracized by her kinsfolk. Alone in her new surroundings, she retains a close connection with some people in Pakistan and ends up a "traitor," sending clothes and arms across the border.[9] This extreme confusion of the protagonist—to an extent that she cannot pin down her loyalties—outraged many people at the time of the film's release, raising demands for a ban on it.[10] The armed incursions of Pakistani nationals into Kashmir around the same time did not help the film's reception either. Magazine readers called the film "Apna Trash,"[11] claiming that its duplicity produced "heartbreak."[12] Yet another reader evoked a widely held view that women, when faced with a choice of betrayal and dishonor or loyalty and death, prefer the latter: "No refugee girl or woman would, nay could, dare of, think of betraying the land, which has given shelter, food, clothing, and above all sympathetic treatment to her. She would prefer to commit suicide, and a good many would have done so, rather than be a traitor."[13] Another viewer from Colombo bemoaned the fact that the film was being shown there; he was worried about the poor impression of Indian womanhood being exported to Ceylon.[14] A review of the film went to the crux of the matter, when it denounced the characterization by comparing it to a pedagogical model of *the Hindu woman*: "If there are Hindu women like that [i.e., like Mohini] in this country we have not yet met them. On the other hand *we have read of* thousands of Hindu women through the ages who have willingly thrown themselves into fire and burnt themselves to ashes to prevent even their dead bodies from being polluted by the gaze of their enemies."[15] The reviewer went on to claim that during the Partition massacre, thousands of women in Punjab lived up to these "hallowed traditions" that "we have read of." Then he launched into a diatribe against the producer and director of *Apna Desh*, purportedly on behalf of Indian women of all times:

> Can you find among these women, one woman with the wicked perversity of the heroine of "Apna Desh"? If the answer is in the negative then this picture must be condemned as an unpardonable insult to our unfortunate sisters whose injuries in the hands of our enemies are still fresh and bleeding.
>
> Isn't their cup of destiny bitter enough already that Producer Shantaram should add poison to it and in doing so insult the entire womanhood of India from Sita down to the humblest housewife of our day.[16]

The reviewer insisted that not a single Indian woman deviated from her cherished nationalist ideal during the collective insanity. He seemed remarkably sanguine about the boundaries between Indian self-concepts and "our enemies," given the recent vintage of the separation. In his Hindu patriarchal universe, there was apparently no room for contention or even confusion; any cultural text that raised challenging questions, or offered alternative visions, had to be "condemned."

By the late 1940s, V. Shantaram was already one of the most respected filmmakers in the country. His films, made at studios that he cofounded (Prabhat Studio in Pune, and later, Rajkamal Kalamandir in Bombay), were characterized by a strong zeal for social reform, and thus dovetailed into a Nehruvian program of modernization. In the post-independence era, Shantaram served on various industry bodies and official film boards, including the 1951 Film Inquiry Committee. In 1985, he was awarded the Dadasaheb Phalke Award, the highest honor bestowed by the Government of India to stalwarts of the film industry. His oeuvre is very much a part of the national cinematic canon: the National Film Archives in Pune, located next to the site of Prabhat Studio, holds copies of most Shantaram films. Yet a print of *Apna Desh* is missing from this official collection; it is not available from distributors who market videocopies of his works. It is impossible to dismiss this absence as happenstance: I shall argue that the "disappearance" of the film indexes the threat it was seen to pose to a cultural and political hegemony.

The curious instance of *Apna Desh* reveals the vicissitudes of a cultural field in confrontation with a critical event. A mainstream filmmaker, himself a pillar of the extant cultural hegemony, produces a text in response to a historical crisis that, like the event itself, challenges and undermines vital institutions of that hegemony. One might argue, following Ernesto Laclau and Chantal Mouffe, that a film like *Apna Desh* becomes a temporary *nodal point* around which a whole range of *elements* coalesce and get articulated as a differentiated ("wicked" and "perverse" in the estimation of the *Filmindia* reviewer) position—as a *moment*—within a fledgling Partition discourse in tension with a centralizing nationalist one.[17] Because of its untimely and out-of-joint nature, this critical moment in Shantaram's much-celebrated career gets marginalized; once relegated to cultural oblivion, it remains overlooked even in the 1980s and 1990s, when Partition discourse finally surfaces with full force in the national imaginary.

Leftist Cultural Initiatives in West Bengal

Chhinnamul and *Natun Yahudi*, two Bengali films arising out of leftist cultural praxis, sought to document the plight of East Bengali refugees and to present their rehabilitation as a national problem. In spite of their exploration of pressing contemporary issues such as the material and psychic dimensions of displacement, and the socioeconomic tensions in the wake of the political division, both films failed at the box office. Yet, while *Chhinnamul* has been canonized by the critical establishment, *Natun Yahudi* has, for all practical purposes, been forgotten.

A brief account of the politically animated cultural field of Bengal is necessary to set the production context for these films. By the early

1940s, left-leaning Indian intellectuals felt the need for a strong cultural movement that would foster the growing political consciousness of peasants, workers, and various subaltern groups and shield it from both the cynical manipulations of communal forces and the two-pronged assaults of imperialism and fascism. Accordingly, the Indian People's Theatre Association, popularly referred to as the IPTA, was established in 1942 in Bombay and Calcutta. It was meant to spearhead a grassroots movement with "its roots deep down in the cultural awakening of the masses of India," one which sought "to revive the lost" in India's "rich cultural heritage . . . by interpreting, adopting and integrating it with the most significant facts of the people's lives and aspirations in the people's epoch."[18] By the mid-forties, the IPTA grew into a nationwide movement. Its Film Division sponsored several landmark projects, including *Udayer Pathey* (1944), *Dharti Ke Lal* (1946) and *Neecha Nagar* (1946), which attempted to develop a new realist idiom in Indian cinema. Both its Song and Dance Division and its Drama Division performed for diverse audiences in cities, towns, and villages, always adapting the performances to local contexts. Culture was deployed to mobilize collective resistance and to organize the struggle for freedom, social progress, and economic justice. As one 1990s estimation of the movement puts it, the IPTA remains the "only instance of a cultural avant-garde in contemporary Indian history,"[19] to which one might also add that at its inception, this vanguardism was of a flexible and populist kind, having substantial overlap and exchange with the mainstream culture industry.[20] The movement's strategy of developing collective objectives in terms of local aspirations and the expression of larger struggles through regional folk performance idiolects enabled "several regional movements to forge new links and to reinvent their own local traditions."[21]

Films like *Chhinnamul* and *Natun Yahudi* emerged out of a tradition of cultural activism that congealed around the IPTA in Bengal. The IPTA-produced play *Nabanna* (*New Harvest*, 1943) about the famine of 1943 set new standards for analytical cultural engagement with contemporary history. At once a moving depiction of the travails of starving peasants and an incisive exposé of the famine as a disaster produced through the greed and indifference of powerful social blocs, the play was riveting entertainment even as it mobilized popular consciousness. Several people involved with this project graduated to cinema, bringing with them a politically charged experimentalism: the playwright Bijon Bhattacharya, actor and director Shombhu Mitra, Ritwik Ghatak, and Nemai Ghosh. Ghosh shot and directed *Chhinnamul*, a film whose cast included both Bhattacharya and Ghatak. The play's influence is evident in *Chhinnamul*'s thematic and formal components. Like the play, the film adopts an episodic narrative structure that seeks to explicate the social structures, political institutions, and economic relations that perpetuate the subjection of the masses. In both texts, suffering villagers migrate to the big city in the hope of alleviating their situation; in each case, while the journey fails to solve their problems, it leads to greater political awareness and agency.

According to Nandi Bhatia, the peripheral status of the IPTA in dominant accounts of Indian cultural history can be attributed in part to the movement's "affiliation with 'popular' drama," and its flouting of "canonical assumptions of 'proper' literary and aesthetic values."[22] Much of this marginalization has to do with the movement's association with the Communist Party of India and the complexities of nationalist politics in the forties. In sharp contrast to Gandhi and the Congress Party's strategy of noncooperation with British war efforts, the CPI decided to back the Allies against the Axis powers, in line with the Soviet position that between the fascists and the imperialists, the former posed a greater threat to an incipient global revolution. If this strategic alignment with the British came to be regarded as an antinationalist act, the doubt about the loyalties of the Indian left was reinforced when the IPTA questioned Gandhi's stringent policy of nonviolence, which had gathered a hegemonic force by the early 1940s, in plays like *Roar China* and *Four Comrades*. Only in recent years has a critical establishment come to recognize the importance of the IPTA[23]—not just as an organ of leftist cultural activism centered on the notion of class struggle, but also as a radical democratic force that enabled the articulation of other regional impulses as nuanced political positions.

Chhinnamul begins with a series of vignettes seeking to establish the symbiotic nature of rural community life: as artisans exchange their products and services with their neighbors, they discuss current events and catch up with each other. They draw on folk cognitive frames to interpret political developments in terms that make sense to them: when one guy dismisses the impending division of the country, saying it is not a vegetable that can be cut up easily, his friend reminds him that land does get divided in agrarian feuds. The camera pans languidly across the river, the landscape, and the houses, generating not only an impression of the lushness of rural Bengal but also a sense of imminent loss. Soon this idyllic world comes under the shadow of trouble brewing elsewhere; Srikanta, the most politically aware individual in the community, brings news of a large meeting in a nearby town of political activists seeking to scuttle the imperialists' and communalists' conspiracy of national bifurcation. At home, a couple of moneylenders—one Hindu, the other Muslim, reflecting the greedy opportunism of certain classes across religious lines—hover like vultures, eyeing the peasants' land.

Focusing on Srikanta and his pregnant wife, their hopes and fantasies, the film develops an idea of home that relies heavily on a bourgeois conception of the nuclear family. An awkward scene, involving close-ups of a bird's nest and the couple's exchange of looks, places a rather literal stress on procreation and domesticity. While the metaphor of a bird's nest in the face of a storm does, at one level, work well to portend the precarious nature of the lives of common people caught in the tumult of history, the focus on one couple reveals a fundamental narrative tension between the social and the individual dimensions. As I elaborate below, even as the film wants to uphold the socialist realist dictum "one for all, all for one,"[24] it tends to relapse into a more humanist focus on a heroic male figure.

Srikanta gets jailed on charges of inciting political unrest, trumped up by an alliance between a nervous police force and scheming economic opportunists (the landlord/moneylender types). Using his wife's distress as a frame, the film presents the Partition as an outcome of broader political intrigues, drawing simultaneously on folk idioms to convey the subjective affect in terms of natural calamities. From a close-up of a lamp flame, the camera pans to an empty pillow, then to the wife's face as she sleeps. Cut to clouds; cut to turbulent waves; thunder and raging storm on the soundtrack; the wife whimpers in her sleep, then wakes up; waves crash on a disintegrating riverbank; a bugle is sounded. The image of swirling waves is superimposed with images of angry congregations in cities: a Muslim leader declares "Pakistan," a Hindu leader proclaims "Hindustan"; these emphatic utterances are crosscut repeatedly, so that they become antagonistic retorts; the congregations turn to violent demonstrations. Riot scenes dissolve into a newspaper headline: "Is Bengal going to be divided?" Two villagers at the grocery store anxiously deliberate the confounding turn of events; the camera tilts down the weighing scale, coming to rest in close-up on a bag made of recycled newspaper: on its side is the telling headline, "Bengal gets partitioned."[25] The truncation insinuates itself into the materiality of quotidian life.

Rumors of spreading brutality circulate across the nervous rural community; a voice-over narration, combining direct expository commentary with reported dialogue, conveys the bewilderment. There is a raw energy at work in these sequences that also bear the marks of a low-budget production. Another striking formal strategy involves the initiation of an action on the soundtrack, and then letting the reactions develop through images. These sound-image montages—which Ghatak refines in his films (see chapter 5)—create a polyvocal texture, engaging multiple subjectivities, attitudes and modalities (urban/rural, haves/have-nots, opportunists/victims). Such density is evident in the sequence in which the two landlords/moneylenders urge villagers to

Chhinnamul: The old woman refuses to abandon her ancestral home.
Courtesy of NFAI.

leave for Calcutta, where the government will provide them with food, shelter, even land: when a disheartened family decides to leave, these connivers buy up all its property at preposterously low prices.

The film captures the trauma of getting uprooted from one's ancestral home, both naturalized and sacralized by generations of forefathers (the phrase *satpurusher bhitey* used in these scenes refers to the home and hearth of seven generations of patrilinear ancestors). Srikanta's wife is convinced by her neighbors to go to Calcutta with them, but she refuses to sell their house, so that he has a home to return to upon his release from jail. A woman neighbor sobs inconsolably as she tries to pack as much as she can, in spite of the long, arduous journey ahead. The wrenching misery of displacement becomes palpable in a heart-rending scene involving an old widow who refuses to leave. Grabbing on to a post supporting the roof, she stubbornly repeats, "Jamu na, jamu na, jamu na" (Won't go, won't go, won't go). Neighbors and members of her family entice her with the prospect of bathing in the holy Ganges water in Calcutta, but she seems more interested in her familial moorings than in such an enforced pilgrimage. Withered, uncomprehending, yet unrelenting, she emerges as an emblematic figure of loss.

The director, Nemai Ghosh, had spent his formative years in East Bengal. The distress of countless refugees from that region moved him to action: as a photographer and documentary filmmaker, he felt an obligation to represent their plight, to analyze the forces that had produced such a social catastrophe. While his experience with the IPTA's drama division inspired him to work within the popular format of fiction film, he incorporated some documentary footage, most notably the high-angle panoramic shots of refugees on the platforms of Sealdah train station in Calcutta; he also included some real-life refugees in the cast. His approach calls into question the traditional polarization of fiction and nonfiction films, shifting the focus to overall discursive strategies. Indeed, *Chhinnamul* displays all the four tendencies of documentary filmmaking that Michael Renov lays out for us: "to record, reveal and preserve" (a real, historical trauma); "to persuade or promote" (the magnitude of the refugees' suffering, the need for their rehabilitation); "to analyze or interrogate" (the national and local forces that caused and intensified the distress); "to express" (a poetics of suffering, e.g., the real-life shot of a naked, emaciated child trying to stand up, and falling down on the pavement).[26] While Ghosh had not seen any Italian neorealist film yet, he had read about, and seen stills from, Vittorio De Sica's *Bicycle Thieves* (1948) and Roberto Rossellini's *Rome, Open City* (1945). In his attempt to fashion a realist idiom that could capture various aspects of a historical tragedy of the magnitude of the Partition, he drew on strategies associated with politically inflected realist film movements.

If Ghosh was obliged to document the travails of people he thought were similar to him, he was also forced to acknowledge their experiential difference from him in the figure of the old refugee woman who played the part of the widow refusing to leave her home. As Ghosh himself narrates in an interview, when he tried to direct her acting in the scene, she quietly pointed out that he could teach her about the technical aspects of filmmaking—lighting, camera movements, even acting techniques; as for the dimension of suffering, he simply did not have the emotional resources to instruct her.[27] Deferring to the truth of her assertion, Ghosh simply supplied her with bits of dialogue. Her performance was improvised, drawing on her own experiences: sitting on her haunches, curled up against a hostile world, bowing her head down to convey both incomprehension and dejection, resolutely holding on to the post, uttering the same words over and over again. Her "acting" emerged as the film's pivotal moment; over time, she became an intertextual presence through similar characters in subsequent Partition narratives—for example, in *Garam Hawa*.[28]

For his part, Ghosh, in attempting to achieve a "documentary realism" by casting real-life refugees, came to bear witness to their predicament: not as much through empathetic identification as through the recognition of their irreducible difference. If the film does not explicitly foreground this aspect of witnessing, it nevertheless impressed many contemporaneous viewers with its "honest" depiction of dislocation and suffering, radically different from the usual reduction of refugees to objects of either derision or pity. One reviewer notes that "possibly for the first time" the East Bengali dialect "ceases to be an object of cheap satire and fun at the hand of vulgarly unimaginative producers."[29] Particularly impressive is the portrayal of a complex array of emotions among refugees on the train: one guy smiles as his fellow refugee dozes off on the floor of the overcrowded compartment; tears well up in another man's eyes as the train crosses the border; as they approach Calcutta, their faces light up with excitement. Once in the city, the narrative focuses on the refugees' struggles: on the station platform, competing with each other for a little space; on the streets, in their frustrating attempts to find jobs; in the empty mansion, which they come to occupy as illegal squatters, and where they have to face the wrath of the unsympathetic landlord and his goons. In each situation, the film adds expressive touches to reveal the ironies of refugee life: punning on the Bengali word *tika*, which means both "vaccination" and "survival," one man comments on their precarious existence in the middle of epidemics—being able to survive only with the help of vaccines; as a girl plays on the railway platform with her toys, a woman wonders when their "doll's house" existence will end; the man who used to be a skilled goldsmith is seen hawking mass-produced plastic combs on the streets; the village ironsmith cannot find a job in the automobile body shops; when the rich landlord calls them illegal squatters, the villagers tell him indignantly that they had once willingly provided shelter to people who lost their homes to an encroaching river.

The strong pressures of life in exile start to split the group up, as various members break away to try their own luck: their sense of community cannot be sustained in the face of competitive pressures and capitalist incentives. At this point, the film itself shifts its focus from the group to an individual. Released from prison, Srikanta comes to Calcutta, looking for his wife and neighbors. As he searches everywhere, we catch glimpses of the city from a newcomer's overwhelmed perspective. When he locates the group after a long search, following a newspaper report about the illegal possession of a building by refugees, the landlord is about to have the group thrown out by force; the narrative ends with the hint that he may be able to avert such eviction. Moving away from a more egalitarian plot foregrounding the collective dimensions of suffering and resistance, the film reveals a deep-rooted investment in the bourgeois notion of an illustrious being—a male subject who is also a natural helmsman. This tilt foreshadows problems that come to plague leftist cultural initiatives by the early 1960s: masculinist cultural vanguardism leading to elitist impulses; democratic norms giving way to a cult of personality; ego clashes splitting cultural groups into competing factions.[30] Although Srikanta turns up to lead his people, his hapless wife dies in childbirth; while the man answers a call to broader social action, the woman pines away for a large part of the narrative and eventually perishes. In this respect *Chhinnamul* aligns itself with a popular Bombay film like *Shaheed*, whose heroine also withers away yearning for her beloved; in this respect, it seems more archaic than other popular films like *Biallish*, *Pahela Admi*, and *Samadhi*, whose female protagonists become active social subjects.[31]

Chhinnamul ran for only two weeks in Calcutta. According to the noted filmmaker Mrinal Sen, it failed at the box office not because of a lack of spectatorial enthusiasm for the subject, but because it failed to engage audiences in terms of a gripping narrative structure.[32] For Sen, while the individual shots were remarkable, the editing left much to be desired: the sequences never flowed together, the denouement was often disappointing. Nevertheless, the film was well received in the international film festival circuit; upon Pudovkin's glowing recommendation, it was widely released and seen in the Soviet Union. This favorable reception by the Soviet cultural establishment turned the film into a treasured art object for the Indian left, ensuring its preservation and continued, if limited, circulation. Half a century later, it remains a remarkable creation of an alternative model of cultural production, one that purports to engage self-consciously in broader sociohistorical struggles. In this, it follows the legendary IPTA play *Nabanna*; in its inauguration of a new realism in Bengali cinema, it prefigures and makes possible the more humanist and more widely celebrated *Pather Panchali* (1955).[33]

Natun Yahudi was produced by members of the *Kranti Shilpi Sangha* (Revolutionary Artists' Union), the cultural wing of the Revolutionary Socialist Party.[34] It was originally produced onstage in 1949—one of several Bengali plays seeking to interrogate the catastrophic sociohistorical milieu of the 1940s[35]—under the apolitical banner of *Uttarsarathi*, in a conscious bid to draw a wider audience. Following the play's success, it was turned into a film by the playwright Salil Sen. I have not seen the film,[36] but by all available accounts, the screen adaptation was a failure: while it ran in Calcutta theaters for about seven weeks, it went practically unnoticed outside the city.[37] The title *Natun Yahudi*, which translates as *The New Jew*, signals a desire to place a specific experience of homelessness in relation to other historical experiences of dispersion, to locate the refugees' hardships within a long tradition of struggles on the part of the displaced. The title invokes, by association, certain tropes of

Soviet poster for *Chhinnamul*. Courtesy of NFAI.

mobility—exile, exodus, search for a homeland, diaspora—that provide a cognitive grid for understanding the displacement of Bengali refugees, for countering the oppressive ossification of categories like nation, state, border and citizenship, and for resisting discrimination based on concomitant antinomies (citizen/alien, resident/exile, ghoti/bangal).

The narrative centers on the woes of a displaced family from East Bengal, consisting of schoolteacher Manmohan Pandit, his wife, their sons Mohan and Duikhya, and their daughter Pari. The memory of Manmohan's eldest son, who died in the freedom struggle, inspires the family to hold on fiercely to an idealism that seems hopelessly misplaced in the post-independence era. Mohan turns down a job to express his solidarity for striking workers, choosing to become a coolie instead. However, Duikhya gives up on high ideals and becomes a crook.[38] The father, originally a teacher, finally gets a job as a cook, but a series of mishaps pushes the already déclassé family over the brink: the father falls sick; Duikhya is run over by a train; to raise money for their treatment, Pari sells herself to a gangster and runs away from home. The father dies of heartbreak, the son of his injury. Finally, the father's delayed pension arrives from East Pakistan—too late to save the family. Through an unrelentingly grim chain of events (repeated with minor variations in later films like *Meghe Dhaka Tara* and *Alo Amar Alo*), the narrative captures the absolute devastation brought upon common people's lives by the political division of Bengali society. In particular, it points to the emergence of a displaced underclass in the absence of proper reparations; it also puts to test an earlier nationalist idealism in the context of the actually existing nation-state.

The film is particularly incisive in exposing the indifference, even outright hostility, which the refugees face in their new surroundings. Upon his arrival in Calcutta, Mohan has a dispute at the train station with volunteers who are supposed to be helping refugees. When the family looks for a place to rent, the landlords raise trivial objections to refuse accommodation. This discrimination by West Bengalis against people who were more or less similar to them was legitimated through the disowning of certain traits (dialect, food habits, deportment), reified— through repetition—as terms of difference. In Homi Bhabha's terms, the hybridity inherent to Bengali identity was concretized and mobilized in post-Partition West Bengal as the "condition of subjection."[39] The culture of Calcutta was enshrined as "modern Bengali culture"—a veritable mother culture in relation to which cultures of other areas of Bengal, including the east, would remain the mutants or bastards. In terms of such a strategy, people who were "quite similar" were turned into people "quite different" and therefore could be treated with arrogant contempt.

Eschewing the mainstream production of the reified bangal type,[40] using East Bengali dialects throughout, and calling attention to the discrimination that refugees were subjected to, *Natun Yahudi* became a polemical intervention within a cultural field whose mediation of social contradictions, brought to the fore by the cataclysm, had been largely indirect, evasive, even conservative. Besides the film's alleged aesthetic limitations, this aspect surely helps explain its failure at the box office. Indeed, one review claimed that the film's extensive use of East Bengali dialects and its critical take on West Bengali attitudes toward the refugees were "flaws" that would antagonize audiences.[41] Not surprisingly, the film also faced objections from censorship authorities over its ironic depiction of the refugees' abject suffering in sharp contrast to the aspirations of the incipient nation-state. The contested scene depicted displaced families huddling at the railway station under government-sponsored posters promoting tourism, with the slogan "See India" inscribed in bold letters; it clearly intended to present homeless refugees as an integral part of India, and to challenge more exalted visions of the national space (e.g., a shot of the Darjeeling mountains). Sensing a subversive intent in this ironic juxtaposition, the censor board demanded that the scene be either cut or reshot. Since there were no funds for reshooting, and since the scene included important dialogue, the production team had to manually scratch out the "See India" inscription, frame

Natun Yahudi: Refugee talks to volunteer at Sealdah station, with tourism posters in background before the legends were scratched out. Courtesy of Biswaranjan Chatterjee.

by frame, from about twenty feet of film. Thus the final cut bore only the emulsion-free trace of a tactical reappropriation whereby a statist directive had been turned into a sardonic articulation of official indifference and ineffectuality regarding a grave and poignant social problem.

National Self-Reflection: New Indian Cinema

Garam Hawa, released in 1973, also encountered initial opposition from the censor board; eventually, it won the President's Gold Medal as the best film of the year. This strange turn in the official evaluation of the film was a sign of more fundamental shifts at a historical conjuncture marked by national self-reflection and flux.

Recent scholarship on the evolution of contemporary India stresses the gradual unraveling of some of the central tenets of a nationalist project of modernization.[42] Bhikhu Parekh describes Prime Minister Nehru's own shift from a program of modernization carried out by an active centralized state, led by a westernized neocolonial elite, to a greater faith in local government (the *panchayati raj*) and indigenous models of development.[43] Moving away from his earlier focus on heavy industries, imported technology, and higher education, Nehru started to advocate agricultural advancement and primary education in the late 1950s. But he did not have a chance to see this transition through: the liberation of Goa from the Portuguese authorities in 1961, the routing of the Indian army in the 1962 border war with China, and dissension within the Congress Party over his foreign policy kept him distracted until his death in 1964. In the post-Nehru era, his cherished democratic ideals suffered serious erosion; the autonomy of the state was compromised by the emergence, through the collusion of an industrial bourgeoisie and multinational interests, of strong and influential lobbying groups. Indira Gandhi responded to the rising popular unrest by initiating a program of socialist centralization, whose linchpin was the ambitious nationalization of private banks. The socialist stance remained mainly a matter of rhetoric: the drive toward further centralization became the preeminent concern and was extended aggressively to the political field. By the early 1970s, the legitimacy of a highly centralized state had come to be widely questioned. Rajni Kothari argues that the state attempted to compensate for this loss of moral authority through the exercise of force.[44] Various antistate mobilizations, of which the extremist Naxalite movement became most prominent, were quashed by the army and paramilitary forces. This tendency was to culminate in the declaration of a state of national emergency in 1975, whereby Mrs. Gandhi's government suspended most civil and political rights in the name of governance and came down severely on its adversaries and all centrifugal forces. Ultimately, this draconian measure would pave the way for the deposition of the Congress Party from power in 1977, after three decades of uninterrupted rule. But the signs of change were well in position by the end of the 1960s.[45]

The crisis of the state engendered a wide sense of disillusionment: Partha Chatterjee refers to his discovery of a "persistent feeling" among Indians in the 1970s "that their leaders and their organization [Congress Party] had betrayed them."[46] They no longer seemed to share a common conception of what they stood for, or what they could be loyal to: in other words, there was a great uncertainty about the very basis of political community. The commemoration of the twenty-fifth anniversary of independence and Partition in 1972 became an occasion for national introspection; the emergence of Bangladesh through the splitting of Pakistan in 1971 revived memories of the earlier bifurcation, producing both nostalgia and a strong awareness of persistent conflicts in the region.

With various elements of the Indian social field coming together in novel constellations, new political imperatives came to be articulated, inaugurating a new discursive regime: a fresh phase in the career of the nation, marked by a greater willingness to confront past traumas and engage with heretofore taboo questions, had begun. This, then, was the context of *Garam Hawa*'s production and reception. A largely bureaucratic censor board's trepidation about a film that addressed the plight of a Muslim family in post-Partition India stemmed largely from a tacit understanding that such issues ought to be avoided—an understanding that dated from the immediate years after the Partition and was driven by a fear of fresh communal flare-ups. But in the transformed atmosphere of the 1970s, social groups were finally willing to address issues and events that had been deflected and repressed for years. Thus, when the film was shown to various members of Parliament and political pundits in Delhi, a majority of them did not find anything objectionable in the narrative: rather, they liked the film's handling of sensitive issues, its sympathetic representation and analysis of the human dimensions of a calamitous moment in terms of the experiences of one upper middle-class family.[47] Prime Minister Mrs. Gandhi and the information and broadcasting minister, I. K. Gujral, actively supported *Garam Hawa*:[48] within an emergent hegemonic formation, the time for such a film had clearly arrived.

Funded by the state-sponsored Film Finance Corporation, *Garam Hawa* is considered part of the "New Indian Cinema"—a body of films from the 1970s that, in some accounts, gets the epithet "Indian *nouvelle vague*." With these cultural texts, low-budget "art films" acquired a new momentum, visibility, and prestige: no longer limited to a singular Ray or a maverick Ghatak, this new spurt of creativity took on the attributes of an aesthetic-political movement, in many ways echoing the earlier moment of cultural activism spearheaded by the IPTA, yet fundamentally different in enjoying official support. This cinema was the result of an alignment of several elements, including the emergence of a new breed of directors, technicians, and actors trained at the Film and Television Institute of India (FTII), a modest-sized audience that had been politicized through the charged confrontations between a mainstream hegemony and its detractors in the 1960s, and a fresh—if ersatz—socialist zeal surging through the ruling Congress Party.

Since this New Cinema included a range of ambitious works by some very interesting filmmakers[49] with diverse agendas, it is difficult to provide a list of defining parameters without running the risk of simplification. But a prevalent tendency was a heightened "realism" that employed deliberate formal techniques to draw attention to deep-rooted social antagonisms, often to propose resolutions in which the state—or, rather, its representative bureaucrats—emerged as the initiator of social reforms. Quite tellingly, many of these narratives incorporated an ex-

pression of a revolutionary consciousness in a climactic scene: for instance, at the end of Shyam Benegal's *Ankur* (1974), a young boy throws
a stone at the landlord's house. In a sense, such moments would serve
a consumerist function by appeasing a politicized audience's desire for
categorical political agency. While it is possible to read such climactic
gestures as resisting hegemonic closure within the text, a contextual
reading would have to take into account the hegemonic sanction—
indeed, exaltation—of such symbolic acts at that particular historical
juncture. Such an official sanction is even thematized in one of Benegal's
subsequent films, *Manthan* (1976), where the bureaucrat protagonist
instigates revolutionary action among villagers.

As Madhava Prasad argues, the realism we encounter in New Indian
Cinema performed a clearly ideological function: by placing all revolutionary impulse within the scope of "a slow developmentalist trajectory," it contained the possibility of social transformation within the
framework of India's state-sponsored passive revolution.[50] This "developmental aesthetic" served the interests of an interventionist state
by underscoring the need for reformatory action and simultaneously
reiterating the ultimate authority of the state in undertaking such ref-
ormation. In this sense, notwithstanding their politicized nature and
claims to alterity, the films of the New Cinema were more or less inscribed within a contemporaneous national-cultural project. Recognition from the international film festival circuit and state-sanctioned
awards at home catapulted the New Indian Cinema, at least for a few
years, to the status of national cinema—in clear preference to the far
more popular commercial film industry.

Garam Hawa and India's "Living Dead"

In September 1948, *Filmindia* magazine described Muslims who remained in post-Partition India as "the living dead": they were "orphans
in their own land," who were paying "for the sins of others" (i.e., the
"sins" of separatist Muslims).[51] *Garam Hawa* represents the predicament of one such Muslim family of Agra. Salim Mirza and Halim Mirza
are two brothers. Salim runs the shoe factory he inherited from his
father; Halim is a Muslim League politician. Both brothers live with
their families and their old mother in their *haveli* (ancestral house), although Halim is the legal owner of the building (his inheritance). Salim
has two sons: Bakr, who is married with a kid, and Sikander, who goes
to college. He also has a daughter, Amina, his favorite child. Amina is
in love with Kasim, Halim's son; since Islamic customs allow nuptials

between first cousins, their wedding seems imminent. But soon after Partition, Halim decides to migrate to Pakistan with his family, while Salim refuses to leave his birthplace; as a result, the lovers are separated. After a few months, when Halim tries to improve his social position in Pakistan by marrying off his son to the daughter of a local family of high standing, Kasim comes back to Agra to marry Amina. But the police deport him, claiming that he does not have the necessary papers: public-domain formalities between the sibling states intervene in the lives of their hitherto single population, causing private heartbreak.[52]

The credit sequence consists of a series of (mostly still) shots, documenting the events surrounding Partition: a topographical map of South Asia, followed by a geopolitical map of undivided India; Gandhi, Nehru, Jinnah and various other nationalist leaders; Mountbatten, the last viceroy; a close-up of a handshake; folk dancers (probably celebrating independence); map of divided India, with a separated Pakistan; a train full of refugees; overcrowded camps. The sequence ends with three gunshots on the soundtrack: a single shot of Gandhi's face, in profile, is made to "topple over" through rapid editing; cut to a dark, empty screen. As a poetic narration laments the brutalization of people and the reduction of cities to funeral pyres, establishing the contiguity of experience across the border, documentary footage of Gandhi's funeral procession and last rites are presented on screen. The soundtrack refers to Partition carnage, but the images bear the trace of another act of violence: their juxtaposition sets in motion a mechanism of displaced mourning. Gandhi emerges as a metonymic figure: his assassination becomes the site of displaced Partition trauma, his funeral an occasion for ritualistic public grieving. Early in the film, the elderly protagonist Salim Mirza claims that the "sacrifice" of Gandhi will not go in vain, that the sad event will galvanize people into overcoming their differences and building the secular community of Gandhi's dreams. Mirza moves from mourning for Gandhi to mourning for the divided national community and hopes that the response generated by one loss will help heal the other wound.

Salim Mirza's optimism is gradually shaken as moneylenders and banks refuse him business loans, fearing that he, too, will go away to Pakistan; the municipal government evicts his family from the ancestral haveli since its legal owner, Halim, has moved to Pakistan; his younger son, Sikander, cannot get a job in spite of doing well at college; his factory is set on fire; he himself is harassed on false charges of espionage. Amina gives up on Kasim and gives in to the romantic overtures of another cousin, Shamsad. But soon, he too accompanies his parents to Pakistan, with promises of returning. When Amina's elder brother

Bakr also leaves with his wife and son, her sadness and mounting disorientation are captured eloquently through her habitual placement of plates—now too many—at dinner. Amina tries to put up a brave face until news arrives about Shamsad's engagement to someone else; devastated by this betrayal, she commits suicide. The tragedy shatters the brokenhearted father's resolve: he decides to leave Agra for Pakistan.

Spaces of Displacement

A core feature of New Indian Cinema is a typically modernist preoccupation with spatial configurations. In *Garam Hawa*, with its central thematic of rootedness and migration, of belonging and alienation, space emerges as the crucial discursive trope: spatial geographies of belonging become the very markers of dislocation. Through its careful elaboration of the spatial dimensions of "home," concretized both as actual place of habitation (the haveli in Agra) and as the psychic domain of affiliation (an intimate, familiar world), the film sets up a dynamic of gradual displacement. The space of the haveli, where the two brothers live with their families, is established in detail: the courtyard, where the women perform their daily chores and socialize; the roof, where the boys fly kites and lovers meet furtively; the room where the two families get together at mealtimes; the bedrooms, where various married couples make their own plans; the cozy corner of the balcony shaded by blinds, where the grandmother reclines in her armchair. After their eviction, Salim Mirza's family has to take up quarters in the cramped space of a rented house: a steep staircase, with a rope instead of a railing to support oneself, leads to a small upper room which Sikandar and Amina are forced to share; an iron grille shows up prominently in various shots, separating members of the family, conveying a sense of their confinement.

As various members of the extended family leave for Pakistan, Salim Mirza sees them off at the station, then returns home in a *tanga* (horse carriage) along the winding lanes of Agra. Every time the driver asks, "Who did you drop off today, *mian*?" These recursive scenes of leave-taking underscore a growing sense of abandonment, a dwindling hope. The very first shot after the credits shows a train as it begins to pull out of the station. Next, we see Mirza in medium close-up, his back toward the camera, face in profile, waving at his departing relatives offscreen. As the tail end of the train goes out of the frame, a mosque is revealed in the background, on the other side of the tracks: with great felicity, the scene conveys the irony of a Muslim left behind by his kinsfolk in a markedly Muslim space, an "orphan" in his "own land."

Garam Hawa: Space of confinement. Courtesy of NFAI.

The predominantly Muslim character of the cultural space of Agra is established by two other scenes at famous historical sites associated with the Mughal empire: Amina decides to forget Kasim and accede to Shamsad's romantic advances at Fatehpur Sikri, in the legendary *Panch-mahal* structure;[53] later, they court on the premises of the Taj Mahal, celebrated as a monument to undying love. The grandeur of Mughal architecture—the precise geometric shapes and patterns, the intricate lattices and filigree works—and the nostalgic evocation of a dazzling Islamic past place their courtship in a collectively shared sensuous frame: the mounting erotic charge is intimated in terms of a rapturous song sung by group of *qawali* singers.[54] The strains of the qawali return hauntingly in two subsequent scenes: first, when Shamsad and Amina's romance is consummated on a boat on the river Yamuna, near the Taj; and finally, during Amina's suicide. The love-making occurs offscreen, partly in deference to norms of cultural discretion, and partly to avoid censorship hurdles; instead, the camera pans languidly across the river, its banks, the reeds growing in the shallow waters, the inverted reflection of the magnificent mausoleum. The soundtrack is a mix of ambient noises (the wind, birds, the water), reverberating echoes of the two lovers calling out each other's names (from an earlier scene at the Taj), and snatches of the qawali. The scene leaves viewers with a rather eerie feeling, mobilizing a complex of emotions with strong historical resonance. Here Amina's loss of virginity rings with the loss of social innocence; her trust of Shamsad opens up the possibility of betrayal and already resounds with the disappointment of a larger broken promise;

Garam Hawa: A mournful Salim Mirza against the Agra cityscape.
Courtesy of NFAI.

the consummation of their love portends the eventual impossibility of
their union, tinged as it is with the pathos of a historical separation.
The possibilities entailed in the moment of Amina's sexual surrender
are thwarted by Shamsad's migration across the border: an intensely
personal moment becomes part of the larger traumatic experience in
which the euphoria of national liberation is overshadowed by a lethal
rupture.

The intimation of personal trauma is finally realized when Amina
hears about Shamsad's engagement to another woman in Pakistan. She
stumbles up the steep staircase to her room in a daze and relives various
scenes of intimacy with him. The soaring qawali returns on the soundtrack, providing the *melos* in this melodramatic depiction of Amina's
psychic disintegration, and underscoring the social dimension of her
private agony. Putting on her bridal veil, she looks in the mirror and sees
Shamsad, dressed as a groom, standing behind her. She swings around
expectantly, only to realize she is hallucinating; shutting the door to
her room, she slashes her wrist with a knife. The qawali stops abruptly:
a close-up shot shows her wince in pain; as she whimpers and moans,
her face goes out of focus. From a medium shot of her lying in bed, the
camera pulls back to reveal blood trickling from under her bangles. The
use of the mirror and variations of perspective in this scene continue the
plastic manipulation of spatial elements, evident throughout the film,
that transmit an embodied social tragedy.

Compared to most other Partition films, a more conscious and formalized melodramatic mode mediates oscillations between unity and separation in *Garam Hawa*. When Halim Mirza's family leaves, the camera starts from a close-up of a lock on the door and pulls back slowly to the sound of a train—the camera's measured movement paralleling a train slowly pulling out of the station—to reveal Amina sitting alone on the porch, knitting for her beloved Kasim. In this early scene, she is still optimistic. Later, when Kasim gets deported to Pakistan, she looks more dejected as she sits like a zombie on the same porch. As a loud train whistle is heard on the soundtrack, the camera captures her dazed expression in close-up. This time, as we hear the train gradually beginning to roll out of the station, the camera advances ever so slowly toward her face, to end in an extreme close-up of her vacant eyes. Every time Salim Mirza returns home from the train station, his sad face is framed against the tanga's shade: here, the actor Balraj Sahani's own history as a person uprooted by Partition adds an extradiegetic punch, an ontological sedimentation that intensifies the emotional impact.[55] In the eviction scene, *Garam Hawa* appears to pay homage to *Chhinnamul*, the seminal Partition film, in its depiction of the grandmother's reluctance to leave the haveli. As the family prepares to move, she hides in a small room used to store firewood. Later, when she is about to die, the new occupant of the building accedes to her wish and allows her to "return." As she is carried back to the haveli, she remembers coming as a teenage bride on a palanquin: her "flashback" consists entirely of wedding music on the soundtrack. When she reaches her old home, she looks around happily, as snatches of past conversation are replayed. This moving scene, leading up to her death, plays out in terms of subjective sound bites, underscoring the hallucinatory quality of psychic displacement and the impossibility of a simple return.

A Critical Politics of Mourning

Produced twenty-five years after independence, *Garam Hawa* participates in a collective reappraisal of the legitimacy of a naturalized nationalist ethos. It becomes increasingly difficult for Salim Mirza to procure business loans, either from the local moneylender or from the banks. Without credit financing, it becomes impossible to compete with mass producers; ultimately, small businessmen like him are forced to exit the market. Several landlords refuse to rent buildings to Mirza, a *mussalman*; finally, he manages to get a house only after paying a whole year's rent in advance. Bakr, his eldest son, has to bribe inspecting officials to get work done. Sikandar, his younger son turns up for interviews, only to be told that the manager has already offered the position to someone else. The reluctant landlords, the bank managers, and the interviewers are only heard in the film, and not seen: these arbiters of power remain nameless, faceless individuals. If their anonymity points to the diffused nature of power, it also underscores the difficulty of organizing resistance: if individuals are caught in an impersonal and oppressive power matrix, without clearly recognizable foci, whom do they oppose? In such situations, Salim and Sikander look directly at the camera, producing the rather unsettling impression that spectators are being implicated in these networks of discrimination. Sickened by the flagrant corruption and nepotism, Sikandar's friends talk about migrating to the West: here, the narrative blames both a lack of opportunities and a collective ethos of unscrupulousness for this "drain" of human resources.[56] At issue is the question of national affiliation in the face of the rapid erosion of nationalist ideals and promises.

Focusing on the gradual economic displacement of the family, several commentators locate in the film an exposé of the way in which religious difference is turned into an instrument of capitalist transformation.[57] The end of the film does appear to corroborate such a reading: on the way to the railway station to catch the train to Pakistan, the truncated family runs into a political procession, several marchers bearing red flags signaling their affiliation to a communist program of revolutionary transformation; others carry placards proclaiming the intent to fight economic injustice through a coalition across religious and caste lines. This promise of a secular class struggle brings Sikander out of his disenfranchised dejection and provides him with a reason to stay on in India. Even the elderly Salim Mirza cannot resist the invitation to collective action; instructing the carriage driver to take his wife back home, he joins the procession. Thus the film ends with a reiteration of the possibility of a nationalist position dedicated to the promotion of secular and democratic ideals. However, this intimation of revolutionary agency in the climactic scene is characteristic of several films belonging to the New India Cinema, whose inception coincided with the rise of a state-backed rhetoric of socialism, and with India's marked alignment with the Soviet bloc, signaled through a new Indo-Soviet treaty signed in 1972. In a sense, then, this symbolic expression is a standard narrative ploy of the parallel cinema—a generic gesture, as it were. A singular emphasis on this aspect is bound to produce a reductive reading of the film which, in spite of its ending, remains remarkably nuanced in its depiction of the plight of minority Muslims in post-Partition India. If a certain economic determinism keeps surfacing, it can be traced back to

Garam Hawa: The walls cave in on Salim Mirza. Courtesy of NFAI.

the backgrounds of some of the key players involved in the production of the film. Ismat Chugtai, whose short story provided the basis of the narrative, Kaifi Azmi, who cowrote the script and recited the couplets at the beginning and end of the film, and Balraj Sahni, who acted as Salim Mirza, were all Marxist intellectuals who came into cultural prominence in the 1950s as members of the Progressive Writers Association; like the director Sathyu, they were involved at one point or another with the IPTA. They longed for an Indian society that would move beyond its sectarian divisions and focus on the realization of economic, political, and social justice.

This decidedly modernist longing blinded many an Indian intellectual, Nehru included, to one inescapable reality of an Indian modernity: the absolute persistence of religion in the daily lives of Indians. Repressed and marginalized, the religious element nevertheless inhered within a purportedly modern Indian identity: archaic religious differences and animosities also survived all secularist proselytizing. Recurrent communal violence pointed to the inadequacies of an idealist secularism that, turned into a venerable institution through official sanction, effectively terminated more dialogic and pragmatic approaches to the problem of religious intolerance.[58] *Garam Hawa* eventually reveals a similar blind spot: in promoting a secular ideal, it explains away religious strife largely in terms of economic conflicts. At times, the film's secularist tenor works to its benefit; for instance, while underscoring the Muslimness of Agra's sociocultural environment, the film avoids turning it into an exclusive attribute. While Mughal architecture, Mughal legends, and qawali are primarily Muslim references, they enjoy wider appreciation as elements of a shared, syncretic Indian cultural lexicon. However, the representation of Salim Mirza remains problematic. He is characterized as a mildly religious man, who often expresses his faith that the Almighty will look after his family. However, his characterization involves a certain emptying out of specificities: the elements constituting his religious difference are made to disappear, even as the fact of this difference is made the basis for his victimization. The Muslim protagonist is turned into a cipher, an idealized embodiment of nationalist discourses of secularism.

It is precisely such leveling of religious difference in the name of secularism (usually interpreted as the equality of all religions) that leads to charges about the imposition of a naturalized Hindu identity upon minorities. From a different perspective, Hindu nationalists see secularism (frequently interpreted as a doctrine of affirmative action: helping minorities achieve equal footing with the mainstream) as the philosophy of endlessly pandering to minority communities, at the expense of the Hindu majority. Some of these misgivings are expressed in a review published in the *Star and Style* magazine in 1974. The title of the piece, "Stunning, Charming, but Late," intimates a laudatory response, and also pithily acknowledges that the country had to wait long for such a thoughtful cinematic meditation of Partition and its aftermath.[59] The review goes on to identify "the subjective self-pity for the minority community" as its major weakness: it is "almost wholly one-sided, keeping itself blind" to what happened to the other communities, "since what happened here was more a reaction." For instance, Salim Mirza gets torn by his external environment but does not undertake "some introspection about his own people." The reviewer is alluding to atrocities perpetrated by Muslims, and the sufferings of Hindu and Sikh communities in Pakistan—as if, somehow, acts of persecution on the other side of the border legitimize the "reaction" here. While asserting that Indian cinema needs more films like *Garam Hawa* to revolutionize it, a surmise based largely on formalist appreciation and the riveting narrative, the review concludes that it is "not exactly a film to promote harmony, integration and all that" because it does not have balanced viewpoints. Note the dismissive "and all that," a phrase that tellingly reveals the reservations about such nationalist shibboleths as "harmony, integration" and, by extension, secularism. Such widespread discontent with state-sponsored secularism gradually annulled its legitimacy and eroded its hegemonic force; by the time the Hindu Right demolished a North Indian mosque on December 6, 1992, the term had lost its relevance and efficacy in its standard formulation.[60]

But we are getting ahead of ourselves. In spite of its idealist aporias, *Garam Hawa* remains a remarkable cinematic attempt at what Adorno called "coming to terms with the past"—in unveiling the objective conditions that produced the religious strife and that continue to inscribe a post-Partition Muslim-Indian subjectivity. In its thoughtful and textured mediation of the distressing aftermath of a social cataclysm, Sathyu's film comes closest to the remarkable "Partition trilogy" of Ritwik Ghatak, the focus of chapter 5.

CHAPTER FIVE

Ghatak, Melodrama, and the Restitution of Experience

RITWIK GHATAK, the maverick Bengali film director, remains the most celebrated cinematic auteur of Partition narratives. Although the reference of his films is, properly speaking, to a broader process of social decay, Ghatak himself claims an originary primacy for the geopolitical division: "The engulfing uncertainty, the fracture that I see—the roots are in the splintering of Bengal."[1] He traces the economic and political decline, the moral and ethical erosion, back to the trauma of the bifurcation—"The present anarchic state of affairs prevailing in the country is the direct result of the shape of independence we got in '47"[2]—revealing the deep imprint of this turbulent historical moment on him. For Ghatak, Bengal is more than a microcosm of the nation: in his affective horizon, it *is* the nation. He carries out his critique of a post-independence nationalist project through an intense focus on the problems facing a truncated Bengal—the displacement of refugees, unemployment, poverty and hunger, corruption, indifference, and cynicism. From his directorial debut, *Nagarik* (1952), to his last feature, the essayistic "road movie" *Jukti, Takko, Aar Gappo* (1976), he maintains a critical engagement with Partition and its repercussions, challenging the hegemonic recasting of the event as an anachronistic aberration. This chapter's auteurist focus on Ghatak allows me to pursue, in a more concrete fashion, one of the central questions animating this book: who is it that undertakes cinematic mourning work? As I hope to demonstrate, Ghatak's career dislodges the very idea of a cogent authorial voice, a coherent subject of mourning: in a sense, he emerges as the emblematic mourner.

After a successful stage career with the leftist Indian Peoples' Theatre Association, Ghatak became increasingly interested in cinema; following stints as actor, scriptwriter, and assistant director in various films, he finally made *Nagarik*, about the proletarization and simultaneous politicization of a dislocated middle-class family. When the film could not find commercial distribution,[3] a dejected Ghatak joined Bombay's Filmistan studios as a scriptwriter for a year. He did pen the script of one Hindi box-office hit, Bimal Roy's *Madhumati* (1958), a romantic thriller masquerading as a haunting ghost story. In the late 1950s, he made the two films, *Ajantrik* (1957) and *Bari Theke Paliye* (1958); two other projects remained unfinished. Following a remarkable three-film creative burst in the early 1960s—*Meghe Dhaka Tara* (1960), *Komal Gandhar* (1961), and *Subarnarekha* (1962)—Ghatak found it increasingly difficult to work in Bengal: in particular, *Komal Gandhar*'s trenchant criticism of the leftist cultural scene produced much antagonism. He had a yearlong reprieve in Poona, where he was assistant director at the Film and Television Institute of India (1964–65).[4] Around this time, his precarious mental and emotional state led to the first of several internments. The birth of Bangladesh in 1971 raised new hopes of pan-Bengali cultural collaboration and provided Ghatak with a chance to shoot *Titash Ekti Nadir Nam* (1973) in his beloved East Bengal. The following year, he made the autobiographical *Jukti, Takko, Aar Gappo*, a self-reflexive mapping of his concerns articulated with renewed urgency in the context of the politically volatile late 1960s and early 1970s. Chronic alcoholism and a bout of tuberculosis took a heavy toll, and Ghatak passed away in 1976.

Focusing on the three Ghatak films that came to be regarded retrospectively as his Partition trilogy, this chapter explores the nature of his cultural-political challenge. *Meghe Dhaka Tara* (*Cloud-Capped Star*) centers on Neeta, the eldest daughter of a Bengali family uprooted by Partition and now trying to eke out a living in a suburban refugee colony. As her father becomes increasingly frail and senile and Shankar, her elder brother, pursues his dream of making it as a singer, Neeta has to work long hours to support her family. The mother, hardened by her travails and anxious about her family's survival, exploits Neeta's labor, masking her own dependence, and her willful disregard for her daughter's hopes and desires, in bitter resentment. Montu, the younger brother, uses his skills as a soccer player to get a factory job, only to become disabled in an industrial accident. Geeta, the wily younger sister, has no qualms in stealing Neeta's beau, Sanat, away from her: she reasons that Neeta will not abandon the family for marital bliss. By the time Shankar achieves success as a singer in Bombay and returns home triumphant, Neeta's physical and psychic exertions prove lethal: she comes down with tuberculosis. As the mother eagerly plans a two-storied house, Shankar arranges for Neeta to spend her last days at a sanatorium in the Shillong hills.

Having lost her family in the riots of 1946, Anasuya, the female protagonist of *Komal Gandhar* (*E-Flat*), seeks to overcome her isolation by joining the vibrant group theater scene. Overcoming hurdles such as ego clashes, petty factionalism within the theater troupe, and jealous acts of sabotage, she eventually finds artistic fulfillment and a new community. She also forges a remarkable intimacy—spanning creative partnership and romantic love—with Bhrigu, the aloof and idealistic leader of the theater unit, who, like her, is a displaced person. In the course of Anasuya's voyage, Ghatak imaginatively explores the possibility of overcoming loss and alienation through active engagement in the cultural sphere. If marriage is his privileged figure of union in this film, then, in locating the romantic duo within the sphere of cultural activism, he spurns the emergent model of autonomous couples (see chapter 3) largely dissociated from community and leads us back to the social.

The following film, *Subarnarekha*, strikes a darker note. Returning to the family as the site of a pitched struggle for meaning and mooring, Ghatak presents a picture of the post-Partition milieu that is at once more disturbing and more utopian than the one in *Meghe Dhaka Tara*. After their parents' death in East Bengal, Ishwar Chakraborty migrates to the west and ends up in a refugee colony with Seeta, his young sister. He also takes in the orphan Abhiram, a boy whose mother is abducted in front of his eyes. Facing the pressure of bringing up the youngsters, Ishwar resigns his position as a teacher in the local school and takes up a job at a foundry, thus alienating Haraprasad, his idealist friend and fellow refugee. The atypical family moves to the picturesque plateaus of western Bengal and sets up home on the banks of the river Subarnarekha. Abhiram is sent away to boarding school, and then to college; he wants to pursue writing after graduation, but Ishwar expects him to study engineering in Germany. As Seeta grows up, she develops impressive musical and domestic talents. She adopts a maternal attitude toward Ishwar ("I *am* your mother," she tells him); at times, they

Komal Gandhar: Bhrigu and Anasuya in Birbhum—from empathy to romance. Courtesy of NFAI.

interact more like a married couple, intimating a deep, unconscious incestuous tension. This constant blurring of kinship boundaries is further complicated when Seeta and Abhiram, brought up as siblings, fall in love. Ishwar's opposition to their union, which stems largely from embedded feelings of loneliness and jealousy masquerading as propriety, hardens with the divulgence of Abhiram's low-caste roots when the latter publicly recognizes a dying homeless woman as his long-lost mother—a revelation that threatens Ishwar's job and his social standing in the small-town community. Seeta and Abhiram run away to Calcutta and get married. After Abhiram's death in an accident, poverty pushes Seeta to the brink of prostitution. In a bizarre turn of events, a

Subarnarekha: Seeta and Ishwar—incestuous proximity?
Courtesy of NFAI.

drunken Ishwar appears as her very first customer: traumatized, Seeta hacks herself to death. In this radical unraveling of familial relations, Ghatak captures a burgeoning sense of national crisis and points to its roots in the contradictions inhering in contemporary social structures. Nevertheless, the film retains an ardent utopian strain: Ishwar returns to the banks of the Subarnarekha with his nephew, Seeta and Abhiram's infant son, keeping alive the quest for a mythic home.

Ghatak's Enigma

These basic storylines indicate some of Ghatak's concerns, but they barely capture the scope and complexity of his aesthetic-political praxis. Deciphering Ghatak remains a daunting challenge even, as Sanjay Mukhopadhyay notes, for avowed "Ritwikists."[5] We might say, echoing popular impressions, that Ghatak's films evince an unbridled passion, a taste for excess and disregard for conventional aesthetic discipline; yet, at the same time, they afford the most subtle, hence all the more searing, insights about the predicaments of individuals caught up in the agonizing unfolding of history. His own personal predilections were equally paradoxical: a Marxist intellectual who was revered for his perspicacity and integrity, he was also dismissed as an inveterate drunk, prone to decadent self-indulgence. But as Pier Paolo Pasolini, himself no stranger to controversy, once declared: "The real marxist must not be a good marxist. His function is to put orthodoxy and codified certainties into crisis."[6] In describing Ghatak as "film director and bohemian, Marxist and alcoholic, craftsman and derelict,"[7] commentators underscore his enigma. Even as he constantly contradicted himself, he never lost "his stature or his arrogant intolerance of fools." Indeed, his reputation as "a film-maker's film-maker, an artiste's artiste"[8]—hyperbole that threatens to upstage his films—has only gathered force over time.

I shall argue that the very disillusionments and frustrations that inspired Ghatak's iconoclastic creativity also fueled his intemperate lifestyle; that through his life and his work he attempted to at least make good, if not overcome his alienation. The textual and biographical registers, when considered against the foil of contemporary history, help us get beyond Ghatak's enigma to a better understanding of both his determination by that history and his authorial project as an intervention in it.

Raymond Bellour, in his inspired attempt to explicate Ghatak's art through a close analysis of *Meghe Dhaka Tara*,[9] finds the filmmaker to be, notwithstanding the classical arc of the narrative, a consummate modernist with a highly developed style all his own. He draws our attention to Ghatak's organization of emotions through the montage of image and sound, to achieve a remarkable form of "expressive modulation." No single Ghatakian element or strategy can be linked reductively to a specific effect all the time; any particular effect is best understood in terms of the dialogic interaction of several elements. Each component is developed gradually to muster great emotional force: Bellour's privileged example is the tree with which the film begins and which appears in six subsequent scenes, but always with a difference (in mood, function, character development, and interaction). He concludes that it is not enough to analyze or critique this work; it begs a somewhat different mode of apprehension—it is a film that we have to "accompany."[10] I take this provocation to mean that Ghatak's thoroughly cinematic figurations—his *audiovisions*[11] bearing his inimitable imprimatur—resist objective explication and demand engagement bordering on immersion.

In spite of Ghatak's strikingly individualist style, we can no longer invoke any romantic notion of the author as a creative genius producing timeless masterpieces in isolation, outside history.[12] It may be more productive to situate Ghatak as a creative node at the intersection of various social determinants, and his films as cultural texts within a larger discursive field. We have to take into account the palpable contributions of the music composer Jyotirindra Moitra, the cinematographers Dinen Gupta and Dilip Ranjan Mukhopadhyay, the sarod maestro Bahadur Khan, and a recurring group of actors (Bijon Bhattacharya, Surpiya Choudhury, and Anil Chatterjee, among others). Furthermore, both Ghatak and his films are available for continuous interpretation and appropriation, from the dismissal of his oeuvre in the sixties as being embarrassingly melodramatic, to the recent critical consecration of Ghatak as the fountainhead of an Indian cinematic avant-garde. Such an approach becomes something of an imperative due to his mode of operation. Through the creative contagion of various discursive units and levels—inducing one argument in the middle of another thought, layering historical moments with mythic allusions, setting up a relay of commentaries between sound elements and images—Ghatak forges a dialogic, intertextual approach. Contradicting himself in his interviews and writings, refusing to explain the articulation of disparate, even conflicting, elements beyond a stubborn assertion that for him they worked together, Ghatak confounds attempts at totalizing readings. In adopting the collision between social and cultural fragments at the core of his aesthetics, he aligns himself with the cultural politics of Bertolt Brecht (two of whose plays, *Caucasian Chalk Circle* and *Galileo*, Ghatak translated into Bengali) and Walter Benjamin, and breaks with a Marxist-realist orthodoxy associated with critics like Georg Lukács.[13] His is a shimmering authorial voice, distinctive not so much for clarity of meaning as for a strong sense of the subjective experience of underlying social contradictions. Like Anasuya and Bhrigu of *Komal Gandhar*, Ghatak strives to overcome alienation by engaging with his sociohistorical conjuncture through the concrete, sensuous activity of cultural production. Thus he seeks to reinstate Partition as an integral part of the mainstream of national life in a characteristically iconoclastic manner. While the public sphere has traditionally marginalized women and dismissed the individual body, affect and desire, Ghatak transforms these elements into privileged discursive tools. Hence the focus on women protagonists, the reinscription of historical trauma on people's bodies, the self-consciously melodramatic mise-en-scènes, and the bold, trenchant exposition of the libidinal underpinnings of the noblest bourgeois fantasies.

Allegories of History

On the evidence of his films, Ghatak appears to share Walter Benjamin's philosophical concerns—especially his critique of Progress and History.[14] The heartbroken characters played by Bijon Bhattacharya (the father in *Meghe Dhaka Tara*, the bungling refugee aspiring to be a playwright in *Komal Gandhar*, the idealist-turned-cynic of *Subarnarekha*), the consumptive protagonist of *Meghe Dhaka Tara*, the abandoned airstrip and the self-mutilated body of Seeta in *Subarnarekha*—they are the detritus of contemporary life, Benjamin's "landscape of ruins." When the film-maker writes that the "fundamental note" in *Komal Gandhar* is one of (the possibility of) unity, and that he has attempted—through the collisions generated within a layered narrative—to realize this "life-truth . . . *like a flash of lightning*,"[15] he practically echoes Benjamin: "To articulate the past historically . . . means to seize hold of a memory as it flashes up at a moment of danger."[16] Looking back in history is not simply a matter of nostalgic reification: it mobilizes a process of anamnesis, whereby the willful forgetting of inconvenient experiences is reversed and "lost" memories are restituted to a community. Intellectually driven by moments of great historical crisis, both Benjamin and Ghatak evince an understanding of temporality that rejects mechanistic chronology and teleology. Both attempt to hold on to critical moments that rend an artificially secured social unity to illuminate underlying contradictions and forgotten possibilities. Benjamin wants to complicate historiography and thus "redeem" history; Ghatak stages a crisis of historical consciousness through his anachronistic allusions, and presents such a riven temporal sensibility as an ethicopolitical necessity. Both strive to produce allegories of their sense of history: this is why Benjamin champions the fragment and the quote, Ghatak works with allusions and incomplete allegories, and both hold on to the flotsam and jetsam of human experience. Ghatak, in particular, returns obsessively to what is, for him, the originary site of trauma, and constantly rewrites the story of his community: he refuses to accept any evasive and official version as the definitive account. It is this will, this urgency, that constitutes the charge of a Ghatak film, the ecstasy of a Benjaminian insight.

Dialogism: Kalidasa, Marx, and Tagore

Ghatak's unrelenting engagement with history takes remarkably eclectic forms. Making classical Sanskrit literary allusions jostle with Marxist thought, placing Tagore and Shakespeare side by side, he brings various cultural archives—regional, national, civilizational, global—into creative dialogue, helping to shape an Indian intellectual modernity.

It was through his association with the IPTA in the 1940s that Ghatak came to subscribe to a politicized view of culture as a cognitive and emotional resource for shaping popular consciousness. However, his association with the communist circles of Bengal proved to be tenuous: he had to leave the IPTA in 1954, the year he produced a controversial document articulating his vision for the organization[17] and was subsequently "purged" from the Communist Party of India. On several occasions, he pointedly referred to his admiration for Marxist *philosophy* and simultaneously distanced himself from the ossified institutions of communist politics. Thus, when asked about the ideological basis of his work, he replied: "The ideological base is fundamental Marxism. Marxism not in the sense of this party or that party. Marxism as can be seen philosophically, psychologically. Marx, Engels, Lenin—many clashes and conflicts [in my films] have touches of their writings."[18] Here, he was moving away from the various leftist factions that had emerged in Bengal by the early 1960s,[19] and from particular orthodoxies within the Indian left.

At the same time, Ghatak was drawing on the writings of Rabindranath Tagore, often dismissed by leftist critics as a bourgeois author from a landed, mercantile family. Ghatak stressed the absolute centrality of Tagore's intellectual legacy to modern Bengali life and identity.[20] He mentioned three Tagore pieces in particular as direct inspirations for *Komal Gandhar* and *Subarnarekha*. Of these, the 1922 essay "The Religion of the Forest" asserted that the classical Sanskrit drama *Shakuntala*—penned by the great Kalidasa at a time (the fourth century CE)[21] when Indian civilization had already crossed over from the age of forest retreats into a more cosmopolitan, urban phase—revealed the continued hold of the ideal of the *ashrama* or hermitage on the Indian imagination. For Tagore, the notion of the hermitage was centered on "the recognition of the kinship of man with conscious and unconscious creation alike. . . . The hermitage shines out, in all our ancient literature, as the place where the chasm between man and the rest of creation has been bridged."[22] Implicit in this ecological formulation was a model of community in which nonalienated living was still possible.

Tagore's revival of this ashrama model of community resonates best with the early Marx, especially the *Economic and Philosophic Manuscripts of 1844*, and *Theses on Feuerbach*. In the *Theses*, Marx proposes a philosophy of praxis as the core of his radical sensual humanism: he stresses that it is concrete, sensuous activity—with a focus on use value, as opposed to exchange value—which defines human beings and provides fulfillment to their existence. In developing the concept of alienation, Marx adds something more to the Hegelian concept of objectification: he insists that alienation involves a radical separation of human beings from their basic attributes. Thus, within a capitalist mode of production, a worker becomes estranged not only from his product but also from his own activity (which should provide the fulfillment of his existence), from himself, and from his environment. The focus on the sensuousness of human existence, which gets lost in the scientificity of Marx's later writings, shares an emphasis on sensory integrity with Tagore's idea of a community in which "the chasm between man and the rest of the creation had been bridged." I am not sure if Ghatak was familiar with Marx's early writings, but he was drawn to the promise of a nonalienated collective life in the classical model of the ashrama. In the fractured context of post-Partition Bengali society and polity, Ghatak sought to articulate this indigenous utopian strand with a Marxist concern for concrete, sensuous activity into a radical cinematic practice.[23]

Consistent with his manifestly discursive approach to filmmaking, Ghatak referred to Eisenstein as his most important cinematic influence: he even called him "the Kalidasa of cinema."[24] In an essay titled "Dialectics in Film," he expressed his fascination for the dialectical approach to reality and to its representation.[25] Combining classical, folk, and popular Indian aesthetics with Jungian psychology and Soviet-style montage was, for him, a legitimate way of forging a new kind of film language. In this respect, Ghatak's work exemplifies the kind of radical dialogism that Mikhail Bakhtin noted in Dostoevsky's novels, consisting of utterances that self-consciously staged their interactions with other utterances, past and future, and achieved their polyvocal signification essentially through such dialogue.[26] The modern novel, according to Bakhtin, brought worldviews and experientialities into dialogue, intensifying the heteroglossia inherent in language through this interaction and its projections in the future. While literary theorists before Bakhtin traced novelistic dialogism to the epics, Bakhtin located its origins in the egalitarianism of satire and the carnivalesque which, in sharp contrast to the epic's preoccupation with Olympian heroes of antiquity, and its aristocratic idealization of a monologic unity, produced proximate and recognizable worlds—not unlike the novel's "zone of familiar contact."[27] Yet Ghatak's dialogism led him to an epic structure—a twist that obliges us to reconsider Bakhtin's influential formulation.

The Epic: Familiar, Contemporary, Discursive

Ghatak's films are reflexive arenas for cultural negotiations. The plot, while remarkable for its meticulous attention to real lifeworlds, is not stymied by the demands of an orthodox realism; instead it attempts, through the self-conscious and heightened interactivity of its elements, to capture the post-Partition milieu in an emotionally proximate way and to highlight rhetorically its deplorable dimensions. Simultaneously, Ghatak's highly formalized melodrama transforms what we understand as dramatic flow, negating the possibility of projective identification even as it produces intense affect, engaging viewers in sensitized and conscious ways. Such an intensified epic form can be traced back not only to Brechtian dramaturgy, but also to India's premodern epics with their many intertwining, mutually commentating narrative strands.[28] Indian epics and mythologies have a direct relevance to contemporary Indian life: as culturally shared cognitive resources, as discursive frames of reference, they remain integral parts of the nation's living traditions. As Ghatak points out: "We are an epic people. We like to sprawl, we are not much involved in story-intrigues, we like to be re-told the same myths and legends again and again. We, as a people, are not much sold on the 'what' of the thing, but the 'why' and 'how' of it. This is the epic attitude."[29]

Bakhtin's analytic distinction between the familiar and quotidian novelistic world and the remote, idealized horizon of the epic does not hold up in the Indian context. Here, the epic is able to engender and engage modern consciousness in direct and proximate ways, through participatory modes of questioning and reworking, unleashing the continuing political promise of the generic form. Through the resignification of various myths (Uma, Seeta, Nachiketa, Shakuntala), Ghatak salvages them from petrification and underscores their relevance in the lives of contemporary Indians.[30] The epic form allows Ghatak to shift his attention from the individual level to the collective, thereby subverting the kind of realism that had come to crystallize around the individual as the psychological and moral center of the narrative. Insisting on the social nature of human existence, Ghatak opens up a space outside a hegemonic cultural project looking for a cogent citizen-subject, a space from where he launches his attacks on bourgeois conceptions of modernity and nationhood.

Following Eisenstein's writings from the 1930s celebrating cinema as a medium that encompasses other aesthetic forms, Ghatak conceived of film as an omnibus art form: he drew upon sources as disparate as classical drama and music, folk theater and music, tribal dance, Buddhist sculpture, the Vedas and the Upanishads, popular music, mythology. Yet, as in the films of Eisenstein, each aesthetic form was allowed a certain autonomy, so that a possibility of dialogue was maintained. Ghatak accepted the Soviet filmmaker/theorist's dictum that meaning is generated from the collision between elements, and not from their union. Thus, in *Subarnarekha*, after Haraprasad stops his friend Ishwar from committing suicide, he brings him to Calcutta to experience the terrifying fun (*bibhatsa maja*) of the big city. As the two weary middle-aged men drown their sorrows in liquor at a cabaret, Haraprasad launches into a diatribe against the decadent apathy of an entire generation, sunken in a nightmare about the famine, the war, the atom bomb, the riots, the Partition. He quotes from ancient Vedic texts, butchering the original Sanskrit with his bangal intonation, mocking all forms of high idealism and simultaneously accentuating a sense of contagion. Here, the soundtrack also features a musical quotation: the music being played in the Western-style bar, already a site of deculturation, is none other than the "Patricia" theme from Fellini's *La Dolce Vita* (1960), which Ghatak takes to be both a celebration and a critique of European decadence. The collision of these wildly divergent elements produces a strong sense of decay and disorientation underlying the sensory indulgence: the orgiastic "fun" reveals itself to be a collective nightmare, setting us up for the subsequent sequence in which a brother turns up as his sister's "client."[31]

The Eisensteinian intuition also informed sound-image relations in Ghatak's films. The famous Eisenstein-Pudovkin-Alexandrov manifesto—"*Only the contrapuntal use* of sound vis-à-vis the visual fragment of montage will open up new possibilities for the development and perfection of montage"[32]—is deployed and extended to stunning effect. Take, for instance, the centuries-old traditional wedding songs that waft nondiegetically throughout *Komal Gandhar* expressing, through their collision with the images of discord, a hope for unity. It is only at the end, when the lovers come together, and the theater group reunites to produce an exciting new play, that the wedding song's celebration of unity is also reflected in the images: in the actual union of the two romantic protagonists, and in the symbolic union of Bengal effected through the juxtaposition of shots of various parts of the province (the rolling hills, the plains, the river banks, the city—literally "flashbacks" of the theater group's travels, figuratively conjuring up the space of Bengal). Through the incorporation of these folk songs, Ghatak invokes a lost Bengali cultural unity, defiantly counterposing it to the current fragmentation.[33]

Consider another instance of sound-image montage from *Meghe Dhaka Tara*. When Sanat visits Neeta's family, her mother comes out of the kitchen to greet him; we hear a crackling noise—ostensibly oil splattering in the wok, or water boiling over—energizing the offscreen space of the kitchen. Later, as Sanat and Neeta go out for a walk, the mother tensely looks on, worried that her breadwinning daughter will marry Sanat and abandon the family: the same crackling noise is reproduced, now dissociated from the kitchen. Repeated yet again with the mother's face in close-up as Sanat chats with Neeta in her room, this recurring acoustic embellishment unifies the disparate scenes into one unfolding anxiety. The kitchen sound not only captures the ambience of a Bengali household but also serves as the acoustic approximation of a vernacular

Meghe Dhaka Tara: The embittered mother, engulfed in smoke from the kitchen oven

expression that describes a soul ravaged by life's hardships as one that has been burnt to cinders.[34] The self-interested acerbity of the mother, an archetypal "cruel woman," is tied to the quotidian activity of cooking and, by extension, to the labors of a life lived in penury.

Archetypes

The notion of archetypes, fundamental symbols that have come to imbibe and signify the deepest attributes of collective human existence, enables Ghatak to elaborate on the indisputable social dimension of human life. Drawing on comparative mythology, particularly the writings of Joseph Campbell, and on Jungian psychology, Ghatak describes archetypes as constituents of the social unconscious. They are the cultural repositories of "the deepest feelings of man," and hence also the sources of "spontaneous human reactions." He writes: "The theory of the collective unconscious revealed that man carries in his brain images that were born long before civilization. We came to know that in the history of different races, certain fundamental archetypes repeat themselves. Throughout history, in the evolution of different civilizations, we see the same complex life image transform into symbols through archetypal images."[35] The privileged archetype for Ghatak is the Great Mother that "still haunts the consciousness of the different races all over the world," from the Pyrenees caves on the Spain-France border to Bengal.[36] In *Meghe Dhaka Tara*, the three female characters are turned into archetypal symbols, embodying three traditional aspects of feminine power: the mother represents cruelty; the heroine Neeta embodies the nurturing aspect of femininity; Geeta, her sister, is the sensual woman.

In invoking Jung's formulation of a collective unconscious, Ghatak becomes vulnerable to charges of a transcultural universalism, and a concomitant belief in essential human nature. It seems, however, that Ghatak's films avoid the problems that mark his subsequent explication. Note the absolute primacy that Ghatak accords to the social existence of humans, his insistence on the materiality of human life. At the same time, he talks about the depths of our being, a level of aesthetic enjoyment that is so deep that it remains indescribable. Even as he harps on the interpersonal nature of human experience, he seems to point to an intensely personal dimension of that experience. This polarized distinction between the personal and the social, the subjective and the objective, is a legacy of idealist philosophies: Ghatak's films, unlike his writings, appear to transcend these oppositions. As Paul Willemen puts it:

> The drama and the analytical presentation of socio-historical processes fit so closely together that it is impossible to say whether the environment is there to explain the characters and their drama, or whether the characters were selected/constructed as exemplary and necessary to convey an analysis of the social. In effect, the question becomes irrelevant: people are presented as living in and determined by history, superseding the false oppositions between the subjective and the social, between the individual and society, as idealist philosophies tend to put it. Ghatak . . . depict[s] social existence, nothing less.[37]

Just as the mother's severity is connected to her daily struggle of feeding her family, concretized through her cooking in the kitchen, Neeta's self-effacement is made palpable in terms of her torn sandal, the sweat that she wipes away from her forehead with her sari, and her bloody handkerchief, bearing the trace of her tuberculosis, that she tries, so desperately, to hide from Shankar. The archetypal characterizations are fleshed out through their corporeality and concrete activities.

What is more stunning is the way in which Ghatak employs the single archetype of the Mother Goddess to capture the ravages of history on individual subjectivities. In Hindu mythology, the Mother Goddess appears in many forms, a few of which are evoked in the trilogy: Uma, the tender virgin; Durga, the benign and familiar mother; Jagaddhatri, the protector of the world; Kali, the angry, cruel and punitive mother. Neeta, born on the day of the annual worship of Jagaddhatri, bears the burden of the family, her own microcosmos; her mother, in her cynical cruelty, approximates Kali. It is not difficult to imagine how someone like Neeta might, through the travails of life, turn into someone like her mother; indeed, toward the end of the film, she speaks to her mother in a harsher tone, impatiently cutting off her nagging complaints. In the theater studios of *Komal Gandhar*, we see a guillotine-like structure (*harikath*), used for animal sacrifice at Kali temples; it is particularly prominent in scenes in which Anasuya feels trapped in, and tormented by, malicious factional squabbles. *Subarnarekha*'s Seeta, once a loving, nurturing figure, stoops to prostitution in order to feed her son and ultimately hacks herself to death, not unlike Kali who, enraged by the sins of mankind, goes on a killing spree—except that Seeta's "sin" leads to traumatized self-destruction. This outcome is portended in the famous scene on an abandoned airstrip, a remnant from the World War II days: young Seeta comes face to face with a Kali impersonator (practicing masquerade as a form of folk entertainment) and is immobilized with fear.[38] Ghatak himself lays out the ecumenical reach of this terrifying encounter: "One archetypal image that has been haunting us from a remote past, is today confronting us all over the world. You may call it by many names: the Hydrogen Bomb, or Strategic Air Command, or De Gaulle, or Adenaur, or some other name you would not like to mention. It is the power of annihilation, the ability to destroy, and per-haps, like little Seeta, we have suddenly found ourselves confronted by it."[39] Ghatak understands the archetype as a cultural sign bearing the sedimentations of one long catastrophic history. And in confronting the archetype, we are compelled to face up to our own shell-shocked complicity in that history.

Without resorting to the Jungian category of a collective unconscious, archetypes may be understood as highly condensed, shared models (of characters, relations, settings) that have congealed over time through the concrete practices of daily life. Thus archetypes are ultimately ma-terially inscribed in the cultural forms and rhythms of social existence and not stored in a presumed social unconscious; the element of uncon-sciousness arises from the unthought automaticity marking the daily structures and activities.[40] These palimpsestic entities gather their signi-fying force by virtue of their historicity, and their continuing relevance in the lived experiences of people; they become the substance of a cul-ture's myths, and provide the contours of a community's identity.[41]

The archetypes in Indian culture are frequently derived from Indian mythology, and from subsequent cultural texts based on them. While they embody important social and cultural values, archetypes are em-ployed to negotiate contemporary contradictions and necessary trans-formations: for instance, while the archetypal mother has to balance her love for her children with her social responsibilities in seminal films like *Mother India* and *Deewar* (1975), the balancing act is always inflected by changing values.[42] Thus, if we look at the genealogies of particular cinematic archetypes, we begin to get a sense of their cultural and historical specificities. Ghatak works with the same cultural/civilizational pool of mythic structures and archetypes as commercial filmmakers like Mehboob Khan and Raj Kapoor; what marks out his invocation of these elements is the way he politicizes them. Unlike Khan's *Mother India* or Kapoor's *Awara*, Ghatak's films do not stage the contradictions only to offer resolutions acceptable to a nationalist bourgeoisie. In his hands, the myths and archetypes disintegrate under the burden of their inherent conflicts; the familiar becomes so strange and disquieting that it fails to bring emotional succor. Instead of shoring up hegemonic structures, Ghatak's mythologies stage irreconcilable differences: they constitute a politics of open-ended criticism.

Subnational Fantasy

The archetype of a hardworking, tired, yet resilient and infinitely patient, young Bengali woman becomes, in Ghatak's imagination, an embodiment of Bengal: "A girl, a very ordinary girl, tired after her day's work, waits near my house at the bus or tram stop, a lot of papers and a bag in her hand, her hair forms a halo around her head and face, some clinging to her face because of perspiration. I discover a history from the subtle lines of pain on her face, my imagination reaches out to the most ordinary, yet unforgettable drama in her strong, firm and determined, yet soft, touching and infinitely patient life."[43] This displacement of the collective history onto the individual mobilizes a powerful fantasy: the image of the young woman comes to be invested with the attributes of an idealized Bengal—lush, tranquil, nurturing. It is important to recognize that this symbology emerges not from some primordial female figure, but from contemporary Bengal. Indeed, the fantasy has its roots in modern poetic imaginings; Ghatak derives its terms from a famed Tagore poem that opens with the line: "I have secretly named her *Komal Gandhar*." The poet describes running into a young girl, who reminds him of the verdant Bengali countryside; there is a sweet and poignant air about her, which makes him think of the minor-key note *komal gandhar*, E-flat. The indelible fullness of the musical note echoes the essence of this image of a young woman; in Ghatak's mind, it comes to resonate with a sense of all that has been lost through the social division and all the potential that remains in spite of the loss.

Komal Gandhar: The idealized woman. Courtesy of NFAI.

The cultural production of this fantasy is reflexively acknowledged in *Komal Gandhar*: as Anasuya, an urban group theater enthusiast, transforms herself into a rural Bengali woman, the camera holds her face in close-up. Offscreen, the play's director instructs her to assume a certain pose and expression. She wears a white sari with a red border[44] and drapes the *anchal* around her head,[45] which is slightly tilted to one side: her makeup consists of a big red dot on her forehead, and kohl around her large, black eyes. The soft light transforms her face into an icon of idealized beauty: serene, tender, seductive. When the theater troupe goes to the hills, the members look down at the lush green plains of Bengal: one of them glimpses in the landscape the *komal* (tender), smiling face of a young girl. Later, as Anasuya stands disoriented in the middle of a political demonstration, her head tilted to one side, a political activist remarks that her pose reminds him of his dead sister: in her intimate iconicity, she points indexically to countless Bengali women who did not survive those turbulent years.

It is around this figure of the young woman that Ghatak articulates his own anger and pathos over the division of Bengal, and his hope of cultural redemption. At the end of *Meghe Dhaka Tara*, as Neeta is dying of tuberculosis in a distant sanatorium, her elder brother sadly looks on as another young woman drags her feet to work in worn-out sandals: the oppressive structures live on, the exploitation continues. Drawing our attention to the continual objectification of women in daily life and within nationalist discourses, Ghatak carries out a protofeminist critique of Bengali society and culture. Feminist scholarship of the past two decades has underscored the critical potential of melodrama in engaging women's life-worlds and subverting narratives that appear to

Meghe Dhaka Tara: The consumptive woman. Courtesy of NFAI.

maintain the status quo of patriarchal oppression.[46] In sharp contrast to Satyajit Ray's *Apu Trilogy*, a bildungsroman charting its male protagonist's gradual maturation as a (male) citizen-subject, Ghatak's "Partition trilogy" focuses on women characters and stages the precariousness of an incipient national subjectivity. While Apu emerges stronger from each successive loss of a female relation (aunt, sister, mother, and wife), the latter's male characters—Shankar, Bhrigu, Ishwar—cannot do without their female counterparts. Ghatak's recording of women's suffering and labor, both in and outside the domestic sphere, and of the virtual erasure of their pent-up hopes and desires, is marked by a deep empathy. Simultaneously, he trains an analytical eye on both the idealization of women as the repository of essential cultural values, and their commodification within a cultural economy. Thus he names Seeta, the woman who falls into prostitution, after the mythic queen of the epic *Ramayana* and the supreme ideal of Hindu womanhood. One could argue that Ghatak himself falls into the trap of romantic idealization when he talks about Bengal as a tender and melancholy girl. But then, his project is one of resuscitating a fragile strain of hope that inheres in the icon: even as he makes explicit the mechanisms and pitfalls of such romanticism, he is unwilling to turn his back on this enchantment and its promises. The tension between analytical revelation and utopian idealism, which emerges as a defining feature of Ghatak's work, indicates his ambivalent, melancholic relationship to nationalism, and secures for his oeuvre a key position among acts of cultural mourning. Besides, Ghatak's idealized women are firmly placed within a network of social relations: there is no enjoying the enchantment without experiencing the heartbreak of the post-Partition Bengali milieu. Anasuya's despondent breakdown at the border between the two Bengals, Seeta's violent suicide, Neeta's final cry at the Shillong sanatorium—three hysterical articulations of anguish and protest that together constitute the emotional and critical core of the trilogy—all rend the circuits of reification and mark the irruptions of irrepressibly real female lives and subjectivities.

Ghatak's Melodrama: Embarrassing Excess?

An extreme melodramatic mode characterizes the entire body of Ghatak's work, and the trilogy in particular. Audiences and critics have expressed their discomfiture with the excessive emotionalism, the incredible coincidences, the theatrical acting: the nondiegetic whiplash sound of *Meghe Dhaka Tara* that conveys Neeta's sense of betrayal as she makes a dazed exit upon discovering another woman in Sanat's apartment—a sound effect that returns several times, most notably as an expression of Sanat's despondence when she rejects his attempts to get back with her; the clumsy juxtaposition of a car crash in the background, when Bhrigu learns in *Komal Gandhar* that Anasuya has a fiancé in faraway France; the incredible series of coincidences that propels the plot of *Subarnarekha*, such as the miraculous arrival of a long-lost Haraprasad as his friend Ishwar is about to hang himself, or Ishwar's drunken binge in Calcutta ending at his sister's door.

For Ghatak, the forced coincidental structure, glaringly evident in this traumatic reunion of brother and sister, is a conscious formal choice. In rendering the situations and actions obvious and simplistic, he hopes to free the viewers from the shackles of a character-driven plot, so that they engage with the rhetorical and contextual implications: "Take, for instance, the brother turning up at his prostitute sister's. If we keep in mind the narrative's thematic thrust, we realize that any prostitute the guy visited would still turn out to be his sister. Here that point has been expounded mechanically: the aim is to allude to the general through the particular."[47] In the scene under consideration, Ghatak carries out this strategy—of taking the most hackneyed plot structures, and playing up the melodrama—with great virtuosity. A drunk Ishwar loses his glasses and stumbles into the semidark room, the music from the bar (the tune from *La Dolce Vita*) still playing on the soundtrack. Seeta looks at the door and sees her estranged brother walk in. Layers of light and darkness lend a charged density: Ishwar haltingly makes his way through it. A close-up of Seeta is followed by an extreme close-up of her eyes, partly out of frame; by now, the music has stopped, and all we can hear

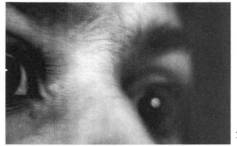

1

2

3

4

5

6

Subarnarekha: Seeta's suicide.
Courtesy of NFAI.

is labored breathing. As Ishwar comes nearer, Seeta takes up a huge kitchen knife; as she hacks herself to death offscreen, blood splatters all over Ishwar in medium shot. The camera frames parts of Seeta's musical instruments, as her body trembles and wheezes against the *tanpura* offscreen, producing a terrifying drone and clatter for several seconds. Ishwar peers at the prone body: Seeta's face gradually comes into focus. Shocked, he picks up the knife and lurches out of the room. In an extreme close-up shot, Seeta's face, eyes wide open, floats in the dense darkness. On the soundtrack, we hear "He Ram"—Gandhi's last utterance right after being shot fatally; with this pithy sound bite, an otherwise common exclamation expressing shock and despair, Ghatak invests this isolated instance of personal violence with the significance of another, more high-profile, brutal act, inscribing both moments within the same pathologically violent public sphere.

In the context of an emergent modernist-realist film aesthetic, dominated by Ray's restrained style, Ghatak's films struck a high-pitched, anachronistic chord. Just as Bengali cinema appeared to be moving beyond its staple sentimentalism, the excessive melodrama of these texts constituted, for bourgeois urban audiences, a regression to an archaic maudlin sensibility. The politicized viewers who formed an alternative audience in Bengal and who were drawn to the overtly political films of Mrinal Sen in the 1960s and the 1970s, were baffled by the centrality that Ghatak accorded to the subjective experiences of his characters, and accused him of self-indulgence, pessimism, nihilism, even decadence. According to the critic George Sadoul, an avowed fan of Ghatak's *Ajantrik*, the melodramatic sequence of Seeta's death in *Subarnarekha* was bound to preempt any chance of the film's favorable reception in Europe: he suggested that Ghatak should rethink the sequence, keeping in mind the devaluation of the melodramatic mode in the 1960s' film festival circuit.[48]

In response to his interlocutors, Ghatak declares: "Melodrama is a birthright, it is a form."[49] This defiant polemic asserts his faith in melodrama as a key register for the aesthetic mediation of social contradictions. Ghatak takes elements of this common and critically discounted mode and employs them in such an exaggerated fashion that their formal operations become clearly visible. Through such self-conscious accentuation, the clichéd components of melodrama are made to subvert their own functions: as the dramatic flow comes to stuttering halts, context triumphs over events and actions, the social dimensions of experience dispel the seduction of individuated subjectivism. Such a tactic of politicizing melodramatic elements, while not altogether rare, musters a singular force in Ghatak's films.[50] Thus, when the whiplash

sounds over Neeta's stupefied exit from Sanat's apartment, the extrava-
gance of this acoustic embellishment, far from focalizing us to Neeta's
mental state, jolts us out of the action into a keen awareness of the level
of betrayal and of the injustice of the situation: we are forced to place
it in the context of larger betrayals and injustices perpetrated not just
by Sanat and Neeta's family, but by many others—by an entire social
system. When Neeta's father learns of her illness, he shouts out in an
automatic reflex: "I accuse . . ." The next shot shows him from behind,
his arm outstretched, finger pointing ahead. Neeta's brother, who stands
facing the father and the camera, asks nervously, "Whom?" In response,
the father, now in a frontal medium shot, only manages a feeble "no-
body" as his face quivers and his hand comes trembling down. Not only
the family, but also a wider, inchoate apparatus of exploitation in modern Bengal, is held responsible for Neeta's tragedy.

The use of melodrama as a way of bringing in the collective level is
evident in the use of folk songs and phrases that are intimately connected to the material practices of Bengali life. These culturally specific
quotations set up an epic relay of exchanges, with the various levels
commenting back on, and amplifying, each other. When the consumptive Neeta starts to cough up blood, and later when she is about to leave
home in pouring rain, a nondiegetic female chorus breaks into a melancholy tune: it is a traditional song sung at weddings, when the young
bride is about to leave for her in-laws' house. In invoking *Gouridaan*, the
archaic Bengali custom of giving away very young girls in marriage, the
song not only underscores the pathos of Neeta's impending separation
from her family in a folk idiom but also becomes a searing comment
on her unwed status, the abrogation of heteronormative expectations
constitutive of her subjectivity.[51] The tune is introduced for the first
time in an instrumental version during the sequence of Geeta's wedding to Sanat; ironically, it is Neeta who is in charge of all arrangements.
The mother, who tacitly supports the nuptials in complete disregard of
Neeta's desires, can barely look at her; nevertheless, she secures Neeta's
consent in giving up her share of the meager family jewels for Geeta's
benefit. The tune comes in at the very cusp of this awkward transaction:
for all the commentary on Ghatak's "unruly" stylistics, it is such formal
precision that remains a defining feature of his work. This sonic intensification sets the stage for, and continues into, the next heartrending
scene between Neeta and her dad. With self-lacerating prescience, the
despondent father observes that in the old days, young girls were dis-
posed of in marriage to much older men; now that we have become
"civilized" and "modern," we educate our daughters and then exploit
them endlessly, wringing the life out of them. Melos, besides intensify-

Komal Gandhar: End of the train line at the border, boats in the background. Courtesy of NFAI.

ing the dramatic tension, becomes a conduit for charged critical intro-spection about a putatively reformulated modern heteropatriarchy.

The single folk phrase *dohai ali*—boatmen's entreaty to god and/or nature to spare and save them from destruction—is transformed in *Komal Gandhar* into a stunning expression of grief and outrage, an index of psychic division. When the theater group goes to perform in Lalgola, a town on the border between the two Bengals, the concrete mark of the division and the proximity of the "other side" unleash strong and conflicting emotions. While conversing on the bank of the River Padma, standing at the end of a railway track, Bhrigu and Anasuya find out that they are both refugees from the east who lost family members in the communal riots. Memories of similar experiences bring them closer; this experiential bond further enhances the attraction they already feel for each other. At this moment of union, the camera pans away to the river, to the accompaniment of music (flute and percussion) and female voices chanting the phrase *dohai ali*. Next, Ghatak introduces a remark-able dolly shot: as the soundtrack gathers speed and rises in volume, so that the chant begins to sound like a cry for help, the camera charges headlong toward the buffer at the end of a railway track. At the moment of impact, the music and chant give way to a shattering explosion: then the screen turns to black, and the soundtrack falls silent. The shot sets up a counterpoint to Bhrigu and Anasuya's romance, reminding us that their union has to transcend the confusing and dislocating traces of an immense social cataclysm. Right after, we see Anasuya break down amid wild reeds, which prompts a concerned Bhrigu to rush to her side. Later, as Anasuya is faced with a choice between Bhrigu and her fiancé who has emigrated to Europe, she stands petrified at the bottom of a staircase: the camera dashes down toward her, and the same plaintive chant is heard on the soundtrack. Through this reiteration, Ghatak places the possibility of further migration in relation to the displacement resulting from the Partition, thereby tracking a wider historical pattern of alienation and dispersion. He appears to suggest that unless the social, economic, and political forces that caused the Partition are recognized and confronted, they will lead to further dislocation. Partition and diasporic migration emerge as two threats to the community at both regional and national levels. If the onrushing camera signals the assault of history, then the mounting chant expresses Ghatak's and the postcolonial nation's agony and apprehension.

Viewers have noted a tendency toward theatrical acting style in the trilogy, particularly in the performances of Bijon Bhattacharya. This actor, who wrote the seminal play *Nabanna*, was associated mainly with the stage, but his theatrical acting on screen might have been a conscious choice, and not a habitual relapse. Bhattacharya acts as Neeta's father in *Meghe Dhaka Tara*, as Gagan—a bangal refugee with theatrical aspirations—in *Komal Gandhar*, and as the idealist-turned-cynic Haraprasad in *Subarnarekha*. In each case, his character is that of a bewildered and disoriented person who cannot come to terms with his dislocation and who does not have the psychic or material resources to overcome his déclassé situation. His bangal dialect, his emaciated frame, and his overdramatic expressions and gesticulations, all marks of his difference as an East Bengali refugee, become the defiant articulations of his identity: he is perhaps an exteriorization of a repressed part of Ghatak's own self—indeed, of every Bengali self. But more than his accent, Bhattacharya's speech pattern takes on a deliberate rhythm and parodic intonation. This studied melodeclamation adds a further formal twist to these films: it frames the dialogue, calls attention to its intent and artifice, and forces viewers to really listen.

In terms of content, the trilogy engages with a world where familiar structures have either disintegrated or become tenuous: the films are populated by characters seeking to overcome their alienation, looking for a home or a community. The family or the home is, of course, the quintessential melodramatic topos. The two main characters of *Komal Gandhar*, having lost most of their family members in the riots, are looking to regain a sense of belonging. They hope to establish a community of like-minded people through their work in theater, but ideological tensions and ego clashes threaten to waylay their endeavors. *Subarnarekha*'s decimated family is the site of confusing relations and

Meghe Dhaka Tara: Wide angle, depth of field shot. Neeta reads Sanat's letter. Courtesy of NFAI.

interactions; the narrative leads up to a troubling incestuous confrontation that, by metonymic extension, reveals the illicit drives underlying nationalist aspirations. If the family is still present in *Meghe Dhaka Tara*, it has also mutated beyond recognition into a parasitic burden that crushes the protagonist. Neeta shares a remarkable intimacy with Shankar, her elder brother: she is closer to him than to Sanat, her beau. When Shankar expresses remorse about his continuing dependence on her, she declares: "I love you all madly." If, in its unconditional and sensuous abandon, her love is of the purest kind, it also puts pressure on social norms and kinship configurations. Within modern society's calculating ambit, this is an impossible form of love—a bit incestuous, not unlike the desire or love for the nation-imagined-as-mother.

The force of Ghatak's melodrama derives largely from its formalization, evident at the microlevel of the shot: richly conceived, flouting standard cinematic notions of perspective and framing to achieve an electrifying expressivity. Practically every shot conveys a charged intensity because of conflicts and tensions innate to it: tensions between bodies caught in odd and continually shifting proxemic relations; between empty space and voluminous bodies; between the crowdedness of bodies and space caught in deep focus; between what is visible and what is blocked from view; between shadow and light; between objective reality and subjective interiority. Then the shots are put together to construct scenes of great emotional potency: eschewing the standard master shot and dismissing any naturalized sense of spatial relation; juxtaposing deep focus, wide angle shots, and crowded medium shots with extreme close-ups, producing disorientation and a sense of cramped doom; music not only acting as a sound bridge across shots, but carrying the shots on its melodic and rhythmic arc. As my halting attempts to describe these thoroughly audiovisual moments reveal, any such endeavor must contend with the limits of verbal explication. Notwithstanding such difficulties, one still gleans from these loaded moments Ghatak's absolute refusal to resolve spatially, and thus to domesticate, contradictions that have no easy resolutions.

For an illustration of Ghatak's formalized melodrama, I want to dwell on a scene that takes the ubiquitous song sequence of Indian popular cinema and turns it into altogether something else. When Neeta learns that Sanat, her boyfriend, has become tired of waiting for her and decided to marry her own younger sister, she tries to hide her feelings. But her distress comes through when she joins her brother in singing a well-known song composed by Tagore.[52] While the lyrics invest the scene with a tremendous emotive charge for Bengali audiences, the impelling melodic signification is not lost on audiences unfamiliar with the language. As in most indoor scenes, light falls directly on odd corners, surfaces and objects, leaving the more significant parts of the frame in a hallucinatory penumbra. Indeed, the wretched refugee colony room becomes an intense, mysterious domain traversed by chiaroscuro lattices. While the siblings sit on a bed and sing, Ghatak presents them in a series of shots that many will find odd or awkward: the camera pans from a close-up of Shankar's eyes to Neeta's face, establishing his deep sympathy for her; as Neeta looks upward, the camera trains its gaze on her throat in close-up from a low angle, her throat muscles moving with the exertion of her singing and simultaneously expressing her agony; Neeta's contorted face, in extreme close-up, emerges from the bottom of the frame and moves out of it (somewhat diagonally across the camera) as she gently sways her head in the act of singing, thereby producing disorientation—even a certain physical distress—in the spectators. (See also the figures on p. 226, four consecutive shots that build up a scene in which Shankar discovers Neeta has tuberculosis.) The proverbial cinematic gaze implodes and disperses as the sheer volume of body parts, captured in extreme close-up and coming into view from unexpected directions, embeds the spectator physically and emotionally in the scene: subjective point of view is developed to the point of palpable embodiment. A typical example: the frontal shot of a head/face rising up and moving away from the camera, followed by a shot of what is essentially the same movement, but now captured as the back of the head rising toward the camera, the two shots together constituting an unusual "cutting on action" and placing the spectator in the "impossible" physical space of the character's head (seen in this song sequence;

Meghe Dhaka Tara:
Ghatak's impossible space.
Sanat finds out that Neeta
has tuberculosis.

in the railway platform scene in *Subarnarekha* where Abhiram recognizes the dying lower-caste woman as his long-lost mother; among the reeds on the river bank in *Komal Gandhar*, when Anasuya is overcome with emotion).

Bellour sums it up when he says that Ghatak's melodrama derives its force from the elements—and from the formalized way in which these elements are brought together—in each shot.[53] When he describes *Meghe Dhaka Tara* as "the film we accompany," he suggests that critique or analysis is not enough in this situation: "The somewhat manic intensity and effort required for this work is always worth it, since it is a question of seeing precisely how the film works to the end." He is suggesting that we give ourselves over to the dialogism that "is the basis of the teaching situation, of seminars, of so many lectures." But I will suggest a different sense of "accompanying" that remains implicit in Bellour. It is the way one accompanies a performance of Indian classical music: from a slow or midtempo introduction and elaboration (*alap*), to a gradual build-up (*jod*), leading up to a fast climax (*jhala*)—a musical jouissance, if you will. Thus Shankar's singing voice gradually gives way to a "vibration" of the sarod rising to a crescendo as the story propels itself inexorably toward the peripatetic moment of Neeta's cry on the Shillong hills. Bellour intuitively stumbles upon the best way "to comprehend the energy and the essence" of Ghatak's cinema "haunted by music": we let ourselves be carried along with it.

Mourning Work

Time and again, a sense of tremendous personal agony erupts into Ghatak's sustained sociohistorical analysis. His obsessive returns to the moment of Bengal's division, his compulsion to trace all social problems of the post-independence period back to the Partition, indicate the extent to which he was personally affected by it. He turns his pain and disillusionment into rare critical charge, training it on the social field and the state. Refusing to accept the official devaluation of Partition as a historical aberration and working against the general silence, he makes the seemingly ungrievable crisis the tenacious core of his cinematic project.

In the penultimate sequence of *Meghe Dhaka Tara*, Neeta's elder brother visits her at the sanatorium up in the mountains. After years of depending on her financially, Shankar has finally become a successful singer and is able to support the family. They both know that her tuberculosis is at a very advanced stage, and not much can be done about it.

Shankar attempts to regale her with chitchat about the family's new-found affluence and about their infant nephew's lively antics. Suddenly, Neeta looks up at him and cries out: "But I did want to live!" An eddying camera captures the mountains around them in a 360-degree pan: Neeta's heart-rending but defiant cry reverberates in all directions. She finally reaches the mountains that she has always dreamt of visiting: but she goes there to live out her last sickly days. In one sense, Neeta allegorizes the predicament of the Indian nation: years of collective dreaming and struggle end in a blighted nationhood. Through the defiant, melodramatic articulation of her desire to live, Ghatak protests the tragic vitiation of nationalist aspirations and the subsequent disillusionment of statehood. But it is possible to read more into this memorable scene; Kumar Shahani, for instance, has claimed that Ghatak's work constitutes a defiant assertion of identity that challenges both indigenous and Western structures of domination: "In an atmosphere where our cultural attitudes and artefacts have been identified with the objectification of effete feudal Brahminism and European humanism inflicted on us by the colonials, Ritwikda's work is *the violent assertion of our identity*. It is the cry of the dying girl in *Meghe Dhaka Tara* that echoes through the hills, our right to live."[54] This two-pronged critique—of the European colonization of the Indian imagination and the reified, bourgeois aesthetics of a domestic cultural establishment—marks Ghatak's oeuvre as a spirited postcolonial intervention.

In many ways, Ghatak displays the symptoms of a melancholic; in terms of a Freudian schema, his engagement with Partition takes the form of primitive mourning work.[55] The melancholic has to work through the loss of self-sufficiency caused by the sudden eruption of an other in the midst of the self. In Ghatak, we see such a loss caused by an exogenous splintering of the ego. The very base of his Bengali identity (the geographic area designated as Bengal, the Bengali people, Bengali culture, Bengali society) is fragmented, and he is suddenly confronted with another Bengal. His films, specially those constituting the Partition trilogy, may be understood as attempts to work through the loss of a unitary Bengali self, to accept the fact of the bifurcation. Unlike the mainstream Calcutta filmmakers (say, the people who produced the Uttam Kumar–Suchitra Sen films, analyzed in chapter 3), Ghatak cannot easily "other" the other Bengal: he cannot fundamentally distinguish himself from the Muslims or the bangals.[56] His melancholia colors the intense narratives of *Meghe Dhaka Tara* and *Subarnarekha* (whose protagonists bear the mark of the ego's destabilization on their bodies); it forces him, in *Komal Gandhar*, to substitute the broken dreams with new dreams of integration, to attempt to transcend the boundaries and forge a new integrative order of identity. In short, melancholia shapes Ghatak's cultural politics. His early mourning work creates a space for future cinematic attempts at working through the collective trauma, without having to demonize the "lost objects" of our national desires.[57]

Beginning with the dislocation of Partition, Ghatak moves to the growing displacement from westward migration. In *Komal Gandhar*, the already uprooted Anasuya faces the choice between staying back in a truncated, decaying Bengal and moving to a more promising world of opportunities. Through her dilemma, Ghatak dramatizes the very palpable costs of severing one's ties with one's homeland, of becoming part of a diasporic drift. In this depiction, there is a distinct—if implicit—critique of the individualist rootlessness generated and encouraged by global capital in its singular focus on self-reproduction and self-augmentation. Even as Ghatak challenges a unitary nationalism, he cannot celebrate unproblematically the so-called transnational trends. He forces us to reconsider the implications of global movements of population in terms of a radical dispersal of community and the concurrent consolidation of neocolonialism. In mourning national scission, he also foregrounds the precarious, spectral status of the nation within capitalist modernity, thus astutely skirting the more recent idealization of diasporic and transnational formations.

CHAPTER SIX

Tamas and
the Limits of Representation

FOUR DECADES after Partition, a five-hour-long television miniseries titled *Tamas* beamed the trauma back into people's homes and forced it out in the public sphere. Presented by the state-owned television network Doordarshan and directed by the reputed "parallel cinema" filmmaker Govind Nihalani, *Tamas* hit a collective raw nerve with its hard-hitting exposé of the political intrigues that led to unimaginable sufferings. Through its vivid depictions of loss and dislocation, the serial—whose title literally means "darkness"—resuscitated experiences that some would prefer to forget. This televisual assemblage of cultural memory, and the impassioned response it evoked from several generations of viewers, brought to the fore the complexities of mass-scale mediations of social trauma. At the heart of the controversy was the vexed question of bringing violence into representation, a question that comes loaded with ethical, epistemological, and political implications and provokes a range of proscriptions.

Tamas begins with a memorable sequence that animates the subsequent narrative chain: following orders from the local *thekedar* (labor contractor), a *chamar* (low-caste worker) called Nathu kills a pig. As man and animal square off, the camera focuses mainly on Nathu's face, contorted in tense revulsion; we hear his panting, thumps, and blows, and the pig's grunts. This opening intimates, by proxy, the brutality at the heart of the Partition saga, and sets a foreboding tone for the entire miniseries. At the same time, Nathu's alienation from his own labor—his manifest loathing of a job that he undertakes for money—divests him, if only partially, of responsibility for the killing, and for subsequent developments. This dissociation of agency and accountability turns out to be significant narrative maneuver, for what happens next gets recast as the outcome of a cynical power play. The carcass of the pig shows up in front of the mosque, angering Muslims in the area, who assume that Hindus are responsible for this act of desecration. As tension mounts, the British administrators refuse to take steps necessary to prevent the full-blown outbreak of communal hostility. Within a matter of hours, terror spreads through the town: a Muslim, weapon in hand, chases a cow (we surmise that the dead cow will show up on the steps of the Hindu temple—a fitting retaliation to the original affront); teenage members of a militant Hindu outfit stab a Muslim; by nightfall, riots break out, and entire neighborhoods go up in flames.

The miniseries goes to great lengths to depict Nathu, and people like him, as being caught in a maelstrom: they are hapless pawns whose actions are not of their own volition. Partition here takes on the force of a natural disaster, an anomaly in the face of the customary unity and camaraderie that mark the daily lives of common people. Both the truncation and the birth of the nation are presented as inevitable: if the division is explained in terms of the political machinations of influential power-mongers, the nation is valorized as the community of well-meaning and humane folks, waiting to come into its own after the departure of the alien rulers. I hope to establish that *Tamas*, produced and aired by the state-owned television network, operates within the contours of a nationalist historiography, its internal mythologies negotiating all along the particularly fraught relationship between representations of social violence and the futures of community.

A Sublime Project?

Beyond the unavoidable gap that opens up between any reality and its representation (by now, a commonplace poststructuralist insight), violence introduces a further torque. In bringing corporeal and psychic violence into representation, we are faced with a quandary: are the resources at our disposal adequate to our mission? Can we find the right words, fitting modes, appropriate strategies? Or does the very attempt to know, comprehend, and depict violence result in a necessary attrition of experience, a draining of affect, a kind of containment? In other words, can violence be represented without perpetrating yet another form of violence?

For Claude Lanzmann, the celebrated documentarian of the Holocaust, any attempt to understand and capture the nature of the experience is, in a sense, obscene: "It is enough to formulate the question in simplistic terms—Why have the Jews been killed?—for the question to reveal right away its obscenity. There is an absolute obscenity in the very project of understanding. Not to understand was my iron law during all the eleven years of the production of *Shoah*. I had clung to this refusal of understanding as the only possible ethical, and at the same time the only possible operative, attitude."[1] Lanzmann's "refusal of understanding" springs from a deep anxiety about the possible trivialization of a catastrophic experience through attempts to make sense of it; he seeks to circumvent this risk by turning his willful "blindness" into the condition of possibility for an ethical act of witnessing, whereby the experience is remembered even as its cataclysmic nature and incomprehensibility are acknowledged.

Human comprehension totters in the face of the great tragedies of the last century—Hiroshima, the Holocaust, famines, pogroms, and war. These collective experiences overwhelm our faculties: they mark the very limits of representation and put into question the continuation of the human species. As pain and grief remain shrouded in silence, as speech and action falter, the search for apposite means of knowledge and representation—means that can somehow do justice to the enormity of suffering—becomes something of a sublime project.[2]

In writing about violence against women in South Asian societies, anthropologist Veena Das has commented on the strain placed on social scientific discourse: "Languages of pain . . . often elude me."[3] The categories and frameworks scholars use in producing knowledge, with their affectations of disinterested objectivity, either overlook important dimensions of suffering or tame the experience by making it fit the contours of normalizing paradigms. For Jean-François Lyotard, both knowing and not knowing can become complicit with the horror. On the one hand, since knowledge is partially mimetic, knowing lends itself to voyeuristic pleasures, to the production of kitsch. The procedures whereby we make sense of violence pave the way for its institutional acceptance and normalization. In the words of Maurice Blanchot, "Knowledge which goes so far as to accept horror in order to know it, reveals the horror of knowledge, its squalor, the discrete complicity which maintains it in a relation with the most insupportable aspects of power."[4] On the other hand, denying or forgetting suffering perpetuates the terror: to be erased from collective memory is to be consigned to a form of social death. The challenge, as Lyotard understands it, is to come up with procedures and phrases that refuse to reduce experience to kitsch, that enable victims to find their voice, that help us bear witness to their suffering.[5]

Treating social trauma in an intensely reverential way—as "negative sublime," if you will—comes with its own set of problems. This kind of sealing off, even sacralization, of violence and suffering leads us into an impasse, where the possibility of agency is foreclosed, where we are left wringing our hands in despair. Lanzmann, Lyotard, or Das warn us about the pitfalls of trying to make sense of debilitating experiences, and they all underscore the necessity of continuous engagement: of anamnesis, of witnessing, of working through. Blanchot brings out the enigma of this twofold challenge with reference to Auschwitz: "The wish of all, in the camps, the last wish: know what has happened, do not forget, and at the same time never will you know."[6]

Coming to Terms with the Past

Bhisham Sahni started working on his Hindi novel *Tamas* in 1971, the year Bangladesh was born through yet another round of civil war and geopolitical truncation in South Asia. The novel, which went on to win the Sahitya Akademi Award—the highest literary honor in India—in 1975, benefited from the passage of time: even as the work powerfully conveyed the horror of the Partition carnage, Sahni was able to strike a detached and analytical note. The six-part miniseries was based on the novel, and on two other short stories by Sahni—*Sardarni* and *Zahud Baksh*. Each episode began with the same short introduction in Hindi by the author, in which he laid out the producers' objectives in making the series in the late 1980s. Such a frame was considered necessary, as the question "Why *Tamas*? Why now?" was on the minds of many at the time of the initial broadcast. According to Sahni, the series creators did not aim to reopen old wounds and reawaken dormant hostilities, or to hold any particular community responsible for the mayhem; rather, they hoped to expose the communal forces that led to the Partition and to call attention to their continued operation in contemporary India. By stressing that he himself had lived through the carnage—an experientiality also emphasized by director Govind Nihalani, who said, "My first memories of fright, panic, and blood are from that period"[7]—Sahni cast the novel/miniseries as an act of bearing witness. He also articulated an abiding commitment to the causes of secularism and national integration. As the director put it, *Tamas* was "an act of faith."[8]

Nihalani was interested in analyzing contemporary conditions through the lens of Partition: he echoed Sahni in reiterating that "the communal elements who created the [Partition] holocaust are still active today and the patterns too remain the same. So I felt the need for a film on the role of these communal elements. The Partition provided a good historical backdrop."[9] His assertion that similar patterns were discernible, and that the same communal elements were still active after four decades, bore a striking resonance with Theodor Adorno's observations from 1959 on the persistence of fascism in Germany: "That fascism lives on, that the oft-invoked working through of the past has to this day been unsuccessful and has degenerated into its own caricature, an empty and cold forgetting, is due to the fact that the objective conditions of society that engendered fascism continue to exist."[10]

"Working through" or "coming to terms with" the past required, for Adorno, an active engagement with it: an analysis of the structures and forces that produced that past. Denying or forgetting would not assuage the problem. One possible answer for "Why *Tamas*? Why now?" can be framed in terms of a need to confront and overcome the past. However, for Adorno, "objective conditions" include the mechanisms that cause such murderous prejudices to fester in people in the first place—mechanisms that are able to pull together psychic predispositions into a historical force. Does *Tamas* offer such a social-psychological perspective? Does it admit of the potential for an element of radical evil in people, waiting to be coaxed and orchestrated into sinister collective expression? Can its progressive optic allow such a critical view of the "masses"? As I argue below, the challenge that the miniseries poses gets domesticated in terms of a nationalist historiography that, in its unproblematic espousal of a community of well-meaning "ordinary folk," effectively divests such a collectivity of historical responsibility. This is where the creators of *Tamas* diverge from Frankfurt School analytics.

All the same, both Sahni and Nihalani are committed to what may be described broadly as leftist cultural politics. Between 1957 and 1963, Sahni spent seven years in the Soviet Union, working as a translator from Russian to Hindi. On his return to India, he directed his energies toward writing and teaching. Nihalani came into prominence as a cinematographer in the heyday of the New Indian Cinema in the 1970s. He made his directorial debut in 1980, collaborating with playwright Vijay Tendulkar on a series of hard-hitting films dealing with corruption and loss of idealism. As I point out in chapter 4, the very notion of "leftist cultural politics" has a complicated history in post-independence

India, as the Left was largely co-opted by the nationalist agenda of the Congress Party. Madhav Prasad has suggested that the reformist works of the New Indian Cinema—typified by the early films of Shyam Benegal, with cinematography by Nihalani—fostered a "developmental aesthetic," upholding official programs aimed at eradication of poverty (*Garibi Hatao*), promotion of cooperative entrepreneurship, and the end of usurious money-lending and exploitation of landless labor.[11]

However, the turn to authoritarian rule in 1975 dealt a severe blow to the institutions of democracy and socialism and prepared the ground for the rapid ideological transformations of the 1980s. As endemic corruption produced a deep skepticism, commercial cinema witnessed the rise of the "angry young man"—a new kind of hero (most notably embodied by superstar Amitabh Bachchan) who appeared from among the ranks of the dispossessed masses and who was not afraid to take matters of justice in his own robust hands. This development—which Prasad places within "an aesthetic of mobilization,"[12] and Ashis Nandy sees as providing "a slum's eye view of politics"[13]—was one kind of response to emergent conditions. The effect on the more politicized, socially engaged quarters of the cultural field was even more striking. The practitioners of parallel cinema evinced a new order of reflexivity about their own position within Indian polity and culture. Two films made in 1980—Mrinal Sen's *In Search of Famine* and Govind Nihalani's *Akrosh*—signaled an introspective turn within leftist cultural politics: while Sen questioned the representational practices of educated, leftist, urban artists (interrogating their obsessions with the rural milieu and idealizations of underprivileged classes),[14] Nihalani revealed the ineffectual attempts of both well-meaning middle-class professionals and radical social workers to "make a difference" in the lives of subaltern groups.

It was the gathering clouds of religious fundamentalism that posed the biggest challenge for the Indian Left.[15] As the nationalist agenda of the earlier era unraveled, and the Congress Party's cynical manipulation of the anxieties of minority religious groups for short-term gains in elections came under public criticism, the secularist doctrinaire lost its legitimacy. Fundamentalist groups that had been effectively marginalized for almost three decades bounced back into the mainstream of national politics, gathering enough popular support by the late 1980s to force a new national agenda. The rewriting of national history from a Hindu chauvinist perspective, whereby all minority religious groups and traditions were reduced to mere appendices within a glorious Hindu heritage, or recast as perilous contagion, fanned xenophobic sentiments and communal tensions. While the demise of secularism was by no means a fait accompli, the shifting winds impelled intellectuals and cultural practitioners to train their critical gaze on the role of religion in history and memory.

Partition did not end Hindu-Muslim enmity: on the contrary, for many, the riots of the late 1940s became further proof of the deep-rooted religious strife. In Pakistan, there was belligerence between Bengali Muslims and Bihari Muslims, between *Mohajirs* (refugee communities) and Pathans or Sindhis. Besides two wars and countless border skirmishes between India and Pakistan, riots broke out periodically (Bhiwandi in 1972, Ahmedabad in 1985, Karachi in 1972 and 1985, Meerut in 1987). As one spectator claimed during the *Tamas* controversy: "We are no better off today. If you add all the communal killings after 1947, more people have died after than during Partition."[16] The sheer weight of this rancorous history posed a perpetual threat to the secularist ideal, providing its opponents with political leverage. The truncation of 1947 also served as a precedent, fueling fresh separatist movements demanding their own homelands as redress for real or imagined grievances. In the South Asian context, such claims to autonomy produced a series of tense faultlines of which East Pakistan, Sri Lanka, Assam, Kashmir, and Punjab were only the most salient examples.

In the 1980s, even in the absence of broad popular support, militants were able to spearhead a strong separatist movement in Punjab. While the demand sprung largely from economic and political imperatives, it was couched in religious terms: Khalistan was envisioned as a homeland for the Sikh community. The irony was that the Sikhs, who had sided with the Hindus against the Muslim community in 1947 and vehemently opposed the division of their province and the country, now clamored for a scission from Hindu-majority India. Things came to a head in 1984 when, in her bid to end terrorism in Punjab, Prime Minister Indira Gandhi sent the army into the Golden Temple of Amritsar. Although the militants had turned this venerated temple into their headquarters, the central government's action—seen as the official violation of a sacred space and of Sikh religious sentiments—caused widespread resentment among the Sikh population. On October 31 of the same year, Gandhi was gunned down by her own bodyguards of Sikh origin. Over the next few days, Sikhs became the targets of sectarian violence all over North India. The rioting was not simply the spontaneous expression of anger and grief that it was made out to be; rather, the violence was organized, with trucks and buses deployed to bring in rioters to Sikh neighborhoods. In the capital city of Delhi alone, more than two thousand Sikhs were beaten or burned to death. While the media attributed the police inaction to a collapse of administration, many have suggested that it marked the administration's complicity.[17] Rajiv Gandhi, who would soon succeed his mother, characterized the anti-Sikh violence as a natural response: appearing on Doordarshan, he commented that when a huge tree falls, the ground is bound to tremble.

For Sikhs, who had lived through the trauma of 1947 or had grown up hearing about the sufferings, 1984 was a nightmarish déjà vu. Many Sikh men had to shave their beards and shed their turbans to avoid attacks, while families worried about the safety of their women. Their experiences tellingly underscored the precariousness of minority lives within a volatile nation. The so-called lumpen classes were not the exclusive provenance of riots and mayhem, for much of the violence occurred in respectable, middle-class neighborhoods, with the active participation of local people. The shock of this revelation—that decent, regular citizens could actually commit or tacitly support the most abominable acts—exposed the aporia of standard Partition historiography, according to which the most heinous and violent acts were always committed "somewhere else" by "others," never "here," and never by "us." The events of 1984 stunned historians, sociologists, and social activists alike, forcing them to reconsider Partition in terms of disconcerting and undertheorized collective proclivities, and to acknowledge continuities with the past.[18] The miniseries *Tamas* was one attempt at this kind of rewriting of national history.

The other significant development in the 1980s was the rise of caste-based politics: the *dalits* (the downtrodden, the untouchables) had organized themselves into a significant political force, with substantial influence on the outcomes of both local and national elections, and with a major stake in the distribution of the social pie.[19] *Tamas*, with its focus on the lower-caste Nathu and his wife Karmo, must have seemed like the ideal text to be adapted for mass broadcast on Doordarshan.

Nihalani came across Sahni's novel in 1982, while working as an assistant director for Richard Attenborough's *Gandhi* (1984).[20] He was entrusted with shooting the scenes of Partition riots for the film, scenes that probably inaugurated the eighties' turn to explicit audiovisual representations of the trauma. If, as I argue in previous chapters, the horror of Partition was frequently displaced onto the shock over the assassination of the "Father of the Nation" in films of earlier decades, now this biopic, an Indo-U.S. coproduction with an international cast and crew, paved the way for more direct mass cultural mediations of 1947. In 1986, the Doordarshan primetime soap *Buniyaad* included episodes depicting the upheaval; then came *Tamas* in 1988.

How does the miniseries approach this complex and incendiary episode, the very mention of which seems to revive disturbing memories and ignite extreme passions? What limits does it defer to, or perhaps press against, in representing experiences that many consider to be too painful and hazardous for recapitulation, let alone audiovisual revivification? To extend this line of enquiry: what does this mass cultural emplotment of history teach us about the potentials and limitations of an admittedly *interested* engagement with the past from its own moment of articulation?

The Masses and the End-Games of Empire

The primary representative of the British colonial administration in the miniseries is the district's deputy commissioner. While the locals refer to him as the DC, an acronym signifying his official position, we also get to know him by his first name, Richard, from the more intimate scenes with his wife Lisa. Richard embodies one of the central paradoxes of British attitudes toward India: on the one hand, he is a scholar of ancient Indian history, with a passionate interest in classical literature and the arts; on the other hand, he has a manifest disdain for Indians and does not believe that they can manage without their alien rulers. We first see him at an archeological excavation site; while the area under his jurisdiction reels from the aftermath of the riots, he sits in his study with its antiques and Buddha statues, entranced by a newly discovered ancient Sanskrit text. The India that interests him is the India of the past, a fascinating object of scholarly perusal. This orientalist obsession produces an India that is frozen in antiquity, whose only contemporary relevance springs from British colonial interests. And these interests require the constant undermining of the Indian struggle for freedom by carefully nurturing the seeds of conflict within it. The DC's reluctance to comply with the local leaders' request to deploy police and military forces, as a way of mitigating the mounting tension, indicates something far more devious than callous indifference. He wants to fan the flames of communal discord and step in only afterward to prove, once more, that the natives are an unruly, barbaric lot. Informed of the outbreak of deadly riots in the middle of the night, he makes a derisive remark about Indians being incapable of self-governance, then goes back to sleep. Both the novel and the miniseries take great pains to link the riots back to agents who are on the payroll of the colonial government: the man who pays Nathu to kill the pig used to vandalize the mosque is an official contractor; dubious characters who hover in the background in the first episode, possibly manipulating the situation as it spins out of control, turn out to be the DC's subordinates.

Richard's cynical detachment is set against his wife's empathy and distraught helplessness. Horrified by the flames in the horizon, the peal of bells, and the howl of crowds in the distance, and upset by Richard's lack of responsiveness, Lisa is sleepless and fretful all night long. After the riots subside, she decides, against Richard's wishes, to volunteer her services at the refugee camps. This stress on the difference in gendered reactions to communal violence underscores the masculinist nature of the projects of empire building and knowledge production; it also follows well-known British cultural works (*A Passage to India* and *Jewel in the Crown*, to mention two significant 1980s screen adaptations) in advancing a critique of colonial attitudes through the lens of a British feminine subjectivity, with its essentialized attributes of empathy and respect.

In foregrounding policies of the colonial state as a key reason for the escalation of sectarian acrimony, *Tamas* adheres to one of the principal tenets of nationalist historiography. The British policy of "divide and rule" has been the subject of extensive documentation and commentary, dwelling on major instances such as the 1905 partition of Bengal and also the myriad, more dispersed ways of playing on the anxieties of religious communities and fomenting mistrust between groups. However, communalism and the eventual truncation cannot be explained exclusively in terms of British tactics: recent historical research points beyond colonial hoodwinking to the complicity of Indian groups. After all, sectarian rancor has persisted five decades after independence; some might argue that as a structural force, communal tensions have intensified. How does *Tamas* contend with this vexed question of Indian responsibility?

The strategy it adopts is rather simple: a sharp distinction is made between the hapless commoners, the "masses," and the politicians, community leaders, and affluent classes, agents who have the power to shape history. I have already noted that the man who kills the pig and unwittingly precipitates the riots is portrayed as a pawn in the hands of sinister schemers, one who can only watch from the sidelines as the horror unfolds. In absolving Nathu, *Tamas* sets up a pattern of divesting common folk of any responsibility. Meanwhile, the powerful are depicted as ruthless, conniving advancers of their own agendas: they cautiously stand by, squabble among themselves, and stoke the volatility. When the riots subside, the merchants and landowners discuss trading opportunities and the value of real estate in the wake of the mass exodus: they are not unlike the vultures circling over the carcasses.[21]

The narrative focuses on two ordinary couples whose paths cross as they flee their own hometowns: Nathu and his pregnant wife Karmo, and the elderly Sikh retailer Harnam Singh and his wife Banto. Deeply anguished by his own unintended involvement in the carnage, Nathu is further unnerved when he accidentally steps on a black magic totem: he feels as if fate is entangling him in a vortex of ill luck. Hoping to protect his wife, his old mother, and his unborn child from the murderous rioters, Nathu leaves home with them; his ailing mother cannot withstand the uprooting and succumbs to the stress of the journey. Fate also seems to play a strong role in the story of Harnam Singh and Banto: they are barely out of their door, heeding the warning of their Muslim neighbor, when the rioters arrive on the scene. In one of the most poignant scenes, we see the elderly couple hiding behind a bush, watching their homefront shop being looted and their ancestral home going up in flames. Eventually these four characters, victims of fate—or fate reconfigured as the relentless march of a history beyond their control—will travel together and take refuge in a *gurdwara*, a Sikh temple.

Tamas goes to great lengths to uphold humanist values that bind people together and function as the cement of community. Just as nationalist historiography endorses acts of courage, compassion, and neighborliness, the miniseries dramatizes instances of valiance, when people risk their own lives to defend their neighbors belonging to another sect. These are the most powerful and moving images that linger in spectators' minds long after the episodes are over: a Hindu woman defends her neighbor, a Muslim teacher she calls her brother, sword in hand; a Muslim woman provides shelter to Harnam and Banto against her family's wishes; Muslim Shahnawaz Khan escorts the Hindu merchant Lalaji and his family to a safe, Hindu-majority neighborhood, without concern for his own safety. Through these representations of selfless acts of compassion, and the heartrending scenes of people watching their lives get reduced to cinders, *Tamas* projects ordinary people as the repository of common sense and humanity. Consider the Muslim scholar of classical Hindu literature, who assures his family that they are safe even in a Hindu neighborhood, for it is *their* neighborhood, where they have lived all along; then, as the rioters force into his home, he watches in disbelief as they set his books—including, ironically, the manuscript of his Urdu translation of the great Sanskrit play *Shakuntala*—on fire. Such hatred, such destructive energy belies normal expectations, it goes against basic human decency: how can regular, caring people become such fiends? In making us ponder such a question along with its characters, the miniseries shepherds us toward an impression of the masses as essentially sensible and peaceful: they form a national community marked by a long tradition of camaraderie and coexistence. In this view, nationhood is a cinch—the nation is a predestined entity, an already existing fetus, waiting to be born with the departure of the British. Not surprisingly, the series derives much of its dramatic energy from the impending fate of Nathu's unborn child, and it concludes with the birth of this child at the camp, signaling the founding of the sovereign state.

The darkness referred to in the title *Tamas* springs from the endgames of a dying empire and the machinations of politicians, community elders, and elite classes who want to secure their positions in the emerging state structure. As these leaders sow the seeds of discord and rend the national community, they vitiate the birthing of the nation. The members of the Muslim League are deeply distrustful of the Congress Party politicians; their leader Hayat Baksh does nothing to quell the rising clamor for a separate Pakistan. The Congress Party functionaries are always squabbling and questioning each other's motives and commitment. The Sikh leader Teja Singh tells the congregation in the gurdwara that they should be ready for any sacrifice; yet, when he has the chance to broker peace by paying a large sum of money, he sends out two emissaries to haggle with the rioters and bring down the amount. Both men are butchered: Teja Singh's call for sacrifice rings hollow. Among local politicians, the two exceptional figures are the elderly Bakshiji, a dedicated Gandhian, and Jarnail Singh, a firebrand revolutionary. Bakshiji's idealism and Jarnail's integrity stand in sharp contrast to the general opportunism; both seem out of sync with the realpolitik of the impending transfer of power. At any rate, in the diegetic world of *Tamas* all politicos are either inept or self-serving.

Tamas does allude to forces beyond this hermetic world, especially the contentious terrain of national politics in which the fate of the country was being decided in August 1947. Without blaming anyone by name, the miniseries strongly conveys the impression that Partition was orchestrated by self-absorbed national leaders interested in carving out their own spheres of influence.[22] In the fourth episode, local Congress leader Bakshiji learns from his Muslim League counterpart that the national leadership of his own party has accepted the proposal for partition. Back at the party office, the local Congress functionaries sit in stunned silence. This scene opens with a slow pan across framed portraits of nationalist leaders on the wall, ending with the portrait of Gandhi, then cuts to a close-up of a dejected Jarnail Singh nodding his head in disbelief. Gradually, the members speak up, trying to come to terms with the news: they question the legitimacy of the national leadership's decision and wonder about Gandhi's earlier assertion that the nation could be truncated only "over his dead body." At a regional level, even the politicians feel like mere puppets at the mercy of national players. The despondent mood of the characters is established through a judicious mix of close-ups and medium shots in a pale blue light. Finally, Jarnail Singh breaks out of his stupor; like a true melancholic, he refuses to accept the loss, and declares that he will not allow the division of his homeland. Rushing to the center of town, he begins addressing the crowd with great passion, asking them to fight this cynical truncation in the name of religious faith. But he is gunned down in the middle of his speech: the bifurcation, now inevitable, is realized "over his dead body."

Tamas reserves its most trenchant criticism for religious fanatics. In the very first episode, the leaders of the Hindu Sabha discuss steps to safeguard Hindu interests, steps that will put their men in direct conflict with Muslims. Another militant Hindu organization, not named in the miniseries but easily identifiable as the RSS (Rashtriya Swayamsevak Sangha) by the khaki shorts and white shirts of its cadres and the fanatical anti-Muslim rhetoric, puts its young volunteers on the road to kill the *mlechchha* (polluting barbarian) enemy; it extols violence as an essential element in the service of community and nation. In an arresting sequence, an RSS instructor exhorts a teenage volunteer named Ranvir to kill a chicken: the exercise is meant to strengthen his confidence and resolve and get him used to bloodshed. At first, Ranvir is unable to butcher the bird and gets nauseous at the very idea of violence, but after a humiliating slap and some rousing words of encouragement, he succeeds. Through a close-up of the young man's triumphant face covered in sweat and blood, eyes wide open and nostrils flaring, we become privy to the process of ideological interpellation, even brutalization, of a young mind.[23] *Tamas* squarely holds religious fundamentalism responsible for sowing the seeds of loathing and violence among otherwise innocent people, transforming them into vicious brutes. Within hours, Ranvir puts a knife in the back of a Muslim whom he knows personally; this unprovoked attack helps convert the festering tension in the region into a full-blown riot.

This narrative polarization between elite ruling classes and the masses, indexical of the series creators' ideological disposition, has echoes in other nationalist cultural projects. For instance, Italian neorealist cinema obsessively recast the hardworking common man into the iconic national subject, the embodiment of a robust humanism, without a trace of the fascist tendencies that seemed to define national character just a few years back; only the decadent elite was held responsible for fascism. If we flash forward to the present, we find neofascist forces making a comeback all over Italy. Left-leaning cultural practitioners and historians do everyone a disservice by stripping subalterns and working classes of all responsibility for a national turn to sinister politics, be it fascism or communalism.[24] Essentializing the masses as the repository of humane values may seem like progressive class politics, but it does not help explain the large-scale participation of common people in forms of social terror, nor does it help us work through and overcome collective violence.

Tamas does include at least one remarkable instance in which class and sectarian affiliations square off in a complex and startling way. Lalaji, a Hindu merchant who lives in a Muslim neighborhood, decides to move with his family to a friend's home in a Hindu area. They leave behind Nanku, a male servant, ostensibly to look after the house, but mainly because there is no space for him at their friend's. A weedy dullard with a high-pitched voice, Nanku looks helpless and pathetic as he stands alone holding a piece of wood as weapon: we know he will not survive the bloodthirsty rioters. Shahnawaz Khan, a Muslim friend, escorts the family to safety across the tense town. When Lalaji's wife discovers she has left behind her jewelry box, Shahnawaz offers to go back for it. Nanku takes a long time in answering the door; as Shahnawaz waits outside, he is taunted by a group of Muslim hoods for sucking up to the Hindus. Once he is inside, Nanku's whiny voice and awkward obsequiousness get on his nerves. Shahnawaz proceeds to the room upstairs where the jewelry box is supposed to be. Through the window, he can see the courtyard of the adjacent mosque, where people sit around a dead body performing funeral rituals. Angry and confused emotions well up in him as he watches this mournful gathering. When he turns around, he finds Nanku staring at him with a wide, stupid grin on his face. Visibly disconcerted, Shahnawaz retrieves the jewelry box, as funeral chants and lamentations continue offscreen. As he comes down the stairs, Nanku in front of him, something implodes in him: he violently kicks the servant, who rolls down the stairs and passes out.

Why does Shahnawaz—a decent, cultured, well-meaning man, by no means a religious zealot—give in to such base passions? What clouds his senses and pushes him over the edge? Does the cumulative stress of the past few days finally get the better of his humanity? The sight of the mourners, people who belong to his own sect, triggers a strong response: he feels outraged at the violence against his community. At the same time, his class affiliations produce anxieties about the well-being of his Hindu friends. These competing loyalties produce a form of cognitive dissonance, blacking out his common sense. A series of facial close-ups convey Shahnawaz's discomfort: can Nanku possibly be laughing at him, just as the Muslims had done a few minutes ago? Whether Nanku was actually mocking him is immaterial: the point is that for Shahnawaz, Nanku's grin becomes the exteriorization of his own torment, of the unbearable irony of his position in a fissured society. Unable to eliminate the root cause of his misery, he lashes out at the easiest target, then proceeds to meet his friends from the other side of the religious chasm.

Shahnawaz's struggle dramatizes the predicament of all people who find themselves bound to others by ties forged through the interactions and exchanges of everyday life. What makes his characterization singular is that it remains the rare instance in *Tamas* when the confusions and actions of those calamitous times are not reductively explained away. Rather, we get a sense of the bewilderment induced in sensible, well-intentioned subjects by irreconcilable obligations. Nevertheless, it is the poor servant who becomes the victim of the upper-class Muslim's momentary lapse of reason. Nanku is expendable to his own master, to Shahnawaz, and to the narrative. The series producers' allegiance to a particular kind of class politics erases any possibility of subaltern agency.

Since the creators reveal a leftist bias in their consistent attempt to exonerate the ordinary people of all malevolence, and to establish that it is the poor who suffer the most in communal fights, one is led to wonder: what evaluation do they offer of the role of the Indian Left during the bloodbath? In general, it is a sympathetic assessment: the communist activists seem genuinely committed to the secular ideal; the local Party chief brings together community leaders and representatives of all the political groups to figure out ways of diffusing tension and maintaining peace; at the height of the riots, they organize themselves into smaller units and work with various sects in different localities to try to keep the bloodshed in check. The film allows the communists a remarkable moment of self-reflection, if only in the form of a dissenting view. During a party meeting, Jamil, a Muslim member, questions the practice of blaming the colonial state for all the woes that beset Indian society and polity. He refuses to ascribe communal strife exclusively to imperialist conspiracy and asserts that it is essential to understand the constitutive role of religious strife in Indian nationalism: without such an understanding, imported political systems such as socialism will never work in this country. Failing to make his compatriots see his point, Jamil storms out. The leader explains away his dissension in terms of an apparent lack of conviction, or a "weak ideological base." Yet the activists who are sent to their own religious communities are scolded and scoffed at when they try to sell the idea that the riots are the product of colonial machinations. For the community leaders, religious conflict is the primary reason for all enmity. Curiously, *Tamas* does not embrace the centrality of religion that it has Jamil spell out; instead, it traces all conflict back either to colonial manipulation, or to the self-promoting moves of the elites and leaders. Religion remains an unexplained structure, a specter hovering above ground-level actions.[25]

Religion, Community, Gender: The Sikh Experience

More than the Hindus and the Muslims, it is the Sikhs who are represented primarily in terms of their religious life in the televisual adaptation of *Tamas*. The novel, which was written in the early 1970s and set in undivided Punjab in the days leading up to Partition, already featured the elderly Sikh couple as two of its main characters; it also included a long segment in the gurdwara at Syedpur. The miniseries, produced soon after the anti-Sikh violence of 1984, expands the roles of the passionate and melancholic Jarnail Singh and the elderly couple. The resonance with contemporary events was not lost on audiences: Jarnail's febrile patriotism and the displaced couple's plight underscored, with great irony, the continuing precariousness of minority life and subjectivity. Moreover, practically all of episode 5 takes place in the gurdwara, ending in what to many is the most moving sequence of the series: to protect the honor of their community and faith, the women embrace death by jumping into a well. While we do glimpse Hindu and Muslim religious rites spread throughout the series, the sheer length of the gurdwara episode, its depiction of Sikh religiosity, and the climactic sacrifice accord to religious faith a centrality that is missing from the rest of *Tamas*.

Harnam Singh and Banto take Nathu and Karmo to Sayidpur, the village where their daughter Jasbir lives. They make their way to the local gurdwara, where everyone has taken refuge. Teja Singh, the head of the congregation, leads them in prayers and gives an inspiring speech, declaring that the moment of sacrifice is near. They spend the night singing hymns and planning strategies. Close-ups of Jasbir reveal to us her courage and determination; she touches her *kirpan*, the ceremonial dagger Sikh women wear on their bodies. An attempt at compromise between the communities, brokered by two communist activists, fails; Nathu, who is sent out as one of the emissaries, gets killed. As the Muslim rioters approach the gurdwara, and their war cry, "Allah ho Akbar," grows louder, the besieged Sikh congregation cries out that the "Turks" are coming: they refer to the Muslims by conjuring up the invading Turks of some eight centuries ago. Such historical reference frames the current conflict in terms of medieval wars: men are summoned to take

Tamas: Sikh women sacrifice themselves. Courtesy of NFAI.

up arms to keep up the valiant tradition of Rajput and Sikh resistance to Muslim marauders; women are called on to protect their honor by embracing death, emulating the example of heroic women down the centuries. The men rush out with their weapons to confront the enemy. As the gurdwara reverberates with the relentlessly rhythmic clash of cymbals, Jasbir sits in front of the *Granth Sahib*, the Holy Book of the Sikhs, and begins a frenzied song about the bravery of those who fight for their faith. As the women join in ecstatically, the song rises to a crescendo, and then ends abruptly. Silence inside, the sound of brutal fighting offscreen; the women seem to be in a trance. Jasbir stands up, announces that it is time for their ultimate sacrifice, and leads the women and children to a well in the courtyard.

The pale blue light of dawn imparts a sense of freshness and purity to this tragic scene. The women rush swiftly through billowing smoke, partly obscured; the smoke not only denotes the fire and destruction all around but also conjures up a mythic dimension—a sense that is augmented by the use of choral music and the low percussive beat. As they reach the well, the music stops: there is a momentary lull, as the early morning appears as tranquil as any other, filled only with the howling of the wind. Then Jasbir murmurs a prayer and jumps in the well: the calm is broken by the sound of her body hitting the water. The music resumes as one by one, the women—some holding their children—jump in the well. In the end, only the well is left in a desolate landscape with the howling wind and the chirp of crickets.

The sequence leaves a strong haptic impression on its audience: shrouded in the enigma of martyrdom, these women march into the annals of history. Enigma—for we shall never know what martyrs feel at the moment of their supreme sacrifice. What we know, we know from romanticized accounts, from legends that turn historic figures into mythic ones. By 1988, the martyrs of 1947, those that had died rather than let the enemy sully them, had also become such mythic figures. *Tamas* evokes the qualities that are necessary to such mythologization: purity, courage, calm resolve, and, yes, enigma. But beyond the smoke, the visual mystification, what sense can we make of this enigma? The entanglement of community, gender, and honor has a long history, as we have seen in previous chapters.[26] In telling its powerful story with all its resonance for contemporary national life, *Tamas* invokes the connections without interrogation or critique. In particular, it reiterates a deeply problematic conception of gender and sexuality in relation to community—namely, women's purity is essential to the strength and honor of a society. Because of such an equation, women are targeted in times of communal aggression. An alarming mutation of such violence takes the form of men killing women of their own community to "save" them from the attackers: otherwise, their bodies are tainted through sexual assault, and their souls are sullied through forcible conversion of faith. Thus, the elderly Harnam Singh, a genteel and compassionate man, repeatedly tells his wife Banto that if the rioters get to them, he will slay her before taking his own life; she looks positively radiant and grateful at such a promise of deliverance. But one is left wondering: does a woman really prefer this final solution to the prospect of a not-so-honorable life?

In such discussions of community and womanhood, the woman is cast either as a victim or as a courageous martyr who gives her own life to save her honor. These polar positions, which appear paradoxical at first glance, turn out to be intimately related: both situations ensure women's subjection. Discourses of sacrifice and of martyrdom appear to offer women an honorable choice, but what kind of choice is death, really? Such ideological interpellation works on the presupposition that the only other position available to women during communal strife is that of the victim. The precedent of valiant Rajput women burning themselves to death to avoid sexual ignominy in the hands of the Muslim invaders is the stuff of legends: it transforms impending victimization into the possibility of glorious consecration in the mythic realm. Such transformation requires a fanatical investment in the mythic structures, an unswerving and ecstatic faith. The build-up to the scene at the well traffics in such frenzied belief, as women heed the call to sacrifice in a trance. In terms of the operative patriarchal logic, such a sacrifice makes rational sense. But women's subjectivities during Partition—the complex and variegated choices real women make under acute duress—remain unexplored in such a mythic representation.

I want to dwell on one particular shot that stands out from the rest of the sequence, perhaps from the rest of *Tamas*. After the women's sacrifice, as the camera pulls back slowly from the well, a mournful male voice begins singing, and a dissolve through the smoke ends in a close-up of Karmo's shell-shocked face. At first, the image is entirely blue; then the smoke clears briefly, revealing the red veil framing her face; as more smoke wafts across, the red bleeds out, and her face becomes a ghostly trace. In this shot, the smoke screen reveals something by obscuring the obvious: it tells us that there is no easy or sanguine way of knowing, of remembering, of representing. As Karmo stares back into the camera and at the audience, she occupies the liminal place of a witness: she witnesses on behalf of an audience from another era, the future generation whose representative she carries in her womb, but also on behalf of those dead women, by placing this audience under an obligation to remember.[27] This one shot of Karmo's face marks, even embodies, the sublime nature of the tragedy: instead of submitting itself to an imperative to mythologize in the name of faith or community, it encapsulates and engages the core challenge of representing suffering— "Know what has happened, do not forget, and at the same time never will you know."

Aporia, Reception, Performance

Tamas embodies a series of contradictions, compromising the grounds for evaluation. The dissident communist activist asserts that any work-

Tamas: Karmo's shell-shocked face. Courtesy of NFAI.

able notion of community in India must recognize the constitutive role of religious faith, yet religion emerges as something vicious (as in the fanaticism of the Hindu fundamentalist groups) or, at best, eerie (as in the more sympathetic portrayal of the ecstatic Sikh women). Purnima Mankekar rightly observes that the representation of the mass suicide of the women in the series is ambivalent: "at the same time that it portrays them as heroines who have the courage to take their own lives, it depicts them as driven by an 'irrational' religious frenzy."[28] Religion, when accorded the attention it deserves in the Indian context, is reduced to a bad object. Such is the dilemma of a television show that wants to uphold a standard version of secularism predicated on a sharp dichotomy between faith and rationality.

As a socially engaged show representing national history, *Tamas* embraces a certain realism to try to lay out for its audience the objective conditions of such a history—to provide a cognitive map, as it were. Yet a mimetic approach to realism leads, after a point, to reification. The reference to Muslims as "Turks" may well be the practice in northwestern parts of the country, but there is a problem in equating medieval invaders with people who were born in India, several generations of whose forebears have called it home. The use of such a reference in the service of verisimilitude, without a critical frame, reiterates disturbing stereotypes and attitudes. The challenge, here, is one of balancing a realist approach to social problems with a transformative cultural politics.

Still another blindness in *Tamas* results from its adherence to a monotonic explanation of mob violence in terms of colonial and elite manipulations, conveying the impression that the masses, on their own, want to coexist without rancor. Partition emerges as the aberrant moment within a grand narrative of national unity. The question is: if 1947 is such an exceptional instance of communal strife, then how do we explain the recurring riots? What is the point of bringing 1947 back into discourse in the late 1980s? In his introduction, Bhisham Sahni argues that the purpose of the show is to expose the communal forces that persist in society; each episode of *Tamas* begins with a title screen that declares: "Those who forget history are condemned to repeat it." Clearly, the miniseries wants to engage with the past in order to learn from it, to better understand the present, and perhaps to transform the future. Yet, in following standard historiography, it mystifies structural conditions and ends up producing a romanticized and idealized view of the nation as the province of caring and courageous folks.

For the first time, *Tamas* made tens of millions of viewers collectively confront the Partition ordeal. The compelling images and sounds— the fire and smoke, the distant roar of fighting mobs, the war cries of the approaching rioters ("Allah ho Akbar" and "Har Har Mahadev"), the dead bodies, the panic on the faces of the protagonists—brought back memories that many would like to forget. Even more overwhelming were the emotions and physical responses that the series induced: the tension that one feels as familiar places turn sinister and the security of one's assumptive world crumbles; the dread that people suffer about their families and loved ones; the terror that overcomes one's senses on being surrounded by a hostile crowd; the shock of coming across dead bodies; the nausea induced by the incalculable destruction. The overwrought psychosomatic reactions involved something beyond the textual: in their unwittingly hysterical experientiality, they compelled audiences to relive the trauma.

This kind of performativity complicates the question of reception. With a forcefully affective text like *Tamas*, the textual dimension becomes entangled with the experiential: reception involves both "reading" and "performance." As such, the potential for divergence between textual intention and reception becomes more acute. What people make of what *Tamas* offers as history is informed by the emotions and prejudices intensified by sectarian memories of violation and betrayal. Is there any absolute guarantee that the powerful revival of these memories on television will steer people beyond the fear and loathing and not charge up these passions even further? The pedagogical intent of the series, what it wants to teach people as desirable attitude and behavior, may be deflected or subverted by its performative aspects. Of course, such potential divergence also presents us with the possibility that the normative nationalist historiography that *Tamas* sticks to will be contested. All the same, an outright ban on such mediations of Partition, which some groups vigorously advocate, precludes any possibility of learning from the trauma by sealing it off. Such an injunction is neither wise nor viable as cultural policy, given the social record of recent decades; it is also unlikely that a prohibition on mass cultural representations of communal violence will prevent its recurrence in contemporary India.

Proscriptions and Standards

Moving from the demand for outright ban to the feasibility of setting up limits and standards for representations of trauma, we face another set of questions: How do we decide what can and cannot be shown in mass media? Who gets to make these decisions? What are the principles that should be followed? For instance, how much violence is "too much"? How do we ascertain these norms? How do we pin down responsibility? How do we own up to our own complicities? Since trauma and violence mark the limits of community life, these become incredibly loaded questions: it is no surprise that *Tamas* turned into the epicenter of a culture war. The public discourse around *Tamas* and the paradoxes and challenges that it shows up indicate intense contestations regarding taste culture, collective principles and intersubjective ethics, and the meaning of concepts like civility and humanity. The controversy also points to a pitched battle over issues of legitimacy, rights, and public culture. In other words, the miniseries marks a crossroads in the evolution of an Indian civil society.

In many ways, objections to cultural representations of violence concern matters of taste. Depictions of violence frequently turn trauma into kitsch, thereby trivializing the experience; they desensitize audiences to the horror, helping to normalize aggression and brutality; they even manage to titillate through forms of sensationalism. *Tamas* manages a thoughtful reticence, avoiding salacious indulgence in, or promotion of, violence. Two of the bloodiest scenes dwell on the slaughters of a pig and a hen, underscoring the bestiality at the heart of aggressive behavior, sharply contrasting the civility that is a basic condition for human community. Most of the bloodshed between humans happens offscreen and is communicated through sound. The violence is made palpable in terms of a pervasive atmosphere of terror: the mounting tension, the ominous lanes, the apprehension on people's faces, the distant flames, the roar of bloodthirsty mobs. The rare instances of explicit physical assault—Shahnawaz kicking the servant down the stairs, Jarnail Singh being shot by a sniper—are all the more shocking because of this general discretion. The one major instance when the narrative upholds violence is in the scene of the Sikh women's mass suicide: this desperate act, where the anticipation of assault leads to preemptive, self-inflicted violence, is romanticized as courageous self-sacrifice. Such is the impact of this masterfully constructed sequence, that even viewers who find it ideologically troubling will have difficulty in dismissing it as kitsch.

Speaking from a feminist position, I can harbor strong reservations about the ideological inscription of the women's suicide within a patriarchal-nationalist articulation of discourses of community honor and sexuality. As a postcolonial critic, I can fly against the grain and question the modernist-secularist qualm about an act of self-sacrifice based on seemingly irrational faith. However, to have lived through Partition, to have suffered and survived the gendered violence, and then to have to make sense of that experience, is an undertaking that I cannot even begin to imagine, let alone comprehend. This absolute and irreducible difference compels me to consider the possibility that for many such subjects, the idealized solution offered in *Tamas* is one way of making sense of women's behavior during the riots. It is entirely possible that some women were overtaken with terror and killed themselves in sheer desperation; it is also possible that some were interpellated to protect their honor. "What really happened" matters far less than how Partition survivors and their families try to understand it. These survivors in real life, like Jarnail's, Jasbir's, and Karmo's shell-shocked faces in the miniseries, place an ethical obligation on us to acknowledge and accept the range of subjectivities and accounts of the trauma. The debates around *Tamas* signal dilemmas that are, in the main, ethical and unresolvable: this acknowledgment, I will maintain, does not empty out the political as much as complicates it.

The political dimension of the controversy was most apparent from the strong polemics regarding the show's representation of religious organizations and political parties. Then–BJP president L. K. Advani, later the home minister, described the series as a "distortion of history" that portrayed the RSS and Arya Samaj cadres as "beastly fanatics," reduced Muslim League members to "mere ruffians," and turned Congress Party functionaries into "anaemic nincompoops." Pramod Nawalkar, leader of the militant Hindu group Shiv Sena, complained that the series was biased in favor of the Muslims.[29] Not surprisingly, the series producers' refusal to blame any one group conflicted with the partisan expectations and chauvinistic historiographies of the dogmatic camps: so the attacks originated across the spectrum of faith-based politics. While the politicized Hindu groups staged demonstrations against what they claimed to be an Islamic slant, a writ petition filed by a Muslim businessman, Javed Ahmad Siddique, in the Bombay High Court after the airing of the first two episodes claimed that the Muslims were "shown in a bad light." Several television stations were ransacked; police had to open fire to control demonstrations in Delhi, Bombay, and Hyderabad. Meanwhile, artists, intellectuals, and social activists staged rallies to express their solidarity with the director and the writer. Bhaskar Ghose, as Doordarshan's director-general, backed the series and its creators all along.

Beyond matters of taste and ethics, contestations erupted over the more practical—and to some, more pressing—issue of law and order: detractors of the show alleged that this retelling of a violent historical episode would reopen old wounds, rekindle sectarian passions, and lead to further acrimony and acting out. They asserted that it "presents a dementia" and has no "educative value," and that in spite of attempts to present instances of inter-faith neighborliness and cooperation, "the images that linger" in spectators' minds "are the ones dealing with violence."[30]

The Public Sphere and the Ideal Citizen-Spectator

The series was the locus of one of those pitched controversies through which civil and political institutions are debated and restructured in the public sphere of postcolonial India. The debate went all the way up to the Supreme Court, which sided with an earlier landmark judgment of the Bombay High Court upholding the broadcast of the miniseries on the state-owned television network.[31] The court battle divulges the contours of an implicit theory of how "official culture" ought to deal with the collective trauma after years of silence. What is the agenda behind this broadcast, and who is its intended audience? What are the expectations and anxieties about differential reception? How are concerns about the possible re-igniting of communal hatred balanced against the need to learn from experience? The debate also brings to light entrenched presumptions about a paternalistic state and a representative, reasonable citizen. However, as I propose to demonstrate, these are not completely immutable paradigms: the verdict contains certain slippages, even contradictions, which point to an awareness on the part of the judges of the evolving nature of both citizenry and state. The moment of adjudication offers, in that sense, a possibility for the transformation of both culture and law.

In the initial stage of the legal battle, Javed Ahmad Siddique was the petitioner seeking to legally block the broadcast of *Tamas*, while the Union of India, the director general of Doordarshan, Blaze Advertising Pvt. Ltd. (the coproducers) and Govind Nihalani, the director, were named the respondents. After a Bombay High Court Division Bench ruled in favor of the broadcast, rescinding an initial stay order, another petition was filed with the Supreme Court by Ramesh Chotalal Dalal, a Bombay advocate. The petitioner argued that in representing Partition violence, the miniseries was "likely to promote . . . on grounds of religion, caste or community, disharmony or feelings of enmity, hatred or ill-will among different . . . groups"; as such, it was prejudicial to national integration, and violated sections 153A and 153B of the Indian Penal Code. According to the petitioner, the serial also violated Section 5B(1) of the Cinematograph Act of 1952, which stated, "A film shall not be certified for public exhibition if, in the opinion of the authority competent to grant the certificate, the film or any part of it is against the interest of the security of the State, friendly relations with foreign States, public order, decency or morality, or involves defamation or contempt of Court or is likely to incite the commission of any offence." *Tamas*, in the petitioner's view, was likely to disrupt "public order," "incite the commission" of certain "offences," and thus threaten "the security of the State." The petition expressed concern about the tremendous reach of television: "persons of all ages" would be exposed to communal animosity and "fail to grasp the message, if any," of the serial. It is not clear if the worry was about younger or older audiences: while young people might have an uninformed, rash reaction, the broadcast could trigger strong memories and passions in older spectators who actually lived through the trauma. Nevertheless, anxieties about the response of spectators of various ages to incendiary situations depicted in *Tamas* raise questions about the program's intended address and potential reception.

Two Supreme Court judges, in upholding the Bombay High Court judgment in favor of the broadcast, cite several prior verdicts in media-related cases as precedents. These model instances reveal embedded definitions of an ideal consumer of mass culture. One such verdict from 1971, in adjudicating on charges of obscenity against a documentary film, observes that "our standards must be so framed that we are not reduced to a level where the protection of the *least capable* and the *most depraved* amongst us determines what the *morally healthy* cannot view or read." An earlier legal opinion from 1947 states that the effects of words ought to be judged from "the standards of *reasonable, strong-minded, firm and courageous men,* and not those of weak and vacillating minds, nor of those who scent danger in every hostile point of view." Another cited verdict, from 1980, considers criteria for ascertaining whether a particular cultural text promotes enmity or hatred: the conclusion is that "the likelihood must be judged from *healthy* and *reasonable standards.*"[32]

Take note of the operative phrasings: "healthy and reasonable standards" cannot be compromised for the protection of the "least capable and the morally depraved," the "weak" and the "vacillating"; ultimately, it is the "strong-minded, courageous, morally healthy" citizens that matter, who are seen as the basis for determining cultural yardsticks. We are left with the cornerstone of modernist law-speak: the notion of an abstract, rational, representative agent who can be a model citizen. Of course, law is not the only realm that invokes such an Olympian model of subjectivity: it is ubiquitous in modern economic theory or political science. The obsessive appeal to rationality helps produce shared perceptions of "reasonable" and "moral" standards, which constitute the normative structures of behavior. The idea of a modern citizenry is based on these putatively universal standards: here, "difference" collapses into "sameness." In other words, modern law suffers from a typically liberal aporia: the failure to recognize adequately the experiential bases of subjectivity, the material and incarnated differences that constitute political agents.[33]

The 1971 judgment, invoked in the *Tamas* verdict, uses highbrow Western literary illustrations as the grounds of universally shared values and morals that redeem certain cultural representations: for instance, incest in *Oedipus Rex* has a pedagogical value; similarly, the rape in Voltaire's *Candide* or in the story of Lucrece is justified for the moral instruction it affords us. Again, these instances from an essentially Eurocentric cosmopolitan cultural imaginary are privileged to think through principles of acceptability. However, midway through the verdict, an interesting slippage occurs: there is a shift away from the modernist notion of a representative, rational subject, toward a greater recognition of the social and material grounds of subjectivity: "Illiterates are not devoid of common sense, or unable to grasp the calumny of the fundamentalists and extremists when it is brought home to them in action on the screen." This faith in the illiterates' "common sense" reveals that they are not summarily dismissed as morally weak or inherently unreasonable: rather, they are considered handicapped by their lack of education. Of course, this acknowledgment of a fractured citizenry due to differential training opens up a role for the educated, the discerning intelligentsia: the "revealing" and "instructive" aspects of a difficult historical moment must be "brought home" to the illiterates, the underprivileged, by cultural arbiters like Govind Nihalani. The requirement of reasonableness is here displaced onto another modernist formulation: the taste, the analytical expertise, and the discriminating acumen of a progressive vanguard—in short, the institution of Culture.

At the heart of this notion of an intelligentsia mediating national history for all other classes is a pragmatic view of historical representation. Indeed, the *Tamas* verdict is quite remarkable for its espousal of a strategic understanding of history. Jettisoning modernist pretenses to objectivity and insistence on truth—the facts and only the facts—the judges declare that "naked truth" is not always beneficial, that "truth in its proper light"—that is to say, truth that is reframed by "timely and harmless concessions" and accommodations—is often more instructive. But even as they uphold pragmatism over a modernist obsession with facticity, they revert back to a vague legalese transcending historical contexts: asserting that *Tamas* is valuable for its strategic mediation of Partition violence "from an average, healthy and commonsense point of view," they invoke an eminently evident and shared ground of mainstream sanity. They continue: "There cannot be any apprehension that it is likely to affect public order or it is likely to incite . . . the commission of any offence. On the other hand, it is more likely that it will prevent incitement to such offences in future by extremists and fundamentalists." Here, the verdict shares the series producers' anathema of political machinations, and their belief in the innocence of the masses. It implies that reasonable and well-adjusted people, who apparently constitute a clear majority of the citizenry, will have no problem with the series: it is only the sectarian political groups who will feel exposed by, and therefore object to, the broadcast.

When the judges proclaim—referring to the series epigram, and practically quoting Benjamin—that "those who forget history are condemned to repeat it," they recognize the need to work through traumatic experiences in order to break recurring cycles. They also acknowledge the possibility that representations of trauma in mass media may constitute legitimate history and may be effective as collective mourning work. One is tempted to discern in the call for strategic deployment of history and in the bracketing of a rigorously factual construal of "what actually happened" implied by such an injunction—that is to say, in the reconceptualization of what constitutes evidence—a postmodern turn in Indian law. If the departure from a strictly "scientific" historiography indicates such a shift, the stress on reason and the average, representative citizen-viewer muddles the picture. Furthermore, South Asia abounds in instances of the purposeful inscription and invocation of history, of pragmatic deliberations and amendments in representing experience. The epics and mythologies, for instance, embody an Indian historical consciousness that does not rest on an absolute demarcation between fact and fiction. These civilizational resources for apprehending history become especially significant in the realm of the popular: as I demonstrate in chapters 1 and 2, these indigenous frameworks are crucial components of popular sense-making practices within an Indian modernity. So a claim about a postmodern turn fails to grasp adequately the cultural layers and epistemological complexities. In recognizing the importance of presenting "truth in its proper light" and simultaneously harping on rationality, the judges effectively open the door to a range of paradigms and influences, not all of which appear easily commensurable.

The legal scuffle over *Tamas* presents a rich moment for studying the contestations and negotiations through which the public sphere in India is continually reconstituted. I will argue that beyond inherited British laws, beyond universalized juridical norms and axioms, Indian law—like all other modern public institutions in India—has to contend with an entire system of popular moral structures and epistemes. But since a penchant for the modern-cosmopolitan requires the constant production of the "indigenous" as an unchanging, parochial, retrograde other, and a disavowal of its influences, a continually evolving and vital popular realm has remained a largely unthought domain. The inconsistent assumptions and argumentations in the verdicts—which invoke the reasonable "average Joe" or, rather, "average Ram" to substitute a modernist myth for the problematic of the vernacular popular—index a lack of legal will to get to the heart of the dispute. This vacillation reflects what Shoshana Felman has called the "juridical unconscious": in spite of its professed transcendence, law's own imbrication in the structures of injustice and inequity prevents it from redressing the injuries of history.[34] As a site of power, law embodies the wider contradictions of contemporary Indian polity. Even for politically astute cultural practitioners like Sahni or Nihalani, the flesh and blood "masses" remain a problem. To draw attention to class and caste oppression, the series stresses that poor people like Nathu have no control over their destiny; but such an insistence also erases any potential for subaltern agency. As recent historiography associated with the Subaltern Studies Group has demonstrated, these dispossessed communities participate in sense-making practices and have unpredictable bearings on collective experience.[35] In life, the masses are susceptible to deep-rooted prejudices and virulent reactions; they do participate in riots and pogroms and are capable of perpetrating the most heinous acts of violence. There is no guarantee that any totalized message of a televisual narrative will get across, as intended, to its vast and segmented audience: hence the volatile responses and anxieties, the pitched debates and legal battles.

Nevertheless, in bringing back Partition into mainstream consciousness and discourse, *Tamas* initiated a process of active mourning work. It precipitated a range of discussions—about representations of social violence on television, about the limits of representation, about television audiences and responsible citizens, about community, about violence, about the possibility of community beyond violence—with profound implications for the public sphere. It unproblematically assumed the existence of modern civil society in South Asia and took its constituent values and institutions for granted without analyzing the myriad negotiations or the role of the masses in such political contestations. Instead, the series and the court verdict called upon an actual citizenry to become a model community by presenting to them desirable modes of social behavior in times of, and during public discussions of, sectarian conflict. How efficacious *Tamas* was in this ideological project remains a matter of debate.

CHAPTER SEVEN

Mourning (Un)limited

Globalization, Religious Nationalism, and Mourning

If the collective catharsis around *Tamas* proved to be a turning point in memorializing and mourning Partition, perhaps the most significant element of that turn was the revelation that the now-distant event continued to shape the trauma of the present. The year 1947 returned with such a force in public discourse—as standard or unorthodox historiography, as literature and film, as political rhetoric—that by the late 1990s, there were derisive references to a veritable "Partition industry." What I find most striking in the shift, and in critical responses to it, is the acute self-consciousness about its conditions of possibility. Recent Partition discourse signals a marked awareness of the forces that shape it, including current political trends (e.g., Hindu triumphalism, caste politics), demands of the culture industry (e.g., the frictions of global media, the premium placed on packaging for a transnational market) and contemporary cognitive frameworks and critical interventions (e.g., language of trauma and loss, feminist rewriting of national history). The field of mass media is keenly cognizant of its own role in creating archives of memory: films now routinely present the modalities of commemoration and witnessing in their content, structure, and style.

Two main contingencies, conveniently captured by the terms *global-*

ization and *religious nationalism*, crucially molded this discursive turn. At first glance, it might seem that the ontological phenomena these appellations index are antagonistic, even irreconcilable. Globalization involves the transcendence of national boundaries and identities through the consolidation of emergent networks, flows, and imaginations. For its proponents, globalization implies a progressive development in which modern values and institutions become universal; for its critics, it involves the subsumption of all other concerns to the logic of capital.[1] Yet others call attention to significant transnational assemblages that challenge top-down, corporatist views of globalization.[2] Champions of contemporary religious nationalisms point to the struggles of sovereign populations against the encroachments of a homogenizing global; its interlocutors decree the fostering of insular societies and parochial identities, and what they see as the grievous unraveling of mid-twentieth-century rational-secular nationalist projects.[3]

Several considerations complicate this polarization, revealing a structural imbrication between nationalism and globalization. One could argue that the resurgence of ethnic and religious nationalisms is a direct response to contemporary geopolitical tectonics, and to the perceived threats to local social formations and identities. The ideological power and efficacy of the national remain largely undiminished in the face of analytical criticism and the cognitive demands posed by rapid transformations precisely because the nation continues to provide necessary moorings in a disorienting world. Nationalism defined in ethnic or religious terms also allows large segments of national populations—whose lives have been, in the main, adversely affected by globalizing forces—to hold on to the possibility, real or chimeral, of political agency. While religion, with its associations to superstition and blind faith, is typically seen as the bête noire of modernity, fundamentalism, in spite of its implications of absolute religious belief and essential identity, has come to denote collective political action by religious movements. Religious fundamentalism, which involves the politicization of religious difference, is a thoroughly modern phenomenon.[4]

Even a schematic account of the Indian context helps bring out the congruencies of—and hidden links between—globalizing trends and fundamentalist politics. While faltering shifts in official policies were already in evidence all through the previous decade, it was in 1991 that India undertook a radical overhaul of its economic institutions and programs in response to a spiraling national debt crisis.[5] The economy was "opened up" through the dismantling of protective tariff structures and regulatory licensing regimes (disparagingly referred to as India's "Licensing Raj"), the initiation of a comprehensive drive to attract foreign capital, and the partial privatization of key sectors, including energy and air transportation. In a series of gradual shifts, the state promoted capital-friendly financial structures, infrastructural development aimed at the private sector, and the establishment of Special Economic Zones (or SEZs) and IT parks. This economic liberalization was concurrent with the emergence of new telecommunication technologies, information networks, and circuits of cultural exchange. By the middle of the nineties, commercial satellite television broadcasting invalidated earlier media policies aimed at securing a relatively insular and "uncontaminated" national televisual culture: within a few years, the number of television channels available to Indian audiences went up dramatically from two to more than thirty.[6] News media consolidated its presence on the Internet, reaching out to a transnational audience in terms of news portals and commercial services. Early in the new century, Indian cinema made astounding strides in expanding its global sphere of operation and influence.[7]

In the 1980s, religious nationalism—the long-repressed other of state-sponsored Indian modernity—made a triumphant comeback around the notion of hindutva, a core, immutable Hindu identity. This resurgence was the outcome of several overlapping historical forces, significant among which were the following: the failure of official programs of the Nehru-Gandhi era to end economic stagnation, ameliorate poverty, and assuage social inequities; the specter of separatist movements fueling the distrust of minority communities; resentments about the "clientelist politics" espoused by the Congress Party in pursuit of demographic vote banks; and tension generated by a radical attempt to extend and deepen affirmative action (the imbroglio of 1990 following efforts to operationalize the recommendations of the Mandal Commission), which strengthened the already widespread impression that the central government served minority groups at the cost of majority, upper-caste Hindu interests. Some of these factors also contributed to the seismic shifts in national policies from the mid-1980s. Beyond this causal congruency, I want to stress a dimension of political mutuality: the consolidation of a refigured nationalism, with its maniacal emphasis on the need to preserve an essentially Hindu Indian-ness, served to deflect attention from the significant loss of national sovereignty and the burgeoning income inequities resulting from the embrace of globalization. Not surprisingly, when the National Democratic Alliance came to power in the mid-1990s, it continued to build on the Congress Party's regime of economic liberalization, even as its Hindu right-wing votaries fanned a sense of panic about the impending loss of cultural identity. For the NDA, as for the Congress Party, the real stake was a political entente that would further the interests of the elite classes, while engaging the masses in this or that ideological red herring. While the outcome of the 2004 elections (the unexpected defeat of the NDA in the wake of the "India Shining" campaign) showed up the limits of this ploy, the confounding entanglement of liberalization and Hindu chauvinism has, so far, framed the Indian experience of globalization.

This, then, is the conjuncture in which Partition returns to public discourse. But what does it mean to claim that India opened up only in the 1990s, in spite of the nation-state's substantial political presence in the global arena through its participation in international forums like the Non-Aligned Movement and initiatives aimed at fostering South–South dialogues? The rhetoric of openness is clearly predicated on economic liberalization, with its twin criteria of large volumes of foreign trade and ease of foreign capital investment, thereby privileging the logic of the market over all other concerns that might inform national policies. This transformation of the project of nationhood in terms of a calculus of efficiency and exchange produces mutations in its social and cultural coordinates. The logic of the market demands that the past, like all other entities, be transformed into a commodity that can enter the nexus of exchange: our memories must be made concrete, and imparted marketable forms. Old and therefore obsolete memory is now repackaged so that it retains the aura of authenticity even as it satisfies current tastes and cultural-political needs; it is subjected to forms of temporal containment so that the past resides in the past without leaking into the present. Under the sign of globalization, cultural memory of Partition must present itself as novel yet authentic, moving yet distant, traumatized yet authoritative.

The recasting of nationalism in terms of hindutva also requires a new version of history. Once the Hindu right wing came to power through a coalition led by the BJP, the Ministry of Education embarked on a systematic program of rewriting national history. School textbooks were supplanted,[8] particular historians and their works were targeted for their "distortion" of the past,[9] new guidelines were set up for government-funded educational institutions and research centers.[10] Selective fixation on certain historical events and the simultaneous erasure of other moments sought to engender a new popular historical consciousness. Since anti-Muslim sentiments and policies were central to hindutva politics, nearly eight centuries of Islamic reign were reduced to a long and scandalous episode of "invasion" marked by pilferage, rape, forced conversion, and murder: the substantial achievements of that era and the remarkably syncretic aspects of the lifeworlds of Indians were strategically elided. The votaries of hindutva sought to achieve closure on the past by consecrating a charged Hindu-chauvinist account as *the* national history.

The conditions under which cultural mourning work proceeded in the past two decades would lead one to expect film narratives that develop their affective charge in terms of reified categories and relations (us and them, loyal and treacherous, compassionate and rapacious); that invoke 1947 to address topical issues and stir up patriotic fervor against Pakistan—and, metonymically, against Muslims in India—in terms of an "original" betrayal (1947 emerging as the urevent of the conflicts of 1965, 1971, and 1999); that reduce the trauma to a palatable, even entertaining, commodity in terms of spectacle and music, manageable myths, and definitive legends (the blithe, apathetic protagonist who becomes a martyr in protecting his community, the brave neighbor who endangers his life to save others); that erase the historical structures at work and transform the particular experience into the self-indulgent and ultimately obscure category of "universal human condition." In short, one would expect most recent Partition films to feature well-crafted, moving narratives that aim for a sense of closure on what remains an essentially incomprehensible and, therefore, open past. One might also expect a small group of films to interrogate or work against these tendencies.

Such a neat categorization, while heuristically useful, is troubled by the analysis of specific films. Most works reveal a great deal of confusion and, in a few cases, even conscious ambivalence. Contemporary cinema is constitutive of the deep social contradictions in South Asia: it performs these conflicts textually and thus engages the split sensibilities of its publics. Nevertheless, when we focus on films that, one way or another, mourn the national division, the question of how they mourn and to what effect remains an important basis for distinction. As the overarching project of this book is to look to the collective past with an eye to the future, such differences in the work of cultural mourning demand particular attention. Because of my interest in a hermeneutic of mourning, I am compelled to take a more critical view of recent Partition films than do some of my colleagues, writing on the same texts from somewhat different angles.[11]

A Freudian paradigm of mourning entails the recognition of loss, the gradual withdrawal of investment from the lost object or ideal, and its retention as a sublated trace. Sublation involves the rational translation of the affective into the cognitive; but this translation is never complete, and residual affect remains. We may recognize the objective conditions that produced the trauma in the first place, but that does not mean we will be able to comprehend or overcome our subjective relations to these objective conditions. In other words, we are never able to confront the trauma quite fully, and mourning is never complete. As long as the individual analysand recognizes this dimension of incompleteness, the gap itself is sublated and he is, in a sense, "cured." The rational-teleological model of "healing" or "moving beyond" depends on this acknowledgment of the residue that resists cognitive assimilation.

At the social level, the persistence of the affective has far more unpredictable consequences, as it remains available for both accidental alignments and orchestrated political mobilizations. It becomes all the more crucial to understand what happens to this volatile residue if we are to understand the precise nature of cultural mourning. The films of this period harness the affective to very different purposes: some, like *Gadar* (2001) and *L.O.C.* (2003), fixate on the figure of the Other in anger and revulsion, and foreground a desire for revenge and retribution; others, like *Pinjar* (2003) and *Way Back Home* (2003), bear witness to the common historical predicament of Self and Other, and register the difficulties of maintaining a clear distinction between the two terms. Furthermore, the films vary in the extent to which they recognize the persistence of trauma; they also differ in the complexity and sensitivity with which this recognition is staged. While *Train to Pakistan* (1997) poses a closure to the trauma in terms of its narrative resolution, *Earth* (1999) acknowledges it as an open wound even as it frames Partition as a temporally distant event; yet other films (*Naseem* [1995], *Zubeidaa* [2001]) capture traumatized subjectivities through intricate flashbacks or intertwined narratives, emphasizing temporal seepage. These divergent approaches to mourning promote different forms of historical consciousness, with distinct implications for the future of community in India.[12]

The Predicaments of Patriotism

The first set of films under consideration explores the question of patriotism through either the direct invocation of Partition or its trace by focusing on the ups and downs in post-1947 Indo-Pakistani relations—especially the conflicts over Bangladesh (1971) and over Kashmir in Kargil (1999). All these films were produced in the period between 1997 and 2004: the BJP-led National Democratic Alliance was in charge of the country; the relations between Hindu and Muslim communities were severely strained due to persistent attempts by Hindu militants to build a temple in Ayodhya at the site of the demolished Babri Masjid;[13] *jehadi* terrorists, allegedly aided by the Pakistani army and the Taliban, spread a reign of terror in Kashmir and even managed to detonate a bomb on the steps of the Parliament building in Delhi; for two months in the summer of 1999, the Indian and Pakistani armies fought in the remote Kargil region—the first war in South Asia in the era of dramatically expanded media networks, thereby garnering immediate, unprecedented, and round-the-clock coverage and causing jingoistic feelings to scale new heights on both sides of the border; the two nation-states, both acknowledged nuclear "powers" since the matching test blasts of 1998, were involved in a long and adamant standoff involving huge armies and nuclear missiles between 2001 and 2003. Patriotism, inflected with strong anti-Pakistani, anti-Muslim sentiments, emerged as a national obsession in India; no doubt, corresponding passions ran amok on the other side of the border.[14]

Released in this vituperative atmosphere, *Gadar* takes us back in time to 1947. Sikh truck driver Tara Singh harbors romantic fantasies about Sakina, who is the daughter of Sharaf Ali, a wealthy Muslim merchant of Amritsar, and a student at a local college. The two are thrown together by chance when Tara Singh rescues Sakina twice: first from marauding hordes of Hindu and Sikh rioters after she gets separated from her family fleeing to Pakistan; and then when she finds her father's watch on the ground, assumes that her family has perished, and is about to fling herself in front of a train. Traumatized, Sakina falls completely silent; Tara treats her with respect, guards her, and cares for her day and night. Romance blossoms, and they get married. Soon, a son is born to the happy couple: for a while, love appears to have surmounted differences of class and religion. But Sakina finds out that her parents are alive and thriving in Pakistan; in fact, Sharaf Ali is now the mayor of Lahore. After initial contact and a tearful phone conversation, Sharaf Ali arranges Pakistani visas in such a way that both Tara Singh and the son will not be allowed to cross the border. Theirs is an educated and "liberal" family, hence they can take back the daughter who has been living with a working-class infidel (unlike so many families who disowned such "sullied" daughters or simply exterminated them). However, there is no place for a *Jat* laborer or his offspring in their respected circles. The family attempts to marry Sakina off against her wishes to a Muslim of high status and with a bright political future. Tara Singh appears with his son in the nick of time and, after a protracted showdown, the family returns safely to India.

Gadar consciously attempts to establish its secular credentials by depicting members of all communities as equally capable of cruelty and compassion: the Muslim female protagonist is chased by Hindu and Sikh plunderers (in contrast to most Indian films, in which only Hindu or Sikh women are actually shown to be tormented by Muslim men) and is eventually saved by a Sikh man; Tara Singh has to contend with his bigoted relatives before marrying Sakina; common people help the beleaguered couple run from the Pakistani police on their way back to India. Sharaf Ali's eldest son, who has gone mad, possibly from the trauma of Partition, keeps talking about *Azad Hindustan*—independent (and undivided) India. However, in the course of its denouement, the narrative undermines its professed neutrality. The film upholds a popular Indian view that Pakistan is the result of paranoid Muslim demand for a separate homeland, implying that Hindu or Sikh leaders and their political calculations are in no way responsible for the division. The centrality of anti-Indian sentiments to Pakistani nationalism is conveyed in the scene of Eid celebrations at the mayor's house: while a group of women dance to a Hindi song (implying the hegemony of Hindi popular culture in South Asia), a couple of guests remark that the celebration should be in Urdu, the national language of Pakistan. The sympathetic portrayal of common Pakistanis gives way to a more negative representation: it turns out that the woman who assists the fugitive protagonists is actually after Sakina's jewelry. The film's investment in Indian patriotism becomes apparent in what is, by far, its most charged sequence, shot in front of a mosque. Out of his love for his wife, Tara Singh gives in to Sharaf Ali's demands and agrees to convert to Islam, then publicly proclaims "Islam Zindabad" (Hail Islam) and "Pakistan Zindabad" (Hail Pakistan) but refuses to utter "Hindustan Murdabad" (Down with India). The staging of this spirited refusal—Singh holding on to his position in the face of a convoy of Pakistani army men, their guns trained on him—is calculated to produce patriotic twangs in the heart of even the most cynical Indian. His refusal is all the more moving because it comes after he agrees to give up his religion (proving his secular disposition) and to praise the breakaway nation (signaling his magnanimity and lack of malice) for the sake of love, the cardinal cinematic emotion. However, Sharaf Ali's demands go too far: for Indian audiences in 2001, this fictitious mayor of late-1940s Lahore becomes all too real, one with the "treacherous" and "bastard" nation of Pakistan that is not content to have been born but continues to threaten India through its alleged involvement in anti-Indian terrorist activities and its overt belligerence. Even romantic love cannot justify such a sacrifice of the national: instead, it serves as the foil for underscoring the absolute primacy of patriotic love. The narrative works hard to stress that Tara Singh is forced by Muslim bigotry to turn against the Pakistani state.

In a hypermasculinist display of Jat patriotism, Tara blasts his way through barriers mounted by the Pakistani authorities, and brings his family back home safely. We should note that an intertextual dimension is at work here for spectators of Hindi films: Tara Singh is played

Gadar: Tara Singh refuses to chant "Down with Hindustan"

by Sunny Deol, a real-life Jat, who reprises his role of a virile one-man army, a vigilante fighting corruption and oppression, from various populist films of the early 1990s—most notably *Ghayal* (1990) and *Narasimha* (1991). Equally one-dimensional is Deol's interpretation of the character of Major Kuldeep Singh in the 1997 film *Border*—whose box-office success provided a shot in the arm for the Indian war film (and its variant, the terrorist film) genre. While this film centers around the famous Battle of Longewala during the Indo-Pak War of 1971, Partition's ambivalent legacy is the substance of the narrative and is explicitly referenced not only in its title but also in the song "Mere dushman, mere bhai, mere humsaye" (my enemy, my brother, my double [reflection/shadow]) which accompanies the end credits. But there is no uncertainty or ambivalence evident in the characterization of Kuldeep Singh, who commandeers an Indian army unit in the deserts of Rajasthan bordering Pakistan. A seasoned military man who also fought in the Indo-Pak War of 1965, Singh displays a steadfast loyalty to the nation, a single-minded sense of purpose, and an insatiable appetite for victory: as he keeps saying, "No one wins a war by being dead," implying that victory will come only if one is able to eliminate the enemy. When some Pakistani spies are caught, Singh kills them off execution-style; he turns livid when his subordinate officer dithers in pulling the trigger. As the two belligerent armies gather in their trenches, Singh stomps out in the open intervening space in broad daylight, defiantly facing the prospect of being hit by snipers' bullets. When a Pakistani officer phones up Singh to rail him, he has a fit and starts shouting abuses, claiming they are scared low-lifes who nag like women: in a move typical of much patriotic rhetoric, the enemy is berated through a feminizing analogy.

The disdainful reference to nagging women ties up with an early scene in which Singh finds out that his wife has been trying to get him transferred, so that he does not have to go to the battlefront. There is no place for such timorous machinations in his relentlessly macho worldview, and Singh responds in anger without stopping to consider his wife's perspective; for him, one's duty to the motherland comes before one's duty to one's family and loved ones. This gendered rendering of patriotic obligation has been a mainstay of Hindi films, be it films representing the freedom movement[15] or the conflicts of the post-independence era: men respond to the public call for heroic sacrifice, women come in their way and are eventually left behind to mourn, to bear the marks of social loss in their psyches and, sometimes, on their bodies. Two other narrative strands, pertaining to the lives of Lieutenant Dharamveer and the Border Security Force (BSF) officer Bhairav Singh, reiterate this ideology—although with greater ambivalence. The celebration of Dharamveer's engagement to Kammo is disrupted by the news of war and the cancellation of his leave: as his blind mother, widowed in the 1965 war, sits shell-shocked on the porch, muttering "I won't let him go" over and over, he quietly bids farewell to his tearful sweetheart and leaves for the front. Bhairav Singh hears of the outbreak of war on his wedding night and has to take leave of his bride the very next morning. Even in the middle of their nuptials, Bhairav has a vision: he splits, and a part of his self runs off with his BSF buddies. The homosocial dimension of military patriotism is alluded to as engendering a realm of belonging in which the only presence women are allowed is in absentia; it is further developed in scenes of camaraderie among the army men, most notably in a musical sequence in which the soldiers read letters from their families, happily engaged in sentimental exchanges.

The youthful Dharamveer, whose father died in the previous war, initially questions military ethics and the unquestioning allegiance expected of soldiers. He recoils in horror at the cold-blooded shooting of enemy informants; his vacillations provoke one of his colleagues to describe him as a boy who is playing with men's toys. In the course of the film, he overcomes all his qualms, learns to appreciate the rules of the warfront, and becomes a hard-boiled soldier. Through his dramatic transformation, the film interpellates its public to military tenets and normalizes the unconditional demands of patriotism. However, the faint trace of a critical consciousness lingers within Dharamveer: he dreams of his mother, already afflicted with hysterical blindness upon losing her husband in the previous war, rushing through the corpses on the battlefield, plaintively calling out his name. In a sense, he anticipates his own impending death and mourns on behalf of his mother—a connection that is established when this vision is repeated at the moment of his martyrdom.

Various characters refer to the nation (-space) as both motherland and mother goddess, thus reproducing the equation of landscape and woman (simultaneously idealized and made available for mastery) and a particular strand of nationalist imagination with strong Hindu under- pinnings. Bhairav Singh, a local Rajput, can sleep all night long on the desert sands: for him, the desert landscape is as cozy and sheltering as a mother's lap. When a colleague berates the harsh terrain, Singh is upset at this affront to his "mother." Loyalty to one's country is naturalized: one should cherish one's motherland because it is "like one's mother." Yet the motherland is placed hierarchically above the mother for pur- poses of patriotic indoctrination. This "confusion" between the primary and secondary terms of the country-as-mother paradigm indexes a structural aporia constitutive of the patriotic subject.

Hit by multiple bullets and delirious with pain, Bhairav Singh picks up a landmine and approaches a Pakistani tank, shouting "Mother, here I come!" One could argue that he is a devoted Rajput soldier, therefore his invocation of *Shakti* is in keeping with the demands of cinematic verisimilitude. But a very particular structure of sentiments, evident to Indian audiences, is being evoked here: it has its roots in the his- torical memory of legendary Rajput resistance to medieval Muslim in- vaders. At another point, when only 120 Indian infantrymen are sur- rounded by some 600 Pakistani soldiers and 40 tanks, Major Kuldeep Singh energizes his men by reminding them of the militant Sikh Guru who declared that one *Khalsa* (pure Sikh) resistance fighter amounted to 125,000 Mughal imperial troops. As mythologized history is evoked to inspire grossly outnumbered men, the secular trappings of the film begin to unravel. And as heavy artillery firing destroys an entire village, only the temple of the mother goddess remains standing: if this miracu- lous "escape" symbolically stems the long history of the destruction of temples by Islamic invaders, it also reveals the film's persistent framing of patriotism in religious terms.

Bhairav Singh is also allowed the most overt and grandiose "secular" gesture in *Border*. When heavy bombing sets homes on fire, he salvages a copy of the Koran for a distraught Muslim villager—an inheritance from his dead father. Overcome with emotion at this magnanimous action, the guy asks why Bhairav would risk his life for a holy book of another faith. Bhairav replies that to him, all religions are equal and all gods are sacred. The villager looks toward the camera in what approxi- mates a direct address to the audience and wonders why some people call Hindus infidels. Referring to the Islamic holy war or *jehad* against infidels, the sequence effectively suggests that contemporary Islamic fundamentalism is misguided in its anti-Hindu and anti-Indian atti- tude; at the same time, it manages to divest Hindus of such bigotry.

The film ends with a series of images which imply that common people on both sides of the border suffer equally: a close-up of a dead Pakistani soldier's hand holding a photo of his beloved; Dharamvir's mother running across the battlefield, his fiancée Kammo waiting at the village bus stop; a group of burka-clad Pakistani women keening on the desert sand. Finally comes the poetic and wistful declaration: "My enemy, my brother, my double." And yet, what goes on before forcefully promotes a Hindu-Indian patriotism whose ire is directed unequivo-cally toward Pakistan. We are informed at the beginning of the film that it is based on "true" events, and that it is dedicated to the memory of the director's brother who died in the 1971 war, but such ontological reference to real, lived experience cannot mask the patent ideological operation of the narrative in its affective address. If, as Fredric Jameson put it, History is what hurts,[16] then in the universe conjured up by *Border*, Pakistan—and, by causal regression, Partition—remains that History, the Other, the untranscendable ground of trauma.

Border aspires to a level of craftsmanship[17] that would compare well with global standards: it is a product of the new Bollywood, the contemporary Bombay film industry that has not only embraced the odd epithet signaling both its acknowledgment of the hegemony of the Hollywood culture industry and its desire to achieve similar levels of success but has also embarked on an ambitious program of "makeover" involving corporatization, adoption of state-of-the-art technologies, and aggressive marketing strategies at home and abroad.[18] Take, for instance, the remarkable scene in which Kuldeep Singh falls down in front of an enemy tank after fighting valiantly all night long. As he lies half-prone in the foreground of the frame, his back to the camera, he helplessly watches the barrel of the tank being lowered to aim straight at him (and at the audience). At this tense moment, an aircraft enters the frame from the background, drops a bomb on the tank, and flies really low over Kuldeep and the camera, making spectators duck ever so slightly. The relief that comes from this appearance of air force backup at the end of a long night of siege is turned into palpable corporeal sensation through this remarkable staging. J. P. Dutta, the director of *Border*, has been producing well-crafted films that are often set in the stunning desert landscape of Rajasthan with its undulating dunes, sandstone palaces and castles, women in vibrantly hued clothes, and lines of camels in the horizon (e.g., *Batwara* [1989], *Kshatriya* [1992]). While these films address the feudal social structures, lifestyles, and caste politics of the region, they also fabricate exotic spectacles with an eye to the diasporic market: as such, the contentious issues that are brought up get resolved in markedly reified and spectacular terms.

Dutta returns to the desert terrain in *Refugee* (2000), also set around the time of the Bangladesh war. This film manages to be far more even-handed in its representation of various communities and state institutions and wants to imagine a world without borders, passports, and visas. But as one commentator on a Web site observes, "One can't help suspect that J. P. Dutta imagines such a world would be established on India's terms rather than Pakistan's," as by the end "there does seem to be something of an 'India good, Pakistan bad' sentiment in the film regardless of its efforts otherwise."[19] The focus is on the travails of a Muslim refugee family fleeing from the former East Pakistan (now Bangladesh) and trying to make it into Pakistan. The complications of being a musalman in South Asia are presented here in terms of the problems the family faces: the "liberation movement" of Bangladesh, based on the issue of language and culture, displaces the Urdu-speaking family; both Indian and Pakistani authorities see the members of the family as illegal aliens or, worse still, destitute refugees who will be a burden to the state. The eponymous protagonist of the film is of unknown origin: he does not belong to any particular religious community or nationality; from his age, we can surmise that he was either separated from his family, or abandoned as a child, around 1947. He carries merchandise and helps people move across the Indo-Pak border, particularly across an arid "no man's land" that he calls home. He begins as an interstitial idealization, somewhat distanced and divorced from forms of family and community life; the narrative then charts his gradual "humanization" through his romantic involvement with Naaz, the daughter of the refugee family. Dutta deploys the figure of this young man to put to question the more sanguine categories from his earlier film *Border*, but romantic love ultimately provides the ground for the resolution—or, rather, displacement—of all difference.

Cinematic patriotism hit a new peak in Dutta's very next film, *L.O.C.* (*Line of Control*, 2003), about the Kargil war. In 1999, terrorists with their base in Pakistan crossed the Line of Control established at the end of the 1971 war and attempted to cut off the Kashmir Valley from Ladakh by closing down the strategically important National Highway One. Pakistani and Indian forces were soon engaged in a bloody conflict in the remote, mountainous region of Kargil. As Pakistani forces and Islamic terrorists had positioned themselves on the upper slopes, Indian troops initially suffered heavy casualties in the war that raged from May until July. The Indian side finally managed to push back the intruders, in large measure by pressing into service the powerful Bofors artillery guns.[20] Once again, Dutta gestures toward unbiased representation: whenever one soldier talks about revenge, another remarks about the families of dead soldiers on both sides; a commander of the Indian army insists on burying the dead Pakistanis; one of the main characters, while reporting victory at a post to his superior officer, admits that the enemies also fought valiantly. However, in the context of the entire narrative, these elements remain ineffectual: if anything, they serve to underscore the humanity of the Indians, their grace under fire, to a national public. The choice invectives that the two sides exchange ("curs," "wolves," "rats," "swine," and *motherchod*—the curiously bilingual form of *motherfucker* that is widely used in the northern half of India) indicates that no love is lost between them on the battlefield. The strong religious dimension of patriotism is underscored through the loud and frenzied invocations of various gods and goddesses of the Hindu pantheon—Kali, Durga, Ram, and Krishna—that rend the air as Gurkha, Jat, and Rajput regiments charge at an enemy perceived to consist of Islamic jehadis. It is reported that Muslim soldiers in the Indian army called out "Allah ho Akbar" and tied green bands over their helmets as they attacked their Pakistani counterparts: apparently, they value their ties to the nation more than their religious affiliations. However, we never hear their chant on a soundtrack that is thick with Hindu incantations. Through such strategies of inclusion/exclusion, *L.O.C.* frames the Kargil battle as a holy war and contributes in effect to the tide of religious nationalism coursing through contemporary South Asia. At the same time, the film wants to maintain a pretense of espousing universalized ideals and institutions. When Lieutenant Colonel V. K. Joshi tells his subordinate that they must under no circumstance cross the L.O.C., the implication is loud and clear: while India respects international laws, it is Pakistan that has broken them repeatedly and thus has become a "rogue country," to use a term that is now a cornerstone of the presiding global hegemonic order.

If recent incursions into Kashmir have become one in popular Indian consciousness with previous raids from across the border dating back to 1948, then *L.O.C.* emerges as the latest entry in a cinematic subgenre that began with the 1950 film *Kashmir* (see chapter 2). In keeping with the current aspirations of the Bollywood culture industry, Dutta wants to invest the film with an epic scope and feel: he borrows liberally from famous war films, including Kurosawa's *Ran* (1985), Spielberg's *Saving Private Ryan* (1998) and Terrence Malick's *The Thin Red Line* (1998). An action sequence from the last film[21] appears to be the model for a scene that is repeated several times with different characters in *L.O.C.*: in each case a soldier risks his life and charges uphill through a fusillade of bullets and throws a hand grenade into the enemy bunker, thereby managing to wrest a strategic location away from the adversaries. The main difference from the sequence in *Thin Red Line* is that in *L.O.C.*, most of these heroic soldiers die in the process of securing victory for their units. This structure of repetition introduces a curious element of banality in the narrative, and the main reason audiences may not find it boring lies in a morbid interest in the violent spectacle of young male bodies being ripped apart by bullets—an interest that is not altogether different from the fascination with repetitive actions in videogames and in pornographic films. Of course, the spectacularization of violence is not the only consideration behind the repetitive structure. Repetition finally achieves commemoration: by the end of the film, its painstaking recording of the battle locations and regiments wrests a mythic domain within the national popular for previously unknown locales like Kukarthang, Tololing, Khallubar, Batalik, and Tiger Hill.[22] Nevertheless, repetition here produces a pornography of violence, bleeding out all ethical charge in the service of a monomaniacal patriotic moral outrage. The film features an unprecedented galaxy of contemporary stars: Ajay Devgan, Akshaye Khanna, Saif Ali Khan, Suneil Shetty, and Abhishek Bachchan play characters that become martyrs; Sanjay Dutt and Manoj Bajpai portray figures that survive; and Rani Mukherjee, Kareena Kapoor, Mahima Chaudhry, and Esha Deol are the wives and girlfriends who are left behind to mourn the dead or take care of the maimed. The characters are drawn from all parts of the country, and while the film is in Hindi, we hear snippets of various regional languages. There is thus a potent sense of the entire nation behind the war efforts at Kargil, just as there is a strong impression of the involvement of the entire film industry in this project of memorialization and mourning.[23]

I want to make two specific but related points about the nature of this mourning work. First, much of the mourning takes place in the intensely homosocial space of the warfront: at various points, army officers express their anguish at the shocking loss of lives, and victorious commanders look positively dejected; on many occasions, characters cradle the dead, shed tears over them, plant a kiss on their foreheads. In this respect, *L.O.C.* presents a far less gendered representation of bereavement than *Border*: both men and women mourn the fallen heroes. However, the film also stresses the heterosexuality of its characters to the point of neurosis: time and again, battle scenes are punctuated with flashbacks of the soldiers' intimate moments with their wives and fiancées. I cannot think of another war film that emphasizes the normativity, even exclusivity, of heterosexual coupling in such an obsessive-compulsive manner, as if the soldiers' sexuality is a matter of national importance and the source of a deep anxiety. I will argue that the anxiety stems from the winds of change that are blowing through

Bollywood: on the one hand, emerging cultural norms must allow for a sensitive and caring masculinity; on the other hand, such accommodations destabilize conventional modes of being a man. Trauma, hysteria, and mourning continue to be viewed as weaknesses associated with women: masculine subjectivities find it difficult to acknowledge such conditions and symptoms publicly. A properly masculine form of mourning must unfold along a logic of displacement, whereby grief is channeled into anger. In a situation of war, loss feeds a craving for revenge: in this film, the death of each soldier incites his colleagues to more violent acts in a bid to avenge his martyrdom. This brings me to my second point about the nature of mourning that *L.O.C.* seems to propose and undertake in its repetitions: it involves an endless cycle of violence. To sum up, the structure of the film reveals, no doubt unwittingly, that a traditionally masculinist conception of mourning—which cannot admit the necessity of public expressions of grief—must unfold as continual and unending rounds of violence.

For a film that is ultimately about the impasse over Kashmir, *L.O.C.* never brings up the question of Kashmiri people's right to political self-determination. Instead, it reduces the issue to a clash between Pakistani aggression and Indian patriotism. While *Border* refers obliquely to Partition, the title of the later film refers back to the Indo-Pak conflicts of 1965 and 1971. The original trauma of Partition has now been replaced by the continuing trauma that is Pakistan. That is to say, the loss of 1947 has itself been lost—or, rather, it has been transformed into the ever-threatening existence of the neighboring country. On the evidence of *L.O.C.*, it appears that more than five decades after the truncation, Indians (and for that matter, Pakistanis) have yet to work through the experience: if anything, they have regressed deeper into a melancholic state so that they now turn their redoubled rage at the breakaway part. The context in which *L.O.C.* was produced, circumscribed by the nuclear standoff, the Kargil war, and the bombing of the Indian Parliament by alleged Pakistan-trained terrorists, would seem to support such a claim about a melancholic drive toward revenge and mutual destruction.

Patriotism is also the focus of three other recent films, *Hey Ram*, *Mission Kashmir*, and *Fiza*, all released in 2000. However, in sharp contrast to *Gadar*, *Border*, or *L.O.C.*, which evoke patriotic loyalty as a self-evident passion and obligation, these films explore the historical contradictions that fester at the heart of Indian patriotism. *Fiza*, written and directed by the veteran film journalist Khaled Mohammed, confronts the charged issues of intercommunity relations and national affiliations from a minority Muslim perspective increasingly under siege from a Hindu right-wing hegemony.[24] The film, which centers on the experiences of a young Muslim woman named Fiza, her brother Amaan, and their widowed mother, is remarkably successful in capturing minority difference without degenerating into exoticism.²⁵ In the fateful days of the 1993 Bombay riots, Amaan has a traumatic encounter with a band of murderous rioters: subsequently, he disappears. Fiza and her mother remain hopeful that he is still alive; even as this hope dwindles with time, they wait patiently for the police to bring them some news. Finally, fed up with six years of official inaction, Fiza herself sets out in search of her brother. Her quest soon takes her to the Indo-Pakistani border, where she discovers that Amaan, convinced that there is no legitimate place for Muslims within the Indian body-polity, has joined anti-Indian Islamic terrorists. In what follows, there is no simple recovery of an innate patriotic self; the narrative ends in tragedy when the law closes in, with Fiza shooting down Amaan at his request so he can escape interminable torture in police custody. This eschewal of a reassuring narrative resolution upset some audiences: in some places like Ludhiana, irate spectators ransacked theaters; others criticized the film for feeding communal passions. Still, the film was a big draw for weeks in cities like Bombay, proving that there was a public who welcomed the thoughtful exploration of seemingly unassailable verities.

Regendering Trauma

A strange gap remains at the heart of *Fiza*, a silence about the precise nature of the trauma that would force a gentle and amiable person like Amaan to act out with homicidal rancor. The extent of his loathing cannot be explained simply in terms of a masculinist exchange of a need to mourn for a need to retaliate. A similar occlusion occurs in *Hey Ram*: it remains less noticeable as the narrative offers a clear and compelling "reason" for the protagonist's transmutation into a fanatical assassin. This film takes us back to 1946, a year before Partition; the setting is Calcutta, where Saketh Ram and his wife Aparna lead the blissful life of newlyweds. But their idyllic world is shattered in August as political forces bent on ensuring the bifurcation of the country orchestrate the outbreak of lethal riots. In a harrowing sequence that remains possibly the most explicit and brutal depiction of Partition violence to date, Aparna is first gang raped and then murdered while her husband remains tied to the piano in the living room. Saketh manages to escape alive and roams around traumatized and disoriented until he comes under the influence of Shriram Abhyankar, a Hindu fundamentalist zealot. Abhyankar, a member of the extremist outfit RSS, convinces him that Gandhi, the most prominent leader of the Indian struggle for independence since 1920, is mainly responsible for the death of thousands of Hindus and for the tragic truncation of the country. For people like Abhyankar, it is Gandhi's insistence on peaceful coexistence and nonviolence that has confused Hindus while Muslims have made the most of the situation by aggressively pursuing their demand for a separate country. As he puts it, the dream of Hindu-Muslim amity is as ludicrous as expecting goats and butchers to live together without bloodshed. This strong acknowledgment of an alternative Hindu chauvinist perspective, noticeably marginalized in the first three decades following independence, brings out the contentious nature of postcolonial nationalism. The balance of this rambling narrative charts the indoctrination of Saketh Ram; his attempts to avenge the betrayal of nationalist dreams and, on a more personal level, Aparna's death, by gunning down Gandhi; and his eventual reconversion to pacifist and secularist ideals after he runs into his old Muslim friend, Amjad Ali Khan. Hearing that Amjad has lost his father and his uncle in the riots, he begins to realize that the other community has suffered the same kind of losses as Hindus. When a murderous Hindu mob descends on a warehouse hiding Muslim women and children, Amjad is wounded. The cry of the terrified reminds Saketh of Aparna's screams: the trauma is revivified, and in his disorientation he ends up protecting the Muslims.

By the time Amjad succumbs to his injuries in the hospital, Saketh Ram has completely snapped out of his fanatical spell—as if it were a pathological condition prompted by one traumatic loss (Aparna's death), now terminated by another (Amjad's death). He ends up a disciple of Gandhi and witnesses his assassination by another member of the RSS. Focalizing us through Saketh's subjectivity, the narrative substitutes the trauma of Partition by the killing of Gandhi, thereby replicating a displacement that is typical of other Partition films (see chapter 4). In spite of this resolution upholding the ideal of communal harmony, the bulk of the film engages the audience in a troubling romance with Hindu rightwing ideology and tendentiously fixates on a deeply reductive notion of the mussalman as the national Other. Given the predominant arc of the narrative, the secularist truisms tagged on at the end ring resoundingly hollow. One is left with the disconcerting feeling that the definitive reinscription of the past in *Hey Ram*, especially the closure it imposes on a traumatic experience, forecloses the possibility of a continuing critical relationship to it: the film cannot imagine a world beyond endless cycles of vengeful acting out. As one commentator surmised from her experience of watching the film, "Gandhi dies many deaths in an upmarket Delhi cinema hall." While *Hey Ram* is "ostensibly a film on communal harmony and on the relevance of Gandhi in contemporary India . . . the audience decides to write an entirely different script. For them, Gandhi is the villain of the piece and they cheer at each potshot taken at him." Furthermore, "loud thumps" of approval "follow when the decimation of Muslims is described as *kartavyapalan* (duty), as war, not murder or crime."[26]

All the same, the film's sense of closure is tenuous because of its marked vacillations and confusions: *Hey Ram* remains an incoherent text. Saketh Ram's pathology, what Amjad calls his "madness," is explained largely in terms of his violent expulsion from normative heterosexual union. Even after he accepts his family's counsel and remarries, he leaves home to join a hypermasculinist, homosocial outfit, whose members consider tolerance as a sign of weakness, as if to compensate for his failure to protect his first wife. The film connects this new affiliation to a community of militant Hindu men not only to a desire for revenge, but also to the threat of physical assault on men. There is an explicit reference to the very real possibility of sexual violation: when the rioters invade Saketh's home and rape Aparna, one of the intruders declares that he "prefers" Saketh to his wife. As Saketh's hands remain tied to the piano the man flips him over, so that he ends up bent over the piano keys, and attempts to sodomize him. While Saketh is able to thwart the sexual assault, the film registers in this episode a dimension of communal violence that usually goes unacknowledged: a very real threat to the male body—not in the form of mutilation or death, but in the form of sexual violation. However, in contrast to the obsessive references, implicit and overt, to the trauma of Aparna's rape and murder, the carnal assault on Saketh is never brought up again. The specific nature of male trauma from riots, whether during 1946–47 or during 1992–93, remains largely unthought and undisclosed. In social mayhem, when desires and actions are not circumscribed by the normative, the vulnerability of the male body, qualitatively speaking, is not too different from that of the female body. While the narrative of *Fiza* does not clarify whether Amaan was sexually assailed, the possibility remains; sometimes the threat is enough to induce trauma. The occlusion we encounter in *Fiza*, which *Hey Ram* partly redresses, points to the gendered nature of much trauma discourse. The sustenance of patriarchal privileges requires a disavowal of such incidences of emasculation, of the vulnerability of the male body and psyche; thus, even as the sexual victimization of women has emerged as a central concern in scholarly and popular accounts of social trauma, this category of male trouble remains outside discourse. Recent films and feminist historiography, in focusing exclusively on women's plight, recognize the differential experience of riots: while the frequency and extent of sexual violence against women justify this focus, the elision I am pointing to is reproduced. I want to stress the need for a greater attention to the plight of men in riot situations from a queer perspective: not of queer men per se, but of men as troubled subjects of heteropatriarchy.[27]

Trauma as Spectacle

With *Hey Ram*, we are in the realm of the spectacularization of Partition violence. Unlike the television series *Tamas*, this film stages the brutality in terms so graphic that they produce physical revulsion in spectators. Consider, for example, the sequence that ends in Saketh Ram's traumatization. On a trip to the store, Saketh encounters packs of rioters butchering people of the other community and pursuing women as fair game. Hurrying back home, he discovers a group of Muslim men trying to break down the door to his apartment. The leader of the group is Altaf, a local tailor whom he knows well: the film here conveys the disquieting sense of betrayal that is a core element of the cultural memory of Partition. Disoriented by a stunning blow to his head, Saketh tries in vain to fight off the intruders as they enter his home and proceed to assail the bedroom door that Aparna has managed to lock from the inside. As he is tied up to the piano in the living room, the men alternately hit him and touch him suggestively. Altaf climbs out of the living room window onto the ledge outside, manages to enter the bedroom from the balcony, and opens the bedroom door; his cronies rush in, leaving behind the guy who "prefers" Saketh to torment him. The camera remains in the living room, and we catch only a glimpse of Aparna's rape in a mirror through the doorway; the horror is captured visually in terms of the assault on Saketh, and in his helpless reactions—for instance, in the way he bangs his head on the piano keys. This visual discretion is more than compensated for at the level of the soundtrack: the ominous music, the pounding on the door, Aparna's screams, the clank produced by the hammering of the piano keys, the noise outside, Saketh's agonized calls for help—all work to produce intense sensations that shock and overwhelm audiences. After an interminable and harrowing scuffle, Saketh manages to survive the assault and enters the bedroom to find a bloody and disheveled Aparna gasping through her last breaths, blood spurting out of her slit throat. Having been privy to the couple's highly romantic and playfully intimate relationship in earlier sequences, spectators are now made to experience and endure Saketh's searing sense of loss: as he lurches out onto the streets, howling in his private grief, re-

Hey Ram:
As Aparna is raped in the bedroom . . .
. . . Saketh remains tied to the living room piano

coiling from the horrors of a public bloodbath, we are drawn right into a world turned upside down. The entire sequence—through its montage of brutality, sexual assault, bloody corpses, convulsive mourners, and terrifying sounds—induces terror and shock.

This mimetic reproduction of Partition as cinematic spectacle is driven in part by the demands of a global media market. It is symptomatic of a cultural trend at the end of a particularly distressing century, a trend that evinces a fascination with the problematic of understanding, memorializing, and mourning traumatic experiences. Framed by a millennial apocalyptic imagination,[28] such fascination veers into nostalgic reenchantments and the mobilization of vicarious trauma.[29] It should come as no surprise that *Hey Ram* was India's official entry to the foreign film category in the Oscars race of 2000: not only was it well-crafted high drama about a traumatic episode, it was also in large measure about Gandhi—one of India's primary cultural exports to the west, and conveniently linked to Richard Attenborough's multiple Oscar–winning *Gandhi*. Recent engagements with Partition trauma are crucially overdetermined by considerations that have little to do with the exigencies of coming to terms with the past, considerations that end up freezing and taming the past. *Hey Ram* begins and ends with a framing narrative about the death of an old and wizened Saketh Ram, himself a Gandhi-like figure by now, which unfolds in the middle of the riots of December 1992. This attempt to connect the past to the present, and the ontological gesture of bringing in Gandhi's real-life great grandson Tushar Gandhi alongside the fictitious character of Saketh's grandson, a writer, would seem to foster a critical historical consciousness on the part of the younger generation. Yet the film ends with shots of photographs of various characters—historical and narrative—on the wall, as Saketh's grandson brings out a box of artifacts that remains locked up and declares that he has an amazing story to tell. What is evoked here is Memory—with a capital *M*—of events that happened long ago and are now mainly of anecdotal value.[30]

Train to Pakistan (1997) and *Earth* (1999), two films made around the time of the fiftieth anniversary of Independence/Partition, also evince an investment in the nostalgic invocation of collective memory and frame their narratives in ways that mark a clear boundary between the past and the present. The first, based on a popular English novel by Khuswant Singh from 1956 and coproduced by Britain's Channel Four, begins as first-person narration by Hukam Chand, a local magistrate in Punjab, shifts to a more collective register in its focalization with multiple characters, and ends with a romantic mythologization of the principal protagonist as one in a long line of legendary heroes who sacrifice their lives for the sake of love. The story focuses on the village community of Mano Majra, caught up in the eye of the storm in 1947 because of its location near the new border. The narrative stresses the importance of the trains, which either stop at or rumble past the local station, in the quotidian lives of the villagers: the schedule of trains helps them mark time throughout the day. The daily pulse is disrupted as trains stop running altogether for a while, and a sense of foreboding engulfs the village as troubling rumors of strife begin to circulate. One dawn, as an unscheduled train from the west draws into the station, the sound wakes up the blind Muslim muezzin Imam Baksh and prompts the Sikh priest in the Gurdwara to break into a prayer. The magistrate and his subordinates enter the untimely train to discover corpses of Hindu and Sikh passengers—refugees ruthlessly butchered before they could get to the safe side of the new border. The scene features ominous music

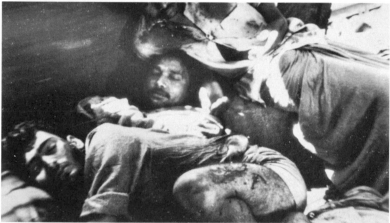

Train to Pakistan:
Untimely train rolls into the station.
Corpses on the train. Both courtesy of NFAI.

on the soundtrack, and the officials cover their nostrils to indicate the stench of rotting corpses, and yet, the visual aestheticization mitigates the horror, the bodies appearing picturesquely calm in the blue haze of dawn.

If the irruption of a wayward rhythm in the form of unscheduled trains points to the temporal complications of a traumatic experience, it still cannot capture the unending nature of trauma: in this diegetic world, once the trains begin to run on time, order will be restored and everyone will return unproblematically to their past subjectivities and lives. Singh's use of train schedules in the novel, evocative as it is, remains circumscribed by his instrumentalist attachment to the measured time of clocks and calendars, while the complications of psychic time belong to an altogether different order. One might note in Singh's defense that he penned the novel not too long after the tumult, so its long-term temporal implications were not evident to him. The film's faithful adherence to this figure of train schedules after another four decades appears far more egregious in its reduction of traumatic temporality to a finite and aberrant episode.

The film reproduces stock dramatic situations with stereotypical characters negotiating emerging threats to communal amity; noble values and acts of kindness are pitted against resurgent prejudices, mounting suspicions, and impetuous vengefulness. While the village elders, particularly the religious leaders, cite centuries of brotherhood and intimate, interdependent lives, and they pray for the well-being of the other community, the younger men grow more angry and unaccommodating as more sepulchral trains roll into the station, corpses float down the Sutlej river, and the stench of burning bodies fills the air. Again, it is possible to defend the novel as an early attempt to come to terms with the fallout of Partition in comfortingly familiar terms, but the film's rehearsal of the same elements after a lapse of decades constitutes a failure to deepen our understanding. Such cultural repetitions, inspired primarily by calculations of topical marketability, seem stuck in the same moment within an unfolding hermeneutic of mourning. As such, the transformatory possibilities of the historically rich material remain underdeveloped. An analytical reading must point to this lacuna in cultural mourning work, and to the measure of banality that accompanies what I have described as a discursive turn regarding Partition.

This banality is compounded in *Earth*, a film that taps into the contemporary global concern with genocides and social traumas. *Earth* is an adaptation of the 1991 English novel *Cracking India* by the Pakistani-born writer Bapsi Sidhwa. The novel, in its concerns, characterizations, and emplotment, is representative of the contemporary crop of South Asian writing in English that has acquired impressive purchase in international cultural circuits. The film, directed by Indian-Canadian filmmaker Deepa Mehta, is even more noticeably pitched at a global audience: its truck with loss and mourning is calculated to achieve currency in the global media market. The narrative unfolds from the point of view of an eight-year-old girl, Lenny, belonging to a Parsee family.[31] As a minority sect, the Parsees found themselves caught in the intercommunity tensions of the 1940s but managed to maintain a neutral position. This neutrality was not only prompted by a political pragmatism, but also stemmed from a detachment that was the result of their investment in a Western lifestyle—an investment that the film establishes through its references to markedly Western practices (celebrating Lenny's birthday with a cake; ballroom dancing) and "progressive" attitudes (women driving cars, frowning upon the marriage of underage girls). The film reflexively interrogates this neutrality: Lenny's mother says it is an uncomfortable position to inhabit, when all their friends are affected by the turmoil; her father quips that if the Swiss can be neutral in a war, so can the Parsees; when Lenny asks her mother if the Parsees are "bum lickers" (an epithet indicating their fondness for a British lifestyle), she says that they are more like chameleons who can adapt to and practically disappear in their environments, prompting the young girl to surmise that Parsees are no bum lickers, they are simply invisible.

One would expect the film to make the most of this outsider's "neutral" perspective to bear witness to the predicaments of its characters within a complex historical setting. But the sense of detachment from the surrounding milieu often works against the film, as it labors to suture us into an individualized tale of a girl's emerging consciousness. A bourgeois conception of subjectivity, coupled with a feminist interest in projecting interiority, turns the narrative into a coming-of-age story: that, by itself, would not be a problem, were it not for the concomitant reduction of a harrowing chapter of modern history to a mere backdrop. The pop-psychological dimension of the story becomes apparent in the phase-oriented denouement of Lenny's gradual "loss of innocence" through dinner table imbroglios, flirtations in the park, and direct encounters with violence. See Lenny learn about communal strife! See Lenny begin to experience sexual attraction and jealousy! See Lenny become an unwitting pawn in a cynical game of betrayal and revenge! What is rendered invisible in the episodic narration is the remarkably fraught historical milieu of late 1940s South Asia.

Since the film includes visual representations of riots, trains full of corpses, and the forced abduction of a central character—all ontological markers of a certain history—this last claim requires further elaboration. By now an iconography of Partition, drawn from photographs, fiction, films, and even oral histories, is in place; films like *Earth* and *Train to Pakistan* turn banal in their recycling of what are, essentially, images of other images.[32] Certain imagery—most notably shots of trains entering a station through clouds of smoke, accompanied by portentous music—conjure up the European Holocaust: in a sense, these films want to turn Partition into an "Indian Holocaust,"[33] as if it has become imperative for all societies to flaunt such afflictions to claim world historical significance. Still, one has to allow for the possibility of differentiated viewing publics: people who know very little about the carnage of 1947 may find *Earth* somewhat moving, even illuminating: the translocal references might help establish a broader framework for understanding the trauma of modernity. But the situations presented in the film are so hackneyed, and so thoroughly geared toward private drama, that they restrict viewers' engagement and understanding. In trying to eschew sensationalism, an aim apparent in the espousal of a "detached" perspective, the film also becomes curiously inert. That is to say, the nature of historical understanding—cognitive *and* affective—that the film affords remains grievously limited. Tableau-like shots of weary refugees streaming into town on foot or in bullock carts, or of the beautifully lit and aesthetically arranged corpses in the train, are presented like a series of picture postcards: as if the past were, indeed, a foreign country, an exotic location in time, now opened up for tourist contemplation and consumption through cinematic time travel. Nowhere is this more apparent than in the very odd sequence in which Lenny, accompanied by her ayah (nanny), Shanta, and her two working-class suitors, the "ice candy man" Dil Nawaz and the masseur Hasan, watches the riotous mobs from the roof of Dil Nawaz's house. As bombs explode all over town, guns are fired, and people are butchered, the group keep watching: only after Lenny has taken in the violence does Shanta drag her away and cover her eyes in the most ineffectual of gestures. The improbability of this scene boggles one's mind: How can Lenny's family allow the nanny to take the child out of the sheltering family quarters, when riots are about to break out any minute? Why does the group, including the sensible Hasan, keep standing on the roof, exposing itself to stray bullets and shrapnel? As the characters point out the various neighborhoods going up in flames and react in either muted satisfaction (Dil Nawaz, who has turned vengeful since the butchering of his sisters) or horror (Hasan, at the burgeoning violence, and Shanta, both at the violence on the streets and inside her friend Dil Nawaz), it becomes clear that this implausible and stilted scene is meant to provide a suturing point of view for an audience that is contemplating the horror from the safety and aloofness of the present moment—distant in time and space (contemporary South Asian and global audiences). This detachment becomes evident at various other moments due to the studied mise-en-scène—for instance, when Hasan watches the refugees, or when Lenny and the servant find Hasan's corpse in a sack—moments that should be upsetting but are not. The annoyingly precious pool of light that hovers in every significant scene, connoting sensuality, beauty, innocence, or pensiveness, ends up being a stylistic distraction. In spite of its patently mimetic realism, *Earth* begins to take on, by default, the attributes of a presentational text: but what it purports to reveal remains unclear.

Even the very last scene, a coda featuring the novelist Bapsi Sidhwa, manages only a facile reflexivity: while it frames the film as a personal narrative of coming into a subjectivity marked by loss ("That day in 1947, when I betrayed my ayah, I lost a part of myself . . ."), it tells us nothing about the workings of memory, let alone the historical conditions of the novel's or the film's production. Sidhwa's reference to history reduces 1947 to its negative aspect, ignoring the remarkable achievement of anticolonial struggle in South Asia: "Two hundred and fifty years of the British Empire ended in 1947—but what's there to show for it, except for a country divided?" Referring to the traumatic violence that Partition unleashed, Sidhwa asks: "Was it worth it?" I have been making a case in this chapter for a feminist critique of self-evident notions and structures of patriotism, yet I have to pause at the tone of Sidhwa's rhetoric. It is one thing to analytically reveal, and to make affectively palpable, the hidden dimensions of heteropatriarchal oppression in the name of the nation; it is quite another thing to suggest, even rhetorically, that 1947 achieved nothing. In negating 1947, Sidhwa and filmmaker Deepa Mehta are contributing to the ideological recuperation of postcolonial experiences by neocolonial frameworks of understanding history. One has to wonder who exactly is the addressee of this rhetoric: are Sidhwa, a doyen of the new South Asian literature in English, and Mehta, a controversial diasporic filmmaker, not pandering to a global gallery in terms that will be most palatable to it?

The film's purposefully global address is also evident in the consciously "multicultural" construction of the working-class group of friends.[34] The ways in which Dil Nawaz and Hasan propose to Shanta, and the manner in which she responds to them, are taken from a contemporary "universalized" script of romantic behavior, and seem ridiculously out of place in the context of plebeian Lahore of the 1940s. When Dil Nawaz refers to the animal inside every person, one that is tamed by civilizing forces but that comes out when the social structures fall apart, the film effectively evokes an innate and purportedly transcultural animal instinct. At least one commentator points approvingly to the film's, and Mehta's, espousal of such a view: "The filmmaker makes a profoundly convincing argument for the idea that war is itself a kind of element, unstable yet *every* bit as permanent as the ground on which we stand."[35] Such recognition of a universal, elemental force *de profundis* effectively divests historical conditions and agents of any conscious responsibility for the recurring atrocities. In Dil Nawaz's line of reasoning, the only thing that can effectively counter this instinct is love, yet another universal element, and so Shanta should marry him. Mehta herself subscribes to such elemental forces, as evidenced in the titles of her films *Fire* (1997), *Earth* and *Water* (2006), especially when their invocation helps sell her films in an international film circuit. After all *Earth* was released in South Asian markets as *1947*—for it was deemed correctly that at least in that part of the world, local history would be a bigger draw than any metaphysical reference.

In their predictable imagery, stereotypical characterizations, and routine dramatic situations, cinematic spectacles of Partition turn trauma into kitsch; in their linear plots and neat closures, the narratives attempt to embalm the past; in their global address and their allusions to other harrowing experiences, allusions that produce a kind of historical transference, these films threaten to erase the particularities of 1947. We are left with the impression that the past is over, done with, and thus cannot affect us anymore; that the main reason we bring up old traumas is to relive them nostalgically for their sensational impact, their entertainment value. Through this disavowal of the persistence of the past, Partition spectacles help sustain the puzzling intensity of trauma. I will even argue that these recent films, in their reifying containment of a difficult past, become effectively the flipside of the silence in the early decades: ultimately, both strategies promote cultural amnesia. If the early silence, dictated by the rawness of a still-fresh trauma and the expectations and demands of a newly independent country, induces one kind of forgetting, the recent explicit representations reiterate a monolithic version of Partition history, closing off the connections to unrealized possibilities and helping us forget the overlooked residues that always complicate the story. If the earlier moment required representations that celebrated the new nation-state and optimistically looked to the future by erasing the past, the present moment of globalization and of a more "open" India—in which an economic amenability to trade and foreign investment and ownership gradually extends to a general willingness to embrace a neoliberal world order at the cost of substantial loss of national sovereignty—promotes a pseudo-openness about the national past, inducing nostalgic invocations of national history that seem to "resolve" fundamentally unresolvable social contradictions and to eliminate the need for continued engagement.

Temporal Seepage

One of the more subtle aspects of coming to terms with a traumatic past is the recognition that it is impossible to overcome or transcend the experience completely: in other words, mourning a loss can "succeed" only through an acknowledgment of its ultimate failure. In Freudian terms, a sublation of the lost object involves an acceptance of the loss itself. Two competing selves, one predating and one following the experience of loss, jostle endlessly to produce a traumatized subjectivity: the past irrupts endlessly in the middle of the present. A politics of mourning that fosters such an insight and reanimates the arrested possibilities helps overcome the tyranny of functionalist teleology and imagine a more utopian future. The two films that I examine in this section engage with the legacy of Partition in bold and inventive ways, promoting precisely such a politics of mourning. The first, *Naseem* (1995), is a fictional feature in Urdu by Saeed Mirza, a filmmaker known for his quirky, offbeat works dealing with the experiences of minority groups in contemporary India. The second, *Way Back Home* (2003), is a Bengali documentary by Supriyo Sen, featuring his own parents.

Produced by NFDC and Doordarshan, *Naseem* was first shown on Doordarshan, followed by very limited theatrical release. It is not so much about Partition as about the social and political conditions which the minority Muslim community confronts daily in contemporary India—conditions whose contours remain crucially inscribed by the simmering traces of 1947. The film focuses on a Muslim family in the months leading up to the destruction of the Babri Masjid on December 6, 1992. The Hindu fundamentalist outfit known as the Viswa Hindu Parishad mobilized its cadres and its allies around the claim that the mosque had been built over the ruins of a Hindu temple that had once marked the birthplace of the Hindu demigod Rama. At stake was the recasting of Indian national space and history in Hindu chauvinist terms, and the further marginalization of minority groups within Indian society and polity. Focusing on the volatile atmosphere that was soon to conflagrate into bloody riots in various parts of the country, most notably in Bombay, the film pointedly explores the dwindling futures of a secular national community.

The protagonist of the film, a teenage girl named Naseem, goes about her humdrum life—attending school, hanging out with her friends, sneaking into a film meant for adult audiences, spending time with her ailing grandfather (her beloved *dadajan*)—even as a sinister and polarizing politics unfolds in the national arena and on television. The strong bond between Naseem and her grandfather constitutes the emotional core of the film: the old man regales his granddaughter with reminiscences of a time when he was young and newly wed, leading a happy life with his wife in Agra before 1947. In his nostalgic recounting, this past life takes on the charming attributes of a prelapsarian existence. At the same time, these enchanting memories serve to mourn forgotten possibilities and to invoke a lost future, a future that could have been. This kind of mourning opens up a parallel temporality: one of lost potentials,

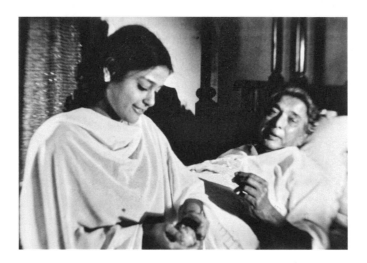

Naseem: Naseem with her grandfather. Courtesy of NFAI.

but one that offers hope of avoiding compulsive antagonism and acting out. Put another way, we are reminded that the past once had many possible futures. Here, memory transmitted across generations brings the characters, and the spectators, out of an inexorable teleology, allowing them to inhabit a more resonant time-space, and to dream of escaping the legacy of a traumatic past. The plot has an interesting structure that breaks temporal order yet obsesses over dates, thus conveying both the apparent inevitability and the randomness that simultaneously characterize the march of history. As the episodic narrative jumps from one month to the next, the sequences are marked by dates, so that we move closer to the fateful day in early December, but the grandfather's recollections pull us out of that inescapable denouement. Two kinds of movements through time—one along a unidirectional vector, the other looping along mnemonic circuits and imaginative planes—capture the continuity and density of the experience referred to as Partition.

The very first shot of the film, repeated about four-fifths of the way into the narrative, establishes the layered temporalities of traumatized collective subjectivities in visual terms. The scene is marked on-screen as occurring on December 4; thus, in terms of calendrical time, it comes after the subsequent sequences that cover the period between June and November (not considering reminiscences in flashback that keep interrupting the present). Naseem sits in front of a large mirror with three panels, brushing her hair, her back to the camera, so that we see her face reflected in the central panel. Somewhere behind her and near the camera is a television set, also reflected in this panel. The two side panels

Naseem: Spatializing temporality. Courtesy of NFAI.

mirror the anxious faces, in profile, of an older woman and a young man who, we soon learn, are her mother and older brother. While the grown-ups seem both riveted and troubled by the television broadcast, Naseem is engrossed in her own reflection. The mirror is the source of enchantment in this scene, not only for the girl but also for the spectators: the three panels present a visual fullness via their multiple perspectives. But the panels fracture this fullness, just as the television signal is always weak and on the verge of disappearing (in several scenes, people fiddle with the controls to adjust the reception). In this narrative, any particular reality has to jostle with, and is constantly under threat of erasure from, other states of being. Through its intimation of this dense ontology, and its spatial mapping of the intertwined temporalities in terms of the multipaneled mirror and the television screen, this very first shot establishes the film's radical sense of time and politics.

Certain incendiary moments of political manipulation—the 1984 pogroms aimed at the Sikh communities, or the 1992–93 riots following the destruction of the Babri Masjid—jolt us out of these parallel temporalities: these moments seem to seal us into a unitary and streamlined teleology of violent acting out. As the promises afforded by the memories of an already lost future appear even more out of reach, disillusionment leads to anger. Naseem's elder brother Mushtaq, who has to deal with the violence of the public sphere, reacts angrily to their grandfather's endless narrations. To him, and to his militant friend Zafar, this is nostalgic escapism: as he declares flatly, the era conjured up in the old man's stories is now over. The reality that matters to the youth is the reality that unfolds around them, a disquieting reality of marginalization and persecution that pushes them further into a confrontational politics underwritten by religious faith; it is a reality that reiterates the particular teleology set in motion with the truncation of 1947.

In presenting these two competing visions, the film achieves a remarkable double articulation of history, already encapsulated in its very first shot. This double vision is further elaborated in the scene of the family's Eid celebrations. Looking all spiffed up in a *sherwani* that Naseem talks him into wearing, the grandfather recites poetry for the guests. When Zafar responds with more couplets, the old man is impressed. But their exchange of poetry and pleasantries gives way to a more pointed debate when Zafar says it is difficult for him to get into the festivities as every day there are reports of more people dead in social altercations, and the dead all happen to be Muslim. The grandfather suggests that it is the poor who die in riots, attempting to advance a materialist understanding of the violence; Zafar retorts that it is the Muslims who have been kept poor in postcolonial India. As Zafar recites from Faiyaz, the old man gently chides him, saying that he is quoting the poet out of context, thereby changing his intended meaning. Claiming that new times require new attitudes and interpretations, Zafar respectfully excuses himself from the family gathering; Mushtaq leaves with him, quietly signaling his agreement. Two very different consciousnesses, shaped and separated by generational experiences and sensibilities, joust in this scene: together, they capture the complexities of a beleaguered community's sense of history, its anticipations of the future, and its present political contingencies.

How is the grandfather's investment in the past different from the fundamentalist invocation of a mythic past—for Islamic fundamentalists, when the great Sultans and Shah-en-Shahs reigned over India, and for Hindu fundamentalists, when the great Rama presided over a just and powerful Hindu domain? These mythic pasts, whether Hindu or Muslim, are exclusionary, as they cannot admit a multiplicity of futures; rather, they each imagine only one totalizing future. In such views, the ideal future has already happened: it is a future that is always already anterior—an anterior future, which simply needs to be replicated. Thus these reenchantments close off the fullness of potentialities that remain submerged in historical memory, invoking a narrowly construed past and mapping it onto the postcolonial narrative of national development, attempting to ensure a strict Hindu or Muslim teleology. The possible critical charge of enchanting memories that resuscitates abandoned pathways and idealisms is, thus, lost.

This loss, intensified by the resurgence of an aggressive Hindu nationalism as the mainstay of Indian national politics, is dramatized in the film in terms of the grandfather's death in the early hours of December 6. As the body is being taken for burial, Zafar brings news of the fall of the mosque. When he remarks that Dadajan has chosen the perfect time for his departure, his comment is as much an indictment of the old man's customary escapism as a deep apprehension about the future. At this point the possibility of peaceful community life in India virtually disappears, the destruction of the mosque having driven, as it were, the last nail into secularism's coffin. The old man's death appears to signal the end of secularist politics as Indians have known it; his passing also points to the apparent end of leftist politics with class inequities, and not religious difference, as its primary focus. In many ways, *Naseem*'s grandfather is the young Sikander of the earlier film *Garam Hawa* (chapter 4). Sikander, like the grandfather in his youth, lived in Agra; he had decided to stay on in India in the hope of finding his true community among leftist activists fighting class oppression and religious bigotry. This intertextual connection is strengthened by the iconic presence of the leftist poet Kaifi Azmi in the role of the grandfather, for it was Azmi who had penned the script for *Garam Hawa*. There is a further, generational link between the two films: Saeed Mirza, writer-director of *Naseem*, happens to be Azmi's nephew in real life. Considered together, the two films from 1973 and 1995 present a deeply affecting portrayal of Muslim-Indian subjectivity ravaged by loss and the irreconcilable demands of a fissured life. The films also appear to suggest, at first glance, the disappearance of precisely that strand within such a subjectivity which would enable the dream of a more harmonious national future.

The kind of disappearance *Naseem* projects through the grandfather's death is not a simple erasure signifying the defeat of secular politics. Instead, the film invokes a *dis*-appearance in the sense of a negative appearance or, better still, a nonappearance: a ghostly intimation of that which is struggling to come into view, but has not yet managed to do so.[36] For death or erasure does not achieve a complete eradication: certain traces remain, insinuate themselves into our consciousness, haunt us. This is the abiding force of every loss—the productive potential that remains in its heart. If secularism as we have known it is dead in India today, its utopian dimension persists in memory. This utopian trace, and the lost possibilities embodied in the recollections of a time before religious differences were turned into murderous rancor, keep *dis*-appearing with a mysterious urgency and impel us to keep working toward a yet-to-be imagined and articulated secularist politics informed both by past mistakes and by forgotten promises. This is why I find *Naseem* to be a remarkably prescient instance of cinematic mourning work, one that seizes a contemporary moment of crisis to reflect on the past and insists on a more textured historical consciousness as a conduit to a better future.

The documentary *Way Back Home* (2003) chronicles the journey undertaken by the parents of filmmaker Supriyo Sen in search of their ancestral homes in the district of Barishal, Bangladesh. This "homecoming" takes place some fifty years after they fled from the region to Calcutta in 1950, when mounting communal tensions made it unsafe for Hindu families to continue living in what was then East Pakistan. Divided into two hour-long parts—*Abar Ashibo Phirey* (a title taken from a famous poem by Jibanananda Das, and translated here as *Way Back Home*, although a more literal translation would be *I Shall Return Yet Again*) and *Kalpanar Swadesh* (*Imaginary Homeland*)—the documentary deftly interweaves archival footage, still photographs, first person testimonials by the elderly couple, cursory lines spoken by various people that the couple encounter on the road and in Barishal, a few songs (including two folk songs traditionally sung by boatmen), and voice-over narration by the filmmaker. In spite of the use of archival material and explicatory commentary, including English intertitles that encapsulate relevant moments from modern South Asian history, *Way Back Home* remains a profoundly subjective work. The film explores how memory, particularly traumatic memory, attempts to resuscitate a sense of wholeness for subjectivities inscribed in loss; it stages the impossibility of return to a prelapsarian state, indexing the inevitable failure of such a project. The way back home turns out to be interminably stretched out, just as mourning work must remain forever incomplete. Yet the film converts this irreducible lack into the very possibility of a transformatory cultural politics. What begins as a quest on behalf of his parents also turns out to be Sen's search for his own identity, his place within a tormented history, as he interrogates the role of what may be called his generation's postmemory in shaping a post-traumatic historical consciousness. Traversing across generations, across borders material and psychic, across the private/public divide, and across subjectivities, *Way Back Home* emerges as a significant new entry into the burgeoning subgenre of autobiographical documentary.[37]

A melancholic and contemplative mood is established early in the film. It begins with a short sequence shot in Barishal, in which Sen's father tentatively looks for a recognizable house, a familiar face, or even a tree after the lapse of half a century. When he declares plaintively that he cannot identify anything, we sense that this journey will be a heartrending one. After brief titles, the film takes us back to the Sen family's present home in Calcutta. The parents reminisce about their life in East

Bengal, stressing the strong bonds among people from different class and religious backgrounds, and the intimate connections one felt to nature—the orchards, the rivers, the sky. They remember a joyous life when the year seemed like an endless series of festivals; the deterioration in the social atmosphere after Partition; the hardening attitude among many Muslims toward Hindus who had chosen to remain in East Pakistan; desperate attempts to maintain communal harmony; fresh bouts of violence in early 1950; and the eventual flight to West Bengal. Seemingly incongruous fragments of memory surface in these testimonials: the kind Muslim neighbors who guarded the mother's family for days but finally advised them to leave; a man named Sikander helping them to reach the border; the father's community wondering how they would protect their women from sexual violence, and even considering the option of killing them with their own hands—purportedly to save their honor; the duplicity of a student leader who attended a peace meeting and then led the rioters the same night; the heckling that Hindus faced even as they departed, leaving behind all their belongings; the apathy, even outright resentment, that the refugees confronted upon crossing the border; the disorientation and penury they experienced in the big city; the demeaning and dehumanizing effects of the Indian government's decision to classify the refugees as a "permanent liability" and attempts to forcibly place them in camps. Tears well up in their eyes, their voices choke, as they recount their experiences; the father punctuates his account with "Can you even imagine?" This iterative query, the faltering enunciations, and the physical articulations intimate the unfathomable. As if to recompense for this gap, the recollections undertake a nostalgic ballasting of the past, display a fetishistic investment in it, and reveal the hope of recovering a fullness of subjectivity through a trip back to the abandoned homeland—a hope whose futility becomes apparent in the second part of the film, and that is achingly presaged in the opening sequence.

The first half puts the personal testimonials about the past in dialogue with archival material, establishing the entanglement of memory and history. Thus, the parents' recollections are placed alongside a "voice-of-god" narration accompanying photographs and film footage of the carnage of 1946, celebrations of independence, refugees in Calcutta, Gandhi's attempts to maintain peace. It is this part that remains closer, at first glance, to a more traditional notion of documentary with its objectives of recording, preserving, and understanding reality and history, while the second part explicitly stages the problematics of subjectivity and historical knowledge. However, the filmmaker's interest in capturing the continual and interminable process of becoming historical subjects is evident throughout the film. The melancholy that imbues the frame in practically every scene, and which stretches across multiple generations, is accentuated in terms of formal and stylistic elements: thoughtful placement and measured movement of the camera (static long shots of the mother standing at a window, or slowly walking down a corridor; languid camera pans across the river at dawn or dusk, or in the moonlight), frequent use of dissolves for transitions between shots (as the father speaks of crossing the border, a series of dissolves take us from his face to still photographs of refugees), complex juxtapositions of image and sound (as the mother speaks of leaving Barishal, a flute is played on the soundtrack, while on-screen a close-up of her face is replaced by a shot of rain on the roof and the trees, followed by a medium shot of a crow in the rain; while father describes the riots, we see mother standing on the balcony, or the camera tilts and presents a panoramic shot of Calcutta through the window); layering of sound and music (as the mother speaks of year-round festivals, we hear ululations and conch shells).[38] A single strand of recollection on the soundtrack is accompanied by a whole range of visuals: for instance, the father's narration of the flight from East Pakistan incorporates shots of him sitting on the bed in Calcutta, standing on the railway tracks at the border, still photographs of refugees, and footage of the Sealdah train station in Calcutta (possibly shot in recent years, but in black and white to make it look "archival"). As past and present seep into each other in the course of this cinematic act of remembering, the labyrinthine nature of mourning becomes apparent.

Even in the first part, the "documentation of the past" accommodates not only the parents' desire to recover what has been lost, but also a more surreptitious form of mourning on the filmmaker's part—mourning the very present, that which will also be lost some day. Sen lovingly presents exquisite shots of Calcutta—the one place he has experienced as home, as opposed to the distant "imaginary homeland" elsewhere, in Barishal. Calcutta is presented not in the manner of famous "city symphonies," cinematic paeans to metropolitan centers that evoke monumental cityscapes; instead, Sen's Calcutta is decidedly low-key, intimate, pensive. The only city landmark that comes into view is the Howrah Bridge, its cantilever towers hovering above a congested and unplanned urban sprawl of residential buildings remarkable only for their general moss-stained dilapidation. Limiting himself to the locality where his parents live, Sen presents us with glimpses of alleys, small storefronts, corridors, balconies, and staircases, taking in the particular furniture and architectural features: high ceilings with fans, red concrete floors, large grilled windows and latticed balcony walls, green wooden shutters, an old and ornate teak bed. In documenting these details, Sen evinces a nostalgia not for the past, but for the present moment: for surely these buildings, and the lifeworld to which they belong, will soon fade away in the face of relentless hypermodern renewal, just as his ancestral homes and orchards have vanished over the last fifty years. In documenting these architectural spaces in Calcutta—which his parents, in their nostalgic enchantment with a Barishal of yore, often discount—Sen mourns their impending disappearance. Indeed, *Way Back Home* communicates, in its overarching introspectiveness, a profound understanding of the mournful drive at the heart of the will to document, photographically and cinematically, reality and human experience—what Bazin had called cinema's "mummy complex."

Part 2 takes place entirely in the present, as Sen and his crew accompany his parents on their passage through Barishal. Sen's dad looks desperately for a familiar human face, or even a tree, that would call out to him. As he locates the police inspector's house and the old Krishna temple but cannot find his ancestral home, he appears lost in the temporal folds of a palimpsestic landscape. His wife is similarly disoriented: if she closes her eyes, she remembers a particular setting that has very little correspondence to the current locale. Visibly upset, he admits he is lost, she declares that her memories were better than this alien reality. The few anchoring traces—his college, her school, the cremation ground, the old mailman, her cousin's daughter, the cousin's tomb—bring forth fragments of memory and overpowering emotions. These halting irruptions call attention to the myriad, often unanticipated, reinscriptions through which subjectivity is constantly being reconstituted. Gradually, the filmmaker's own stake in the journey to Barishal becomes apparent to us. Born into a refugee family, his sense of self is constituted by a historical loss that predates him. We learn from his own testimonial, largely off camera, that he has grown up hearing about, and dreaming of, a verdant elsewhere with green groves and blue skies, wide rivers and open fields, that is able to transcend "all that is impure, ominous and dark." But this mythic elsewhere also creates a gaping hole at the heart of the here and the now. Since Partition not only produced a geopolitical division, but also introduced "a great psychological divide" between the two main religious communities of South Asia, Sen's Hindu-Bengali identity is circumscribed in a web of dislocations and belongings. The film is his attempt to come to terms with the multiple levels, personal and social, of loss inaugurated by the truncation of 1947.

At the end of the journey, Sen finds only obscure traces of torn-down houses and dead kinsfolk; without concrete, ontological basis, the homeland of his dreams turns out to be imaginary. The past, now even farther than a foreign country encircled by barbed wires, remains beyond his reach. Through his recognition of this impossibility of recovery or return, Sen comes to embrace his self with its deep marks of loss—in a sense, he overcomes the trauma of Partition. This autobiographical register takes center stage as we finally catch a glimpse of Sen's face, in close up, toward the end of the film. As he stares out of a car window, staring at the lush green landscape with its rice fields, hamlets and coconut trees, we hear his reflections on the soundtrack: "All this time, I used to dream of my own homeland—I thought it existed somewhere in this sub-continent, that I had to reach it someday. I wanted to reconstruct a land without bloodshed where people are as generous as the river."[39] However, this dream of reconstituting the self in spatial terms falls apart. Confronting the material, institutional, and psychic markers (borders and checkposts, passports and visas, attitudes and passions), Sen realizes that the social relations that constitute space have changed radically over time. Once in contemporary Bangladesh, the fossilized spatial imaginings of a nostalgic self cannot be sustained.

Sen's admission of the impossibility of this long-cherished project comes immediately after footage of the February 2002 carnage in Gujarat, in which fascist forces of hindutva, encouraged by the complicitous inaction of the state government, carried out a genocide aimed against Muslims, killing several thousand in the process (the official count of casualties being 2,000). Through a lucid dissolve from scenes of mayhem to the filmmaker's contemplative face, the film articulates the impossibility of a personal return with the hopelessness of collective attempts to recover either a nostalgic secularism or a mythic Hindu past. The loss marking individual subjectivity is connected to the challenges confronting the national body and polity.

While the dream of the unproblematic recovery of a unified self—individual or national—is acknowledged to be only a dream, Sen defiantly holds on to its utopian potential. In a structural choice that reveals the political imperative driving his work of cinematic mourning, Sen returns us in the very next sequence, the film's finale, to his mother's search for her long-lost cousin Kamala in Barishal. We know from the mother's earlier musings that Kamala (or, as she refers to her, Kamlididi) was a beautiful, personable woman, an accomplished singer, who dared to antagonize her own Hindu community to marry her Muslim beau; that she had to convert to Islam, was shunned by her family, and was left behind in East Pakistan in 1950. After a long search, our team locates her daughter Minu and learns from her that Kamala passed away a year ago. Minu talks about her mother's syncretic lifestyle, her continuing investment in Hindu religious and cultural practices, and her critical avoidance of certain aspects of Islam. She also places her own investment in secular structures in relation to the rising tide of Islamic fundamentalist politics in Bangladesh: she mentions, in particular, her attempts to save Hindu women from harassment, and the persecution by religious fanatics of people in her locality, including her own eighteen-year-old son, because of their support of a secularist candidate in the middle of the general ascendancy of diehard Islamists in the elections of 2000. The legacy of the courageous and broad-minded Kamala lives on in her offspring.

As Sen's mother lights a candle and incense sticks at Kamala's grave, Sen's voice-over musings deftly dovetail a personal quest into the social:

> Finally we find her, . . . the woman known as Kamala Dasgupta or Aleya Begum, who has linked me in blood to her Muslim offsprings. This is the person that Gandhi had searched for—in Noakhali, Bihar, Punjab—during the riots-torn days of Partition. Now she lies in peace, underneath ancient trees and an open sky, in a remote village of the subcontinent ravaged by religious loathing, nuclear face-offs and border skirmishes. She is the person in whose quest we have traveled so far.[40]

Kamala emerges as the embodiment of a dream that her death cannot extinguish, just as secular harmony remains an ideal that refuses to go away in spite of Partition, in spite of the repeated social conflagrations. As the group lights candles at her grave both to mourn her and to celebrate her legacy, *Way Back Home* mourns 1947 and its long aftermath, as it simultaneously holds onto the remarkable possibilities that remain embedded in memories of the trauma. This is the film's critical enchantment.

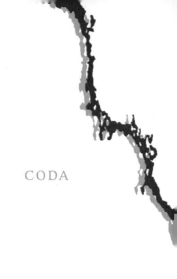

The Critical Enchantment
of Mourning

ANCHORED IN THE THREE CATEGORIES of nation, trauma, and cinema, *Mourning the Nation* is an interrogation of one national cinema's ongoing labor of mourning a collective loss. If mourning is an interminable process, then this book, itself a work of mourning, cannot presume to be conclusive in the standard sense of the term. Still, some tentative observations regarding its methods, revelations, and limitations are in order. I want to foreground, in particular, the possibility—indeed, necessity—of a critical optic in engaging acts of cultural mourning. The very notion of crisis, which animates this book, invites such a criticality: as Susan Rubin Suleiman reminds us, "crisis" shares with "criticism" the Greek root *Krinein*—"to discriminate, to separate, to choose."[1]

This book engages two major questions: (1) How does cinema mourn? (2) How does national cinema mourn its own intrinsic fissures? While the first question is primarily about the medium specificity of cinematic mourning, the second is mainly one of cultural politics. At issue is a theory of cinematic mourning work in the context of national dissimulation and dispersion. The concrete historical experience in terms of which these general queries are explored is the South Asian Partition of 1947. Thus the scope of this project is brought into focus around a specific event and a singular cultural context.

The very notion of the *event*, hovering at the intersection of contingency and structure, ephemera and meaning, permanence and loss, poses a set of representational possibilities and challenges that is constitutive of the cinematic medium.[2] In that sense, cinema—which unfolds in, even as it freezes, time—is preternaturally suited to the task of mourning. But this is not just any event: Partition happens to be a shocking collective experience with continuing repercussions. The temporality of the event is complicated by its traumatic nature: it is experienced over time only as it seeps gradually into conscious comprehension, and as it is relived and repeated in unforeseen, intractable ways.

The cultural and historical dimensions of 1947 matter to this book in at least two significant respects. First, the episode sets in motion a very particular regional history rife with its own alignments and animosities, hopes and anxieties. I have situated the task of mourning in relation to this larger history at whose core is India's constantly evolving project of nationhood. Second, the textures, rhythms, and repertoires of local lifeworlds mold the specific modalities of mourning. Thus the preceding pages devote considerable attention to the strategies and tropes that comprise Indian cinema's mourning work. Without claiming an exceptional status for Indian cinema, or delinking it from global networks and energies, I have attempted to flesh out the singularity of its labors of mourning. If historical specificity complicates generalized rubrics of structural lack, trauma, and mourning, the haptic and affective dimensions of the experience infiltrate and shape its archives, expanding the notion of historical evidence.

My central argument in the book congeals around a hermeneutic of mourning that I assemble retroactively from the early silences surrounding Partition and the more recent "return of the repressed" in the form of explicit mediations. I show that the trauma enters films from before the eighties not so much as well-thought-out narrative episodes and elements, but more as displaced and inchoate citations, images and phrases—cinematic "runes" that become legible only through an allegorical reading practice. In the last two decades, the event practically explodes in cinema as part of a broader public discourse, the mid-1980s being a watershed moment. While this particular hermeneutic is shaped by the traumatic nature of the experience, it is also crucially inflected by shifts in nationalist ideologies and programs.

Mourning does not occur in a vacuum; therefore I move beyond structural and medium-specific understandings of the process to argue for a situated politics of mourning. Such a politics entails making an analytical distinction between two types of films. The first kind blocks critical engagement with the past in terms of its nostalgic ossification as spectacle; disavows the past's continuing relevance through its demarcation as a time that is now distant and done with; imposes a reductive clarity on experiences that defy forced explication; induces vicarious trauma in spectators, transmuting a horrifying episode to fodder for entertainment; and raises the specter of further acting out. The second kind of mourning proceeds from very different ethicopolitical grounds, seeking to overcome the concrete conditions that led to the trauma in the first place, and to foster the more radically utopian promises that remain unrealized and overlooked in every community. The uncertainty about the ends of mourning makes it imperative for us to distinguish films that produce totalizing and narcissistic visions of national identity, closing off collective history, from films that refuse such closure.[3] In a sense, mourning work has to keep "failing" in order to ensure its continued efficacy: if it were to reach a conclusion, it would "succeed" at the cost of critical relevance.

How does one retain a productive critical position in the face of concerns that emerge in a social field marked by anxiety and agonistics, fascination and projection? An intrinsic stage of mourning is the revival of affective investment in the past in terms of desire and fantasy: that is to say, mourning always involves *enchantment*. Cinema, in particular, provides a powerful and captivating means of cultural memorialization; it pulls together the fragments and reassembles the past via considerable acts of imagining. This form of cultural recall entails, beyond a simple recovery of the past, the creative revivification of an archive of inert data and fragmentary evidence. And yet, if we do not subject traumatic experiences and mourning work to critical interrogation, we risk foreclosing the possibility of social transformation. Mourning, a task at once intractable and essential, must simultaneously come to grips with criticality and enchantment. The articulation of these two irreconcilable positions has been the core challenge informing this book. By way of a last word, I want to propose that at its best, mourning becomes a form of critical enchantment.

How can cinema (and cinema studies) fulfill this seemingly implausible demand for critical enchantment? Several distinct approaches have emerged in the preceding pages: a reflexive presentation of the procedures of cinematic memorialization, especially the problematic of representing traumatic loss; a realist narrative that performs the vicissitudes of traumatized subjectivities through an intensely melodramatic address, revealing the underlying social conflicts; the recuperation of lingering utopian impulses from a forgotten past in the service of a transformed future. Any of these approaches, in and of itself, does not ensure critical acuity. As I have demonstrated, the standard polarizations between modernist reflexivity and realist transparency, between art cinema and commercial cinema, are ultimately not that illuminating: their limitations are repeatedly revealed through the largely unconscious irruptions in otherwise closed texts, and through the hegemonic undertones of supposedly oppositional texts. A film's critical function cannot be assessed and established without taking into account its context of production, its public, and the evolving discursive field within which it is located.

These considerations suggest two distinct modes of engaging the historicity of the films—one focusing on their context, the other on their dialogic transactions with the past.[4] The first mode involves a focus on a text's conditions of possibility, especially the objective conditions of its own time, while the second takes a more anachronistic approach, interpreting the film mainly through the lens of contemporary exigencies. While the first mode (contextualization) tends to ignore the continuing relevance of past representations in the present through its obsessive stress on the film's embeddedness in structures concurrent to its production, the second (doing history from the present) erases the specificities of the past in its reinscription of the film in terms of current concerns. I have been arguing for a more capacious approach, one that is able to apprehend the diachronic emergence of Partition discourse without sacrificing historical contingencies, in terms of the constitutive location of various films within an overall hermeneutic of mourning.

I choose to end this book with *Naseem* and *Way Back Home*—from 1995 and 2003 respectively—not out of any naive concern for chronology, but because these films strike a fine balance between contextualization and dialogic interpretation, thereby staging, en abyme, a hermeneutic of mourning within their plots. *Way Back Home* closely parallels the concerns of this book, especially a strong interest in fostering a post-traumatic subjectivity: a subjectivity that has worked through, come to terms with, *post*ed the trauma of Partition not in terms of a pretense that the loss is a matter of the past, but in the sense of learning to live with the loss and accepting the impossibility of either recovering plenitude or achieving retribution. If this film also works through a structure of repetition, it is repetition with a difference—it does not replicate violent acting out but frees subjects from such compulsions. The filmmaker Supriyo Sen and I belong to the same generation, and we share similar (culturally) Hindu, middle-class, refugee-family backgrounds: to an extent, I can claim as my own the tentative historical consciousness that struggles to emerge in this autobiographical documentary.[5]

A further question springs from my transferential relation to the past and to its reconstructions: to what extent do the problems I investigate inhere in my work? Disavowal, nostalgia, fetishism, fixation, and cultural bias tend to persist in disguised ways: one ends up replicating these tendencies when one is dealing with enchantments. My upbringing makes it easy for me to fall into a Hindu majoritarian predisposition for hegemonic assimilation, if not subtle discrimination; my ideological proclivities nudge me toward the habitual espousal of a secularist apologia for tendentious minority politics. Concerns about a manageable scope lead to yet another problem: I focus exclusively on Indian films, ignoring their Pakistani and Bangladeshi counterparts, as if Partition were an experience affecting only Indian nationals.[6] Attending to cinematic mediations from the sibling states will help understand how the trauma is dealt with from their perspectives; it will enable us to discover, and articulate, cultural endeavors across the region that imagine realms of post-traumatic affiliations transcending the official borders—the most glaring material markers of Partition. The future of South Asia demands the forging of a post-traumatic consciousness through such transborder initiatives, and future film scholarship has an important role to play in this ongoing, collective project of cultural mourning.[7]

To return to the broader concerns of this book, since the nation is always born and experienced through loss—be it the loss of difference, the loss of other forms of community life, even the loss of idealism that drives nationalist imagination and creativity—nationhood always entails a dimension of mourning. Behind the exulting notes of various national anthems one can discern the faintly audible minor-key undertones: the sadness born of sacrifice, disillusionment, and even defeat. Mourning the nation involves mourning a political form that has made collective mourning a modern imperative. To mourn the nation is, therefore, also to mourn the political conditions that make for the possibility of social mourning itself. To mourn the nation, thus, is also to try to envisage a time and a place in which mourning would no longer constitute a necessary element of the political, a future in which one would no longer need to mourn in order to be a political being—that is, in order to constitute communities. It is a task whose contours are not yet discernible; it is a task that began with the nation.

Notes

Introduction

1. I remember high school history textbooks from the 1970s celebrating the struggle for freedom culminating in independence; the throwaway references to Partition riots did not provide any sense of their nature, extent, or long-term effects.

2. Here, the field of cinema is being broadly construed: I also study one important television miniseries. While the institutions and modalities of television broadcast (e.g., discrete episodes, commercial breaks, massive simultaneous reach) are quite different from those of film exhibition—differences that become apparent in chapter 6—the series in question was shot on film, by one of the preeminent filmmakers of India. The entire series, on film, is part of the holdings at the National Film Archive of India in Pune.

3. Anderson, *Imagined Communities*; Balibar, "The Nation Form," 86–106; Hobsbawm, *Nations and Nationalism since 1780*, 1–14.

4. See P. Chatterjee, *The Nation and Its Fragments*; Agamben, *Means without End*; Mignolo, "On Subalterns and Other Agencies."

5. Connor, "A Nation Is a Nation."

6. Cheah, *Spectral Nationality*; Appadurai, "Disjuncture and Difference in the Global Cultural Economy." See also the various essays in Shapiro and Alker, *Challenging Boundaries*.

7. Here I am drawing on Dominic LaCapra's useful distinction between "structural absence" and "historical loss," delineated in his essay "Trauma, Absence, Loss."

8. Žižek, introduction to *Mapping Ideology*.

9. Rogoff, *Terra Infirma*, 1–7.

10. P. Chatterjee, *Nationalist Thought and the Colonial World*, and *The Nation and Its Fragments*.

11. Ngũgĩ provides one example of the radical disruption that colonial systems wrought on the experiential world of the colonized subject: after the introduction of English in the Kenyan education system, students caught lapsing into their native tongue (Gĩkũyũ) were subjected to corporeal punishment. Ngũgĩ wa Thiong'o, *Decolonising the Mind*.

12. See, for instance, P. Chatterjee, *Nationalist Thought in the Colonial World*; Spivak, "Can the Subaltern Speak?," Chakrabarty, *Provincializing Europe*; Moreiras, *The Exhaustion of Difference*; and Cooper, *Colonialism in Question*.

13. Chakrabarty, *Provincializing Europe*, 76.

14. Fritz Breithaupt points out that the extreme idealism of the late eighteenth century ("the German period of *Sturm und Drang*") led to inevitable disillusionment about selfhood, so that "the battle cry for self" soon turned "into a lamentation about its unachievability." Thus, the idea of trauma took shape "as a possible remedy for the impossibility of self." One might note in this formulation the kernel of the "truth" of trauma in its most universal form: an insurmountable structural lack. Breithaupt, "The Invention of Trauma in German Romanticism," 78. Some might trace the origins of modern trauma back to an earlier moment: Descartes's rationalist separation between the mind and the body in the seventeenth century, producing a split in the notion of the human.

15. Freud, *Beyond the Pleasure Principle*, first published in German in 1920 as *Jenseits des Lustprinzips*.

16. For one example of the fascinating work on mourning from the fields of anthropology and religious studies, see Bard, "'No Power of Speech Remains.'"

17. For a fascinating discussion of the transactions between indigenous and imported forms of public mourning in colonial Bengal, see P. Chatterjee, "Two Poets and Death."

18. See, for instance, Caruth, *Unclaimed Experience*; see also essays by Emmanuel Levinas in *The Levinas Reader*, especially 166–210.

19. For essays on the anthropology of death, see Robben, *Death, Mourning and Burial*.

20. See Kakar, *The Colours of Violence*, and Pandey, *Remembering Partition*.

21. I am referring to the plenary session of the Annual South Asia Conference (2000) at the University of Wisconsin, Madison: the panel included, among others, historian Dipesh Chakrabarty and social psychologist Ashis Nandy.

22. Shibnarayan Roy speaks of a similar disorientation in his Bengali book *Swadesh, Swakal, Swajan*, consisting of his musings on national identity and community at the height of the Hindu nationalist movement.

23. This is why I have dispensed with the standard practice of relegating the affective and the personal to a preface, a practice that typically helps secure the impression of a certain kind of scholastic hermeticism.

24. I have benefited from the theoretical models and critical insights in sev-

eral volumes on memory and trauma studies, including Caruth, *Trauma*; Bal, Crewe, and Spitzer, *Acts of Memory*; Radstone, *Memory and Methodology*; Belau and Ramadanovic, *Topologies of Trauma*; and the excellent critical overview by Karyn Ball, "Introduction: Trauma and Its Institutional Destinies."

25. Recent decades have seen some remarkable instances of cinematic commemoration that effectively recover repressed memories on behalf of entire collectivities. Taiwanese filmmaker Hou Hsiao-hsien's elegiac work *City of Sadness* (1989) was instrumental in bringing back a forgotten episode of national history—the massacre of leftist intellectuals by a beleaguered KMT government on February 28, 1947. Most Taiwanese nationals growing up in the intervening decades had no knowledge of the bloodbath, so thorough was its erasure from public and private accounts. The Senegalese film *Camp de Thiaroye* (1987), co-directed by Ousmane Sembene and Thierno Faty Sow, recalls for postcolonial Africa a shocking incident from 1944 that the French would probably have preferred to expunge from memory: the French army's cold-blooded massacre of Senegalese *tirailleurs* in their sleep. The tirailleurs, who had fought valiantly to defend French interests in the war, had incurred the wrath of their European superiors by challenging the double standards of the French colonial army and legitimately demanding the same treatment and pay as their white compatriots. In both instances, cinema undertook the task of witnessing on behalf of wounded groups, recovering dimensions of experience that had been erased from historiographic accounts.

26. Sturken, *Tangled Memories*.

27. See, for instance, Klein, "On the Emergence of *Memory* in Historical Discourse."

28. One could argue, of course, that the obsession with criticality is itself a modernist enchantment.

29. For a useful discussion, see LaCapra, "Reflections on the Historians' Debate," in *Representing the Holocaust*.

30. Mowitt, "Trauma Envy."

31. Churchill, *A Little Matter of Genocide*.

32. There are signs that Partition is becoming another paradigmatic case for thinking globally about collective traumas. For instance, in the 2004 volume *Divided Countries, Separated Cities*, edited by Ghislaine Glasson Deschaumes and Rada Ivekovic, the South Asian scission emerges as a reference point for thinking about partitions all over the world. The preeminence of this one truncation over others may have to do with the scale of the experience (if one can talk about comparative scales with respect to trauma). But this salience must also be situated in relation to India's current geopolitical significance and to the sheer number of scholars working on South Asia.

33. See Zertal, "From the People's Hall to the Wailing Wall."

34. Amin, "On Retelling the Muslim Conquest of North India," 30.

35. Caruth, *Unclaimed Experience*, 24, 8.

36. Around August 16, 1946, between five and ten thousand people were butchered in Calcutta alone. See Gordon, "Divided Bengal," 308.

37. Cleary, *Literature, Partition and the Nation-State*, 19.

38. Chatterji, *Bengal Divided*; Jalal, *The Sole Spokesman*; Pandey, *Remembering Partition*; Singh, *The Origins of the Partition of India*; Tan and Kudaisya, *The Aftermath of Partition in South Asia*.

39. See, for instance, Talbot, "Literature and the Human Drama of the 1947 Partition," and various articles in Settar and Gupta, *Pangs of Partition*, vol. 2. For an exception, see the all-too-short discussion of popular Bhojpuri performance related to Partition in Tiwari, "Partition Memory and Popular Culture," 69–73. Folk performance as a way of commemorating Partition is also the focus of Nijhawan, "Partition Violence in Memory and Performance."

40. Butalia, *The Other Side of Silence*; V. Das, "The Act of Witnessing"; Menon and Bhasin, *Borders and Boundaries*.

41. Rare exceptions include the chapter on the television series *Tamas* in Mankekar, *Screening Culture, Viewing Politics*, and the limited discussions in Rajadhyaksha, "Strange Attractions," 31; Vasudevan, "Dislocations," and P. Kumar, "Testimonies of Loss and Memory." One recent book significantly extends the notion of "historical evidence" by analyzing the concerns and anxieties expressed in political cartoons in the English-language press: Kamra, *Bearing Witness*.

42. See, for instance, Zelizer, *Remembering to Forget*. Also note the singular focus on art cinema in Eric Santner's excellent book *Stranded Objects*.

43. I am referring to dramatizations on television, and not documentaries such as *Heimat* and *Shoah*.

44. Bazin, "The Ontology of the Photographic Image," 9.

45. Ibid., 12.

46. Barthes, *Camera Lucida*, 6.

47. Bazin, "The Ontology of the Photographic Image," 15, emphasis added.

48. Bazin, "Death Every Afternoon," 30.

49. Khalid Mohammed states, "At a modest estimate at least 9,000 Hindi language films—this is news as well as a comment—have just skedaddled with the wind." "Canned Forever," *Hindustan Times*, June 23, 2008.

50. Rosen, "Subject, Ontology and Historicity in Bazin," 3–41.

51. See the brief discussion of the film in Winters, "The Great War and the Persistence of Tradition," 33–45.

52. I am referring here to West German cinema of the period between 1945 and 1989. The East German experience is somewhat different: the films made under the DEFA (Deutsche Film–AG), such as *The Murderers Are among Us* (*Die Mörder sind unter uns*, 1946), *Stronger than the Night* (*Stärker als die Nacht*, 1954), and *I Was 19* (*Ich war neunzehn*, 1968), addressed questions of responsibility and atonement, and the roots of fascism, early on.

53. Rentschler, *Ministry of Illusions*.

54. See Elsaesser, *New German Cinema* and *Fassbinder's Germany*; Kaes, *From Hitler to Heimat*.

55. We should note that modernist reflexivity and affect are not mutually exclusive: Santner (*Stranded Objects*, 155–66), for one, stresses the importance

of affect for mourning and makes a distinction between Kluge's emotionless irony and the strong role that affect plays in a feminist work like *Germany, Pale Mother*. More recently, Caryl Flinn (*The New German Cinema*) attends to the role of music in New German Cinema's cultural mourning work.

56. Hirsch, *Afterimage*, 19.

57. LaCapra, *Writing History, Writing Trauma*, 185–86.

58. For some critics, Spielberg turned the Holocaust into something of a theme park; indeed, his side projects, like the ambitious recording of camp survivors' testimonies, reminded many of the synergistic side projects that accompany a high-concept blockbuster film.

59. My brief account of the criticisms above is based on Miriam Hansen's useful summary in her essay "*Schindler's List* Is Not *Shoah*."

60. Lanzmann, "Why Spielberg Has Distorted the Truth," quoted in Hansen, "*Schindler's List* Is Not *Shoah*," 301.

61. Hansen, "*Schindler's List* Is Not *Shoah*," 302–3.

62. Ibid., 306. There are signs that film scholarship is finally moving beyond these categorizations to engage overall discursive strategies. See recent works such as Gertz and Khleifi, *Palestinian Cinema*; Lowenstein, *Shocking Representation* (on horror films); Kaplan, *Trauma Culture* (covering ground from Duras to Hitchcock); and Kaplan and Wang, *Trauma and Cinema*. Walker addresses home movies, autobiographical documentaries, recorded testimonies, and reenactments in *Trauma Cinema*.

63. See Crary, *Techniques of the Observer*; and Kelly, *Iconoclasm in Aesthetics*.

64. Jain, *Gods in the Bazaar*, 12–13.

65. Hansen, "America, Paris and the Alps."

66. By now, there is a significant body of scholarly work on the significance of frontality, iconicity, tableau, and the darshanic mode in modern Indian aesthetics. See Kapur, "Revelation and Doubt"; Jain, *Gods in the Bazaar*; Pinney, *Camera Indica*; Rajadhyaksha, "The Phalke Era"; and Vasudevan, "The Politics of Cultural Address." Vasudevan, for instance, characterizes frontality not so much as a matter of placing characters and objects at a 180-degree angle to the camera, but more as a direct and familiar form of address through "iconic condensation," drawing on the cultural knowledge of the vernacular audience. "This position of knowledge is not one which relays the spectator through a hermeneutic play, the enigma of what is to come, but through existing paradigms of narrative knowledge, although these may be subject to reworking" (138). Likewise, while the arc of the darshanic or the devotional might suggest a hierarchical social or narrative placement, Vasudevan argues that the cinematic mobilization of this mode is far more fluid, having to do with "the localised deployment of filmic techniques in the micro-narration of a scene—editing, shot-distance and angle, camera movement, lighting, sound elements" (140). Therefore, Vasudevan argues, cinematic narration and the darshanic enframe and reconstitute each other.

67. This is not to discount Indian popular cinema's considerable role in estab-

lishing and maintaining hegemonic structures, but to mark the qualitative difference from cinema's aestheticization of toxic politics during the Third Reich.

68. For recent developments in the study of traumatic experiences, both personal and social, see Belau and Ramadanovic, *Topologies of Trauma*; and Caruth, *Unclaimed Experience*. Also see Caruth, *Trauma*; Kleinman, Das, and Lock, *Social Suffering*; La Capra, *Writing History, Writing Trauma*; and van Alphen, "Symptoms of Discursivity."

69. Butalia, *The Other Side of Silence*; Das, "The Act of Witnessing"; Kakar, *The Colours of Violence*; Menon and Bhasin, *Borders and Boundaries*; Pandey, *Remembering Partition*.

70. Pandey, "In Defense of the Fragment."

71. For a succinct critical-historical discussion on timelines, see Rosenberg, "The Trouble with Timelines."

72. See chapters 1 and 2 in Kakar, *The Colours of Violence*, for examples of the kinds of citations and linkages I am evoking here.

73. This is the structure of trauma that Joshua Hirsch (*Afterimage*) also indexes; however, in contrast to his singular focus on modernist attempts at finding a form adequate to this structure, I locate a pervasive structure of deferral and displacement in the field of popular cinema.

74. On the precariousness of traumatized subjectivities, and the (im)possibility of witnessing, see Agamben, *Remnants of Auschwitz*.

75. Mourning the national partition is closely related to the specific history of an evolving nationalist project. Perhaps a comparative reference to the particular experience of Korea will help clarify this point. Until the 1970s, for older generations, national bifurcation was a source of sadness and suffering. With the rapid development of the South Korean economy, and the strengthening of prodemocratic forces in the 1980s, there was a distinct shift in national perceptions and attitudes. For generations growing up in the 1970s and 1980s, reunification emerged as a collective goal and was tied to the project of democratization. This optimistic mood received a strong boost in 1989: with the end of military rule in South Korea, reunification also appeared imminent. Thus the existence of another Korea across the border was no longer a source of national melancholy: rather, younger generations looked forward to the day when all of Korea would come together as a strong democratic nation. In South Asia, in the absence of any realistic hope for reunification of the three territories, melancholia becomes far more endemic. Lacking the celebratory optimism of the Koreans, South Asians become bitter and resentful: minor tensions rapidly escalate into belligerent face-offs.

76. Schleiermacher, *Hermeneutics and Criticism and Other Writings*, 90–157. See also the excellent survey article by Tilottama Rajan, "Hermeneutics," 486–89.

77. See Benjamin, "Theses on the Philosophy of History"; Gadamer, *Truth and Method*; Derrida, *The Ear of the Other*; Derrida, *Specters of Marx*; Koselleck, *The Practice of Conceptual History*; Jameson, *The Political Unconscious*. The fraught history of the contemporary invocations of romantic hermeneutics, particularly

in relation to questions of agency and politics, points to the difficulty of simultaneously acknowledging one's debt to Gadamer and Derrida. I find Gadamer useful for his application of philosophical hermeneutics in understanding the past and imagining the future—that is, in construing the realm of the political. See Gadamer, *Philosophical Hermeneutics*. I am also influenced by Derrida's incisive critique of Gadamer's faith in "good will" as the guarantor of a progressive politics, and for his interrogation of an unproblematic presumption of psychoanalytic coherence or unity in the midst of an agonistic social. See Derrida, "Interpreting Signatures (Nietzsche/Heidegger)," 1–17. I invoke the two thinkers together in order to resuscitate a utopian vestige of romantic hermeneutics, traced back to Schleiermacher in the 1830s and now refracted through the lens of antifoundational thought.

78. Chakrabarty, *Provincializing Europe*; Mignolo, *Local Histories/Global Designs*; Povinelli, *The Cunning of Recognition*.

79. Nandy, *The Savage Freud and Other Essays*; Abbas, *Hong Kong*; Mbembe, *On the Postcolony*.

80. There are many commentaries on the twilight rituals at Wagah; see, for instance, A. Kumar, "Splitting the Difference."

81. Growing up in Calcutta in the 1960s and 1970s, I never heard of the gendered nature of Partition violence in everyday conversation or even in history classes.

82. Ramaswamy, "Visualising India's Geo-body."

83. While I borrow this phrase from the influential study of the post–World War II German scenario by the Mitscherlichs, the psychodynamics that I advance for the Indian experience, following recent postcolonial theory, is critically different from the German case, in which the collective loss was precipitated by the dissolution of the idealized figure of the Führer as the locus of German pride. Mitscherlich and Mitscherlich, *The Inability to Mourn*.

84. Freud, "Mourning and Melancholia."

85. Ibid., 244–45.

86. Freud, *The Ego and the Id*.

87. Butler, *The Psychic Life of Power*, 183.

88. Ibid.

89. There is no reason to believe that the Nehruvian version of secularism was the only one in the 1950s, although it was the hegemonic one; in fact, recovering alternative secular visions—which do not summarily dismiss the question of faith—ought to be a central concern of any project aimed at a reformulation of the secularist agenda. Likewise, social *forgetting* was a rather intricate phenomenon, not all of whose motivations were state-driven. Since social violence marks the limits of community, and certain painful experiences threaten life, all kinds of denials and repressions were necessary to secure collective and individual survival following 1947.

90. Laplanche and Pontalis, *The Language of Psycho-analysis*, 485.

91. Adorno, "The Meaning of Working through the Past."

92. With the rise in collective political action by various religious movements,

the term *fundamentalism* has come to denote forms of religiosity that are essentialist and conservative. Thus fundamentalist religion is posed as antithetical to modernity; yet the politicization of contemporary religions is a characteristically modern phenomenon.

93. A more thoughtful articulation of this argument appears in Alam and Sharma, "Remembering Partition."

94. "Grisly Discovery Reopens Old Wounds in India," *New York Times*, March 20, 2006, emphasis added.

95. The excerpt is from Faiz's Urdu poem, *"Subh-e-Azaadi* (August 1947)" (The Dawn of Freedom [August 1947]). This translation, slightly modified here, appears in Genoways, "Let Them Snuff Out the Moon," 111.

96. During the Indo-Pakistani cricket series of 2004, thousands of Indian sports fans went to Pakistan to watch the matches and were accorded a warm welcome by the local people. Such warmth and affection came as something of a surprise after all the belligerence of the previous six years, yet many people remarked that it was only natural—these wildly divergent reactions revealing, once again, the deep ambivalences that mark popular sentiments in this region.

97. My invocation of the temporality of the "anterior future"—a future that still was possible in the past—is a play on the more familiar "future perfect" or "future anterior" tense—a past that is still a future but that will become a past sometime in the future. So the future anterior involves two events, A and B, both of which will transpire in the future, but in a chronology such that A will already have happened by the time B happens. So, although A and B are both located in the future, A is anterior to B.

1. Cinema's Project of Nationhood

1. Steve Curry's haunting photograph of an Afghan refugee girl, which adorned the cover of the June 1985 issue of *National Geographic*, comes to mind.

2. These ideas are developed by Barthes, *Camera Lucida*, 26–28 and 40–45.

3. I use the term *decade* in a loose, experiential sense, so that the period extends back to a few years before Partition, and forward to 1962, when the Chinese invasion and the consequent military humiliation ended the nationalist euphoria from the first flush of independence.

4. Paz, *In Light of India*, 73–133.

5. Ibid., 75.

6. Ibid., 76.

7. See, for instance, Chakrabarty, *Provincializing Europe*; Gaonkar, *Alternative Modernities*; Mbembe, *On the Postcolony*; Guha, "The Small Voice of History"; and also see the essays in Loomba et al., eds., *Postcolonial Studies and Beyond*.

8. Nehru, "The Discovery of India."

9. Dalle Vacche, *The Body in the Mirror: Shapes of History in Italian Cinema*, esp. 254–58.

10. Burgoyne, *Film Nation*.

11. Rajadhyaksha, "Introduction," *Encyclopedia of Indian Cinema*, 10.

12. For a remarkable and extended discussion of European thought on the relation between cultural institutions and the modern state, see Lloyd and Thomas, *Culture and the State*.

13. P. Chatterjee, "On Civil and Political Society in Post-colonial Democracies."

14. See chapters 2 and 3 in Dipesh Chakrabarty, *Provincializing Europe*.

15. Berlant, *The Anatomy of National Fantasy*, 5.

16. Ibid., 4.

17. According to Partha Chatterjee's influential formulation ("The Nationalist Resolution of the Women's Question"), nationalist thought, confronted with the West's proven dominance in material and worldly affairs, asserted the East's (which, in this nationalist instance, implied India's) ascendancy in the inner realm of the spirit. This counterbalancing claim rested on a series of polarities—East/West, inner/outer, spiritual/material—aligned together to establish the primacy of the first set of terms over the second.

18. Guha-Thakurta, "Marking Independence," 95.

19. Ibid., 90.

20. Guha-Thakurta, introduction to *Sites of Art History*, 5.

21. Guha-Thakurta, "Marking Independence," 90.

22. Ibid.

23. Ibid.

24. The press was often critical of the government, chastising it for its general indifference and occasional acts of hostility toward the industry—such as levying entertainment tax at rates ranging between 25 and 75 percent of the price of admission to the theater.

25. A politician from the ruling Congress Party quoted off the record in *Filmindia*, September 1947, 3.

26. "Writing on the Wall," *Chitrabani*, April–May 1953, 5.

27. *Report of the Film Enquiry Committee*, 3.

28. *Filmindia*, July 1948, 7.

29. Letter to the editor from Mrs. Sharada Devi Awasthi of Cawnpore, *Filmindia*, June 1947, 51.

30. *Filmindia*, May 1947, 7; and *Filmindia*, October 1947, 59.

31. This section draws on reports in *Filmfare* magazine, and the discussion of the controversy in Chakravarty, *National Identity in Indian Popular Cinema*, 75–77.

32. *Filmfare*, February 27, 1959. In keeping with his philosophy, Salil Chowdhury did not hesitate to raid the high canon of Western classical music, successfully adopting the opening strains of Mozart's fortieth symphony in a Hindi song.

33. *Filmfare*, June 19, 1957, 19.

34. *Filmfare*, July 9, 1954.

35. *Chitrabani* [in Bengali], May–June 1954, 3.

36. *Chitrabani* [in Bengali], June–July 1954, 3.

37. Guha-Thakurta, "Marking Independence," 100.

38. Ravi Varma was an immensely popular artist in the nineteenth century, whose prints enjoyed wide circulation among the upper and middle classes. He provided an alternative to the "Company" style of British and most British-trained Indian painters; hence, by many accounts, he is the first modern nationalist painter of India. His art went on to influence mass-produced calendar art forms in the twentieth century.

39. While traditional art-historical narratives have undertaken the devaluation of Ravi Varma's oeuvre as sentimental kitsch, and the concomitant valorization of the Bengal School as the true moment of inauguration of Indian modernism, recent accounts of modern Indian art have questioned such a hierarchical evaluation. See Guha-Thakurta, "Visualizing the Nation."

40. See, for instance, Pinney, "The Nation (Un)Pictured"; Jain, "Producing the Sacred"; Uberoi, *Freedom and Destiny*; and Jain, *Gods in the Bazaar*.

41. The frescos on the cave walls at Ajanta constitute one of the most important bodies of classical Indian art.

42. Jain, "Producing the Sacred," 63. Abanindranath Tagore was a primary figure of the Bengal School, whose aesthetic forms privileged spiritual essence over corporeal presence.

43. While my focus here is on representations of the female body, it is worth noting that calendar art also subjects male bodies to modes of sensualization.

44. See Jain, *Gods in the Bazaar*.

45. For instance, women in the domain of calendar art routinely wear cut-offs, referred to as *choli*, that reveal most of the torso. The rather salacious hit song "Choli ke pichhe kya hai" ("What's behind a Choli") from the blockbuster film *Khalnayak* (1995) encapsulates the semantic oomph that the choli enjoys in Indian popular imagination.

46. These iconographic conventions crystallized to such an extent that the opposition of costumes could denote schizophrenic fragmentation in *Raat aur Din* (*Night and Day*, 1967). Manoj Kumar structured his nationalistic tale of the superiority of the East (i.e., India) over the West around such polarities in *Purab aur Paschim* (*The East and the West*, 1970).

47. By far the best discussion of this issue appears in Prasad's engaging chapter, "Guardians of the View," in *Ideology of the Hindi Film*, 88–114.

48. Prasad, "The State in/of Cinema," 127.

49. Ibid. Prasad refers to Noel Burch's classic, *Theory of Film Practice*, 123.

50. "Slandering a Nation," *Filmindia*, January 1950, 3–4.

51. I believe the commentator means "unwed mothers."

52. Ibid., 7.

53. *Filmfare*, July 9, 1954.

54. *Filmindia*, April 1947, 49.

55. Anand Patwardhan explores the complex relations between mass cultural representations, popular appropriations, religion, gender, and sexuality in his documentary *Father, Son and Holy War* (1993). In a chilling sequence, a group of

otherwise unremarkable young men express their readiness to engage in sexual molestation as a routine form of amusement. The sequence suggests that both sexual atrocities committed during riots and the more quotidian—and shockingly normalized—harassment of women in public spaces of metropolitan centers such as Delhi belong to a single behavioral order. This order is framed by a disavowal of the irrepressible presence of sexual fantasy in public life, and by the cancerous mutations of fantasy wrought by social regulation.

56. Official financial backing came only after some filmmakers, most notably Satyajit Ray and Mehboob Khan, won international recognition, and cinema started to look like a worthwhile national cultural activity.

57. Prasad, "The State in/of Cinema."

58. Ibid., 132.

59. Ibid., 126.

60. Rajadhyaksha and Willemen, *Encyclopaedia of Indian Cinema*, 298.

61. Three other factors must be taken into account to explain the ascendancy of Bombay. First, it was the financial capital of the country and had gained most from wartime expansion. Second, the Partition dealt a crippling blow to the Calcutta industry, by bifurcating its Bengali audience. The Pakistan government would not allow the export of Bengali films to the Bengali-speaking East Pakistan. Third, with Lahore going to Pakistan, a large section of the artists and technicians from the Lahore studios migrated to Bombay, bringing in a new spurt of talent and energy. Of course, the fact that most Bombay films were produced in Hindi (officially recognized to be the national language) or its close kin, Hindustani, helped to secure for it a wider market.

62. I am indebted to Ashish Rajadhyaksha for drawing my attention to Filmistan's role in the consolidation of genres in popular Hindi cinema.

63. Rajadhyaksha and Willemen, "All-India Film," *Encyclopaedia of Indian Cinema*, 41.

64. The term was coined by Chidananda Dasgupta in his 1968 essay "The Cultural Basis of Indian Cinema," reprinted in an anthology of his essays, *Talking about Films*.

65. See Vasudevan, "Addressing the Spectator of a 'Third World' National Cinema."

66. Ibid., 311–12.

67. "*Barsaat* makes New Box-Office Records! Raj Kapoor's Artistic Triumph!" *Filmindia*, May 1950, 51.

68. Vasudevan, "Addressing the Spectator of a 'Third World' National Cinema," 312, emphasis added.

69. Saratchandra Chattopadhyay and Munshi Premchand are two towering figures associated with social reformist literature.

70. Geeta Kapur develops this point in "Cultural Creativity in the First Decade," 22.

71. Brooks, *The Melodramatic Imagination*.

72. See, for instance, Shepherd, "Pauses of Mutual Agitation."

73. "'Beware of Films!' Says Debaki Bose!" *Filmindia*, August 1951, 49–51.

74. Ibid., 51.

75. Kaviraj, introduction to *Politics in India*, 7.

76. Ibid., 29.

77. See Willemen, "Negotiating the Transition to Capital."

78. See Sumita Chakravarty's discussion of *Mother India* in her book, *National Identity in Indian Popular Cinema*, 149–56. See also G. Chatterjee, *Mother India*.

79. *Filmindia*, August 1948, 70–71.

80. See, for instance, T. N. Madan, "Secularism in Its Place," and Bilgrami, "Two Concepts of Secularism," 349–61.

81. P. Chatterjee, "Religious Minorities and the Secular State"; V. Das, "Communities as Political Actors."

82. Vasudevan ("Dislocations") provides a more sympathetic reading of *Nastik*: he claims that the film calls for a "revised conception of Hindu community," pointing to the transformation of the "venal" and "worldly" priest into "a figure of pathos who abandons everything for the love of his daughter" (115). He goes on to point out how "the re-location effected by *Nastik* has implications for the way minority identities were repressed by dominant national formations" (116). But Vasudevan does not consider the ways in which the film subtly feeds into anti-Muslim sentiments by implying the purity and wholeness of a Hindu nation-space, uncontaminated by Muslims, which enables the protagonist to regain his faith.

83. Pandey, "Community and Violence"; Kakar, *The Colours of Violence*, 36.

84. For that matter, Madhubala was born Muslim, her original name being Mumtaz Jehan.

85. "Dilip Kumar Must Return Award—Munde," *Indian Express*, July 12, 1999. See also his interview in the *Hindustan Times*, July 11, 1999.

86. In Jia Zhangke's remarkable film about social and cultural change, *Zhantai* (aka *Platform*, 2000), a group of friends in a Chinese small town circa 1980 attend a screening of *Awara*: they are seen watching the scene in which the protagonist Raj sings that very song. (Of course, the voice we actually hear belongs to Mukesh, Kapoor's favorite "playback singer.") I also came across a clip of the song on YouTube, posted by Kirpi, a forty-seven-year-old Turkish fan of *Avare*. Recently, scholars have begun to research and document the transnational popularity of *Awara* and other Kapoor films; see, for instance, Rajagopalan, "Emblematic of the Thaw."

87. See G. Chatterjee, *Awara*, esp. 109–18.

88. In a letter to the editor published in the June 1950 issue of *Filmindia* magazine, thus predating the film's release, one D. G. Gokhale of New Delhi expressed his shock upon hearing that Raj Kapoor was making a film in which father and son coveted the same girl. While this angle was definitely played down in the final version, certain scenes with the judge, Raj, and Rita do seem to support such a reading.

89. *Filmindia*, November 1948, 47.

90. *Filmindia*, April 1950, 49.

91. Ibid. My emphases.

92. I am thinking of the contributions of Geeta Kapur, Ashish Rajadhyaksha, and Ravi Vasudevan, among others. See Kapur, "Revelation and Doubt"; Rajadhyaksha, "The Phalke Era"; and Vasudevan, "Shifting Codes, Dissolving Identities."

93. For discussions of the darshanic mode in Indian visual arts and cinema, see Vasudevan, "The Politics of Cultural Address in a 'Transitional' Cinema"; and Jain, *Gods in the Bazaar*.

94. On the continuing dialogic relevance of the *Ramayana*, see the essays in Richman, *Questioning Ramayanas*.

95. For a discussion of the links between the epics and Hindi commercial cinema, see Booth, "Traditional Content and Narrative Structure in the Hindi Commercial Cinema."

96. In Corey Creekmur's provocative words, "Bombay cinema is not appropriately or even usefully represented as a unique or exotic case radically distinct from Western norms; Indian popular cinema can serve to challenge central and overgeneralized claims of (implicitly Western) film theory and history." Creekmur, "Picturizing American Cinema," 376.

97. Anderson, "Imagined Communities," 10.

98. Ibid., 11.

99. Chatterjee argues persuasively—in response to Benedict Anderson's ("Imagined Communities") claim that the nationalist elites in Asia or Africa have been able to choose from a set of modular national forms already established through the historical experience of nationalism in Western Europe, the Americas and in Russia—the "most powerful" and "creative" achievements of postcolonial "nationalist imagination . . . are posited not on an identity but rather on a *difference* with the 'modular' forms of the national society propagated by the modern West." Chatterjee, *The Nation and Its Fragments*, 5.

Various commentators have pointed to the indigenous inflections that notions of civil society, community, and state acquire in their Indian manifestations. Sudipta Kaviraj provides a perceptive discussion of how the various elements expected to usher in modernity—"representative democracy, . . . developmental planning, secularization, elimination of caste practices in favour of a common modern citizenship"—did not work together to yield expected results in the Indian context. Thus the exigencies of electoral politics actually strengthened caste, religious and regional loyalties. Kaviraj, *Politics in India*, 14–25.

2. Runes of Laceration

1. The social position of theater and film artists remains tenuous for decades: in Guru Dutt's remarkable film *Kagaz ke Phool* (*Paper Flowers*, 1959), the protagonist is estranged from his aristocratic wife on account of being a film director.

2. Nirmala leaves for London with her husband within the week, abandoning the play. It is worth noting that in Ritwik Ghatak's Bengali film *Komal Gandhar*

(1961), the female protagonist is involved in a stage production of *Shakuntala*, and has a fiancé who wants her to join him in Europe; in this politicized narrative, she chooses to remain in Calcutta.

3. The fact that the character is played by Nargis, the legendary actress who goes on to portray the abducted woman in *Lahore* and to embody the woman-nation idealization in *Mother India*, brings a retrospective charge to *Aag*.

4. This idea is developed further in chapter 5, in relation to the female lead's self-mutilation in Ritwik Ghatak's *Subarnarekha* (1962).

5. Benjamin, *The Origin of German Tragic Drama*.

6. De Man, "The Rhetoric of Temporality."

7. Benjamin, *The Origin of German Tragic Drama*, 162.

8. This idea is developed by Paul de Man in his various essays, especially "The Rhetoric of Temporality"; and "Semiology and Rhetoric."

9. De Man, "Semiology and Rhetoric," 204.

10. Ibid., 208, emphasis added. For de Man, while the symbol allows a subject to seek "refuge against the impact of time in a natural world" ("The Rhetoric of Temporality," 206) to move nostalgically toward some authentic wholeness, allegory forces it to confront its "temporal destiny": "Whereas the symbol postulates the possibility of an identity or identification, allegory designates primarily a distance in relation to its own origin, and renouncing the nostalgia and the desire to coincide, it establishes its language in the void of this temporal difference. In so doing, it prevents the self from an illusionary identification with the non-self, which is now fully, though painfully, recognized as a non-self" (207).

11. Benjamin, *The Origin of German Tragic Drama*, 166.

12. Ibid., 167.

13. Ibid., 166.

14. Or, as Benjamin puts it: "The greater the significance, the greater the subjection to death, because death digs most deeply the jagged line of demarcation between physical nature and significance" (ibid.).

15. Benjamin focuses specifically on the melancholy figure of the brooding prince in Baroque funereal pageants.

16. Ibid., 185.

17. Ibid., 176. Extrapolating from the Baroque context, and in accordance with Benjamin's characterization of all of human history as a landscape of ruins, Fredric Jameson (*Marxism and Form*) points to the relevance of the allegorical mode in the modern world: "Allegory is precisely the dominant mode of expression" of a melancholy world "in which things have been for whatever reason utterly sundered from meaning, from spirit, from genuine human existence" (71). In fact, allegory is a pathology familiar to our times: "The privileged mode of our own life in time, a clumsy deciphering of meaning from moment to moment, the painful attempt to restore a continuity to heterogeneous, disconnected instants" (72). Or, as Julia Kristeva (*Black Sun*) argues, a proliferation of allegorical signs enthralls us in the face of meaninglessness because it holds for us the promise of "melancholic jouissance" (100).

18. See, for instance, Bürger, *The Theory of the Avant-Garde*.

19. Benjamin, *The Origin of German Tragic Drama*, 216.

20. As de Man (*The Resistance to Theory*) asserts, Benjamin's "fragments are fragments, and . . . they remain essentially fragmentary. They follow each other metonymically, and they never constitute a totality" (91).

21. Shohat, *Israeli Cinema*, 11.

22. Williams, "Film Bodies."

23. In tracing the history of calendar art, Kajri Jain (*Gods in the Bazaar*) writes: "Over the second half of the nineteenth century lithographs occupied a liminal zone between 'industrial' and 'fine' art, between artisans and the gentry, between woodcuts and oil paintings, and, significantly, between devotional, political, and 'cultural' or 'aesthetic' images. On the one hand these prints addressed a consuming public that was buying pilgrim souvenirs, hagiographic images, icons for domestic worship, and secular, satirical, or allegorical images for decoration, amusement, and, increasingly, political participation. On the other hand, in their use of Western naturalist techniques such as perspective, anatomy, modeling, and shading, they also lent themselves to the reformist repudiation of idolatry that accompanied several nineteenth-century reformulations of 'Hindu' identity" (97).

24. For a discussion of nested narratives in Hindu epics, and the performative practices they engender, see Lutgendorf, "The View from the Ghats."

25. Pollock, "Ramayana and Political Imagination in India."

26. Guha-Thakurta, "Visualizing the Nation," 11.

27. Ibid., 24.

28. Ibid., 26.

29. In a sense, I imagine myself to be dialectically positioned between the allegorist and the collector of Benjamin's critical imagination. Benjamin writes: "The allegorist develops the counterpole to the collector, one might say. He has abandoned the investigative effort to illuminate how the things relate to, fit in with one another. He tears them from their contexts and from then on leaves it to his *Tiefsinn* to illuminate the meaning of the things. The collector, on the other hand, unites that which belongs together; in this fashion he is able to instruct himself about things through their relationship or their temporal position." But he goes on to declare that "there hides an allegorist in every collector, and a collector in every allegorist," revealing the dialectical relation between their roles. Quoted in Pensky, *Melancholy Dialectics*, 244.

30. Personal conversation, Mumbai, July 1998.

31. Foucault, *The History of Sexuality*, 1.27.

32. Until the 1990s, the Bombay film "industry" consisted of remarkably informal and slack enterprises, notoriously negligent in maintaining archival records. Many of the films from the period in question are lost. The estimate I provide here is based on the understandably imprecise recollections of industry insiders (B. R. Chopra, Yash Chopra, Shyam Benegal, and Govind Nihalani); conversations with film historians and archivists (Moinak Biswas, Suresh Chhabria, Gayatri Chatterjee, Sohini Ghosh, P. K. Nair, Ashish Rajadhyaksha, Ravi Vasudevan); and film reviews, industry reports, and print advertisements in magazines like *Filmfare* and *Filmindia*. The estimate for the absolute number

of films containing explicit and significantly long representations of Partition may be somewhat off, but the proportion of such films in total production was undoubtedly minuscule.

33. The English press is covered extensively in Kamra, *Bearing Witness*.

34. *Filmindia*, April 1947, 33.

35. *Filmindia*, June 1947, 29.

36. *Filmindia*, October 1947, 23.

37. See, for instance, the April 1947 issue of *Filmindia*, esp. 3–9 ("What Price Freedom?") and 13–15 ("New Anti-Indian Racket in Pakistan").

38. Ibid., 3.

39. *Filmindia*, May 1952, 3.

40. Ibid., 5.

41. *Filmindia*, March 1952, 3–5. According to a report in the June 1952 issue of *Filmindia*, the magazine was banned in Pakistan soon after the publication of that incendiary editorial; Pakistani state ministers presided over open-air bonfires of *Filmindia* in Karachi and Lahore.

42. Chakravarty, *National Identity in Indian Popular Cinema, 1947–1987*, 69.

43. This provocative idea is developed in Kuran, "The Unthinkable and the Unthought."

44. *Filmindia*, February 1948 and April 1948.

45. *Filmindia*, November 1947, 10.

46. Ibid., 9.

47. *Filmindia*, January 1951, 11.

48. *Filmindia*, March 1949, 10.

49. *Filmindia*, March 1950, 53. Evidently, the film had made a sham of Hindu matrimony by having the married heroine look back "emotionally to her pre-marital love affair several times in a manner that spells disloyalty to her husband." According to the reviewer, Hindu married women would not act in such a way.

50. Ibid., 57. See my discussion of Ghatak's *Subarnarekha* (1962) in chapter 5.

51. *Filmindia*, June 1948.

52. *Filmindia*, April 1950.

53. *Filmindia*, May 1950.

54. Turim, *Flashbacks in Film*. See esp. chapter 6.

55. I am indebted to P. K. Nair for pointing out this phenomenon (personal conversation, January 1998).

56. *Filmindia*, June 1950, 45.

57. Nandy, "An Intelligent Critic's Guide to Indian Cinema."

58. Some of the biggest films in the 1990s have featured doubles (*Judwaa*, *Duplicate*), undoubtedly in response to the rapid transformations under the signs of liberalization and globalization.

59. *Filmfare*, March 7, 1952, 5. The piece refers to other films with double roles: *Chamkee* (1952), *Anhonee* (1952), *Ghungroo* (1952), and *Paapi* (1953).

60. Kewal's scorched face operates much like the paralyzed face of the female protagonist in German filmmaker Helma Sanders-Brahms's remarkable *Germany, Pale Mother* (1979).

61. Precisely such conventions are discernible in Indian mass culture, most obviously in the sphere of calendar art.

62. His temporary proletarianization is similar to that of Raj in *Awara*.

63. As Kapoor explained, *Boot Polish* extends the social reformist message of *Awara*. The earlier film tried to demonstrate that criminals are "not born, but created in the slums of our modern cities, in the midst of dire poverty and evil environment." *Boot Polish* "shows the problem of destitute children, their struggle for existence and their fight against organized beggary. The purpose of this film is to bring home to you that these orphans are as much your responsibility as that of the government of India." *Filmfare*, January 8, 1954, 1.

64. *Filmfare*, October 15, 1954.

65. A notable work of such critical demystification is in Kandiyoti, "Identity and Its Discontents." With respect to Partition violence, see Didur, *Unsettling Partition*.

66. "It was stated in the Indian Constituent Assembly in December 1949 that 33,000 Hindu or Sikh women had been abducted by Muslims, and the government of Pakistan held that 50,000 Muslim women had been abducted by Hindu or Sikh men." Kleinman, Das, and Lock, introduction to *Social Suffering*, xv.

67. As Arthur Kleinman, Veena Das, and Margaret Lock note: "Precise estimates are not possible, but . . . the Constituent Assembly listed the number of women 'recovered' through the army evacuation services as 12,000 from India and 6,000 from Pakistan" (ibid., xv–xvi).

68. Das, "Language and Body," 87.

69. Recent feminist historiography documenting women's experiences of the Partition point to the complications arising from statist interventions. See, in particular, Butalia, *The Other Side of Silence*; and Menon and Bhasin, *Borders and Boundaries*.

70. Das, "Language and Body," 84.

71. Butalia (*The Other Side of Silence*), among others, records the official invocation of Sita's story to promote the rehabilitation of abducted women (121).

72. Rajadhyaksha, "Strange Attractions," 31.

73. Ibid.

74. I am grateful to Gayatri Chatterjee and Corey Creekmur for useful discussions on this point.

75. Just to take one example, Ramanand Sagar migrated to Bombay in 1947 and wrote a Hindi novel *Aur Insaan Mar Gaya* (*And Man Died*, 1948) about Partition carnage. He started out in the film industry as a scriptwriter, graduating to the role of a producer/director. His early scripts encompassed the dark world of *Barsaat* (1949), doubles in *Insanyat* (1955), political exile in *Raj Tilak* (1958), and proletarianization due to the obfuscation of lineage in *Paigham* (1959). The enduring effect of Partition—the deep scar it left, and the rancor it engendered—is detectable in his communally charged works for television created

since the mid-1980s. The immensely successful ninety-one-episode television serial *Ramayan* (1986–88), followed by *Krishna* (1989), dovetailed into a general resurgence of rabid Hindu chauvinism.

76. Vasudevan, "Dislocations," 112.

77. Ibid., 103.

78. Ibid., 102–3.

79. Ibid., 112–13.

80. "Train from Lahore," *Bombay Times*, April 29, 1997.

81. These lines were projected in theaters in the late 1940s and early 1950s before the screening of films. Audiences cheered madly, revealing the affective investment in Lahore as the symbol of a lost fullness.

82. He also offered some possible reasons for the evasion, of which the two most important ones were lack of audience enthusiasm and the overwhelming impact of the cinematic representation of social traumas.

83. Filmmaker Govind Nihalani, whose work is the focus of chapter 6, also expressed a similar impression, although he could not recollect a single title that I was not aware of already.

84. Rachel Dwyer corroborates this allegorical reading in her auteur study, *Yash Chopra*.

85. The phrase is taken from Žižek, *The Sublime Object of Ideology*.

3. Bengali Cinema

1. While Pheng Cheah develops the idea of spectral nationality with respect to the global, I locate a similar spectrality of the subnational in relation to the national (an iterative mise en abyme structure). See Cheah, "Spectral Nationality."

2. Kaviraj, "The Imaginary Institution of India."

3. Ibid., 16.

4. Quoted in Sarkar, *The Swadeshi Movement in Bengal, 1903–1908*, 19–20. Emphases mine.

5. H. H. Risley, quoted in Sarkar, *The Swadeshi Movement in Bengal, 1903–1908*, 17.

6. This antipartition movement, which claimed the cultural and political unity of the people of Bengal, derived its name from a stress on self-reliance through indigenous practices of economic and cultural production. Imported European goods were consigned to public bonfires; domestic production of the articles of everyday use was encouraged. This stress on self-reliance exerted a lasting influence on subsequent Indian political thought: it can be seen in Gandhi's call for community-based models of economic production, and the postcolonial state's fetishization of self-reliance. Interestingly, the poet-philosopher Rabindranath Tagore—who took an active part in fostering cultural and communal unity during the Swadeshi movement—was critical of the extreme indigenist focus. See the Tagore novel *Ghare Baire*, and the discussion in Nandy, *The Illegitimacy of Nationalism*.

7. The term (literally, gentleman) has taken on a complex valence through the sedimentation and interaction of multiple layers: class investments, regional affiliations, cultural pride. Simply put, it refers to the educated, enlightened, cultivated bourgeois class in Bengal, connoting an idealized subjectivity marked by genteel sophistication.

8. Recent historiographic contributions include S. Bose, *Agrarian Bengal*; S. Das, *Communal Riots in Bengal, 1905–1947*; Chatterji, *Bengal Divided*; Datta, *Carving Blocs*.

9. See Datta, *Carving Blocs*.

10. See, for instance, Samaddar, "The History That Partition Creates," and P. Chatterjee, "The Second Partition of Bengal." Chatterjee, in particular, writes about "the highly contingent and strategic nature of the various positions taken on the question of religion and national status by organizations and individuals in the months preceding August 1947" (47).

11. P. Chatterjee, "Bengal Politics and the Muslim Masses, 1920–47," and L. Gordon, "Divided Bengal."

12. As Joya Chatterji (*Bengal Divided*) puts it: "When push came to shove, bhadralok Hindus preferred to carve up Bengal rather than accept the indignity of being ruled by Muslims" (266).

13. Ibid., 259–65.

14. For a discussion of the production of communal discord around the fear of abductions, see "*Abductions* and the Constellation of a Hindu Communal Bloc," chapter 4 of Datta, *Carving Blocs*.

15. Dipesh Chakrabarty points out that Hindu Bengali nationalism had created a sense of Bengal as home, combining a patrilinear sacredness ("This is the land of our ancestors, and hence it is sacred") with the beauty of an idealized—and idyllic—pastoral landscape (developed in nationalist Bengali literature from the late 1800s). This sacred-aesthetic realm did not preclude Muslims: "The Muslim Bengali had a place created through the idea of kinship. But the home was Hindu in which the non-Muslim League Muslim was a valued guest. Its sense of the sacred was constructed . . . through an idiom that was recognizably Hindu." Referring to this conception of homeland, Chakrabarty reveals an aporia in Hindu discourses: "What had never been thought about was how the Hindu might live in a home that embodied the Islamic sacred." It was this aporia that made the Hindus oblivious of their own prejudice, and turned the "Bengali Muslim's ethnic hatred" into "something inherently inexplicable." Chakrabarty, "Remembered Villages," 129.

16. See, for instance, Butalia, *The Other Side of Silence*; Kaul, *The Partitions of Memory*; Menon and Bhasin, *Borders and Boundaries*; and Samaddar, *Reflections on Partition in the East*.

17. Chakrabarty, "Remembered Villages," 110.

18. See Chakrabarti, *The Marginal Men*; Ray, "Growing Up Refugee"; Sandip Bandyopadhyay, "The Riddles of Partition"; and P. Bose, "Memory Begins Where History Ends."

19. Dipesh Chakrabarty ("Remembered Villages") writes about memories of

violence: "They are the helpless recall of a victim overtaken by events rather than of one in narrative control of them. . . . History seeks to explain the event, the memory of pain refuses the historical explanation and sees the event causing the pain as a monstrously irrational aberration" (113).

20. I have already discussed this point in the previous chapter, following Gyan Pandey's analysis in "Community and Violence: Recalling Partition."

21. East Bengal, which became East Pakistan, was separated from West Pakistan by all of post-Partition India: indeed, the two parts had very little in common, other than predominantly Islamic populations. The initial euphoria over a separate Muslim state did not last for long. By 1952, a strong language movement was afoot in East Pakistan, to stave off the imposition of Arabic and Urdu on a Bengali population. The thorny relations between West and East Pakistan culminated in a popular movement for secession in the east. Following a genocide carried out by the Pakistani army, India got involved in the conflict, and after a war in 1971, East Pakistan emerged as the sovereign nation-state of Bangladesh.

In talking about Bengal's Partition, it is really difficult to leave out Bangladesh. Indeed, to do so is to accept statist configurations unproblematically. Yet acknowledging the reality of Partition also forces us to accept the reality of separate nation-states in South Asia, with different institutional structures and different histories.

For a recent contribution that considers testimonies of the displaced on both sides of the border, and includes the experience of a Muslim refugee family in East Pakistan, see Guhathakurta, "Families, Displacement." See also the essays in Bagchi and Dasgupta, *The Trauma and the Triumph*.

22. Chatterji, *Bengal Divided*, 266.

23. Chakrabarty, "Remembered Villages," 115.

24. Ibid.

25. In Bengal, lighting a lamp at sundown in one's ancestral home involves not just a prayer to the family deities, but also keeping the lineage alive. Countless Bengali films (e.g., *Pather Panchali* [1955]) depict this ritual, accompanied by the blowing of conch shells, as evening falls over the Bengali countryside.

26. Chakrabarty, "Remembered Villages," 117.

27. Ibid., 118.

28. Ibid., 121.

29. Ibid., 123.

30. A. Sen, *Poverty and Famines*, especially "The Great Bengal Famine," 52–85.

31. Ibid., 63.

32. Sen notes the long-term effects of the famine: "While the gigantic size of excess mortality attributable to the famine is of a certain amount of interest, the *time pattern* of mortality is of possibly greater relevance. Very substantially more than half the deaths attributable to the famine of 1943 took place *after* 1943. The size of mortality did not return to the pre-famine situation for many years after the famine, and the epidemics of malaria and other fevers, cholera,

smallpox, dysentery, and diarrhoea that sprung up during and immediately after the famine went on raging for a long time" (ibid., 215).

33. Raha, *Bengali Cinema*.

34. Dilip Sarkar, in a personal interview, Calcutta, April 1998. His father, B. N. Sarkar, was the founder of New Theatres, the premier Calcutta (and for a while, Indian) studio of the preindependence years.

35. The title may be translated as "The Voice of Cinema" or, more literally and awkwardly, as "The Message of the Picture."

36. *Chitrabani* [in Bengali], September 1948, 5–7. All quotes from Bengali sources will be in my translation, unless noted otherwise.

37. The Bengali word, *sustha*, implies "clean," "healthy," "robust," "tasteful," "upstanding."

38. *Chitrabani*, June 1949, 36.

39. *Chitrabani*, January 1955, 12–14.

40. See, for instance, Muralidhar Chattopadhyay, "1952," *Chitrabani*, September 1952, 7.

41. *Chitrabani*, January 1949, 29.

42. "The denial of lower, coarse, vulgar, venal, servile—in a word, natural—enjoyment, which constitutes the sacred sphere of culture, implies an affirmation of the superiority of those who can be satisfied with the sublimated, refined, disinterested, gratuitous, distinguished pleasures forever closed to the profane. That is why art and cultural consumption are predisposed, consciously and deliberately or not, to fulfill a social function of legitimating social differences." Bourdieu, *Distinction*, 7.

43. The Bengali term *matragyan* points to a sense of boundaries, knowing when to draw the line, what forms of representation are acceptable. It crops up repeatedly on the pages of *Chitrabani*: see, for instance, the review of the Hindi film *Shaheed* (which I discuss in the previous chapter) in the issue of October 1948, 47.

44. Quoted in English in *Chitrabani*, July–August 1949, 7.

45. Ibid.

46. Roy was a legendary physician, widely respected by proletarian groups for his altruistic social work. To the middle class, he was a towering figure in the Congress leadership who could stand up to Prime Minister Nehru. In an era of Bengal's diminished stature in the all-India political arena, when the province seemed increasingly like a colony of North India, Roy was an icon of regional pride.

47. *Chitrabani*, July–August 1949, 7.

48. Ibid., 8.

49. *Chitrabani*, December 1949, 60.

50. I trace the influence of the IPTA on Nemai Ghosh (chapter 4) and Ritwik Ghatak (chapter 5), whose works display a more pronounced critical alterity in relation to a cultural mainstream.

51. *Chitrabani*, September 1948, 41–43.

52. *Chitrabani*, January 1952, 5.

53. Kinder, *Blood Cinema*. In discussing the position of Catalan cinema as parts of both Spanish national cinema and European media, Kinder writes that "regionalism . . . may refer to geographic areas that are both *smaller* and *larger* than a nation. Thus, the terms 'microregionalism' and 'macroregionalism' help us to understand the regional/national/global interface" (389).

54. *Chitrabani*, July–August 1952, 5–7.

55. For instance, a review of the Hindi film *Parineeta* (1953), an adaptation of a novel by the famous Bengali author Sarat Chandra Chatterjee, commended its Bengali director Bimal Roy for eschewing tacky Bombay formulae and keeping superior Bengali aesthetic sensibilities alive. There was a tenacious projection of the idea that Bengali culture was the savior of Bombay cinema. *Chitrabani*, July–August 1953, 40.

56. *Chitrabani*, February 1952, 63.

57. A review of *Maraner Pare* (1954) criticized the film for its capitulation to Bombay standards and incorporation of *baiji* (courtesan) dancing, crude lyrics, and murder and violence. *Chitrabani*, July 1954.

58. Bose opposed Gandhi's strategy of nonviolent civil disobedience and favored more militant methods of fighting the British colonizers. Jailed by the Raj, he miraculously escaped from prison and from the country, organized the Indian National Army with expatriate Indians, and—aided by the Japanese— fought with the British army all over southeast Asia. The fact of his death in a plane crash has been frequently questioned, leading to wild speculations. He remains a legend, a source of Bengali pride.

59. Of course, people from Maharashtra had their own All-India leader in Sardar Patel.

60. *Chitrabani*, May 1950.

61. *Chitrabani*, June 1950, 23–24.

62. This version of realism subscribes to the belief that the photograph always points back indexically ("There it is!") to the reality it has, supposedly, captured: as Barthes put it, the referent *adheres*. Barthes, *Camera Lucida*.

63. *Chitrabani*, June 1950, 62.

64. The cinematic depiction of Jesus Christ has a complicated history. While some of the early narrative films were passion plays (about a dozen in 1903), famous Hollywood biblical spectacles of the 1950s and 1960s—*Ben Hur* (1959), for example—avoided frontal representations of Christ. The face of Christ emerged as a kind of structuring absence in these films, the absence serving to heighten the sacral aura. I am indebted to Charles Wolfe for this insight.

65. Review of *Patri Chai* in *Chitrabani*, January 1952, 76.

66. In his book *Bengali Cinema*, Kiranmoy Raha argues that from the very beginning, mythological and devotional themes were not as preponderant in Bengali cinema as in films from other parts of India: several films with "social themes and modern story lines" were commercially successful (4–8). Thus, while the first full-length Bengali feature film, *Bilwamangal* (1919), was based on a traditional tale, 1921 saw the box office triumph of *Bilet Pherat*, a social satire about an England-returned Bengali character. Throughout the twenties and

thirties, Bengali cinema drew on the rich literary tradition of modern Bengal—particularly the writings of Bankimchandra Chatterjee, Rabindranath Tagore, and Saratchandra Chatterjee, and popular plays from the Calcutta stage—incorporating a strong social reformist rhetoric in the process. By the mid-thirties, melodrama had established itself as the privileged mode, especially in the melancholic films of Pramathesh Barua. A maudlin sentimentality came to characterize narratives involving a disintegrating aristocracy, and families afflicted with pressures of modernization, poverty, and disease.

67. *Chitrabani*, October 1951, 70.

68. These were heady years for Bengali cinema: the same period saw the release of Satyajit Ray's *Apu Trilogy* and *The Music Room*.

69. Elsaesser, "Tales of Sound and Fury," and Brooks, *The Melodramatic Imagination* provide the two seminal exegeses.

70. Such formal strategies were employed with remarkable facility in films such as *Sagarika* (1956) and *Saptapadi* (1961); Western viewers unfamiliar with these films can find a Hollywood parallel in the rhapsodic pairing of Montgomery Clift and Elizabeth Taylor in George Stevens's *A Place in the Sun* (1955).

71. Biswas is familiar to Western audiences as the aging, imperious *zamindar* of Satyajit Ray's elegiac film, *Jalsaghar* (*The Music Room*, 1958); Sanyal played the genial father in a later Ray film, *Days and Nights in the Forest* (1967).

72. Kleinhans, "Notes on Melodrama and the Family under Capitalism."

73. Mulvey, "Notes on Sirk and Melodrama"; Cook, "Melodrama and the Women's Picture"; Williams, "Melodrama Revisited."

74. Moinak Biswas refers to this space of romance as the "non-space" of the couple in two respects. It is an impossible space where reason/history and occult/destiny collide. It is also the actual physical space between the couple, always eliminated through their final embrace at the moment of union. Thus this space marks a "desire for the private, the autonomous, the modern," but is now crucially inflected in vernacular terms. Biswas, "The Couple and Their Spaces," 141.

75. *Chitrabani*, September 1954.

76. Decorative designs made with a paste prepared from grains, to mark auspicious occasions.

77. *Chitrabani*, September 1954.

78. In keeping with the custom of "playback singing" in post–World War II Indian cinema, Uttam Kumar's songs were often sung by Hemanta Mukherjee, whose rich and sonorous baritone dominated the Bengali pop music scene for nearly four decades. Suchitra Sen's singing voice was provided by the shimmering dulcet tones of Sandhya Mukherjee, who had perfected a fluid, romantic style. Indeed, it is impossible to think of Uttam and Suchitra films without these two playback voices. The popularity of these songs, set to tune by such legendary composers as Anupam Ghatak and Rabin Chattopadhyay, remain undiminished to this day; indeed, they often provide the soundtrack to contemporary nostalgia across the Bengali diaspora.

79. The Muslim–Bengali modernity that was emerging in East Bengal, with its center in Dhaka, was made to play second fiddle to the Calcutta formation.

80. It is a common view that the tremendous popularity comedies enjoyed in the fifties was due largely to their ability to provide Bengali audiences with a welcome, entertaining respite from the harrowing difficulties of their lives: the films engaged their daily concerns only in the most facetious ways. While I do not disagree, I keep wondering about the strong undercurrent of sentimentality that marks these funny films. Why do commercial Bengali films, even comedies, verge on the maudlin? In the context of this project, one is tempted to ascribe this lachrymose tendency to Bengali experiences of the 1940s. However, that causality would be too reductive and would not be able to explain the extreme sentimentality in the literary works of Saratchandra Chatterjee in the early part of the twentieth century, or in the films of Pramathesh Barua in the 1930s.

An obvious and, unfortunately, common strategy is to think of sentimentality as a natural Bengali trait, but it evades explanation rather than provide one. Besides, as recent cultural theories have taught us, the very idea of a "natural" attribute should alert us to the necessity of historicizing it. If one were looking for cultural antecedents that would help explain an overtly sentimental modern Bengali soul, one would have to address the continuing influence of the late-medieval Bhakti and Sufi movements. The followers participate in singing sessions that thrive on overt sentimentality: people are transported to an ecstatic state, in which they feel united—in body and soul—to a divine being. In such a cathartic scenario, people express their emotions freely, primarily through gestures. One would also have to consider the place of sentimentality in the emergence of the modern bourgeois subject, and the influence of Victorian sensibilities on modern Bengali subjectivity. While such a project of cultural history is well beyond the scope of this book, it holds great promise.

81. He had a more serious role in *Natun Yahudi* (1953), a film I discuss in the following chapter.

82. When a member of the ghoti family complains about the incomprehensibility of bangal rhetorical digs, the character played by Bhanu Bandyopadhyay retorts: "Well, how will you understand our lingo? After all, we speak in *bilayti* language." The word *bilayti* connotes "foreign" in general, and "European" in particular. Thus the retort takes on dual valence. On the one hand, the bangal character chides his ghoti interlocutor for treating him like a foreigner (in that the ghoti finds the bangal way of speaking so alien and incomprehensible). On the other hand, he implies that bangal expressions are as sophisticated as European idioms: how will a lowly ghoti follow the refined nuances? The double-edged sarcasm leaves the opponent reeling: at least for now, the displaced person can savor his moment of triumph.

83. These pressing questions, which keep recurring all through this book, are discussed at some length in the introduction, and in chapters 4 and 6.

84. Interestingly, their bangalness is not in evidence: as far as cinematic representation is concerned, cultural assimilation seems to have run its course by the early 1970s.

85. Rice pudding, a traditional birthday dish.

86. *Alo Amar Alo* bears some intriguing resemblances to Ritwak Ghatak's "Partition trilogy": refugee colony life (and even the colony's name), memories of past birthdays, father figures tormented by their complicity in the woman protagonist's abjection (see chapter 5). Nevertheless, the Ghatak films predate *Alo Amar Alo* by more than a decade; this chronology not only establishes a chain of influences (Ghatak's *Meghe Dhaka Tara* [1960] is, without doubt, an urtext for the 1972 film) but also points to the revolutionary nature of Ghatak's work. By the time *Alo Amar Alo* was made, such explicit mediations of Partition trauma were becoming acceptable to a cultural establishment—the same mainstream that had recoiled at the untimely and bold acuity of Ghatak's cinematic vision in the early 1960s.

4. Dispersed Nodes of Articulation

1. Ghatak was involved in the making of *Chhinnamul*, a film that belongs to the previous category of leftist films; his first directorial venture, *Nagarik* (1952), would also fit into this genre of political films. However, the films comprising his "Partition trilogy" of the early 1960s, distinguished in their remarkable expressive power and paradigmatic complexity, constitute a significant leap beyond the IPTA-influenced films of the previous decade.

2. My discussion of an amorphous discursive formation is informed by Ernesto Laclau and Chantal Mouffe's post-Marxist formulation of the *discursive* as an unsutured field constituted by differential moments of articulation. Laclau and Mouffe, *Hegemony and Socialist Strategy*.

3. I came across a print of *Amar Rahe Yeh Pyar* at the National Film Archives in Pune, only to find it had disintegrated in its cans.

4. My use of the term *estrangement* needs qualification. It invokes the Brechtian notion of defamiliarization, with its implications of analytical and polemical engagement, whose applicability in the present context is only partial. I shall argue that the sequences in question draw their inspiration not only from Soviet, German, and Hollywood montage and mise-en-scène techniques, but also from Southeast Asian shadow puppetry, Indian folk theater, and other influences. Some of these formal strategies—for example, the musical commentary—are parts of an indigenous realist tradition and should not be read according to Western frameworks of modernist cultural politics. As Noel Burch pointed out with reference to Japanese cinema, Japanese art is *presentational*—it does not try to cover up its status as artifice and is upfront about the fact that it is only a *re*-presentation (Burch, *To the Distant Observer*). Of course, Burch's insight remains problematic, formulated as it is in Western terms with their implications of political intervention. Just because Japanese—or Indian—art is presentational does not mean that it becomes oppositional art. The specificities of the Indian cultural scene complicate the already loaded terms *political*, *oppositional*, and *critical*. My basic point is that the defamiliarizing techniques, deployed to avoid the ethical problems of representing contemporary violence, fall within the ambit of mainstream cultural forms.

5. Nargis, who invests the character with a tragic grandeur, emerges through

such roles as the icon of Indian womanhood—simultaneously transcendent and tormented.

6. A string instrument played with a bow to produce an achingly sad sound.

7. The problem of the rehabilitation of abducted women concerned several artists and intellectuals of the period. In 1949, Prithviraj Kapoor directed the play *Ahooti* in Bombay, about a Hindu woman who was raped by Muslims and driven to suicide by her subsequent ostracization. Like the film *Lahore*, this play called upon society to take back its lost women and to help them reclaim their lives.

8. Ritwik Ghatak takes recourse to the same plot conceit in *Subarnarekha* (1962)—see chapter 5.

9. Since I could not track down the film, this synopsis is based on discussions in print media.

10. *Filmindia*, September 1949, 65–69.

11. *Filmindia*, July 1949, 61.

12. *Filmindia*, September 1949, 65.

13. *Filmindia*, June 1949, 72.

14. *Filmindia*, November 1949, 79.

15. *Filmindia*, September 1949, 43, my emphasis.

16. Ibid., 44.

17. In *Hegemony and Socialist Strategy*, Laclau and Mouffe provide a model of "articulation" for the contingent coming together of radical democratic impulses emanating from a dispersed field, to produce a temporary political mobilization.

18. Pradhan, *Marxist Cultural Movements in India: Chronicles and Documents, 1936–47*, 129.

19. Rajadhyaksha and Willemen, *Encyclopaedia of Indian Cinema*, 102.

20. Many stalwarts of the Bombay film industry, such as screenwriter/director K. A. Abbas, actor Balraj Sahni, and producer/director B. R. Chopra, were associated with the IPTA in the 1940s.

21. Rajadhyaksha and Willemen, *Encyclopaedia of Indian Cinema*, 102.

22. Bhatia, "Staging Resistance," 434.

23. Pradhan, *Marxist Cultural Movements in India: Chronicles and Documents, 1936–47*; Pradhan, *Marxist Cultural Movements in India: Chronicles and Documents, 1947–1958*; Bhattacharya, "The IPTA in Bengal"; Bhatia, "Staging Resistance."

24. Such an approach was inaugurated in the first flush of the Soviet Revolution by Eisenstein's epochal film *Potemkin* (1925), which Ghosh watched repeatedly, frame by frame, using a hand-cranked projector. See the interview with Nemai Ghosh in *Chitrabhas* (Bengali) 19, no. 1–2 (1984): 9.

25. In South Asia, old newspapers and magazines are routinely turned into paper bags and widely used for carrying groceries: recycling, prompted by economic necessities, has been an integral part of Indian modernity.

26. Renov, "Toward a Poetics of Documentary," 21.

27. Interview with Nemai Ghosh, *Chitrabhas*, 9. What the old woman said can

be translated roughly as: "The consuming fire that ignites in one's heart when one is forced to abandon one's home, the soil one grew up on—you cannot teach me; that is something I am going to *show* you."

28. Another example is the character of the old woman in Asghar Wajahat's play, *Jis Lahore Nehi Dekha* (*The Lahore I Have Not Seen*), adapted for television by Habib Tanveer.

29. Review from *Amritabazar Patrika*, quoted in *Chitrabhas* 19, no. 1–2 (1984): 15, original in English. Another commentator commends the director for his sensitivity, dedication, and honesty. Review from *Desh*, quoted in *Chitrabhas* 19, no. 1–2 (1984): 16, my translation.

30. Ghatak addresses these unfortunate developments in the context of the Calcutta group-theater movement in his film *Komal Gandhar* (1961).

31. I discuss these films in preceding chapters.

32. Mrinal Sen, "Bangla Cinemar Darshak O *Chhinnamul*."

33. *Chhinnamul* is a precursor to *Pather Panchali* in another respect: it helped inaugurate and define an alternative Indian cinema that, because of its laudatory international reception, came to officially represent "Indian national cinema." Interestingly, Ray had wanted Ghosh to be the cinematographer for his directorial debut; but the latter had already left Bengal, following the disappointing popular reception of his film, and become involved with the film industry in Madras.

34. The RSP subscribes to a Marxist-Leninist ideological framework; in the 1940s and 1950s, its estimation of Stalin as a deviation within the Communist movement set it apart from the more influential Communist Party of India.

35. The most famous of these plays about the famine of 1943 and the Partition are *Banglar Meye, Bastubhita* and, of course, *Nabanna*.

36. My account here is based largely on an interview with Biswaranjan Chatterjee (Calcutta, September 1998), who received credit as assistant director of the film and also had a small acting role.

37. According to one review, the film was theatrical, incoherent, and devoid of emotional appeal. *Chitrabani* 5, no. 7 (March 1953): 73.

38. When the family refuses to accept his earnings, Duikhya quietly starts saving for his sister's wedding. The narrative divulges a sentimental streak in the way it humanizes the "fallen" brother through his unwavering familial love and loyalty. Here the sentimentality is not simply a matter of being overly maudlin; rather, it derives from elements of real historical experience: a sense of disenfranchisement, a loss of control, sadness over the family's loss of status, disillusionment with ideals, fear for the sister's future. Duikhya is played by the comedian Bhanu Bandyopadhyay, in a rare dramatic appearance.

39. In a discussion of cultural colonialism, Homi Bhabha writes: "Produced through the strategy of disavowal, the *reference* of discrimination is always to a process of splitting as the condition of subjection: a discrimination between the mother culture and its bastards, the self and its doubles, where the trace of what is disavowed is not repressed but repeated as something *different*—a mutation, a hybrid." Bhabha, "Signs Taken for Wonders," 111.

40. I discuss this "type" in chapter 3.

41. *Chitrabani* 5, no. 7 (March 1953): 73.

42. See, for instance, the various essays in Baxi and Parekh, *Crisis and Change in Contemporary India*; Chatterjee, *Wages of Freedom*.

43. Parekh, "Jawaharlal Nehru and the Crisis of Modernization," 21–56.

44. Kothari, "Interpreting Indian Politics."

45. For a detailed account of the lived social dimensions of the Emergency, see Tarlo, *Unsettling Memories: Narratives of the Emergency in Delhi*.

46. Chatterjee, introduction to *Wages of Freedom*, 5.

47. The only change that was finally required was the addition of two couplets at the beginning and the end of the film: a poetic meditation on the similarity of the subjective experience on both sides of the bifurcating line. The implication was that minority Hindus faced the same kinds of hardships in Pakistan as minority Muslims did in India.

48. See the interview with M. S. Sathyu under the section "Censorship" in Baghdadi and Rao, *Talking Films*.

49. Mrinal Sen, Mani Kaul, Sathyu, Kumar Sahani, Pattabhi Rama Reddy, Shyam Benegal, and B. V. Karanth are among the most famous.

50. Prasad, *Ideology of the Hindi Film*, 188–216.

51. *Filmindia*, September 1948, 21.

52. This theme becomes the driving force of the narrative in Shyam Benegal's *Mammo* (1995), which reflexively references *Garam Hawa*: the three central protagonists of *Mammo* attend a screening of the earlier film and discuss the plight of its characters.

53. Fatehpur Sikri is a walled Mughal city in the outskirts of Agra, dating from the sixteenth century. Panchmahal, a beautiful five-storied gazebo, is reputed to have been a meeting place for royal lovers.

54. *Qawali* is a devotional music form associated with the Sufi strand within Islam: both the singers and the listeners are supposed to be transported to a heightened emotional state through the music. In the 1990s, the Pakistani singer Nusrat Fateh Ali Khan turned qawali into popular "world music."

55. The actor's brother Bhisham Sahni penned the novel *Tamas* and adapted it for television; see chapter 6.

56. Ghatak addresses this issue of migration to the West in his film *Komal Gandhar*; see chapter 5.

57. See, for instance, Pushan Bandyopadhyay, "Uttapta Batash Trishnarta Mati Samne Sathyu."

58. This contentious field is discussed from divergent perspectives in the various essays in Madan, *Religion in India*.

59. "Stunning, Charming, but Late," *Star and Style*, June 1974, 21.

60. The elderly Muslim protagonist of Sayeed Mirza's *Naseem* (1997), a film set in 1992, is a leftist intellectual who has been an ardent believer of the secularist ideal all his life. He could well be the young Sikandar of *Garam Hawa*. See chapter 7.

5. Ghatak, Melodrama, and Experience

1. R. Ghatak, "Manabsamaj, Amader Aitihya, Chhabi-kara o Amar Pracheshta," 9 (translation mine).

2. Interview with Ghatak, *Chitrabeekshan* (1975), reprinted in English, translated by Mitra Parikh, in Rajadhyaksha and Gangar, *Ritwik Ghatak*, 96.

3. The film was believed to be lost for a long time; it was finally released when a partially damaged positive print was found in the 1970s. It remains Ghatak's most explicitly political film, incorporating the communist anthem *Internationale*.

4. Ghatak has described this stint at the FTII as one of the happiest times of his life. His students from that period include directors John Abraham, Mani Kaul and Kumar Sahani, and cinematographer K. K. Mahajan.

5. Mukhopadhyay, "Beejer Balaka." He employs the Bengali neologism *Ritwik-tantra*, Ritwikism, to refer to the filmmaker's cult status.

6. Quoted in Mukhopadhyay, "Beejer Balaka," 226.

7. Anil Saari, writing in *Indian Express* in 1981. Quoted in Banerjee, *Ritwik Ghatak*, 103.

8. Ibid., 103–4.

9. Bellour, "The Film We Accompany."

10. Constance Penley writes that in his essay Bellour "focuses on the interior figuration of the shot and the emotional relation to elements in it." For Bellour, *Meghe Dhaka Tara* is a film whose "system calls for a method of analysis that can respond to the emotion organized by the mise-en-scène. It is not so much a film that one critiques or analyzes after the fact but a film that one accompanies." Penley, introduction to Bellour, *Analysis of Film*, xiv.

11. I use this term in the sense developed by Michel Chion in his book *Audio-vision*.

12. For recent work on cinematic authorship—beyond the structuralist controversy and its poststructuralist elaborations—see D'Lugo, "Buñuel in the Cathedral of Culture"; Elsaesser, *Fassbinder's Germany*; and Benamou, *It's All True*.

13. Lukács assumed, in a Hegelian vein, that reality could be apprehended in its totality. Capitalist reification produced the subject/object dichotomy as a roadblock to knowledge; as a result, the world appeared alien and immutable, impervious to purposive human action. For Lukács, a realist aesthetic could perform the cognitive function of revealing the structures of social and economic life, thus helping us understand reality. Balzac and Tolstoy remained his privileged authors for the portals they provided to an ontological totality. In contrast, for Bertolt Brecht, the novels of these nineteenth-century authors were determinate products of a superseded phase of class history, and therefore were of little value in understanding the social struggles of his era. Brecht considered Lukács to be transhistorical in his adherence to a nineteenth-century model of writing. The radically transformed social reality of twentieth-century capitalism required new "realist" approaches for cognitive and representational

purposes. Brecht claimed that while Lukács had criticized modernist art's use of techniques of fragmentation and estrangement as formalist reification, "it was Lukács himself who had fallen into a deluded and timeless formalism, by attempting to deduce norms for prose purely from literary traditions, without regard for the historical reality that encompasses and transforms all literature in its own processes of change." Quoted in R. Taylor, *Aesthetics and Politics*, 63. While Lukács's insistence on a universalized realist aesthetics limited the usefulness of his approach for radical filmmaking practices, Brecht remains a towering influence.

14. The affinity between Ghatak's approach and Benjamin's philosophy has been noted by at least one commentator writing in Bengali. See the evocative essay by Shibaji Bandyopadhyay, "Smaran-Pratismaran: Ritwik Ghataker Shilpa."

15. R. Ghatak, "Manabsamaj, Amader Aitihya, Chhabi-kara o Amar Pracheshta," 9. The original in Bengali is "bidyuter jhiliker moto . . . jibansatya" (my translation, my emphasis).

16. Benjamin, "Theses on the Philosophy of History," 255.

17. R. Ghatak, *On the Cultural Front.*

18. Interview in Bengali in the annual number of *Chitrabeekshan* (1975), reprinted in part in Dasgupta and Bhattacharya, *Sakshat Ritwik*, 72–80. The quotation appears in the English translation in Rajadhyaksha and Gangar, *Ritwik Ghatak*, 103; however, based on my understanding of the original, I have altered the last sentence.

19. These include the Forward Bloc, RSP, SUC, CPI, the CPI (Marxist), and the CPI (Marxist-Leninist).

20. "I cannot speak without him. That man has culled all my feelings long before my birth. He has understood what I am and he has put in all the words. I read and I find that all has been said and I have nothing new to say. I think all artistes, in Bengal at least, find themselves in the same difficulty." Interview in *Film Miscellany* (1976), reprinted in Banerjee, *Ritwik Ghatak*, 100. In the same interview, Ghatak lashes out at the interviewer for calling Tagore an excessive romantic: "You people have not read Rabindranath. You are yet to know of his anger. From the lowest rung of society to the highest he spared no one" (101).

21. Some historians dispute this dating, but most believe Kalidasa lived sometime in the first four centuries of the common era.

22. Rabindranath Tagore, "The Religion of the Forest" (1922), excerpted in Rajadhyaksha and Gangar, *Ritwik Ghatak*, 74–75.

23. The influence of such a global humanist archive is most evident in Ghatak's *Ajantrik.*

24. Interview in *Film Miscellany* (1976), reprinted in Banerjee, *Ritwik Ghatak*, 100.

25. R. Ghatak, "Chhabitey Dialectics," 43–47.

26. Bakhtin, "Discourse in the Novel."

27. Bakhtin, "Epic and Novel."

28. It is said of the epic *Mahabharata* (which translates literally as "The Great Bharata," *Bharata* being the ancient name of India) that "What is not in the *Mahabharata* is not in Bharata." Thus the epic is traditionally understood to be a totalized representation of the Indian social formation that is, nevertheless, open to transformation through constant interpretation and embellishment. The Indian epics have a direct relevance to modern Indian life, as they are integral parts of the nation's living traditions.

29. R. Ghatak, "Music in Indian Cinema and the Epic Approach," 21.

30. Once again, Ghatak appears to echo Benjamin—here, the latter's populist understanding of the epic in his essay "The Storyteller."

31. As Kumar Shahani has put it so eloquently: "In *Subarnarekha* the dramatic element disintegrates, its *cliches* are turned against itself; the traumatic prostitution of our culture is exemplified as Sanskrit becomes part of La Dolce Vita in one of the world's poorest cities. We are made to face our self-destructive incestuous longings which are otherwise so delicately camouflaged by both our sophisticated and vulgar film-makers." Shahani, "Violence and Responsibility," 62.

32. This injunction, dating back to 1928, follows a prediction that, in hindsight, seems to have been remarkably astute: that sound application will probably occur "along the least line of resistance, i.e. *in the field of the satisfaction of simple curiosity*," leading to "its unimaginative use for 'dramas of high culture' and other photographed presentations of a theatrical order." Eisenstein, Pudovkin, and Alexandrov, "Statement on Sound." Emphasis in original.

33. While the songs are in a local dialect and may not be understood clearly by all Bengalis, the sentiments they express are shared all over Bengal.

34. In Bengali, "Mon-ta joley purey khak hoye gechhey."

35. R. Ghatak, "On Art and the Archetype," 14–15.

36. Ibid., 14.

37. Willemen, "Tyneside Festival Notes 2," 64.

38. R. Ghatak describes the impersonator (*bohurupee*) both as Kali and as the eschatological figure of Time (*Mahakal*): either way, he represents the trauma of History.

39. Interview in Bengali originally published in *Movie Montage* (1967), reprinted in English translation in Banerjee, *Ritwik Ghatak*, 70.

40. This reformulation of archetypes is underwritten by a notion of daily concrete structures and practices that draws on Pierre Bourdieu's conception of *habitus*. Bourdieu argues that the real divisions within society are materially inscribed as public cultural forms in a person's objective environment, providing the parameters of personal identity. In living out those forms, the person comes to embody the assumptions underlying them and takes them for granted: thus, the real social divisions get naturalized. See Bourdieu, *Outline of a Theory of Practice*.

41. The materialist historian D. D. Kosambi developed such a concept of archetypes, rooted in the concrete structure and practices of quotidian life, in his writings. See, for instance, *Myth and Reality*.

42. See the insightful discussion of the continuities and the shifts in the cultural figure of the mother in Thomas, "Sanctity and Scandal."

43. Ghatak's comments published originally in Bengali in *Chitrapat* 10, reprinted in English translation in Banerjee, *Ritwik Ghatak*, 51.

44. Such is the hold of this iconic representation on the Bengali imagination, that even the black and white film leaves no doubt in a Bengali audience about the colors of the sari.

45. The *anchal*, or loose end of the sari, when draped around the head, produces a *ghomta* or veil effect. In this particular representation, the red and white ghomta on jet-black hair serves to frame and accentuate the face.

46. See, for instance, Gledhill, "The Melodramatic Field"; and Williams, "Melodrama Revisited."

47. R. Ghatak, "*Subarnarekha*," 41. My translation.

48. Sadoul's letter to Ghatak, dated February 11, 1965, is quoted in Bengali translation in Parthapratim Bandyopadhyay, "Filmey Melodrama," 80.

49. Rajadhyaksha and Gangar, *Ritwik Ghatak*, 103.

50. I can think of only a few directors who attain such levels in politicizing melodramas: Rainer Warner Fassbinder, Arturo Ripstein, Douglas Sirk, and, to a lesser degree, Luchino Visconti.

51. In conjunction with other narrative elements, the reference to *Gouridaan* mobilizes a symbology of Uma, the Mother Goddess in her youth. According to popular Bengali legends, Uma or Gouri is a daughter of Bengal, who eventually marries Lord Shiva, and becomes the Great Mother. In the film, Neeta happens to have been born on the day on which Jagaddhatri—the benign, protective avatar of the Mother Goddess—is worshipped annually. She finally goes to a sanatorium in the mountains, her passage (and her impending death) marking her union with Shiva (who, according to Bengali legend, resides in the mountains).

52. "Je raate mor duarguli bhanglo jhare" (the night the doors to my room came crashing down in the storm).

53. Bellour, "The Film We Accompany."

54. Shahani, "Violence and Responsibility," 59.

55. Outlined in the introduction of this book. For a superb articulation of the political potential of melancholia, see David Eng, "Melancholia in the Late Twentieth Century."

56. Ghatak's trilogy engages only the struggles of middle-class Hindu-Bengali subjects in post-1947 West Bengal: Muslims remain conspicuously absent. While this singular focus suggests a perspectival bias, Ghatak was probably unwilling to speak for the Muslim community.

57. I have in mind M. S. Sathyu's *Garam Hawa*, Shyam Benegal's *Mammo* (1995), and Sayeed Mirza's *Naseem* (1997).

6. *Tamas* and the Limits of Representation

1. Claude Lanzmann, quoted in Caruth, *Unclaimed Experience*, 123–24n13.

2. Here I am invoking a Kantian notion of the sublime as something so magnificent that it resists description and transcends language.

3. V. Das, "Language and Body," 67.

4. Blanchot, *The Writing of the Disaster*, 82.

5. Lyotard, *The Differend*.

6. Blanchot, *The Writing of the Disaster*, 82.

7. Nihalani, introduction to Sahni, *Tamas*, 8.

8. Ibid.

9. Quoted in Ramindar Singh and M. Rahman, "Communal Controversy," *India Today*, February 29, 1988.

10. Adorno, "The Meaning of Working Through the Past," 98.

11. Prasad, *Ideology of the Hindi Film*.

12. Ibid.

13. Nandy, introduction to *The Secret Politics of Our Desires*.

14. See my essay "The Inward Look."

15. Economic liberalization and increasing privatization, while subjected to rhetorical challenge, were in effect supported by most leftist political units: thus Jyoti Basu, a stalwart of the Communist Party of India (Marxist) and head of the regional government in the left-inclined state of West Bengal, actively sought out foreign capital by promoting investment opportunities, providing pro-capital incentives and building infrastructure in the 1990s.

16. Singh and Rahman, "Communal Controversy."

17. See Axel, *The Nation's Tortured Body*; Chakravarti and Haksar, *The Delhi Riots*; Crossette, "India's Sikhs."

18. Both Veena Das and Urvashi Butalia have written about the impact of 1984 on their research agendas. Butalia, *The Other Side of Silence*; V. Das, introduction to *Mirrors of Violence*.

19. See Omvedt, "Ambedkar and After"; Jaffrelot, *India's Silent Revolution*.

20. Nihalani, personal interview, Mumbai, January 1998.

21. Note a similar narrative thread in *Chhinnamul*, discussed in chapter 4.

22. For revisionist accounts of the Partition that explicitly hold the national leadership responsible for the division, see Jalal, *The Sole Spokesman*, and A. Roy, "The High Politics of India's Partition."

23. Nihalani has explored the process of brutalization as constitutive of certain kinds of masculinities: for instance, in his film *Ardh Satya*, aka *The Brutalization of Anant Velankar* (1983), a sensitive and conscientious policeman cracks under patriarchal expectations and the strains of his job, turning to lethal torture.

24. For a comparative discussion of the neofascist undertones of contemporary mass movements, from the Alleanza Nazionale of Italy to the Bharatiya Janat Party of India, see Gregor, *The Search for Neofascism*.

25. As Purnima Mankekar argues, "As in much nationalist discourse on com-

munal conflict, the potency of religious identity, the role of politics within and between communities, and the power of religion as worldview and a cosmology are here rendered epiphenomenal." Mankekar, *Screening Culture, Viewing Politics*, 321–22.

26. The ideology of honor does not come into play only in exceptional times: it has a function in everyday life, although with far less macabre implications. For a study of the role of honor in social reproduction, see Baviskar, "Community and the Politics of Honor."

27. Karmo's face brings to mind Agamben's discussion of the harrowing case of the *mussalman* and of the (im)possibility of witnessing in *Remnants of Auschwitz*.

28. Mankekar, *Screening Culture, Viewing Politics*, 314.

29. Singh and Rahman, "Communal Controversy," 72.

30. Ibid., 72.

31. All quotations in this section are from the Verdict of the Supreme Court of India, Writ Petition (Civil) No. 107 of 1988 (February 16, 1988).

32. All emphases in this paragraph are mine.

33. For theoretical attempts to think beyond this abstract legal subject, see Cheah and Grosz, "The Body of the Law"; Coombe, "Is There a Cultural Studies of Law?"

34. Felman, *The Juridical Unconscious*.

35. See, for instance, Shahid Amin's brilliant study of the role of the common people in the antipolice riot of Chauri Chaura. Amin, *Event, Metaphor, Memory*.

7. Mourning (Un)limited

1. Bhagwati, *In Defense of Globalization*; Stiglitz, *Globalization and Its Discontents*; see also the essays in Appelbaum and Robinson, *Critical Globalization Studies*.

2. Bello, *Deglobalization*; Tarrow, *The New Transnational Activism*.

3. Kinvall, *Globalization and Religious Nationalism in India*; Brosius, *Empowering Visions*; Hansen, *The Saffron Wave*; and Appadurai, "Patriotism and Its Futures," offer a range of nuanced arguments.

4. Ali, *The Clash of Fundamentalisms*.

5. Bhaduri and Nayyar, *The Intelligent Person's Guide to Economic Liberalization*.

6. For an account of this transitional phase, see S. Kumar, *Gandhi Meets Primetime*, especially chapter 2.

7. Kohli-Khandekar, *The Indian Media Business*.

8. The press regularly documented the controversy over school history curricula. See, for instance, the report "'Saffronisation' Alarms Historians: Walkout by BJP-backed Forum Members," *Chandigarh Tribune*, December 31, 2002. The controversy was brought up in global discussions on teaching history (often alongside the contentious German and Japanese cases). See "Getting the Spin Right on History," *UNESCO Courier*, November 2001.

9. Subhash Gatade, "Hating Romila Thapar," *Himal South Asian*, June 2003, www.himalmag.com/2003/june/.

10. Vinay Lal provides a useful contextualization of these changes in *The History of History*.

11. Some scholars, seduced by the tight and moving plotlines and technical finesse of these films, eschew criticality altogether. Rachel Dwyer, for instance, calls *Border* (1997) a timely and "moving glimpse into the work, life and death of soldiers," singling out its careful historical verisimilitude for praise: "One of the strengths of the film is the attention to detail, for example the use of the right kind of military hardware for the time." Dwyer, *One Hundred Bollywood Films*, 55.

12. Considerations of space keep me from examining several films that I consider important to the concerns of this chapter: these include *Pinjar*, *Zubeidaa*, and *Shaheed-e-Mohabbat* (2000, in Punjabi), which directly address Partition, and a host of films that explore its complex legacies—*Henna* (1991), *Bombay* (1995), *Mammo* (1996), and *Zakhm* (1998).

13. For a discussion of the repercussions of the Ayodhya episode on Indian cinema, see Mishra, "After Ayodhya."

14. The long shadow of Partition is evident in the coverage of continuing Indo-Pakistani animosity—not only in linguistic discourse, but also at the level of the iconographic. For instance, the cover of the August 10, 1998, issue of *India Today*, reporting the breakdown of talks between India and Pakistan, places a jagged "crack" between photographs of the then heads of state, Vajpayee and Nawaz Sharif.

15. See my discussion of the film *Shaheed* (1948) in chapter 2.

16. Jameson, *The Political Unconscious*, 100–102.

17. For an appreciative account of the auteurist elements in J. P. Dutta's films, see Gopalan, *Cinema of Interruptions*, 63–105.

18. See my essay "The Melodramas of Globalization."

19. "Well-Developed Story of Personal Lives Falling Victim to Politics," online posting, September 24, 2001, *Internet Movie Database*, www.imdb.com/title/ (accessed July 2003).

20. Even the rugged landscape of the Kargil sector could not stop the Bofors guns, which were thus redeemed from the scandal surrounding their purchase—a scandal about paybacks that involved the highest levels of the government, including the office of the prime minister.

21. The sequence I have in mind features the actor Dash Mihok as Private Doll.

22. In fact, the film even lists the names of various regiments who fought valiantly at Kargil but who could not be represented in its four-plus-hour running time.

23. Three of the biggest contemporary stars, Amir Khan, Salman Khan, and Shah Rukh Khan, all Muslims, are conspicuously absent from this lineup.

24. For a more substantial discussion of the film, see P. Kumar, "Islamic 'Terrorism,' Secularism and Visions of Justice in India."

25. This balance is achieved possibly due to Khaled Mohammed's encyclope-

dic knowledge of cinematic conventions and his familiarity with the lifeworld of Bombay Muslims.

26. Namrata Joshi, "Mahatma Amid the Mob," *Outlook*, March 6, 2000, 48.

27. For a discussion of the threat to the male body in riot situations, see Bacchetta, "When the (Hindu) Nation Exiles Its Queers."

28. See Jay, "The Apocalyptic Imagination and the Inability to Mourn."

29. Ravi Vasudevan makes the useful observation that the film's evocation of melodrama within a refigured ambit of the sacred, now overshadowed by the deified-yet-secularized icon of Gandhi, and its staging of "identity as spectacle" aided by digital simulation, produce a deeply ambiguous address. Vasudevan, "Another History Rises to the Surface."

30. In his sympathetic reading of the film, Philip Lutgendorf claims that this end (he calls attention to the opening of shutters to let the light in) points "toward a barely-imaginable redemption." Referring to the polarized reception of the film, he argues: "such glaringly bi-polar interpretations at least suggest the intentional complexity of this courageous and groundbreaking film about individual and collective madness." Lutgendorf, "*Hey Ram*," www.uiowa.edu/incinema/HEYRAM.html (accessed March 2007).

31. The Parsees are members of the Zoroastrian community that migrated to India from Persia centuries ago. In modern India, Parsees became influential as industrialists, merchants, bankers and philanthropists.

32. One should also note the recurrence of one sound bite—Jawaharlal Nehru's famous "Tryst with Destiny" speech—in most of these films. While it is possible to defend the use of the recording in terms of verisimilitude, or even irony, it also becomes, across multiple films, something of an acoustic cliché.

33. At least one commentator has noted the way in which Partition films are "haunted" by Holocaust films: Barenscott, "This Is Our Holocaust."

34. The film leaves out a character of Chinese origin who appears in the book, since his ethnicity does not bear on the conflict that provides the historical background of *Earth*.

35. Hazel-Dawn Dumpert, "*Earth*," *L.A. Weekly*, September 8, 1999.

36. My invocation of disappearance is informed by the work of Ackbar Abbas and Avery Gordon. See Abbas, *Hong Kong*; Gordon, *Ghostly Matters*.

37. See Janet Walker's useful discussion of the autobiographical documentary in part 3 of her book *Trauma Cinema*. I extend the scope of this genre by locating an implicit autobiographical imperative in the biographical works of contemporary documentary filmmaker Isaac Julien: Sarkar, "Tangled Legacies."

38. This last evocation of a sensuous fullness echoes a similar moment in Ghatak's *Komal Gandhar* (chapter 5).

39. My translation.

40. My translation.

Coda

1. Suleiman, *Crises of Memory*, 1.

2. Mary Ann Doane provides an illuminating discussion of the "event" in relation to early cinema's experiments with capturing time. See Doane, *The Emergence of Cinematic Time*, especially 140–71.

3. As I demonstrate, this distinction does not reinstate a strict opposition between modernist and populist films: rather, it forces us to attend to common strategies of mourning in relation to overarching ideological-discursive formations.

4. My observations here echo Dominick LaCapra's thoughtful ruminations in the introduction to his book, *Representing the Holocaust.*

5. Of course, my location complicates the legitimacy of such a claim because of the differences arising from diasporic life; location, as we know, also intervenes in terms of the constitution of my audience, overarching research paradigms and frameworks of knowledge.

6. *Khamosh Pani* (aka *Silent Water*, 2003), directed by Pakistani filmmaker Sabiha Sumar, is one celebrated example of such cultural mourning work.

7. Although the scope of the book sanctions the omission of the fecund field of theater, where many of these interventions occur, it does not explain my neglect of other "cinematic arts" like video installations. Paucity of space, while a binding factor, seems like a weak excuse for ignoring a work like Nalini Malani's *Remembering Toba Tek Singh* (1998–99).

Bibliography

Abbas, Ackbar. *Hong Kong: Culture and the Politics of Disappearance.* Minneapolis: University of Minnesota Press, 1997.

Adorno, Theodor. "The Meaning of Working through the Past." In *Critical Models: Interventions and Catchwords*, 89–104. 1959; New York: Columbia University Press, 1998.

Agamben, Giorgio. *Means without End: Notes on Politics.* Translated by Vincenzo Binette and Cesare Casarino. Minneapolis: University of Minnesota Press, 2000.

———. *Remnants of Auschwitz: The Witness and the Archive.* Translated by Daniel Heller-Roazen. Brooklyn, N.Y.: Zone Books, 2002.

Alam, Javeed, and Suresh Sharma, "Remembering Partition." *Seminar* 461 (January 1998): 71–74.

Ali, Tariq. *The Clash of Fundamentalisms.* London: Verso, 2003.

Amin, Shahid. *Event, Metaphor, Memory: Chauri Chaura, 1922–1992.* Berkeley: University of California Press, 1995.

Amin, Shahid. "On Retelling the Muslim Conquest of North India." In *History and the Present*, edited by Partha Chatterjee and Anjan Ghosh, 19–32. New Delhi: Permanent Black, 2002.

Anderson, Benedict. *Imagined Communities: Reflections on the Origin and Spread of Nationalism.* 1983; London: Verso, 1991.

Andrew, Dudley. "Film and History." In *The Oxford Guide to Film Studies*, edited by John Hill and Pamela Church, 176–89. Oxford: Oxford University Press, 1998.

Appadurai, Arjun. "Disjuncture and Difference in the Global Cultural Economy." *Public Culture* 2, no. 2 (1990): 1–23.

———. *Modernity at Large: Cultural Dimensions of Globalization.* Minneapolis: University of Minnesota Press, 1996.

———. "Patriotism and Its Futures." *Public Culture* 5 (1993): 411–29.

Appelbaum, Richard, and William Robinson, eds. *Critical Globalization Studies.* New York: Routledge, 2005.

Axel, Brian Keith. *The Nation's Tortured Body: Violence, Representation, and the Formation of a Sikh "Diaspora."* Durham: Duke University Press, 2001.

Bacchetta, Paola. "When the (Hindu) Nation Exiles Its Queers." *Social Text*, no. 61 (1999): 141–66.

Bagchi, Jasodhara, and Subhoranjan Dasgupta, eds. *The Trauma and the Triumph: Gender and Partition in East India.* Calcutta: Stree, 2003.

Baghdadi, Rafique, and Rajiv Rao. *Talking Films.* New Delhi: Indus, 1995.

Bakhtin, Mikhail. "Discourse in the Novel." In *The Dialogic Imagination: Four Essays*, edited by Michael Holquist, translated by Caryl Emerson and Michael Holquist, 259–422. Austin: University of Texas Press, 1981.

———. "Epic and Novel." In *The Dialogic Imagination: Four Essays*, edited by Michael Holquist, translated by Caryl Emerson and Michael Holquist, 3–40. Austin: University of Texas Press, 1981.

Bal, Mieke, Jonathan Crewe, and Leo Spitzer, eds. *Acts of Memory: Cultural Recall in the Present.* London: Dartmouth College/University Press of New England, 1999.

Balakrishnan, Gopal. "The National Imagination." In *Mapping the Nation*, edited by Gopal Balakrishnan. London: Verso, 1996.

Balibar, Etienne. "The Nation Form: History and Ideology." Translated by Chris Turner. In Etienne Balibar and Immanuel Wallerstein, *Race, Nation, Class: Ambiguous Identities*, 86–106. London: Verso, 1991.

Ball, Karyn. "Introduction: Trauma and Its Institutional Destinies." *Cultural Critique* 46 (2000): 1–44.

Bandyopadhyay, Parthapratim. "Filmey Melodrama: Ritwik Kumar Ghatak" [in Bengali]. In *Ritwik o Tar Chhabi*, edited by Rajat Roy, 81–90. Calcutta: Annapurna Pustak Mandir, 1983.

Bandyopadhyay, Pushan. "Uttapta Batash Trishnarta Mati Samne Sathyu" [in Bengali]. In *Cinemar Shatabarshay Bharatiya Cinema*, edited by Pralay Sur, 238–41. Calcutta: Nandan, 1995.

Bandyopadhyay, Samik, ed. *Govind Nihalani: A Celluloid Chapter Documentation.* Jamshedpur: Celluloid Chapter, 1992.

Bandyopadhyay, Sandip. "The Riddles of Partition: Memories of the Bengali Hindus." In *Reflections on Partition in the East*, edited by Ranabir Samaddar, 59–72. New Delhi: Vikas Publishing House for Calcutta Research Group, 1997.

Bandyopadhyay, Shibaji. "Smaran-Pratismaran: Ritwik Ghataker Shilpa" [in Bengali]. *Chitrabhabna: Ritwik Special Issue* (Calcutta: Federation of Film Societies of India, 1997), 22–36.

Banerjee, Shampa, ed. *Ritwik Ghatak*. New Delhi: Directorate of Film Festivals, National Film Development Corporation, 1982.

Bard, Amy. "'No Power of Speech Remains': Tears and Transformation in South Asian 'Majlis' Poetry." In *Holy Tears: Weeping in the Religious Imagination*, edited by Kimberley Christine Patton and John Stratton Hawley, 145–64. Princeton, N.J.: Princeton University Press, 2005.

Barenscott, Dorothy. "This Is Our Holocaust: Deepa Mehta's *Earth* and the Question of Partition Trauma." *Mediascape* 1, no. 2 (2006), available at www .tft.ucla.edu/mediascape/features/barenscott.pdf.

Barker, Francis. *The Culture of Violence: Tragedy and History*. Chicago: University of Chicago Press, 1994.

Barrett, Michèle. "Ideology, Politics, Hegemony: From Gramsci to Laclau and Mouffe." In *Mapping Ideology*, edited by Slavoj Žižek, 235–64. London: Verso, 1994.

Barthes, Roland. *Camera Lucida: Reflections on Photography*. Translated by Richard Howard. New York: Hill and Wang, 1981.

Basu, Kaushik, and Sanjay Subrahmanyam, eds. *Unravelling the Nation: Sectarian Conflict and India's Secular Identity*. New Delhi: Penguin, 1996.

Baviskar, Amita. "Community and the Politics of Honor." In *The Village in India*, edited by Vandana Madan, 252–66. New Delhi: Oxford University Press, 2002.

Baxi, Upendra, and Bhikhu Parekh, eds. *Crisis and Change in Contemporary India*. New Delhi: Sage, 1995.

Bazin, Andre. "Death Every Afternoon." Translated by Mark Cohen. In *Rites of Realism: Essays on Corporeal Cinema*, edited by Ivone Marguelies, 27–31. Durham, N.C.: Duke University Press, 2002.

———. "The Ontology of the Photographic Image." In *What Is Cinema?* vol. 1, edited and translated by Hugh Gray. Berkeley: University of California Press, 1967.

Belau, Linda, and Petar Ramadanovic, eds. *Topologies of Trauma: Essays on the Limit of Knowledge and Memory*. New York: Other Press, 2002.

Bello, Walden. *Deglobalization: Ideas for a New World Economy*. London: Zed Books, 2005.

Bellour, Raymond. "The Film We Accompany." Translated by Fergus Daly. *Rouge* 3 (2004). www.rouge.com.au.

Benamou, Catherine. *It's All True: Orson Welles's Pan-American Odyssey*. Berkeley: University of California Press, 2007.

Benjamin, Walter. *The Origin of German Tragic Drama*. Translated by John Osborne. London: NLB, 1977.

———. "The Storyteller." In *Illuminations*, edited by Hannah Arendt, 83–110. New York: Schocken, 1969.

———. "Theses on the Philosophy of History." In *Illuminations*, edited by Hannah Arendt, 253–64. New York: Schocken, 1969.

Berlant, Lauren. *The Anatomy of National Fantasy: Hawthorne, Utopia and Everyday Life*. Chicago: University of Chicago Press, 1991.

Bhabha, Homi. "DissemiNation: Time, Narrative, and the Margins of the Modern Nation." In *Nation and Narration*, edited by Bhabha, 291–322. London: Routledge, 1990.

———. "Signs Taken for Wonders: Questions of Ambivalence and Authority under a Tree outside Delhi, May 1817." In *The Location of Culture*, 102–22. New York: Routledge, 1994.

Bhaduri, Amit, and Deepak Nayyar. *The Intelligent Person's Guide to Liberalization*. New Delhi: Penguin, 1996.

Bhagwati, Jagdish. *In Defense of Globalization*. New York: Oxford University Press, 2004.

Bhargava, R. "Religious and Secular Identities." In *Crisis and Change in Contemporary India*, edited by Upendra Baxi and Bhiku Parekh, 317–49. New Delhi: Sage, 1995.

Bhatia, Nandi. "Staging Resistance: The Indian People's Theatre Association." In *The Politics of Culture in the Shadow of Capital*, edited by David Lloyd and Lisa Lowe, 433–60. Durham, N.C.: Duke University Press, 1997.

Bhattacharya, Malini. "The IPTA in Bengal." *Journal of Arts and Ideas* 2 (1983): 9–26.

Bilgrami, Akeel. "Two Concepts of Secularism." In *Politics in India*, edited by Sudipta Kaviraj, 342–48. New Delhi: Oxford University Press, 1997.

———. "What Is a Muslim? Fundamental Commitment and Cultural Identity." *Critical Inquiry* 18 (1992): 821–42.

Biswas, Moinak. "The Couple and Their Spaces: *Harano Sur* as Melodrama Now." In *Making Meaning in Indian Cinema*, edited by Ravi S. Vasudevan, 122–42. New Delhi: Oxford University Press, 2000.

———. "Her Mother's Son: Kinship and History in Ritwik Ghatak." *Rouge* 3 (2004). www.rouge.com.au.

Blanchot, Maurice. *The Writing of the Disaster*. Translated by Ann Smock. Lincoln: University of Nebraska Press, 1986.

Booth, Gregory. "Traditional Content and Narrative Structure in the Hindi Commercial Cinema." *Asian Folklore Studies* 54, no. 2 (1995): 169–90.

Bose, Pradip Kumar. "Memory Begins Where History Ends." In *Reflections on Partition in the East*, edited by Ranabir Samaddar, 73–86. New Delhi: Vikas Publishing House for Calcutta Research Group, 1997.

Bose, Sugata. *Agrarian Bengal: Economy, Social Structures and Politics, 1919–47*. Cambridge: Cambridge University Press, 1986.

Bourdieu, Pierre. *Distinction: A Social Critique of the Judgement of Taste*. Translated by Richard Nice. Cambridge, Mass.: Harvard University Press, 1984.

———. *Outline of a Theory of Practice*. Translated by Richard Nice. Cambridge: Cambridge University Press, 1977.

Brass, Paul R. "Introduction: Discourses of Ethnicity, Communalism and Violence." In *Riots and Pogroms*, edited by Brass, 1–55. London: Macmillan, 1996.

Bratton, Jacky, Jim Cook, and Christine Gledhill, eds. *Melodrama: Picture, Stage, Screen*. London: British Film Institute, 1994.

Breithaupt, Fritz. "The Invention of Trauma in German Romanticism." *Critical Inquiry* 32 (2005): 77–101.

Brooks, Peter. *The Melodramatic Imagination: Balzac, Henry James, Melodrama and the Mode of Excess*. New Haven, Conn.: Yale University Press, 1976.

Brosius, Christiane. *Empowering Visions: The Politics of Representation in Hindu Nationalism*. London: Anthem, 2005.

Burch, Noel. *Theory of Film Practice*. New York: Praeger, 1973.

————. *To the Distant Observer: Form and Meaning in the Japanese Cinema*. London: Scolar, 1979.

Bürger, Peter. *The Theory of the Avant-Garde*. Minneapolis: University of Minnesota Press, 1992.

Burgoyne, Robert. *Film Nation: Hollywood Looks at U.S. History*. Minneapolis: University of Minnesota Press, 1997.

Butalia, Urvashi. *The Other Side of Silence: Voices from the Partition of India*. New Delhi: Viking, 1998.

Butler, Judith. *The Psychic Life of Power: Theories in Subjection*. Palo Alto, Calif.: Stanford, 1997.

Caruth, Cathy, ed. *Trauma: Explorations in Memory*. Baltimore, Md.: Johns Hopkins University Press, 1995.

Caruth, Cathy. *Unclaimed Experience: Trauma, Narrative, and History*. Baltimore, Md.: Johns Hopkins University Press, 1996.

Chakrabarti, Prafulla. *The Marginal Men: The Refugees and the Left Political Syndrome in West Bengal*. Kalyani: Lumiere Books, 1990.

Chakrabarty, Dipesh. "Postcoloniality and the Artifice of History: Who Speaks for 'Indian' Pasts?" *Representations* 37 (1992): 1–26.

————. *Provincializing Europe*. Princeton, N.J.: Princeton University Press, 2000.

————. "Remembered Villages: Representations of Hindu-Bengali Memories in the Aftermath of the Partition." *South Asia* 18 (1995): 109–29.

Chakravarti, Uma, and Nandita Haksar. *The Delhi Riots: Three Days in the Life of a Nation*. New Delhi: Lancer International, 1987.

Chakravarty, Sumita S. *National Identity in Indian Popular Cinema, 1947–1987*. Austin: University of Texas Press, 1993.

Chatterjee, Gayatri. *Awara*. New Delhi: Wiley Eastern Limited, 1992.

————. *Mother India*. London: British Film Institute, 2002.

Chatterjee, Partha. "Bengal Politics and the Muslim Masses, 1920–47." In *India's Partition: Process, Strategy and Mobilization*, edited by Mushirul Hasan, 258–78. New Delhi: Oxford University Press, 1994.

————. "The Nationalist Resolution of the Women's Question." In *Recasting Women: Essays in Indian Colonial History*, edited by Kumkum Sangari and Suresh Vaid, 233–53. New Brunswick, N.J.: Rutgers University Press, 1990.

————. *Nationalist Thought and the Colonial World: A Derivative Discourse?* Minneapolis: University of Minnesota Press, 1986.

————. *The Nation and Its Fragments: Colonial and Postcolonial Histories*. Princeton, N.J.: Princeton University Press, 1993.

————. "On Civil and Political Society in Post-colonial Democracies." In *Civil Society: History and Possibilities*, edited by Sudipta Kaviraj and Sunil Khilnani, 165–78. Cambridge: Cambridge University Press, 2001.

————. "Religious Minorities and the Secular State: Reflections on an Indian Impasse." *Public Culture* 8 (1995): 11–39.

————. "The Second Partition of Bengal." In *Reflections on Partition in the East*, edited by Ranabir Samaddar, 35–58. New Delhi: Vikas Publishing House for Calcutta Research Group, 1997.

————. "Two Poets and Death: On Civil and Political Society in the Non-Christian World." In *Questions of Modernity*, edited by Timothy Mitchell, 35–48. Minneapolis: University of Minnesota Press, 2000.

————, ed. *Wages of Freedom: Fifty Years of the Indian Nation-State.* Calcutta: Oxford University Press, 1998.

Chatterji, Joya. *Bengal Divided: Hindu Communalism and Partition, 1932–47.* Cambridge: Cambridge University Press, 1995.

————. "The Fashioning of a Frontier: The Radcliffe Line and Bengal's Border Landscape, 1947–52." *Modern Asian Studies* 33 (1999): 185–42.

Chattopadhyay, Muralidhar. "1952" [in Bengali]. *Chitrabani* 5, no. 1 (1952): 7.

Cheah, Pheng. "Spectral Nationality: The Living On [*sur-vie*] of the Postcolonial Nation in Neocolonial Globalization." *Boundary* 2 26, no. 3 (1999): 225–52.

————. *Spectral Nationality: Passages of Freedom from Kant to Postcolonial Literatures of Liberation.* New York: Columbia University Press, 2003.

————, and Elizabeth Grosz. "The Body of the Law: Notes toward a Theory of Corporeal Justice." In *Thinking Through the Body of the Law*, edited by Pheng Cheah, David Fraser, and Judith Grbich, 3–25. New York: New York University Press, 1996.

Chion, Michel. *Audiovision.* New York: Columbia University Press, 1994.

Chitrabhabna. Special issue on Ritwik Ghatak. Calcutta: Federation of Film Societies of India, Eastern Region, 1997.

Chitrabhas. Special issue on Nemai Ghosh [in Bengali], 19, no. 1–2 (1984).

Churchill, Ward. *A Little Matter of Genocide: Holocaust and Denial in the Americas, 1492 to the Present.* San Francisco: City Lights Books, 1998.

Cleary, Joe. *Literature, Partition and the Nation-State: Culture and Conflict in Ireland, Israel and Palestine.* Cambridge: Cambridge University Press, 2002.

Connor, Walker. "A Nation Is a Nation, Is a State, Is an Ethnic Group, Is a . . ." *Ethnic and Racial Studies* 1 (1978): 379–88.

Cook, Pam. "Melodrama and the Women's Picture." In *Gainsborough Melodrama* (British Film Institute Dossier 18). London: British Film Institute, 1983.

Coombe, Rosemary. "Is There a Cultural Studies of Law?" In *A Companion to Cultural Studies*, edited by Toby Miller, 36–62. Oxford: Blackwell, 2001.

Cooper, Frederick. *Colonialism in Question: Theory, Knowledge, History.* Berkeley: University of California Press, 2005.

Crary, Jonathan. *Techniques of the Observer: On Vision and Modernity in the Nineteenth Century.* Cambridge, Mass.: MIT Press, 1992.

Creekmur, Corey. "Picturizing American Cinema: Hindi Film Songs and the Last Days of Genre." In *Soundtrack Available*, edited by Pamela Robertson Wojcik and Arthur Knight. Durham, N.C.: Duke University Press, 2001.

Crossette, Barbara. "India's Sikhs: Waiting for Justice." *World Policy Journal* 21, no. 2 (2004).

Dalle Vacche, Angela. *The Body in the Mirror: Shapes of History in Italian Cinema*. Princeton, N.J.: Princeton University Press, 1992.

Das, Suranjan. *Communal Riots in Bengal, 1905–1947*. New Delhi: Oxford University Press, 1991.

Das, Veena. "The Act of Witnessing: Violence, Poisonous Knowledge, and Subjectivity." In *Violence and Subjectivity*, edited by Veena Das, Arthur Kleinman, Mamphela Ramphele and Pamela Reynolds, 205–25. Berkeley: University of California Press, 2000.

———. "Communities as Political Actors: The Question of Cultural Rights." In *Gender and Politics in India*, edited by Nivedita Menon, 441–71. New Delhi: Oxford University Press, 1999.

———. "Introduction: Communities, Riots, Survivors—The South Asian Experience." In *Mirrors of Violence*, edited by Das, 1–36. New Delhi: Oxford University Press, 1990.

———. "Language and Body: Transactions in the Construction of Pain." In *Social Suffering*, edited by Arthur Kleinman, Veena Das, and Margaret M. Lock, 67–91. Berkeley: University of California Press, 1997.

———, ed. *Mirrors of Violence: Communities, Riots and Survivors in South Asia*. New Delhi: Oxford University Press, 1990.

———. "The Spatialization of Violence: Case Study of a 'Communal Riot.'" In *Unravelling the Nation: Sectarian Conflict and India's Secular Identity*, edited by Kaushik Basu and Sanjay Subrahmanyam, 157–203. New Delhi: Penguin, 1996.

Dasgupta, Chidananda. "The Cultural Basis of Indian Cinema." In *Talking about Films*. New Delhi: Orient Longman, 1981.

Dasgupta, Shibaditya, and Sandeepan Bhattacharya, eds. *Sakshat Ritwik*. Calcutta: Deepayan, 2000.

Datta, Pradip K. *Carving Blocs: Communal Ideology in Early Twentieth-century Bengal*. New Delhi: Oxford University Press, 1999.

Deleuze, Gilles, and Félix Guattari. *A Thousand Plateaus: Capitalism and Schizophrenia*. Translated by Brian Massumi. Minneapolis: University of Minnesota Press, 1987.

de Man, Paul. *The Resistance to Theory*. Manchester: Manchester University Press, 1986.

———. "The Rhetoric of Temporality." In *Blindness and Insight: Essays in the Rhetoric of Contemporary Criticism*, 187–228. Minneapolis: University of Minnesota Press, 1983.

———. "Semiology and Rhetoric." In *Allegories of Reading: Figural Language in Rousseau, Nietzsche, Rilke and Proust*, 3–19. New Haven, Conn.: Yale University Press, 1979.

Derrida, Jacques. *The Ear of the Other*. Translated by Avital Ronell and Peggy

Kamuf, edited by Christie McDonald. Lincoln: University of Nebraska Press, 1985.

———. "Interpreting Signatures (Nietzsche/Heidegger): Two Questions." In *Looking After Nietzsche*, edited by Laurence Rickels, 1–17. Albany: State University of New York Press, 1990.

———. *Specters of Marx: The State of the Debt, the Work of Mourning and the New International*. Translated by Peggy Kamuf. New York: Routledge, 1994.

Deschaumes, Ghislaine Glasson, and Rada Ivekovic, eds. *Divided Countries, Separated Cities: The Modern Legacy of Partition*. New Delhi: Oxford University Press, 2003.

Didur, Jill. *Unsettling Partition: Literature, Gender, Memory*. Toronto: University of Toronto Press, 2006.

Dirks, Nicholas B., Geoff Eley, and Sherry B. Ortner, eds. *Culture/Power/History*. Princeton, N.J.: Princeton University Press, 1994.

D'Lugo, Marvin. "Buñuel in the Cathedral of Culture: Reterritorializing the Film Auteur." In *Luis Buñuel's "The Discreet Charms of the Bourgeoisie,"* edited by Marsha Kinder, 101–10. Cambridge: Cambridge University Press, 1999.

Doane, Mary Ann. *The Emergence of Cinematic Time: Modernity, Contingency, the Archive*. Cambridge, Mass.: Harvard University Press, 2002.

Duara, Prasenjit. *Rescuing History from the Nation: Questioning Narratives of Modern China*. Chicago: Chicago University Press, 1995.

Dwyer, Rachel. *One Hundred Bollywood Films*. London: British Film Institute, 2005.

———. *Yash Chopra*. London: British Film Institute, 2002.

Eisenstein, Sergei, Vsevolod Pudovkin, and Grigori Alexandrov. "Statement on Sound." In *S. M. Eisenstein: Selected Works, Volume 1: Writings, 1922–1934*, edited and translated by Richard Taylor, 113–14. London: British Film Institute, 1988.

Elsaesser, Thomas. *Fassbinder's Germany: History Identity Subject*. Amsterdam: Amsterdam University Press, 1996.

———. *New German Cinema: A History*. New Brunswick, N.J.: Rutgers University Press, 1989.

———. "One Train May Be Hiding Another: History, Memory, Identity and the Visual Image." In *Topologies of Trauma: Essays on the Limit of Knowledge and Memory*, edited by Linda Belau and Petar Ramadanovic, 61–71. New York: Other Press, 2002.

———. "Tales of Sound and Fury: Observations on the Family Melodrama." *Monogram* 4 (1972): 2–15.

Eng, David. "Melancholia in the Late Twentieth Century." *Signs* 25 (2000): 1275–81.

Erikson, Kai. "Notes on Trauma and Community." In *Trauma: Explorations in Memory*, edited by Cathy Caruth, 183–99. Baltimore, Md.: Johns Hopkins University Press, 1995.

Felman, Shoshana. *The Juridical Unconscious: Trials and Traumas in the Twentieth Century*. Cambridge, Mass.: Harvard University Press, 2002.

Flinn, Caryl. *The New German Cinema: Music, History and the Matter of Style.* Berkeley: University of California Press, 2004.

Foucault, Michel. *History of Sexuality*, vol. 1. Translated by Robert Hurley. New York: Vintage Books, 1980.

———. "Nietzsche, Genealogy, History." In *Language, Counter-Memory, Practice.* Edited by Donald F. Bouchard and translated by Donald F. Bouchard and Sherry Simon, 139–64. Ithaca, N.Y.: Cornell University Press, 1977.

Freud, Sigmund. *Beyond the Pleasure Principle.* New York: W. W. Norton, 1990.

———. *The Ego and the Id.* Translated by Joan Riviere, edited by James Strachey. 1923; New York: W. W. Norton, 1960.

———. "Mourning and Melancholia." In *The Standard Edition of the Complete Psychological Works of Sigmund Freud*, translated by James Strachey, 14:243–58. London: Hogarth, 1958.

———. "Remembering, Repeating and Working Through." In *The Standard Edition of the Complete Psychological Works of Sigmund Freud.* Translated by James Strachey, 12:145–56. London: Hogarth, 1958.

Gadamer, Hans-Georg. *Philosophical Hermeneutics.* Berkeley: University of California Press, 1976.

———. *Truth and Method.* Lanham, Md.: Sheed and Ward Ltd., 1989.

Gaonkar, Dilip Parameshwar, ed. *Alternative Modernities.* Durham, N.C.: Duke University Press, 2001.

Genoways, Ted. "'Let Them Snuff Out the Moon': Faiz Ahmed Faiz's Prison Lyrics in *Dast-e Saba.*" *Annual of Urdu Studies* 19 (2004): 94–119.

Gertz, Nurith, and George Khleifi. *Palestinian Cinema: Landscape, Trauma and Memory.* Bloomington: Indiana University Press, 2008.

Geyer, Michael. "The Politics of Memory in Contemporary Germany." In *Radical Evil*, edited by Joan Copjec, 169–200. London: Verso, 1996.

Ghatak, Ritwik. *Chalacchitra, Manush Ebang Aro Kichhu* [in Bengali]. Calcutta: Sandhan Cooperative Publishing, 1975.

———. "Chhabitey Dialectics" [in Bengali]. In *Chalachchitra, Manush Ebang Aro Kichhu*, 43–47. Calcutta: Sandhan Cooperative Publishing, 1975.

———. "Manabsamaj, Amader Aitihya, Chhabi-kara o Amar Pracheshta" [in Bengali]. In *Chalachchitra, Manush Ebang Aro Kichhu*, 3–10. Calcutta: Sandhan Cooperative Publishing, 1975.

———. "Music in Indian Cinema and the Epic Approach." In *Rows and Rows of Fences*, 21–23. Calcutta: Seagull, 2000. Originally published in *Artist* 1, no. 1 (1963).

———. "On Art and the Archetype." In *Ritwik Ghatak*, translated and edited by Shampa Banerjee, 11–17. New Delhi: Directorate of Film Festivals, National Film Development Corporation, 1982. [Translated from the original Bengali essay, "Manabsamaj, Amader Aitihya, Chhabi-kora o Amar Pracheshta."]

———. *On the Cultural Front: A Thesis Submitted by Ritwik Ghatak to the Communist Party of India in 1954.* Calcutta: Ritwik Memorial Trust, 2000.

———. "*Subarnarekha*: Parichalaker Baktabya" [in Bengali]. In *Chalacchitra,*

Manush Ebang Aro Kichhu, 38–43. Calcutta: Sandhan Cooperative Publishing, 1975.

Ghatak, Surama. *Ritwik* [in Bengali]. Calcutta: Anushtoop, 1996.

Gledhill, Christine, ed. *Home Is Where the Heart Is: Studies in Melodrama and the Woman's Film*. London: British Film Institute, 1987.

———. "The Melodramatic Field: An Investigation." In *Home Is Where the Heart Is: Studies in Melodrama and the Woman's Film*, edited by Christine Gledhill, 5–39. London: British Film Institute, 1987.

Gopalan, Lalitha. *Cinema of Interruptions: Action Genres in Contemporary Indian Cinema*. London: British Film Institute, 2002.

Gordon, Avery. *Ghostly Matters: Haunting and the Sociological Imagination*. Minneapolis: University of Minnesota Press, 1996.

Gordon, Leonard. "Divided Bengal: Problems of Nationalism and Identity in the 1947 Partition." In *India's Partition: Process, Strategy and Mobilization*, edited by Mushirul Hasan, 279–321. New Delhi: Oxford University Press, 1994.

Gould, William. *Hindu Nationalism and the Language of Politics in Late Colonial India*. Cambridge: Cambridge University Press, 2004.

Gregor, A. James. *The Search for Neofascism*. Cambridge: Cambridge University Press, 2006.

Guha, Ranajit. "The Small Voice of History." In *Subaltern Studies IX: Writings on South Asian History and Society*, edited by Shahid Amin and Dipesh Chakrabarty, 1–12. New Delhi: Oxford University Press, 1996.

Guhathakurta, Meghna. "Families, Displacement." In *Divided Countries, Separated Cities: The Modern Legacy of Partition*, edited by Ghislaine Glasson Deschaumes and Rada Ivekovic, 96–105. New Delhi: Oxford University Press, 2003.

Guha-Thakurta, Tapati. Introduction to *Sites of Art History: Canons and Expositions*, special issue of *Journal of Arts and Ideas* 30–31 (1997): 1–6.

———. "Marking Independence: The Ritual of a National Art Exhibition." *Journal of Arts and Ideas* 30–31 (1997): 89–114.

———. "Visualizing the Nation." *Journal of Arts and Ideas* 27–28 (1995): 7–40.

Hansen, Miriam. "America, Paris and the Alps: Kracauer (and Benjamin) on Cinema and Modernity." In *Cinema and the Invention of Modern Life*, edited by Leo Charney and Vanessa Schwartz, 362–402. Berkeley: University of California Press, 1995.

———. "*Schindler's List* Is Not *Shoah*: The Second Commandment, Popular Modernism, and Public Memory." *Critical Inquiry* 22 (1996): 292–312.

Hansen, Thomas Blom. *The Saffron Wave*. Princeton, N.J.: Princeton University Press, 1999.

Hasan, Mushirul. *Legacy of a Divided Nation: India's Muslims Since Independence*. New Delhi: Oxford University Press, 1997.

Higson, Andrew. "The Concept of National Cinema." *Screen* 30, no. 4 (autumn 1989): 36–47.

Hirsch, Joshua. *Afterimage: Film, Trauma, and the Holocaust*. Philadelphia: Temple University Press, 2004.

Hobsbawm, E. J. *Nations and Nationalism since 1780: Programme, Myth, Reality.* Cambridge: Cambridge University Press, 1990.

Hobsbawm, Eric, and Terence Ranger, eds. *The Invention of Tradition.* Cambridge: Cambridge University Press, 1983.

Horowitz, Donald. *The Deadly Ethnic Riot.* Berkeley: University of California Press, 2003.

Jaffrelot, Christophe. *The Hindu Nationalist Movement and Indian Politics.* New Delhi: Penguin, 1996.

———. *India's Silent Revolution: The Rise of the Lower Castes in Northern India.* New York: Columbia University Press, 2002.

Jain, Kajri. *Gods in the Bazaar.* Durham, N.C.: Duke University Press, 2007.

———. "Of the Everyday and the 'National Pencil.'" *Journal of Arts and Ideas* 27–28 (1995): 57–90.

———. "Producing the Sacred: The Subjects of Calendar Art." *Journal of Arts and Ideas* 30–31 (December 1997): 63–88.

Jalal, Ayesha. *The Sole Spokesman: Jinnah, the Muslim League and the Demand for Partition.* Cambridge: Cambridge University Press, 1985.

Jameson, Fredric. *Marxism and Form: Twentieth-Century Dialectical Theories of Literature.* Princeton, N.J.: Princeton University Press, 1971.

———. *The Geopolitical Aesthetic: Cinema and Space in the World System.* Bloomington: Indiana University Press, 1992.

———. *The Political Unconscious: Narrative as a Socially Symbolic Act.* Ithaca, N.Y.: Cornell University Press, 1981.

———. "Third-World Literature in the Era of Multinational Capitalism." *Social Text*, no. 15 (1986): 65–88.

Jassal, Smita Tewari, and Eyal Ben-Ari, eds. *The Partition Motif in Contemporary Conflicts.* New Delhi: Sage, 2007.

Jay, Martin. "The Apocalyptic Imagination and the Inability to Mourn." In *Force Fields: Between Intellectual History and Cultural Critique*, 84–98. New York: Routledge, 1993.

Kaes, Anton. *From Hitler to Heimat: The Return of History as Film.* Boston, Mass.: Harvard University Press, 1989.

Kakar, Sudhir. *The Colours of Violence.* New Delhi: Penguin, 1996.

Kamra, Sukeshi. *Bearing Witness: Partition, Independence, End of the Raj.* Calgary: University of Calgary Press, 2002.

Kandiyoti, Deniz. "Identity and Its Discontents: Women and the Nation." *Millennium Journal of International Studies* 20, no. 3 (1991): 429–44.

Kaplan, E. Ann. *Trauma Culture: The Politics of Terror and Loss in Media and Literature.* New Brunswick, N.J.: Rutgers University Press, 2005.

———, and Ban Wang, eds. *Trauma and Cinema: Cross-Cultural Explorations.* Hong Kong: Hong Kong University Press, 2004.

Kapur, Geeta. "Cultural Creativity in the First Decade: The Example of Satyajit Ray." *Journal of Arts and Ideas* 23–24 (1993): 17–50.

———. "Further Narratives." *Journal of Arts and Ideas* 20–21 (1991): 99–115.

———. "Revelation and Doubt: *Sant Tukaram* and *Devi.*" In *Interrogating*

Modernity: Culture and Colonialism in India, edited by Tejaswini Niranjana, P. Sudhir, and Vivek Dhareshwar, 19–46. Calcutta: Seagull, 1993.

Kaul, Suvir, ed. *The Partitions of Memory: The Afterlife of the Division of India.* Bloomington: Indiana University Press, 2002.

Kaviraj, Sudipta. "The Culture of Representative Democracy." In *Wages of Freedom: Fifty Years of the Indian Nation-State*, edited by Partha Chatterjee, 147–75. New Delhi: Oxford University Press, 1998.

———. "The Imaginary Institution of India." In *Subaltern Studies VII*, edited by Partha Chatterjee and Gyanendra Pandey, 1–39. New Delhi: Oxford University Press, 1992.

———, ed. *Politics in India*. New Delhi: Oxford University Press, 1997.

Kelly, Michael. *Iconoclasm in Aesthetics*. Cambridge: Cambridge University Press, 2003.

Khan, Yasmin. *The Great Partition: The Making of India and Pakistan*. New Haven: Yale University Press, 2007.

Khilnani, Sunil. *The Idea of India*. London: Hamish Hamilton, 1997.

Kinder, Marsha. *Blood Cinema: The Reconstruction of National Identity in Spain.* Los Angeles: University of California Press, 1993.

Kinvall, Catar. *Globalization and Religious Nationalism in India*. London: Routledge, 2006.

Klein, Kerwin Lee. "On the Emergence of *Memory* in Historical Discourse." *Representations* 69 (2000): 127–50.

Kleinhans, Chuck. "Notes on Melodrama and the Family under Capitalism." *Film Reader* 3 (February 1978): 40–47. Reprinted in *Imitations of Life*, edited by Marcia Landy, 197–204. Detroit: Wayne State University Press, 1991.

Kleinman, Arthur, Veena Das, and Margaret Lock, eds. *Social Suffering*. Berkeley: University of California Press, 1997.

Kohli-Khandekar, Vanita. *The Indian Media Business*. 2nd ed. New Delhi: Response Books, 2006.

Kosambi, D. D. *Myth and Reality: Studies in the Formation of Indian Culture.* Bombay: Popular Prakashan, 1962.

Koselleck, Reinhart. *The Practice of Conceptual History: Timing History, Spacing Concepts*. Translated by Todd Samuel Presner. Stanford, Calif.: Stanford University Press, 2002.

Kothari, Rajni. "Interpreting Indian Politics: A Personal Statement." In *Crisis and Change in Contemporary India*, edited by Upendra Baxi and Bhiku Parekh, 150–68. New Delhi: Sage, 1995.

Kristeva, Julia. *Black Sun: Depression and Melancholia*. New York: Columbia University Press, 1989.

Kumar, Amitava. "Splitting the Difference." *Transition*, no. 89 (2001): 44–55.

Kumar, Priya. "Testimonies of Loss and Memory: Partition and the Haunting of a Nation." *Interventions* 1, no. 2 (1999): 201–15.

———. "Islamic 'Terrorism,' Secularism and Visions of Justice in India." In *Cinema, Law and the State in Asia*, edited by Corey Creekmur and Mark Sidel, 63–82. New York: Palgrave Macmillan, 2007.

Kumar, Radha. In *Divide and Fall? Bosnia in the Annals of Partition*. London: Verso, 1997.

Kumar, Shanti. *Gandhi Meets Primetime: Globalization and Nationalism in Indian Television*. Urbana: University of Illinois Press, 2006.

Kuran, Timur. "The Unthinkable and the Unthought." *Rationality and Society* 5 (1993): 473–505.

LaCapra, Dominick. *History and Criticism*. Ithaca, N.Y.: Cornell University Press, 1983.

——. *Representing the Holocaust: History, Theory, Trauma*. Ithaca, N.Y.: Cornell University Press, 1994.

——. "Trauma, Absence, Loss." *Critical Inquiry* 25 (1999): 696–727.

——. *Writing History, Writing Trauma*. Baltimore, Md.: Johns Hopkins University Press, 2001.

Laclau, Ernesto, and Chantal Mouffe. *Hegemony and Socialist Strategy: Towards a Radical Democratic Politics*. London: Verso, 1985.

Lal, Vinay. *The History of History: Politics and Scholarship in Modern India*. New Delhi: Oxford University Press, 2003.

Landy, Marcia. *Cinematic Uses of the Past*. Minneapolis: University of Minnesota Press, 1996.

——. *Film, Politics and Gramsci*. Minneapolis: University of Minnesota Press, 1994.

Laplanche, Jean, and J.-B. Pontalis. *The Language of Psycho-Analysis*. New York: W. W. Norton, 1974.

Levinas, Emmanuel. *The Levinas Reader*, edited by Sean Hand. Malden, Mass.: Blackwell, 1989.

Liao, Ping-hui. "Rewriting Taiwanese National History: The February 28 Incident as Spectacle." *Public Culture* 5 (1993): 281–96.

Lloyd, David, and Paul Thomas. *Culture and the State*. New York: Routledge, 1998.

Loomba, Ania, Suvir Kaul, Matti Bunzl, Antoinette Burton, and Jed Esty, eds. *Postcolonial Studies and Beyond*. Durham: Duke University Press, 2006.

Low, D. A., and Howard Brasted, eds. *Freedom, Trauma, Continuities: Northern India and Independence*. New Delhi: Sage, 1998.

Lowenstein, Adam. *Shocking Representation: Historical Trauma, National Cinema and the Modern Horror Film*. New York: Columbia University Press, 2005.

Ludden, David, ed. *Contesting the Nation: Religion, Community and the Politics of Democracy in India*. Philadelphia: University of Pennsylvania Press, 1996.

Lutgendorf, Philip. "The View from the Ghats: Traditional Exegesis of a Hindu Epic." *Journal of Asian Studies* 48 (May 1989): 272–88.

Lyotard, Jean-François. *The Differend: Phrases in Dispute*. Translated by Georges Van Den Abbeele. Minneapolis: University of Minnesota Press, 1988.

Madan, T. N., ed. *Religion in India*. New Delhi: Oxford University Press, 1992.

——. "Secularism in Its Place." In *Religion in India*, edited by T. N. Madan, 394–409. New Delhi: Oxford University Press, 1992.

Mahajan, Sucheta. *Independence and Partition: The Erosion of Colonial Power in India*. New Delhi: Sage, 2000.

Mallick, Ross. "Refugee Resettlement in Forest Reserves: West Bengal Policy Reversal and the Marichjhapi Massacre." *Journal of Asian Studies* 58, no. 1 (1999): 104–25.

Mankekar, Purnima. *Screening Culture, Viewing Politics: An Ethnography of Television, Womanhood, and Nation in Postcolonial India*. Durham, N.C.: Duke University Press, 1999.

Marx, Karl. "The Economic and Philosophic Manuscripts of 1844." In *The Economic and Philosophic Manuscripts of 1844 and the Communist Manifesto*, by Karl Marx and Frederick Engels, translated by Martin Milligan, 13–168. Amherst, N.Y.: Prometheus Books, 1988.

———. "Theses on Feuerbach." In *The Marx-Engels Reader*, edited by Robert C. Tucker, 142–46. New York: W. W. Norton, 1978.

Mayaram, Shail. "Speech, Silence and the Making of Partition Violence in Mewat." In *Subaltern Studies IX*, edited by Shahid Amin and Dipesh Chakrabarty, 126–64. New Delhi: Oxford University Press, 1996.

Mayne, Judith. *Cinema and Spectatorship*. London: Routledge, 1993.

Mbembe, Achille. *On the Postcolony*. Berkeley: University of California Press, 2001.

Menon, Ritu, and Kamla Bhasin. *Borders and Boundaries: Women in India's Partition*. New Delhi: Kali for Women, 1997.

Mignolo, Walter. *Local Histories/Global Designs: Coloniality, Subaltern Knowledges, and Border Thinking*. Princeton, N.J.: Princeton University Press, 2000.

———. "On Subaltern and Other Agencies." *Postcolonial Studies: Culture, Politics, Economy* 6, no. 4 (2005): 381–407.

Mishra, Vijay. "After Ayodhya: The Sublime Object of Fundamentalism." In *Bollywood Cinema: Temples of Desire*, 203–33. New York: Routledge, 2001.

———. "Decentering History: Some Versions of Bombay Cinema." *East-West Film Journal* 6, no. 1 (1992): 111–55.

Mitscherlich, Alexander, and Margarete Mitscherlich. *The Inability to Mourn: Principles of Collective Behavior*. New York: Grove, 1975.

Moreiras, Alberto. *The Exhaustion of Difference: The Politics of Latin American Cultural Studies*. Durham, N.C.: Duke University Press, 2001.

Mowitt, John. "Trauma Envy." *Cultural Critique* 46 (2000): 272–97.

Mukhopadhyay, Sanjay. "Beejer Balaka" [in Bengali]. In *Cinemar Shatabarshey Bharatiya Cinema*, edited by Pralay Sur, 219–27. Calcutta: Nandan, 1995.

Mulvey, Laura. "Notes on Sirk and Melodrama." *Movie* 25 (1977–78): 53–56. Reprinted in *Home Is Where the Heart Is: Studies in Melodrama and the Woman's Film*, edited by Christine Gledhill, 75–79. London: British Film Institute, 1987.

Nandy, Ashis. *The Illegitimacy of Nationalism: Rabindranath Tagore and the Politics of Self*. New Delhi: Oxford University Press, 1994.

———. "An Intelligent Critic's Guide to Indian Cinema." In *The Savage Freud*, 196–236. Princeton, N.J.: Princeton University Press, 1995.

————. "Introduction: Indian Popular Cinema as a Slum's Eye View of Politics." In *The Secret Politics of Our Desires: Innocence, Culpability and Indian Popular Cinema*, edited by Ashis Nandy, 1–18. New Delhi: Oxford University Press, 1998.

————. *The Savage Freud and Other Essays in Possible and Retrievable Selves*. Princeton, N.J.: Princeton University Press, 1995.

————, ed. *The Secret Politics of Our Desires: Innocence, Culpability and Indian Popular Cinema*. New Delhi: Oxford University Press, 1998.

————. "Shamans, Savages and the Wilderness: On the Audibility of Dissent and the Future of Civilizations." *Alternatives* 14 (1989): 263–77.

Nehru, Jawaharlal. *The Discovery of India*. New York: John Day, 1946.

Ngũgĩ wa Thiong'o. *Decolonising the Mind: The Politics of Language in African Literature*. London: James Curry, 1986.

Nichols, Bill. *Representing Reality: Issues and Concepts in Documentary*. Bloomington: Indiana University Press, 1991.

Nietzsche, Friedrich. "On the Uses and Disadvantages of History for Life." In *Nietzsche: Untimely Meditations*. Translated by R. J. Hollingdale, edited by Daniel Breazeale, 57–124. Cambridge: Cambridge University Press, 1997.

Nihalani, Govind. Introduction to *Tamas*, by Bhisam Sahni, translated by Jai Ratan, 5–8. New Delhi: Penguin, 1988.

Nijhawan, Michael. "Partition Violence in Memory and Performance: The Punjabi *Dhadi* Tradition." In *The Partition Motif in Contemporary Conflicts*, edited by Smita Tewari Jassal and Eyal Ben-Ari, 145–166. New Delhi: Sage, 2007.

Niranjana, Tejaswini, P. Sudhir, and Vivek Dhareshwar, eds. *Interrogating Modernity: Culture and Colonialism in India*. Calcutta: Seagull, 1993.

Nora, Pierre. "Between Memory and History: *Les Lieux de Memoire*." Translated by Mark Roudebush. *Representations* 26 (1989): 13–25.

Omvedt, Gail. "Ambedkar and After: The Dalit Movement in India." In *Social Movements and the State*, edited by Ghanshyam Shah, 267–92. New Delhi: Sage, 2002.

Pandey, Gyanendra. "Community and Violence: Recalling Partition." *Economic and Political Weekly*, August 9, 1997, 2037–45.

————. "In Defense of the Fragment: Writing about Hindu-Muslim Riots in India Today." *Representations* 37 (1992): 27–55.

————. *Remembering Partition: Violence, Nationalism and History in India*. Cambridge: Cambridge University Press, 2002.

Panigrahi, D. N. *India's Partition: The Story of Imperialism in Retreat*. New York: Routledge, 2004.

Parekh, Bhikhu. "Jawaharlal Nehru and the Crisis of Modernization." In *Crisis and Change in Contemporary India*, edited by Upendra Baxi and Bhikhu Parekh, 21–56. New Delhi: Sage, 1995.

Paz, Octavio. *In Light of India*. Translated by Eliot Weinberger. London: Harvill Press, 1997.

Penley, Constance. Introduction to *Analysis of Film*, by Raymond Bellour. Bloomington: Indiana University Press, 2002.

Pensky, Max. *Melancholy Dialectics: Walter Benjamin and the Play of Mourning.* 1993. Amherst: University of Massachusetts Press, 2001.

Phillips, Richard. "Interview with Deepa Mehta." *World Socialist Website,* www .wsws.org, 1999.

Pinney, Christopher. *Camera Indica: The Social Life of Indian Photographs.* Chicago: University of Chicago Press, 1998.

———. "The Nation (Un)Pictured? Chromolithography and 'Popular' Politics in India, 1878–1995." *Critical Inquiry* 23 (1997): 834–67.

Pollock, Sheldon. "Mimamsa and the Problem of History in Traditional India." *Journal of American Oriental Society* 109 (1989): 603–10.

———. "Ramayana and Political Imagination in India." *Journal of Asian Studies* 52 (May 1993): 261–97.

Povinelli, Elizabeth. *The Cunning of Recognition: Indigenous Alterities and the Making of Australian Multiculturalism.* Princeton, N.J.: Princeton University Press, 2002.

Pradhan, Sudhi. *Marxist Cultural Movements in India: Chronicles and Documents, 1936–47.* Calcutta: National Book Agency, 1979.

———. *Marxist Cultural Movements in India: Chronicles and Documents, 1947–58.* Calcutta: Navana, 1982.

Prasad, Madhava. "Cinema and the Desire for Modernity." *Journal of Arts and Ideas* 25–26 (1993): 71–86.

———. *Ideology of the Hindi Film: A Historical Construction.* New Delhi: Oxford University Press, 1998.

———. "The State in/of Cinema." In *Wages of Freedom: Fifty Years of the Indian Nation-State,* edited by Partha Chatterjee, 123–46. New Delhi: Oxford University Press, 1998.

Puri, Balraj. "Indian Muslims Since Partition." *Economic and Political Weekly,* October 2, 1993, 2141–49.

Radstone, Susannah, ed. *Memory and Methodology.* Oxford: Berg, 2000.

Raha, Kironmoy. *Bengali Cinema.* Calcutta: Nandan, 1991.

Rajadhyaksha, Ashish. "The Epic Melodrama." *Journal of Arts and Ideas* 25–26 (1993): 55–70.

———. "The Phalke Era: Conflict of Traditional Form and Modern Technology." In *Interrogating Modernity: Culture and Colonialism in India,* edited by Tejaswini Niranjana, P. Sudhir, and Vivek Dhareshwar, 47–82. Calcutta: Seagull, 1993.

———. "Strange Attractions." *Sight and Sound,* n. ser. 6, no. 8 (1996): 28–31.

———, and Amrit Gangar, eds. *Ritwik Ghatak: Arguments/Stories.* Bombay: Screen Unit, 1987.

———, and Paul Willemen. *Encyclopaedia of Indian Cinema.* New Delhi: Oxford University Press, 1994.

Rajagopalan, Sudha. "Emblematic of the Thaw: Early Indian Films in Soviet Cinemas." *South Asian Popular Culture* 4.2 (2006): 83–100.

Rajan, Tilottama. "Hermeneutics: Nineteenth Century." In *The Johns Hopkins Guide to Literary Theory and Criticism,* 2nd ed., edited by Michael Groden,

Martin Kreiswirth and Imre Szeman, 486–89. Baltimore, Md.: Johns Hopkins University Press, 2005.

Ramaswamy, Sumathi. "Visualising India's Geo-body: Globes, Maps, Bodyscapes." In *Beyond Appearances? Visual Practices and Ideologies in Modern India*, edited by Ramaswamy, 151–89. New Delhi: Sage, 2003.

Ray, Manas. "Growing Up Refugee: On Memory and Locality." *History Workshop Journal* 53 (2002): 149–79.

Renov, Michael. *The Subject of Documentary*. Minneapolis: University of Minnesota Press, 2004.

———. "Toward a Poetics of Documentary." In *Theorizing Documentary*, edited by Michael Renov, 12–36. New York: Routledge, 1993.

Rentschler, Eric. *Ministry of Illusions: Nazi Cinema and Its Afterlife*. Cambridge, Mass.: Harvard University Press, 1996.

Report of the Film Enquiry Committee. New Delhi: Government of India Press, 1951.

Richman, Paula, ed. *Questioning Ramayanas: A South Asian Tradition*. Berkeley: University of California Press, 2001.

Ricoeur, Paul. "The Human Experience of Time and Narrative." In *Reflection and Imagination: A Paul Ricoeur Reader*, edited by Mario J. Valdes, 99–117. Toronto: University of Toronto Press, 1991.

Robben, Antonius C. G. M., ed. *Death, Mourning and Burial*. Malden, Mass.: Blackwell, 2005.

Rogoff, Irit. *Terra Infirma: Geography's Visual Culture*. London: Routledge, 2000.

Rosen, Philip. "Subject, Ontology and Historicity in Bazin." In *Change Mummified: Cinema, Historicity, Theory*, 3–41. Minneapolis: University of Minnesota Press, 2001.

———. "Traces of the Past: From Historicity to Film." In *Meanings in Texts and Action: Questioning Paul Ricoeur*, edited by David Klemm and William Schweiker, 67–89. Charlottesville: University of Virginia Press, 1993.

Rosenberg, Daniel. "The Trouble with Timelines." In *Histories of the Future*, edited by Daniel Rosenberg and Susan Harding, 281–95. Durham, N.C.: Duke University Press, 2005.

Ross, Kristin. *Fast Cars, Clean Bodies: Decolonization and the Reordering of French Culture*. Cambridge, Mass.: MIT Press, 1995.

Roy, Asim. "The High Politics of India's Partition: The Revisionist Perspective." In *India's Partition: Process, Strategy and Mobilization*, edited by Mushirul Hasan, 102–32. New Delhi: Oxford University Press, 1994.

Roy, Rajat. *Ritwik o Tar Chhabi* [in Bengali]. Calcutta: Annapurna Pustak Mandir, 1983.

Roy, Shibnarayan. *Swadesh, Swakal, Swajan* [in Bengali]. Kolkata: Papyrus, 1996.

Sahni, Bhisam. *Tamas*. Translated by Jai Ratan. New Delhi: Penguin, 1988.

Samaddar, Ranabir. "The History that Partition Creates." In *Reflections on Partition in the East*, edited by Ranabir Samaddar, 1–34. New Delhi: Vikas Publishing House for Calcutta Research Group, 1997.

————, ed. *Reflections on Partition in the East.* New Delhi: Vikas Publishing House for Calcutta Research Group, 1997.

————, ed. *Refugees and the State: Practices of Asylum and Care in India, 1947–2000.* New Delhi: Sage, 2003.

Sangari, Kumkum. "Figures for the 'Unconscious.'" *Journal of Arts and Ideas* 20–21 (1991): 67–84.

Santner, Eric L. *Stranded Objects: Mourning, Memory, and Film in Postwar Germany.* Ithaca, N.Y.: Cornell University Press, 1990.

Sarkar, Bhaskar. "The Inward Look: the Politics and Practice of Cinematic Representation." In *The Enemy Within*, edited by Sumita Chakravarty, 98–130. London: Flick Books, 2000.

————. "The Melodramas of Globalization." *Cultural Dynamics* 20, no. 1 (March 2008): 31–51.

————. "Tangled Legacies: The *Autos* of Biography." *Rethinking History: Theory and Practice* 7, no. 2 (June 2003): 217–34.

Sarkar, Sumit. *The Swadeshi Movement in Bengal, 1903–1908.* New Delhi: People's Publishing House, 1973.

Schaeffer, Robert. *Warpaths: The Politics of Partition.* New York: Hill and Wang, 1989.

Schleiermacher, Friedrich. *Hermeneutics and Criticism and Other Writings.* Translated and edited by Andrew Bowie. Cambridge: Cambridge University Press, 1998.

Sen, Amartya. *Poverty and Famines: An Essay on Entitlement and Deprivation.* Oxford: Clarendon, 1981.

Sen, Mrinal. "Bangla Cinemar Darshak O *Chhinnamul*" [in Bengali]. *Chitrabhas* 19, no. 1–2 (1984): 17–22.

Settar, S., and Indira Gupta, eds. *Pangs of Partition*, vol. 1–2. New Delhi: Manohar, 2002.

Shahani, Kumar. "Violence and Responsibility." In *Ritwik Ghatak: Arguments/Stories*, edited by Ashish Rajadhakshya and Amrit Gangar, 59–63. Bombay: Screen Unit, 1987.

Shapiro, Michael J., and Hayward R. Alker, eds. *Challenging Boundaries: Global Flows, Territorial Identities.* Minneapolis: University of Minnesota Press, 1996.

Shepherd, Simon. "Pauses of Mutual Agitation." In *Melodrama: Picture, Stage, Screen*, edited by Jacky Bratton, Jim Cook, and Christine Gledhill, 25–37. London: British Film Institute, 1994.

Shohat, Ella. *Israeli Cinema: East/West and the Politics of Representation.* Austin: University of Texas Press, 1989.

Singh, Anita Inder. *The Origins of the Partition of India, 1936–1947.* New Delhi: Oxford University Press, 1987.

Sobchak, Vivian, ed. *The Persistence of History: Cinema, Television, and the Modern Event.* New York: Routledge, 1996.

Sorlin, Pierre. "How to Look at an 'Historical' Film." In *The Historical Film: History and Memory in Media*, edited by Marcia Landy, 25–49. New Brunswick, N.J.: Rutgers University Press, 2000.

Spivak, Gayatri Chakravorty. "Can the Subaltern Speak?" In *Marxism and the Interpretation of Culture*, edited by Cary Nelson and Lawrence Grossberg, 271–314. Chicago: University of Illinois Press, 1987.

Stern, Frank. "Antagonistic Memories: The Post-War Survival and Alienation of Jews and Germans." In *Memory and Totalitarianism*, edited by Luisa Passerini, 21–43. Oxford: Oxford University Press, 1992.

Stiglitz, Joseph E. *Globalization and Its Discontents*. New York: W. W. Norton, 2003.

Sturken, Marita. *Tangled Memories: The Vietnam War, the Aids Epidemic, and the Politics of Remembering*. Los Angeles: University of California Press, 1997.

Suleiman, Susan Rubin. *Crises of Memory and the Second World War*. Cambridge, Mass.: Harvard University Press, 2006.

Sur, Pralay, ed. *Cinemar Shatabarshay Bharatiya Cinema* [in Bengali]. Calcutta: Nandan, 1995.

Tagore, Rabindranath. *Ghare Baire* [Bengali, published in 1915]. *The Home and the World*. English translation by Surendranath Tagore. London: Penguin Classics, 2005.

Talbot, Ian. *India and Pakistan (Inventing the Nation)*. New York: Hodder Arnold, 2000.

———. "Literature and the Human Drama of the 1947 Partition." In *Freedom, Trauma, Continuities: Northern India and Independence*, edited by D. A. Low and Howard Brasted, 39–55. New Delhi: Sage, 1998.

Tambiah, Stanley J. *Leveling Crowds: Ethnonationalist Conflicts and Collective Violence in South Asia*. Berkeley: University of California Press, 1996.

Tan, Tai Yong, and Gyanesh Kudaisya. *The Aftermath of Partition in South Asia*. New York: Routledge, 2002.

Tarlo, Emma. *Unsettling Memories: Narratives of the Emergency in Delhi*. Berkeley: University of California Press, 2003.

Tarrow, Sidney. *The New Transnational Activism*. Cambridge: Cambridge University Press, 2005.

Taylor, Charles. *Modern Social Imaginaries*. Durham: Duke University Press, 2004.

Taylor, Ronald, ed. and trans. *Aesthetics and Politics*. London: Verso, 1977.

Thomas, Rosie. "Sanctity and Scandal: The Mythologization of Mother India." *Quarterly Review of Film and Video* 11, no. 3 (1989): 11–30.

Tiwari, Badri Narain. "Partition Memory and Popular Culture." In *Pangs of Partition* vol. 2, edited by S. Settar and Indira Gupta, 69–73. New Delhi: Manohar, 2002.

Turim, Maureen. *Flashbacks in Film: Memory and History*. New York: Routledge, 1989.

Uberoi, Patricia. *Freedom and Destiny: Gender, Family and Popular Culture in India*. New York: Oxford University Press, 2006.

van Alphen, Ernst. "Symptoms of Discursivity: Experience, Memory and Trauma." In *Acts of Memory: Cultural Recall in the Present*, edited by Mieke

Bal, Jonathan Crewe, and Leo Spitzer, 24–38. London: Dartmouth College/ University Press of New England, 1999.

Varshney, Ashutosh. "Battling the Past, Forging a Future? Ayodhya and Be-yond." In *India Briefings*, edited by Phillip Oldenberg, 9–42. Boulder, Colo.: Westview, 1993.

Vasudevan, Ravi S. "Addressing the Spectator of a 'Third World' National Cinema: The Bombay 'Social' Film of the 1940s and 1950s." *Screen* 36 (1995): 305–24.

———. "Another History Rises to the Surface: *Hey Ram*—Melodrama in the Age of Digital Simulation." *Economic and Political Weekly*, July 13, 2002, 2917–25.

———. "Dislocations: The Cinematic Imagining of a New Society in 1950s India." *Oxford Literary Review* 16 (1994): 93–124.

———. "The Politics of Cultural Address in a 'Transitional' Cinema: A Case Study of Indian Popular Cinema." In *Reinventing Film Studies*, edited by Christine Gledhill and Linda Williams, 130–64. London: Arnold, 2000.

———. "Shifting Codes, Dissolving Identities: The Hindi Social Film of the 1950s as Popular Culture." *Journal of Arts and Ideas* 23–24 (1993): 51–84.

Walker, Janet. *Trauma Cinema: Documenting Incest and the Holocaust*. Berke-ley: University of California Press, 2005.

White, Hayden. "The Modernist Event." In *The Persistence of History: Cinema, Television, and the Modern Event*, edited by Vivian Sobchak, 17–38. New York: Routledge, 1996.

Willemen, Paul. "Negotiating the Transition to Capital: The Case of *Andaz*." *East-West Film Journal* 5, no. 1 (January 1991): 56–65.

———. "Tyneside Festival Notes 2." *Framework* 30–31 (1986). Reprinted in *Rit-wik Ghatak: Arguments/Stories*, edited by Ashish Rajadhyaksha and Amrit Gangar, 64–65. Bombay: Screen Unit, 1987.

Williams, Linda. "Film Bodies: Gender, Genre and Excess." *Film Quarterly* 44, no. 4 (1991): 2–13.

———. "Melodrama Revisited." In *Refiguring American Film Genres*, edited by Nick Browne, 42–88. Berkeley: University of California Press, 1998.

Winters, J. M. "The Great War and the Persistence of Tradition: Languages of Grief, Bereavement and Mourning." In *War, Violence and the Modern Condi-tion*, edited by Bernd Hüppauf, 33–45. Berlin: Walter de Gruyter, 1997.

Zelizer, Barbie. "Reading the Past against the Grain: The Shape of Memory Studies." *Critical Studies in Mass Communication* 12 (1995): 214–39.

———. *Remembering to Forget: Holocaust Memory through the Camera's Eye*. Chicago: University of Chicago Press, 1998.

Zertal, Idith. "From the People's Hall to the Wailing Wall: A Study in Memory, Fear and War." *Representations* 69 (2000): 96–127.

Žižek, Slavoj. Introduction to *Mapping Ideology*, edited by Žižek, 1–33. London: Verso, 1994.

———. *The Sublime Object of Ideology*. London: Verso, 1989.

Index

BHASKAR SARKAR
is an associate professor of film and media studies
at the University of California, Santa Barbara.

Library of Congress Cataloging-in-Publication Data
Sarkar, Bhaskar
Mourning the nation : Indian cinema in the wake of Partition /
Bhaskar Sarkar.
p. cm.
Includes bibliographical references and index.
ISBN 978-0-8223-4393-6 (cloth : alk. paper)
ISBN 978-0-8223-4411-7 (pbk. : alk. paper)
1. Motion pictures—India. 2. India—In motion pictures.
3. India—History—Partition, 1947. I. Title.
PN1993.5.I8.S27 2009
791.43'65835404—dc22   2008052621